The Fry Chronicles

STEPHEN FRY

PENGUIN BOOKS

PENGUIN PICKS

UK | USA | Canada | Ireland | Australia
| India | New Zealand | South Africa

Penguin Books is part of the Penguin Random House group of companies
whose addresses can be found at global.penguinrandomhouse.com.

First published by Michael Joseph 2010
Published in Penguin Books 2011
This Penguin Picks edition published 2018

001

Copyright © Stephen Fry 2010
The moral right of the author has been asserted

Printed in Great Britain by Clays Ltd, St Ives plc

A CIP catalogue record for this book is available from the British Library

ISBN: 978–1–405–93372–8

www.greenpenguin.co.uk

To M'Coll

Contents

Illustrations

A moment later, responding to Tony Slattery and revealing an unsurprising cigarette. (Cambridge Mummers)

The Snow Queen, 1980. My first Footlights appearance. (Cambridge Footlights. Reproduced by kind permission of the Syndics of Cambridge University Library: UA FOOT 2/5/30, UA FOOT 2/8/95)

With Kim outside the Cambridge Senate House, celebrating our Tripos results. I was insanely in love with that Cerruti tie. (Andrew Everard)

In room A2, Queens'. Graduation day: posing with sister Jo. (Author's collection)

Rowan Atkinson presents Hugh with the Perrier Prize cheque. Edinburgh, 1981. (Perrier)

The Cellar Tapes closing song. I fear we may have been guilty of embarrassing and sanctimonious 'satire' at this point. Hence the joyless expressions. (BBC Photo Library)

Photo call in Richmond Park for BBC version of *The Cellar Tapes*. (BBC Photo Library)

The same: ultimately a git with a pipe stuck in his face. (BBC Photo Library)

Performing the 'Shakespeare Masterclass' sketch with Hugh. (BBC Photo Library)

With Emma in 'My Darling' – a Robert and Elizabeth Barrett Browning sketch. (BBC Photo Library)

Hugh in Crete. We rented a villa for the purposes of writing comedy. (Author's collection)

A cretin in a Cretan setting. (Author's collection)

Hugh prepares to demolish me at backgammon. The retsina was satisfyingly disgusting. (Author's collection)

Hugh, Emma, Ben, self, Siobhan and Paul: *There's Nothing to Worry About*, Granada TV, 1982. Oh, but there was . . . (ITV/Rex Features)

I host a bed party in my room at the Midland Hotel. We seem happy. I think perhaps we were. (Photo by Robbie Coltrane)

An *Alfresco* sketch that a merciful providence has erased from my memory. (ITV/Rex Features)

The only time in my life I ever wore a donkey jacket. *Alfresco*. (Photo by Robbie Coltrane)

Providence has once again been merciful. *Alfresco*. (ITV/Rex Features)

Alfresco, series 2: The Pretend Pub. (ITV/Rex Features)

A twat in tweed and cravat: inexcusably slappable. *Alfresco*. (ITV/Rex Features)

'We cannot be said to have been the prettiest quartet ever to greet a television audience.' *University Challenge*. (ITV/Rex Features)

The Young Ones. Comic heroes. (BBC Photo Library)

David Lander, earnest investigative reporter in a badly behaved blond wig. (Courtesy of Hat Trick Productions, Channel 4 and Screenocean)

The Crystal Cube, with Emma and Hugh. (Author's collection)

The Crystal Cube. The warty look was created using Rice Krispies. True story. (Author's collection)

The man who put the turd in *Saturday Live*. I cannot recall a single thing about that sketch. Why the rolled-up trouser leg? (ITV/Rex Features)

As Lord Melchett in *Blackadder II*. (BBC Photo Library)

More *Saturday Live*: with Hugh, Harry Enfield and Ben Elton. Why the electric carving knife, if that's what it is? I remember *nothing* of this moment. (ITV/Rex Features)

The Tatler celibacy article. (Photo – Tim Platt/Tatler © Condé Nast Publications Ltd. Words – Stephen Fry/Tatler © Condé Nast Publications Ltd)

From *Forty Years On*, Chichester, 1984. Self, Doris Hare, Paul Eddington and John Fortune. (Picture courtesy of the Chichester Observer)

Celebrating Christopher Richardson's birthday and Uppingham School leaving party – I remember that Paul Smith shirt . . . (Author's collection)

Emma (Ted Blackbrow/Daily Mail/Rex Features)

First-night party for the *Forty Years On* 'transfer', Queen's Theatre, London, 1984. Katie Kelly (back to us, shiny bun), boys from the cast, self, Hugh Laurie, sister Jo.

Me and My Girl. Robert Lindsay and Emma Thompson. (Alastair Muir/ Rex Features)

The French's acting edition of *Me and My Girl*. (Noel Gay Organisation)

Me and My Girl. Emma's dressing-room on the first night. (Ted Blackbrow/ Daily Mail/Rex Features)

One hour before *Me and My Girl*'s Broadway opening. Between my cousin Danny and his grandmother, Great-Aunt Dita.

Experimenting with a new pair of glasses in the kitchen of my parents' house in Norfolk. (Author's collection)

Work is more fun than fun
Noël Coward

I really must stop saying sorry; it doesn't make things any better or worse. If only I had it in me to be all fierce, fearless and forthright instead of forever sprinkling my discourse with pitiful retractions, apologies and prevarications. It is one of the reasons I could never have been an artist, either of a literary or any other kind. All the true artists I know are uninterested in the opinion of the world and wholly unconcerned with self-explanation. Self-revelation, yes, and often, but never self-explanation. Artists are strong, bloody-minded, difficult and dangerous. Fate, or laziness, or cowardice cast me long ago in the role of entertainer, and that is what I found myself, throughout my twenties, becoming, though at times a fatally over-earnest, over-appeasing one, which is no kind of entertainer at all, of course. Wanting to be liked is often a very unlikeable characteristic. Certainly I don't like it in myself. But then, there is a lot in myself that I don't like.

Twelve years ago I wrote a memoir of my childhood and adolescence called *Moab is My Washpot*, a title that confused no one, so clear, direct and obvious was its meaning and reference. Or perhaps not. The chronology took me up to the time I emerged from prison and managed somehow to get myself accepted into university, which is where this book takes up the story. For the sake of those who have read *Moab* I don't mean to go over the same ground. Where I mention events from my past that I covered there I shall append a superscribed obelus, thus: †.

This book picks up the threads and charts the next eight years of my life. Why so many pages for so few years? It was a late adolescence and early manhood crowded with incident, that is one answer. Another is that in every particular I fail Strunk's *Elements of Style* or any other manual of 'good writing'. If a thing can be said in ten words, I may be relied upon to take a hundred to say it. I ought to apologize for that. I ought to go back and ruthlessly prune, pare and extirpate excess growth, but I will not. I like words – strike that, I *love* words – and while I am fond of the condensed and economical use of them in poetry, in song lyrics, in Twitter, in good journalism and smart advertising, I love the luxuriant profusion and mad scatter of them too. After all, as you will already have noticed, I am the kind of person who writes things like 'I shall append a superscribed obelus, thus'. If my manner of writing is a self-indulgence that has you grinding your teeth then I am sorry, but I am too old a dog to be taught to bark new tunes.

I hope you forgive the unedifying sight of my struggle to express some of the truths of my inner self and to measure the distance between the mask of security, ease, confidence and assurance I wear (so easily that its features often lift into a smirk that looks like complacency and smugness) and the real condition of anxiety, self-doubt, self-disgust and fear in which much of my life then and now is lived. It is a life, I suppose, as interesting or as uninteresting as anyone else's. It is mine and I can do what I like with it, both in the world in the real plane of facts and objects and on the page in the even more real plane of words and subjects. It is not for me to be so cavalier with the lives of others, however. In much of my life from 1977 to 1987 people appear who are known in the public world and to whom I cannot give convincing pseudonyms. If I told you, for example, that at university I met a man called Lew Horrie and that we embarked on a comic career together it might not take great insight or too much Googling on your part to know that I was writing about a real person. It is not for me to go blabbing about his life and loves, personal habits, mannerisms and modes of behaviour, is it? On the other hand, were I simply to say that everyone I met in my journey through life was darling and gorgeous and super and lovely and talented and dazzling and sweet, you would soon enough be arcing streams of hot vomit all over the place and in every probability short-circuiting your eBook reader. I don't doubt for a minute that my publishers have already made it clear in the small print of the contract I signed with them that I, the author, am responsible for all lawsuits appertaining to, but not restricted to, emetic and bodily fluid damage to electronic reading devices in this and all territories. So I am sailing between the Scylla of protecting the wholly reasonable privacy of friends and colleagues and the Charybdis of causing you, the reader, to sick up. It is a narrow course, and I shall do my best to steer it safely.

These pages deal with some of the C-words that have dominated my life. Before the chronology of the chronicles commences, let me catalogue a couple more Cs. To put you, as it were, in the mood . . .

C is for C$_{12}$H$_{22}$O$_{11}$

. . . for Cereal
. . . for Candy
. . . for Caries
. . . for Cavities
. . . for Carbohydrates
. . . for Calories

Shades of the prison-house begin to close upon the growing boy
William Wordsworth, 'Intimations of Mortality'

To care about my body would be to suggest that I had a body worth caring about. Since my earliest years I felt nothing but shame for the useless casing of flesh I inhabit. It couldn't bowl, bat or catch. It couldn't dance. It couldn't ski, dive or leap. When it walked into a bar or club it didn't attract lustful glares of desire or even faint glances of interest. It had nothing to recommend it beyond its function as a fuel cell for my brain and a dumping ground for toxins that might reward me with rushing highs and reasons to be cheerful. Perhaps it all comes down to breasts. Or the lack of them.

While it is true that I was once a babe I was never, I think, a suckling. I have no memories of being clamped to the nipple and believe myself to have been bottle-fed from the beginning. There are psychologists schooled in this tradition or that, whether Kleinian, Freudian, Adlerian, Jungian or Insertnamehereian I cannot say, who hold that the Tit or Teat issue has a significant, even crucial, bearing on human development. I can't recall whether the theory suggests it is the denial of mother's milk or the over-abundant supply of it that stores up problems for later life. Possibly both. A lot of bosom pressed into your face at a tender age and you could grow up with a Russ Meyer or Jonathan Ross breast fixation. Nothing but bottle to suck and you develop a horror of bosoms. Or a propensity towards drink in general. Or perhaps the other way around. All absolute poppywash, of course. False mammary syndrome. There are plenty of brothers and sisters, identical twins even, fed on the same infant diets, who have turned out different in every particular – except the irrelevant one of physical appearance. My brother and sister were treated just as I was in infancy, and we could not be, fortunately for them and the world, less alike. So let us suppose that the vices and weaknesses that I am going to tell you about now are peculiar to me and were bestowed upon me at birth along with the moles on the backs of my legs and the whorls on the pads of my fingers. Which is not to say that I am uniquely alone in the possession of these weaknesses. Far from it. They might almost be called the failings of my generation.

Once we get beyond milk, whether breast or formula, we move on to the hard stuff. Solid food. Pappy spoonfuls of apple sauce and beef casserole are pushed into us until we can wield cutlery for ourselves. One of the first and most forcible ways in which a child's character begins to express itself is through its attitude to food. In the late 1950s and early 1960s food meant breakfast cereal and sweets. I was one of the first wave of infants to be exposed to child-targeted advertising. Sugar Puffs were born, as was I, in

1957. That cereal, which no one could pretend had any ambition to be eaten by adults, was represented, a decade before the arrival of the Honey Monster, by a real live bear called Jeremy. He led a busy life being photographed for the carton and filmed for television commercials until he was finally retired into private life, ending up, after a short period at Cromer Zoo, in Campertown, Dundee, where he died peacefully in his sleep in 1990. I visited him at Cromer, the first celebrity I ever saw in the flesh, or in the fur, and believe me, what the A-listingest Hollywood babe or pop idol is to a child now, Jeremy the Bear was to me then. You have to understand the passion, the love, the greed and the need.

Sugar Puffs were pellets of wheat that had been puffed up under heat and coated in a syrupy and slightly sticky fructose and glucose glaze. All you had to do to enjoy their glory was to pour on cold milk. Hot milk was possible for winter days, but it created a soggy bowlful closer to soup than cereal. Besides, hot milk that approached boiling point could form a surface skin, and a skin on milk caused me to vomit. To this day the sight or smell of boiled milk makes me keck and puke. I am put in mind of the cock tales they tell of Cocteau's cocktail parties. They say that Jean Cocteau, to amuse his friends, could lie back naked on a table and bring himself to full ejaculatory orgasm without touching himself, through the power of imaginative thought alone. I have a similar gift. I can make myself vomit by picturing skin on hot milk, custard or coffee. We can both make hot fluids spit and spurt from our bodies. I can't but feel that Cocteau's party piece is always likely to be more in demand than mine.

The breakfast table was where the seeds of my sorrow

were sown. I am sure that I am right in locating my first addiction here. Sugar Puffs were the starting link in a chain that would shackle me for most of my life. To begin with, as you might imagine, they were a breakfast habit. But soon I was snacking on them at any time of day until my mother began to sigh at the number of packets she was forced to buy. I would eat the sweet pellets loose from the box. One after the other, without stopping, into the mouth they would go. I was like an American at the cinema with popcorn: eyes glazed, hand rising and falling pack-to-mouth, pack-to-mouth, pack-to-mouth like a machine.

'Eyes glazed'. Is that important? A child at the breast or bottle has that look. There is a sexual element to such unfocused fixity. Until I was about eight or nine I sucked the first two fingers of my left hand. Almost all the time. While twiddling the hair on the crown of my head with the fingers of the right hand. And always with that glazed, faraway look, with parted lips and laboured breath. Was I giving myself the breast treat that I had been denied? These are dark waters, Watson.

Cereal-packet lists of ingredients and serving suggestions were my literature; thiamine, riboflavin and niacin my mysterious invisible friends. Sold by weight not volume. Contents may have settled during transport. Insert finger under flap and move from side to side. They're Gr-r-r-r-r-r-eat! We like Ricicles, they're twicicles as nicicles. And so they were. In fact, as I liked to say, they were *thricicles* as nicicles. Certainly much nicicler than their staid, unsweetened parent, Rice Krispies, the cereal that said, if you listened carefully, Snot, Pickle and Crap. To have Rice Krispies when you could have Ricicles, to have Cornflakes when you could have Frosties. Who could imagine such a dull life? It was like deliberately choosing to watch the news on television or preferring to drink unsweetened tea. I lived for one thing and one thing only. $C_{12}H_{22}O_{11}$. Perhaps this is why I should have been American, for they have sugar everywhere in the United States. In bread, in bottled water, in beef jerky, pickles, mayonnaise, mustard and salsa. Sugar, sugar, sugar.

My relationship with this beguiling and benighted substance is complicated. I should never have been born if it weren't for sugar, and yet it came close to killing me too.

I told elsewhere[†] the story of the role of my mother's father in bringing sugar to Britain. I latterly found out more as a result of taking part in the BBC's genealogy programme *Who Do You Think You Are?* My grandfather Martin Neumann came to Bury St Edmunds (not to praise him) all the way from the land of his birth, which was originally Hungary, although the 1920 Treaty of Trianon later absorbed his home town of Nagysurány into the newly expanded Czechoslovakia. For the purposes of history, however, he was from Hungary. A Hungarian Jew, as he liked to observe, is the only man who can follow you into a revolving door and come out first.

He came to Britain at the invitation of the Ministry of Agriculture in Whitehall, whose more far-sighted functionaries realized that if there was, as seemed increasingly likely, to be another world war the Atlantic would almost certainly be cut off, as it so nearly had been at the height of the German U-boat threat of 1917. The West Indies and Australia would be out of reach, and there would be no sugar for the British cup of tea, a disaster too horrible to contemplate. Britain was entirely without native sugar capacity, its farmers never having grown a single beet, its industrialists never having refined a single ounce. Back in Nagysurány, now Šurany, my grandfather had been the manager of what was then the largest sugar refinery in the world, so he seemed like a natural candidate for British recruitment. In 1925 he and his brother-in-law Robert Jorisch came to build Britain its first sugar beet refinery in Bury St Edmunds, Suffolk, where it stands to this day, emitting a rich and bitter pong faintly reminiscent of burnt peanut butter. Had Martin and his wife and family remained in Šurany they would, being Jews, have been exterminated in the Nazi death camps, as were his mother, sister, parents-in-law and the dozens of other family members who stayed in Europe. I should never have been born, and the paper or digital display technology that has gone into the production of the book you are now reading with such unalloyed pleasure would have been put to other uses.

So sugar gave me life, but it exacted a price – slavish adherence. Addiction to it and an addiction to addiction in addition.

Sweetened breakfast cereals were one thing, and relatively harmless at that. Weekly boxes of Sugar Puffs, Ricicles and Frosties would be ordered by my mother over the telephone and delivered along with the rest of the groceries by Mr Neil, who always called me 'young man' and who drove the van for Riches, the little store in the village of Reepham, which lay some two or three miles away from our home hamlet of Booton. Men like Mr Neil no longer exist; little stores like Riches no longer exist.

As a result of Mr Neil's weekly deliveries, I could eat almost as much breakfast cereal as I wanted without having to spend any money. My sugar hit was free. Of course it was. Why wouldn't it be? I was a child who lived in a house where there were always Sugar Puffs in the cupboard. Perfectly normal and natural. All this changed when at the age of seven I was sent to a Gloucestershire preparatory school almost exactly 200 miles from our Norfolk home.

My introductory morning at Stouts Hill, for such was the school's name, presented the first in what was to be a long line of disappointments. After a night of homesick weeping and lonely hiccupping I had awoken to the bumptious din and frightening mystery of an alien institution going about its daily rites.

'You! What are you doing? You should be in the refectory,' a prefect shouted at me as I caromed panic-stricken down random corridors.

'Please, what's a refectory?' A picture of some kind of medieval punishment chamber arose in my terrified mind.

The prefect grabbed me by the shoulders and steered me down a passageway, and down another and finally through a door that led into a long, low dining-room crowded with loudly breakfasting boys sitting on long, shiny oak forms, as benches used to be called. He marched me to one, prised two boys apart, hoisted me up and wedged me into the space between. I sat there blinking with frightened embarrassment. Timidly raising my head, I saw that there was cereal available. Cornflakes or lumpy cooked porridge. Of Sugar Puffs, Frosties and Ricicles there was no sign. I might make the claim that life was never the same again, that trust, faith, hope, belief and confidence died in me that day and that thenceforward melancholy marked me for her own, but perhaps that would be pitching it a touch strong. Nonetheless I was shocked. Was there now to be no sweetness in my life?

The school did have one institution that counterbalanced the troubling deficiencies of the refectory. 'Tuck', as you may know, is an old-fashioned English school slang word for sweets. What Americans call candy. While I had encountered sweets before, of course I had, they had usually come in quarter-pound bags scooped from large glass jars in Riches or Reepham Post Office. Pear drops, sherbet lemons, toffee eclairs, humbugs and fruit bonbons: all rather dowdy, respectable and pre-war. The Stouts Hill School Tuck Shop offered wilder excitements in this, the rising golden age of confectionery. Cadbury's, Fry's (hurrah!), Rowntree's, Nestlé's, Mackintosh's, Mars and Terry's were still individual independent manufacturers. From Mackintosh's came Rolos, Caramac and Toffee Crisp, from Fry's (hurrah!), Turkish Delight, Crunchie bars and Chocolate Cream. Cadbury's gave us the Picnic and the Flake as well as their signature Dairy Milk wrapped in delicate purple foil. The Bournville giants were even then preparing to launch within one year of each other the legendary Curly Wurly and the Greatest Chocolate Bar in the History of the World, the Aztec. Nestlé's meanwhile offered us the Milky Bar, Rowntree's had the Aero, KitKat, Fruit Pastilles, Fruit Gums, Smarties and Jelly Tots, Mars had the Milky Way, Mars bar, Maltesers and Marathon. Bless my soul! I never noticed till now that the Mars products all began with M. Marathon would many years later be rechristened Snickers, of course (and I would help launch the new name by recording the voice-over for its advertising campaign: if I had known such a thing might happen back then I might well have exploded), just as Mars' Opal Fruits would one day become Starburst. Doubtless they had their reasons. They also produced Spangles, the square boiled sweet that has become shorthand for just the kind of lazy, overwrought nostalgia in which I am now wallowing. But hang in there if you will; there is a point to all this beyond the mere fevered recitation of brand names.

The Stouts Hill Tuck Shop was open for business on different days for each of the four houses into which the school was divided: Kingfishers, Otters, Wasps and Panthers. I was an Otter, and our tuck day was Thursday. First you queued up for cash. Whatever pocket money your parents had allocated you was kept in trust and doled out in instalments by the master on duty, who recorded the withdrawn sum on your individual page in the pocket-money ledger. As the term wore on I watched in dismay as my capital dwindled away. Desperate letters were written home begging for a ten-shilling note to be sent as soon as possible. 'Please, Mummy, please. All the other boys have got enough money to last them for *ever*. Oh *please, please, please . . .*'

And so it began.

Glorious as the Stouts Hill Tuck Shop may have been, it was but a John the Baptist to the messianic radiance of the Uley village shop, unworthy to tie its red liquorice bootlaces or lick its sherbet dabs. The little post office and general stores was just half a mile from the school gates, and we would pass in crocodile formation on supervised walks through the village, turning our heads in unison towards its inviting windows like cadets honouring their monarch with an eyes right. On the shelves of that shop gleamed, glistened and twinkled the most exotic, colourful and sugary-sweet treasure I had ever seen or had ever dreamed of. Jamboree Bags. Trebor Refreshers. Fruit Salads and Blackjacks a farthing each (that's four for one old penny). Foam shrimps. Rice-paper flying saucers filled with sherbet. Swizzels Matlow Twizzlers that fizzed and popped in the mouth like fireworks. Love Hearts. Chewy sour cola bottles and rubbery white milk bottles. Chocolate buttons sprinkled with hundreds and thousands. Strips of Wrigley's Juicy Fruit and Spearmint, boxes of Chiclets and Pez, loose cubes of Bazooka Joe and packs of Beatles- branded bubblegum, each one with a card inside that offered a picture and priceless biographical information: 'John hates marmalade but Ringo is very fond of lemon curd!', 'George is the tallest Beatle, but only by half an inch!' and other devastating and valuable secrets, all finished with the exclamation marks that remain a characteristic of fan literature to this day. On other shelves there were gobstoppers, aniseed balls and everlasting strips. Sherbet fountains, dabs and dips. Wine Gums, Wagon Wheels and Walnut Whips. Forgive the accidental rhyming. There was the much-prized Spanish Gold, pouches of yellow waxed paper with a picture of a red galleon on the front packed with strands of shredded coconut browned with chocolate powder to make it look like rolling tobacco. Liquorice curved into a Sherlock Holmes pipe, complete with bowl and stem. White candy cigarettes with red ends and rice-paper-wrapped chocolate cigarettes presented in a fake Chesterfield's carton.

All the elements were now in place. Sugar. White powder. Tobacco. Desire. Lack of money. The forbidden.

Yes, forbidden. The village shop was out of bounds to all boys. The extra sugariness of the sweets, the blindingly bright cheerfulness of the wrappers and the loutish American informality of chewing-gum and gobstoppers offended the mostly military sensibilities of the staff. The produce was all somehow just a bit vulgar, just a bit . . . well, frankly just a bit working class. Heaven knows what those same poor schoolmasters would have made of Haribo Starmix or the Kinder Happy Hippo. It is perhaps as well that they predeceased such unpleasantnesses, for I'm sure their hearts would have given out.

Seven years old, 200 miles from home and a deprived addict. There are plenty of stories of children younger than seven who are already full alcoholics or were born addicted to crack cocaine, crystal meth and Red Bull, and I am fully aware that my sugar dependency reads as tame by comparison. The fact of it is an indictment of nothing and a lesson to nobody. Nor is it satisfactorily explicable. I have given you the outline of it but that does not suggest necessary or sufficient cause for so compulsive and all-consuming an addiction. After all, my contemporaries were subjected to the same advertising, had available the same cereals, candies and comestibles and were compounded of the same organs, senses and dimensions. Yet from my very earliest consciousness I sensed with savage unswervable certainty that other people were not seized by the same rapacious greed, insatiable hunger, overmastering desire, shivering lust and terrible, hurting need that had me in its grip almost every hour of every day. Or if they were they had levels of self-control that entirely shamed me. Perhaps, I wondered, perhaps everyone but me was strong, characterful and morally assured. Perhaps only I was so weak as to succumb to appetites that others could control. Perhaps everyone else was equally gnawed by equally keen desires, but had been granted by nature or the almighty an ability to master their emotions that in my trembling desolation I had been denied. We should consider that the atmosphere of my school, like that of any given private school in those days (and many today) quivered with righteous religiosity (today's schools quiver with righteousness without the religiosity, which is only just an improvement). You might be able to imagine then something of the spiritual torture that accompanied my more corporeal agonies. The Bible is crammed from end to end with stories of temptation, interdiction and chastisement. A forbidden fruit hangs from a tree on the very first page, and as we go through we are given more terrible lessons on how greed is punished and lust accursed until we reach the full, final and insane damnations and ecstasies of St John's Revelations, having passed through wildernesses and desert trials, locusts, honey, manna, ravens, sores, boils, plagues, scourges, tribulations and sacrifices. Lead us not into temptation. Get thee behind me, Satan. Vengeance is mine, saith the Lord, I will repay.

In such an atmosphere, with a physiological craving already in place, it is little wonder that guilty connections came to be made in my mind between sugar and desire and satisfaction and desire and satisfaction and shame. All this years before the even fiercer terrors and torments of sex were to make themselves known to me and carve in my heart and bowels the same pattern; gouging it, of course, with deeper and crueller cuts. I say, I *am* a self-dramatizer, aren't I?

Since 90 per cent of my schoolfellows appeared immune

to all this trauma, introspection, shame and temptation I still wonder, looking back, whether I was especially weak, especially sensitive or especially sensual.

To pay for sweets I stole from shops, from the school and, most shamefully of all, from other boys. These acts of theft were conducted, like the eating, in an almost trance-like state. Shallow of breath, eyes glazed over, I would ransack the changing rooms and desks, my insides churning with fear, elation, dread and passionate self-disgust. At night I would raid the school kitchens, homing in on a cupboard in which were stored great catering-sized blocks of raw jelly that I tore with my teeth, like a lion tearing an antelope.

I chronicled in *Moab* the occasion when I was found by a prefect to be in possession of contraband sweets, bubblegum and sherbet fountains that could only have come from the village shop.[†] I persuaded a good-natured little fellow called Bunce, who quietly hero-worshipped me, to take the rap. I had been guilty of so many prior transgressions that one more would result in a severe caning, whereas Bunce, who had no form and no record, would be let off with a warning. It all backfired, of course, and the headmaster saw through our little stratagem. My reward was an extra special beating for having been so wicked as to lure an innocent like Bunce into my web of sin.

The real-life Bunce and I have been in touch since the publication of *Moab*. He was very good-natured about it and reminded me of an event I had entirely forgotten.

Very early on in my school life I had told Bunce that my parents were dead.

'How terrible for you!' Bunce, always kindly, was deeply moved.

'Yes. Car crash. I have three aunts that I get handed around during the school holidays. You must swear not to tell anyone, though. It's a secret.'

Bunce nodded, a look of stout defiance on his downy face. I knew that he would sooner cut out his own tongue than say a word to anyone.

Towards the end of term, I asked Bunce what plans he had for Christmas. He looked uncomfortable as he confessed that he was off with his family to the West Indies.

'What about you?' he asked.

'Derr . . . in Norfolk with my parents, of course. Where else?'

'B-b-but . . . I thought your parents were dead and that you lived with aunts?'

'Ah. Mm. Yes.'

Damn. Busted.

Bunce looked hurt and confused.

'You mustn't mind me,' I said, staring at him fixedly, 'You see . . . I . . .'

'Yes?'

'*I say these things.*'

We never spoke of it again. Not until Bunce reminded me of it forty-five years later. He remembered the incident with absolute clarity. 'I say these things,' were, he maintains, my exact words.

Regularly caned, always in trouble, never stable, never settled in or secure, I left prep school a sugar addict, thief, fantasist and liar.

The pattern continued at my next school, Uppingham in Rutland. More stealing, more sweets. By this time

the sheer quantity of sugary food I had gorged upon
was beginning to take a real and painful physical toll.
Not in the waistline, for I was as skinny as a pencil, but
in the mouth. Caries, cavities and cankerous ulcers were
constant companions. By my fourteenth birthday I had
lost five of my back teeth for ever. The need for sugar
was destroying me. The rush of excitement as I stole
and the rush from the sugar as I sat and feasted on my
kill inevitably ended, such is the way of passion, in the
crash of guilt, melancholia, nausea and self-disgust that
follow all such addictions . . . sugar, shopping, alcohol,
sex, you name it.

More stealing resulted in a rustication, which was the
public-school word for being sent home for a few weeks:
'suspension' I suppose one would call it now. Finally the
school could put up with me no longer, and I was expelled.[†]
I had gone to London on an officially sanctioned weekend
away to attend a meeting of the Sherlock Holmes Society
of London, of which I was an enthusiastic member. Instead
of being in London for just two nights, as agreed, I stayed
away for a week, blissfully locking myself into cinemas
watching film after film after film. Enough, as parents and
schoolmasters never tired of saying, was enough.

Tobacco's bitter juices will soon take over the story. Once
that loveable leaf had me folded in its fond embrace, sugar
never had quite the same hold over me again. But there is
a little more yet to tell of my troubled relationship with
$C_{12}H_{22}O_{11}$.

As I grew to late adolescence and early manhood my
loyalty to Sugar Puffs was little by little replaced with
a passion for Scott's Porage Oats, made with cold milk,

but generously sprinkled, to be sure, with spoonfuls of granulated sugar. At the same time, my childhood adoration of sherbet and fizzy chews gave way to a more adult preference for that altogether more sophisticated confection, chocolate. And of course there was coffee.

It is 1982, and I am in a shabby set of rooms in London that belong to Granada Television. Ben Elton, Paul Shearer, Emma Thompson, Hugh Laurie and I are gathered there to rehearse for the first series of what will later become a TV sketch show called *Alfresco*. The title of this first series is *There's Nothing to Worry About*. I wanted it to be called *Trouser, Trouser, Trouser* but was, perhaps rightly, overruled.

We are in our early twenties and have left university eight months earlier. Everything should be wonderful in our lives, and I suppose it is. Hugh, Emma, Paul and I have won the first Perrier Award at the Edinburgh Festival for our university revue; a tour of Australia has followed. We have just come from filming that revue for the BBC and now we are about to create our very own television series.

Big sticky tins of Nescafé and boxes of PG Tips teabags stand on a trestle table at one end of the room. There is something about rehearsal that encourages the consumption of great quantities of tea and coffee. This morning, as a sketch is being run through that everyone is in except me (it involves music and dancing), I make coffee for them all and realize, as my hand goes towards the teaspoon, that I am the only one who takes sugar.

There I am, teaspoon poised over an open bag of Tate and Lyle. Suppose I were to give it up? I have always been told that tea and coffee are infinitely better without it. I look across at the others and vow there and then that

I will go sugar-free for two weeks. If, after a fortnight of unsweetened coffee, I have failed to acquire a taste for it, I shall return to my two and a half teaspoonfuls none the worse off.

I light a cigarette and watch the others. A rather splendid swell of proud elation surges up inside me. Perhaps I can do it.

And I do. Ten days later somebody hands me a coffee to which sugar has been added. I leap and start at the first sip as if I have been given an electric shock. It is the most wonderful shock of my life for it tells me that I have succeeded in giving something up. It is far from the greatest tale of triumph over adversity you ever read, but that memory of myself staring at the bag of sugar and wondering if I really could quit never left me. It was to be the one faint whisper of hope in the bottom of Pandora's box. I can still smell that rehearsal room and hear its piano. I can still see the packets of biscuits on the trestle table and the Tate and Lyle bag, some of the sugar gathered into translucent crystalline lumps from the repeated insertion of a wet teaspoon.

I saw and smelt and relived that scene once more twenty-seven years later in a room at the Hotel Colbert in Antananarivo, Madagascar. It was very, very hot and very, very humid, and I was wearing nothing but boxer shorts. An approaching thunderstorm growled menacingly, and the hotel's internet connection, flaky at the best of times, failed. As I stood up from the desk to go to the bathroom a terrible sight caught my eye.

An enormously fat man with gigantic drooping bosoms and a vast overhanging belly was crossing the room. I checked, turned back and stared in horror and disbelief. There he was again, filling the wardrobe mirror, a comically overweight middle-aged man, as grotesquely obese as anyone I had seen since I had filmed in the American midwest the year before. I inspected the bulk of this disgusting mountain of blubber from tip to toe and began to weep.

I had spent the last quarter-century seeing myself on large and small screens and photographed in newspapers and had never been under any illusions concerning my physical appearance. But for some reason on that evening in that room I saw myself as I was. I did not shudder, cover myself up and move on. I did not pretend that everything was fine. I did not say to myself that I was tall enough to carry a little extra weight. I cried at the terrible thing I had become.

There were scales in the bathroom. One hundred and thirty-nine kilograms. What was that in old-fashioned English? I had an app for that on my phone. Twenty-one stone and twelve pounds. Holy imperial hell. Twenty-two stone. Three hundred and six pounds.

I remembered that rehearsal room in 1982. I had managed to give up sugar in tea and coffee. Now it was time to give it up in all its manifestations: puddings, chocolates, toffee, fudge, mints, ice-cream, doughnuts, cakes, buns, tarts, flans, flapjacks, jelly and jam. I would have to exercise too. It could not be a diet, it could only be a complete change in the way I ate and lived.

I won't claim that not a single grain of sugar has passed my lips since that moment of epiphanic horror in Madagascar, but I have managed to avoid such tempting patisserie, puddings, candied fruits, chocolates, ices, *petits fours* and *friandises* as waiters present to one at the sort of restaurants in which me and my spoilt kind hang out. Combined with a regime of daily walks, thrice-weekly gym visits and the general avoidance of starchy and fatty foods, this steadfast forbearance has allowed my weight to drop to something below sixteen stone.

I have not the slightest doubt that I could easily balloon again and find myself hurtling back up past the twenty-first, twenty-second, twenty-third, twenty-fourth and twenty-fifth floors like a cartoon character in an express lift. Constant vigilance is the watchword. It is no part of my business with you to maintain that I now fully know myself, but I think I can profess convincingly that I do at least know myself well enough to be nothing but doubtful and distrustful when it comes to any claims of solutions, cures and arrivals at final destinations.

Take smoking, for instance . . .

C is for Cigarettes

. . . for Convict
. . . for Cundall
. . . for Corporal Punishment
. . . for Common Pursuit
. . . for Cessation

All they that love not tobacco and boys are fools
Christopher Marlowe

Given that I was so disruptive, disobliging and disobedient as a schoolboy it is perhaps surprising that I didn't smoke my first cigarette until I was fifteen. As if to compensate for being an early bloomer in matters of the mind I had always been a late developer in matters of the body. My first orgasm and my first cigarette came later to me than they did to most of my contemporaries, and, looking back, it is as though I spent decades trying to make up for lost time. I think I have always linked smoking and sex. Maybe this is where I have been going wrong all my life.

In 1979, towards the end of my first year at Cambridge, I wrote a play called *Latin! or Tobacco and Boys*. Dominic Clarke, the hero, if such a title can used of so warped a character, delivers a speech in the second act in which he describes and conflates his first sexual and smoking experience.

One of those painful steps towards manhood was my first smoke. It was behind the fives courts of my house at school, with a boy called Prestwick-Agutter. I can remember it as if it were five minutes ago. Prestwick-Agutter opened his packet of Carlton Premium and drew out a short, thin . . . cigarette. As my lips rounded about the tip I began to feel panic. I could hear my boyhood being strangled inside me and a new fire awakening. Prestwick-Agutter lit the end, and I sucked and inhaled. The ears buzzed, the blood caught fire and somewhere in the distance my boyhood moaned. I ignored it and sucked again. But this time my body rejected it, and I coughed and expectorated. My boy's lungs couldn't take the filthy whirl of smuts I was so keen to introduce to them and so I coughed and kept on coughing. Despite my inner excitement and my great coughing fit, I managed to maintain a cool, unruffled exterior, with which to impress Prestwick-Agutter, who was amused by my coolness and pluck. British Phlegm and British Spunk flowed freely in me and out of me, and the Public School Spirit was born. After about an hour, it began to rain, so we dashed into the nearest fives court and leant against the buttress. It was an afternoon of rare agony. It was later that evening, when a horde of uncouth Philistines was raiding my study, Prestwick-Agutter amongst them, that my voice broke. Really quite suddenly. I was nearly seventeen, rather embarrassing really.

While that speech was not (I assure you) autobiographical on my part, Dominic's response to sex and cigarettes does correspond largely to my own. I coughed and vomited rather badly. Not after sex, I should say, but after my first smoke. And after my second and third. Nature was giving me powerful hints that I chose to ignore.

I was at home, fifteen years old, disgraced and expelled[†] when I started to smoke. My parents had chosen for me the Paston School in North Walsham, Norfolk, a direct-grant grammar whose major claim to fame was having had Horatio Nelson as an unhappy pupil. To get there every morning required a ride on a motor coach that passed, on its way to the school, through the market town of Aylsham. After a few weeks of the Paston I found myself getting off the bus at Aylsham and spending the day in a small café, where I could smoke, drink frothy coffee and play pinball until the coach came back through on its return journey. This chronic truancy resulted, of course, in another expulsion. Next I was sent to NORCAT, the Norfolk College of Arts and Technology in King's Lynn. Whatever money I could beg, borrow or steal from my mother's handbag went on cigarettes. As an addiction it was more expensive than Sugar Puffs or sweets and almost as disastrous to teeth, yet wholly more acceptable socially.

The average tuck shop ciggie brands for poor students were Players Number Six, Embassy, Carlton and Sovereign. If I had enjoyed a win at three-card brag I might lash out on Rothmans, Dunhill or Benson and Hedges, but when I was truly in the funds the tobacco equivalent of the Uley village shop beckoned. My obsession with Oscar Wilde, Baron Corvo and the appealingly poisonous world of late nineteenth-century decadence resulted in a pretentious preference for exotic brands. Sobranie Cocktails, Passing Cloud, Sweet Afton, Carroll's Major, Fribourg & Treyer and Sullivan Powell Private Stock were the most desirable, especially the last two, which could only be bought from one specialist tobacconist's shop in all of Norfolk or from their very own premises in London's Haymarket and Burlington Arcade.

It was to London that I went when at last I ran away

from King's Lynn. The threatening approach of exams and the probability that I would fail them had combined with a tiresome adolescent 'I don't need no education' attitude, all of which resulted in a cutting and running. Like Dr Watson in the first Sherlock Holmes story, I found myself drawn to Piccadilly, 'that great cesspool into which all the loungers and idlers of the Empire are irresistibly drained'. Now I had someone else's credit cards[†] to keep me in the very choicest brands of cigarette. Perched on a barstool in the American Bar of the Ritz Hotel, I would sip cocktails, puff Sobranies and think myself urbane. Somewhere along the way I had snaffled and kept my grandfather's old collars and the leather box shaped like a horseshoe in which they were kept. Not only was I a seventeen-year-old trying to look like a compound of Wilde, Coward, Fitzgerald and Firbank, I was a seventeen-year-old in a Gatsby-style suit and starched wing collar smoking coloured cigarettes through an amber cigarette holder. It is extraordinary that I escaped a violent beating.

What I did not escape was arrest. The police caught up with me in Swindon, and after a night in the cells I found myself banged up in a young offenders institution with the endearingly quaint Cotswold name of Pucklechurch.

Tobacco, as is well known, is the major currency on the inside. Relative peace, control and stability are achieved within prison walls through structured jobs, but no convict could ever be relied upon to work were it not that the wages of his labour are the only means by which he can buy his snout, his burn, his baccy. He who has the most tobacco has the most status, influence, respect and contentment. This was certainly true in my day, it may all have changed since then.

You might think that the really smart gaolbird would therefore be a non-smoker or at least have the sense to become one. There are almost none that smart, of course. There are plenty of clever gaolbirds, but very few clever in quite that way. You can almost define a convict as one who lacks precisely the kind of wisdom and self-control necessary to derive long-term advantage from short-term discomfort. This deficiency is what will have turned them to crime in the first place and what will have caused them to be inept enough at it to get caught and captured in the second. To expect a convict to have the strength to give up smoking is to expect a leopard to change his spots, become vegetarian and learn to knit, all on the same day.

I was a natural criminal because I lacked just that ability to resist temptation or to defer pleasure for one single second. Whatever guard there is on duty in the minds and moral make-ups of the majority had always been absent from his post in my mental barracks. I am thinking of the sentry who mans the barrier between excess and plenty, between right and wrong. 'That's enough Sugar Puffs for now, we don't need another bowl,' he would say in my friends' heads or, 'One chocolate bar would be ample.' Or 'Gosh, look, there's some money. Tempting, but it isn't ours.' I never had such a guard on duty.

Actually that isn't quite true. Where Pinocchio had Jiminy Cricket I had my Hungarian grandfather. He had died when I was ten, and ever since the day of his going I had been uncomfortably aware that he was looking down and grieving over what the Book of Common Prayer would call my manifold sins and wickedness. I had erred and strayed from my ways like a lost sheep, and there was no health in me. Grand-daddy watched me steal, lie and cheat; he caught me looking at illicit pictures in magazines and he saw me play with myself; he witnessed all my greed and lust and shame; but for all his heedful presence he could not prevent me from going to hell in my own way. If I had been psychopathic enough to feel no remorse or religious enough to believe in redemption through a divine outside agency, perhaps I should have been happier; as it was I had neither the consolation that I was free of guilt, nor the conviction that I could ever be forgiven.

In gaol, everyone inside rolled their own cigarettes. A week's wages could buy *nearly* enough Old Holborn or Golden Virginia tobacco to last the seven days until next payday. The cigarette papers, for no good reason that I could understand, were the usual Rizla+ brand, but presented in a buff-coloured pack with the words 'H M Prisons Only' printed at an angle across the flap. I hoarded as many of these as I could and contrived to smuggle them out on my release. For years afterwards I would refill these from the standard red, blue and green Rizla+ packs commercially available on the outside and enjoy the bragging rights of being seen with prison-issue rolling papers. Pathetic. I want so much to go back and slap myself sometimes. Not that I would pay the slightest attention.

As the prison week ended and the less careful inmates began to run out of burn they went through a peculiar begging ritual that I, never one to husband resources either, was quick to learn. You would spot someone smoking and slide ingratiatingly up to them. 'Twos up, mate,' you would wheedle and if you were the first to have got the request in you would be rewarded with their fag-end once they had done with it. These soggy second-hand butts, whose few remaining strands of precious tobacco were all bitter and tarred by the smoke that had passed through them, were as a date palm in the desert, and I would smoke them right down until they burnt and blistered my lips. We all know the indignities to which enslaved humans will submit themselves in order to satisfy their addictions, whether for narcotics, alcohol, tobacco, sugar or sex. The desperation, savagery and degradation they publicly display make truffling pigs seem placid and composed by comparison. That image of myself scorching my mouth and fingertips as I hungrily hissed in a last hit of smoke should have been enough to tell me all I needed to know about myself. It wasn't of course. I had decided at school, when it had been borne in on me how hopeless I was at sport, that I was a useful brain on top of a useless body. I was mind and spirit, while those around me were mud and blood. The truth that I was *more* a victim of physical need than they were I would angrily have repudiated. Which just goes to show how complete an arse I was.

After a month or so of remand in Pucklechurch I was at last sentenced by the court to two years' probation and released back to my parents. This time around I managed to enrol myself at a college and to sit for A levels and the Cambridge entrance paper.[†]

Prison appeared to have marked the lowest point of my life. The suicide attempts,[†] tantrums and madness of my mid-teens seemed to be over. Back home in Norfolk I concentrated on academic work, achieved A grades and won a scholarship to read English at Queens' College, Cambridge.

Now that I had the good news of my acceptance, I

faced the problem of what to do with the months leading up to the first term. Unlike today's intrepid, elephant-hair-braceleted student adventurers and gap-year eco-warriors who hike the Inca trail, work with lepers in Bangladesh and dive and ski and surf and hang-glide and Facebook their way around the world having sex and wearing baggy shorts, I chose the already hideously old-fashioned challenge of teaching in a private school. I always believed that I was born to teach, and the world of the English prep school was one whose codes and manners I thoroughly understood. All the more reason for a stylish person to avoid such a place and seek new worlds and fresh challenges, one might suppose, but the systole and diastole of my disowning and belonging, rejecting and needing, escaping and returning was well established. I resist and scorn the England that bore me with the same degree of intensity with which I embrace and revere it. Perhaps too I felt that I owed it to myself to put right the failures of my own schooling by helping with the schooling of others. There was also the example of two of my literary heroes, Evelyn Waugh and W. H. Auden, who had each trodden this path. Waugh had even got material for his first novel out of the experience. Perhaps I would too.

I had added my name to the roll of would-be schoolmasters, a roll that resided somewhere in a copperplate hand amongst the roll-top desks, deckled ledgers and Eastlight boxfiles in the cosy, womblike offices of the scholastic agency Gabbitas-Thring, in Sackville Street, Piccadilly. Just two days after registering, a thin, piping voice called me up in Norfolk.

'We have a vacancy at a very nice prepper in North Yorkshire. Cundall Manor. Latin, Greek, French and a little light rugger and soccer refereeing. As well as the usual duties, of course. Does that appeal?'

'Gosh. That's great. Do I have to go up for an interview?'

'Well now, the happy fact is that Mr Valentine, the father of Cundall's headmaster Jeremy Valentine, lives not far from you in Norfolk. He will see you.'

Mr Valentine was kind and cardiganned and very interested in my views on cricket. He poured me a generous schooner of amontillado and conceded that, while this young Botham chap could certainly swing the ball, his line and length were surely too erratic to trouble any technically correct batsman. Of Latin and Greek there was no discussion. Nor, thankfully, of rugger or soccer. I was commended on my choice of college.

'Queens' used to have a pretty decent Cuppers side in my day. Oliver Popplewell kept wicket. First class.'

I forbore to mention that this same Oliver Popplewell, a friend of the family and now a distinguished QC, had just a few months earlier stood up in his wig and gown and spoken on my behalf at a criminal hearing in Swindon.[†] It didn't seem like the right moment.

Valentine Senior stood up and shook my hand.

'I expect they'll want you as soon as possible,' he said. 'You can catch the fast train to York at Peterborough.'

'So I've . . . you're . . .'

'Heavens yes. Just the sort of chap Jeremy will be delighted to have on the staff.'

I caught the train and arrived at Cundall a teacher and 'just the sort of chap'.

Was I now so very different a figure from the thieving, deceitful little shit who had been such a torment to his family for the past ten years? Was all the fury, dishonesty and desire gone? All passion spent, all greed sated? I certainly didn't believe that I was likely to steal again. I had grown up enough to know how to focus and work and take responsibility for myself. All the adult voices that had shouted in my ear (Think, Stephen. Use your common sense. Work. Concentrate. Consider other people. Think. Think, think, *think!*) seemed finally to have got through. I had an honest, ordered, respectable and unexciting life to look forward to. I had sown my wild oats and it was time to grow sage.

Or so I imagined.

I was still a smoker. In fact, to suit my new role of schoolmaster I had moved from hand-rolled cigarettes to a pipe. My father had smoked pipes throughout my childhood. Sherlock Holmes, veneration of whom had been the direct cause of my expulsion from Uppingham,[†] was the most celebrated pipe smoker of them all. A pipe was to me a symbol of work, thought, reason, self-control, concentration ('It is quite a three pipe problem, Watson'), maturity, insight, intellectual strength, manliness and moral integrity. My father and Holmes had all those qualities, and I wanted to reassure myself and those around me that I did too. Another reason for choosing a pipe, I suppose, was that at Cundall Manor, the Yorkshire prep school at which I had been offered a post as an assistant master, I was closer in age to the boys than to the other members of staff and I felt therefore that I required a look that would mark me out as an adult; a briar pipe and a tweed jacket with leather patches at the elbows seemed to answer the case perfectly. The fact that a lanky late-adolescent smoking a pipe looks the worst kind of

pompous and pretentious twazzock did not cross my
mind, and those around me were too kind to point it out.
The boys called me the Towering Inferno, but, perhaps
because the headmaster was also a pipe smoker, the habit
itself went unchallenged.

I still had no need to shave, and the flop of straight
hair that to this day I can do nothing about continued to
contradict my desire to project maturity. Looking more
pantywaist than professorial and more milquetoast than
macho, I puffed benignly about the school as happy as I
had ever been in all my young life.

Having said which, the first week had been hell. It had
never occurred to me that teaching could be so tiring.
My duties, as a valet would say, were extensive: not just
teaching and keeping order in the form-room but preparing
lessons, correcting and marking written work, giving
extra tuition, covering for other masters and being on call
for everything and everyone from the morning bell before
breakfast to lights-out at night. Since I lived in the school
and had no ties of marriage outside it, the headmaster and
other senior staff were able to make as much use of me as
they wished. I had ostensibly been hired as the replacement
for a sweet, gentle old fellow called Noel Kemp-Welch,
who had slipped on the ice and fractured his pelvic girdle
at the beginning of term. The kernel of my work therefore
was to take his Latin, Greek and French lessons, but I very
soon found myself standing in for the headmaster and
other members of staff giving classes in history, maths,
geography and science. On my third day I was told to go
and teach biology to the Upper Fifth.

'What are they covering at the moment?' I asked. My
knowledge of the subject was sketchy.

'Human reproduction.'

I learnt a great deal that morning both about teaching and, as it happens, about human reproduction too.

'So,' I had said to the class. 'Tell me what you know . . .'

I made it sound as if I was testing them, and nodded importantly as they replied; in fact, of course, I was temporizing wildly. I listened fascinated, repelled and disbelieving as they outlined the details of pipes and glands and flaps and protuberances of which I had heard but with whose forms, features and functions I was entirely unfamiliar. The *vas deferens*, the Fallopian tubes, the epididymis, the clitoris and the frenulum . . . it was engrossingly gross. I left the science room most impressed by the depth and range of the Upper Fifth's knowledge.

When there were no lessons the Cundall Manor timetable was devoted to manly pursuits. Without the slightest familiarity with the rules of either game I found myself running around rugby and soccer fields with a whistle between my teeth. I discovered that if I blew it, dug my heel randomly into the mud, pointed goalward and announced a scrum-down or indirect free kick every five or ten minutes or so I seemed to be able to get by.

'But, sir! What was the offence?'

'Don't think I didn't see, Heydon-Jones.'

'Surely it should be a direct free kick, sir?'

'If it was a direct free kick I would have awarded a direct free kick, wouldn't I?'

If it was a great joke that I, a sports-hating, disruptive, anti-social, rebellious triple-expulsee probationary criminal should now be dishing out punishments, blowing referee's whistles and calling for silence at morning prayers, then it was not a joke that I ever much stopped to examine or smile over. So far as I was concerned my reinvention was complete, and the sly, furtive Stephen who had slunk about on the outside of the healthy decent world was dead and wholly unconnected to the amiable young fogey who made puns in Latin and threatened to flog the Fourth Form to within an inch of their miserable lives if they couldn't keep quiet for a second, damn it all to Hades and back – and face the front, Halliday, or I shall whip you with scorpions, by the bowels of Christ I shall.

Such threats were comic hyperbole, of course, but corporal punishment did still exist in those days and at that school. Did I ever raise my hand in violence to a child in the name of discipline and good order? Yes, I confess that I did. I had been beaten myself at school and had never questioned the role of the cane, ruler or slipper in school life. Before you wring your hands or make to wring my neck, let me explain.

It came about like this . . .

I am on duty one evening about a month into my first term. This means that I have to settle the boys down for the night, put out the lights and remain on call for any emergencies and unexpected crises. The dormitories at Cundall are named after seabirds: Avocet, Guillemot, Oystercatcher, that sort of thing. At my own prep school they had been named after trees – Beech, Elm, Oak and Sycamore. I suppose in the twenty-first century's more sophisticated, child-friendly establishments school sleeping quarters are now called Ferrari, Aston Martin, Porsche and Lamborghini or Chardonnay, Merlot, Pinot Noir and Shiraz, or even Beyoncé, Britney, Jay-Z and Gaga, but in my era, the era of Peter Scott, Gerald Durrell and the Tufty

Club, nature and woodland creatures were considered the most meet and seemly sources for boyhood inspiration.

I switch out the lights in Tern and Puffin and walk along the top landing towards Cormorant, from which dormitory issues an inordinate amount of noise.

'All right, settle down in here! Why is it always Cormorant?'

'Sir, sir, my pillow's broken.'

'Sir, there's a terrible draught in here.'

'Sir, I'm sure I saw a ghost.'

'We're scared, sir.'

'Look. Enough. I'm turning the lights out. Not a squeak. Not. A. Squeak. And yes, Phillips, that does include you.'

Downstairs I go and into the staffroom. A fire is blazing, and I sit down with a pile of exercise books for marking. Before I begin the business of correcting I fish the pipe from the pocket of my tweed jacket. I bring out with it a Smoker's Friend – combination pen-knife, reamer, tamper and bradawl. I fiddle and scrape and poke for a while, banging out the dottle from my previous pipeful into an ashtray and puffing down the stem like a horn player warming up his trumpet. Next I prise open a tin of Player's Whisky Flake and peel back a single layer of firm, slightly moist tobacco. The sweet woody smell laced with something that may or may not be the whisky that the brand name promises rises up to greet me like a holy balm. I lay the wedge in my left hand and with the tips of the fingers of my right I begin to massage it into the palm with a firm circular motion. Most pipe smokers prefer a pouch of ready-rubbed, but for me the ritual of loosening and shredding a pressed wafer of tobacco is almost as important as the inhalation of smoke itself.

There is an excellent line in Ian Fleming's last Bond novel, *The Man with the Golden Gun*: 'The best drink in the day,' he observes, 'is just before the first one.' So it is with my habit. The best smoke for me is the one I have in my head while I am priming the pipe and preparing to puff.

Just as I am about to pack the bowl and fire up I hear above me the thudding of bare feet on floorboards.

Cormorant.

With an exasperated sigh, I lay down the pipe and next to it the tangle of freshly rubbed tobacco. As I ascend the stairs I hear stifled giggles and slaps, snaps and whispers. I stride in and switch on the lights. A ritualized fight is in progress, now frozen in the sudden illumination. School ties are being cracked and flicked like whips. I remember these fights from my own dormitory days.

'Silence! Back into bed all of you. Right this minute!'

A scramble as they leap into their beds and instantly pretend to be asleep.

I switch out the lights. 'One more sound from this dormitory and whoever is responsible will be for the whack. Do you understand? For the whack. I mean it.'

Back in the study I note with disappointment that the two or three minutes that the ball of tobacco has spent on my desk has been enough to dry its loosened shreds a little. I fill the bowl and press the tobacco down with my thumb. Still moist enough to pack well. Firm, with a hint of springiness.

Now comes the moment my brain and lungs have been aching for.

Only Swan Vestas will do at this point, no other incendiary device is quite up to the mark: not specialized pipe-smoker's lighters, however cunning and elaborate, not Bryant and May matches, not a Bic, Clipper, Zippo,

Ronson, Calibri, Dupont or Dunhill, excellent in their own ways as they all may be. Swan Vestas are *real* matches, which is to say you can scrape their magenta heads against any rough surface, not just the shiny brown strips to which the safety match is restricted. You can use a brick in the wall or, like a cowboy, the heel of your boot. The sandpaper provided on the yellow Swan Vesta box is golden, and nothing else scratches like it. I pull the match towards me. I know that one is supposed to strike away in case fragments of burning match-head fly into the face, but I prefer the scooping inwards motion, the way one finishes by bringing the flaring match up before one's eyes.

The sulphurous incense tingles in my nostrils as I tip the lit match at an angle over the bowl and then slowly flatten it out. Each inhalation sucks the flame downwards over the prepared tobacco which fizzes and bubbles in welcome, its moist freshness imparting a thick sweetness to the smoke. Finally, when the whole surface area is lit and just before my fingers burn, three flicks of the wrist extinguish the match. It tinkles as it hits the glass of the ashtray. Matches charred almost to the end have always been a revealing clue for Columbos and Sherlocks. 'A pipe smoker did this deed, Watson, you mark my words . . .'

I am puffing now. One, two, three, four, five draws on the pipe, smacking the lips at the side of the mouth. Each hard suck stokes up the boiler so that, on the sixth or seventh pull, I can breathe in a whole lungful. The hot smoke instantly penetrates the bronchioles and alveoli of the lungs, sending its gift of nicotine rushing through the blood to the brain. So powerful a hit can cause giddiness and sweating in even the most hardened pipe smoker. But the bang deep inside, the grateful surge of encephalins and endorphins, the thudding kick to the system followed by the sweet electric buzz and hum as the body's benign pharmacopoeia is released in a single torrent – what are coughs, nausea, burns to the tongue and mouth, bitter tar in the spittle and the slow degradation of pulmonary capacity compared to that spinning, pulsing burst of love, that shuddering explosion of joy?

That first dose is really what the experience is all about. From then on the trick is to keep the pipe alight with gentle, infrequent tuts and puffs on the stem; smaller cigarette-sized inhalations of smoke will follow until the remaining plug, which has acted as a filter for the tobacco above it, is so fouled and contaminated with tar and toxins that the pipe may be declared dead and ready for the cleaning, scraping and reaming routine to be undertaken all over again.

I am at the steady puffing stage now, as content as any human on the planet – a self-fulfilling contentment that only a pipe can provide: pipe smokers look content, they know themselves to be a symbol of old-fashioned contentment and therefore they are content – when a loud skittering above my head jerks me up from the exercise book I am marking.

Damn it to hell.

It was just one little noise, like a mouse in the wainscotting. I can ignore it.

But no, another sound, that unmistakable thud made by bare feet on floorboards.

A wrathful tide engulfs me. I am now precisely as irate as I was content. Had I been less placidly, pipe-smokingly serene, I would not now be streaking up the stairs with such fury.

'Phillips! Of course. Who else? Right. Well. What did I

say? I said the next culprit was going to be for the whack and I meant it. Dressing-gown and slippers, outside the staffroom. *Now!*'

As I make my way downstairs ahead of him I realize the magnitude of what is about to happen. I threatened the whack, which at Cundall meant not the cane, or a ruler, or a slipper, but a plimsoll. I go into the staffroom. Pipe smoke hangs in rooms in a quite different manner to cigarette smoke. Heavy layers of it are wafted into corrugated waves by the draught of my entrance. I close the door. In a cupboard under the master's pigeonholes I find the official small black gym shoe which I pick up and flex, bending it back on itself and letting it spring back.

What have I done? If I fail to go through with the threatened beating then such authority as I have will be undermined and I will never be able to control the boys again. But how hard does one beat? Suppose I make him cry? Oh good lord.

I pace up and down, slapping the sole of the gym shoe on to my palm hard, then harder and harder until it stings fiercely.

A timid knock at the door.

I clear my throat. 'Enter.'

Phillips shuffles in. His face is set and serious. He is frightened. It is known that I have never administered the whack before, and I must suppose he cannot be certain that I will not be brutal. He seems to know the form better than I do, for he removes his dressing-gown and hangs it on a hook at the back of the door in a manner that suggests he has done this many times before.

'I told you that whoever I caught mobbing about next was for the whack, didn't I, Phillips?'

'Yes, sir.'

Why doesn't he beg for mercy? Then at least I might be in a position to relent. Instead he stands there, fearful but maddeningly resolute, leaving me very few options.

'Right. Well. Let's get it over with then.'

I have absolutely no idea how things should proceed at this point, but once again Phillips leads the way. He approaches the leather armchair in front of the fire and bends over its arm, presenting his posterior in the approved fashion.

Oh God. Oh hell.

I swing my arm upwards and bring the gym shoe down.

It connects.

There is a silence.

'There. Right. Well.'

Phillips twists his head round and shoots a look up at me. It is a look of complete shock. He is astounded.

'Is that . . . is that it, sir?'

'And let that be a lesson! When I say no messing around, I *mean* no messing around. Go on then, back to bed with you.'

'Sir.'

Barely concealing his smirk, Phillips straightens, collects his dressing-gown and departs.

The force with which the rubber sole of the gym shoe connected with his bottom would not have bruised a mosquito. If, instead of striking down, I had dropped the shoe on to him it would have hurt more. It might as well have been a tissue as a plimsoll. It had been not a whack but a feeble tap.

I drop into the armchair, shaking all over. Never again. Never again would I threaten corporal punishment.

And never again did I.

★

The tall, mostly humorous pipe-smoking oddity who taught all manner of subjects, refereed junior matches and made himself useful to staff and boys as much as he could enjoyed himself at Cundall. And Cundall seemed to like him, for when he said goodbye at the end of the summer term the headmaster asked if he might be able to come back for the next term.

'But that's when I start at Cambridge.'

'Michaelmas term at Cambridge doesn't begin till October. Our term starts a month earlier.'

And so for the next two years I came back to Cundall and taught either side of the short Cambridge terms. In the summer I drove the tractor that pulled the gang-mower around the cricket square and I umpired cricket matches. In the winter months I took the boys for walks and on rainy Sundays I compiled quizzes and competitions to keep them occupied.

There was no question in my mind that teaching would be my career. It was my true calling and one that sounded in my head as loud as any school bell. Whether I would teach in a place like Cundall, at university level or somewhere in between only my time at Cambridge would decide. If I had the intellectual heft to make it as an academic then perhaps I would make scholarship my life. I imagined that Shakespearean studies would be my *métier* and tweed and briar my constant accoutrements.

It was a pleasant enough prospect. I was over that terrible sugar addiction and the madness and disruption it had caused. It had been replaced by a woody, tweedy, old-fashioned masculine dependency which, so long as the supply was there, did not modify mood or behaviour and which also served to remind me that I was now a mature, sober, rational adult. I made no allowance for love, sex or the body of course. I was fire and air – in other words, smoke: my other elements, like Cleopatra, I gave to baser life . . .

Ten years later, in 1988, I met one of Britain's greatest smokers. He was at the time a premier drinker too.

'I come,' he told Rik Mayall, John Gordon Sinclair, John Sessions, Sarah Berger, Paul Mooney and me as we gathered for the first rehearsal of his play *The Common Pursuit*, 'from the booze and fags generation.' He slumped his shoulders down ruefully to emphasize that this was an ineluctable fact in whose remorseless face he was powerless.

Simon Gray was then, I realize with a slight shudder, exactly the age I am as I write this now. He had, like his favourite actor Alan Bates, a full flop of black hair, but his physique was less solid. Years of drinking had bulged his tummy into a gentle pot while simultaneously wasting his lower half, so that he was spindle-shanked and all but arseless. I almost never saw him without a cigarette in one hand and a drinking receptacle in the other. In the mornings he gulped down champagne, which in his eyes barely counted as alcohol. From lunchtime onwards he sipped at endless coffee mugs or plastic cups of Glenfiddich whisky. It was the first time I had been at close quarters with an authentic alcoholic. Some of my generation drank more than was good for them and would go on to develop into the real thing, but for the moment youth was on their side.

Unusually for the professional theatre, rehearsals for *The Common Pursuit* would begin after lunch. We all decided early on that this was because Simon, who was directing the production, was not able to function before that time. In fact, as I found out, it was because he spent the mornings at his desk. No matter how much he drank, he always seemed able to put in plenty of daily writing hours as a playwright and diarist. Just occasionally I caught sight of him early in the morning, before his first champagne. It was a ghastly sight. His face sagged, his eyes were dull, rheumy and bleared, his voice creaked huskily, and his whole being looked defeated and incapable of thought, action or purpose. One sip of an alcoholic drink, however, and he revived like a desert flower in the rain. He seemed to grow inches taller in front of you, a light and sparkle appeared in his eyes, his complexion smoothed and brightened, and his voice strengthened and cleared. Simon Gray, I decided when I first witnessed this frog into prince transformation, did not have a drinking problem. He had a drinking solution.

Rik Mayall's nickname for him was Mr Drinky. We adored him and he appeared to adore us. 'I know nothing of your generation,' he would say. 'I don't watch television so I haven't seen "The Young Ones" or "Blackadder" or whatever the things you do are called. They told me to audition you, and so I did. You all seem absurdly young and confident, and I am assured that you will bring an audience into the theatre.'

That we seemed young to him I can imagine, but that we gave the impression of confidence seemed extraordinary in any of us except of course Rik Mayall. Rik was a force of nature who appeared charismatically invincible and fearlessly uninhibited from the moment he burst on to the comedy scene with his friend Ade Edmondson in the early eighties. I suppose that I too, as ever, emanated waves of looming self-confidence that I most certainly did not feel.

The title of Simon's play came from a phrase coined and used as the title of a collection of essays by the critic and academic F. R. Leavis, who founded a whole school of English-literature studies whose high seriousness, attention to detail and earnest moral purpose were legendary. Simon Gray had been taught by Leavis himself at Cambridge and remained hugely influenced by him. For myself, I'd always thought Leavis a sanctimonious prick of only parochial significance (my own brand of undergraduate sanctimoniousness at work there, I now see) and certainly by the time I arrived at Cambridge his influence had waned, he and his kind having been almost entirely eclipsed by the Parisian post-structuralists and their caravanserai of prolix and impenetrable evangels and dogmatically zealous acolytes. Stories of Frank Leavis and his harridan of a wife, Queenie, snubbing, ostracizing, casting out and calumniating anyone who offended them went the rounds, and those English academics at the university who had been in their orbit were callously dismissed by the elite as dead Leavisites.

Leavis's intense, suspicious propensity to explode in wrath and to anathematize anyone who dared disagree with him I saw again in Harold Pinter, whose close but combustible friendship with Simon Gray and Simon's wife, Beryl, was an eternal source of delight to me and John Sessions in particular, as ardent connoisseurs of literary eccentricity. I remember once John and I were sitting in the back brasserie of the Groucho Club. Harold, his wife, Lady Antonia, Beryl and Simon had a corner table. Suddenly Harold's booming voice burst out. 'If you are capable of saying such a thing as that, Simon Gray, it is perfectly clear that there is no further basis for our friendship. We are leaving.'

We peeped round to see Harold rise with massive black-polo-necked dignity, stub out a cigarette, toss down the remnants of a whisky and sweep past us, growling all the while. That massive dignity was a little punctured by his realization that the faithful Pakenham hound was not at his heels. He turned and barked across the room, 'Antonia!'

Lady Magnesia Fridge-Freezer, as Richard Ingrams liked to call her, jerked herself awake (her defence against the madness of Harold's tantrums was always simply to fall asleep. She could do this in the middle of a meal or sentence, a kind of traumatic symplegia, a condition known only to cats in P. G. Wodehouse, but which I think refers to what we would now call narcolepsy) and softly gathered up her coat. By this time the whole back brasserie was watching the scene unfold and greatly enjoying the embarrassed lacunae, charged glances and menacing exchanges that one associates with the authentically Pinteresque. Antonia smiled seraphically at the Grays and went to join her husband. As she passed our table she stopped and gathered the loose wool at the shoulder of my pullover.

'Oh, what a lovely jumper,' she sighed, fingering it for a second.

'Antonia!'

And she drifted away. I can almost bring myself to believe that the room burst into applause, but I think that would be an instance of the wish being father of the thought.

I raise the issue of Leavis because the moral seriousness he inculcated into the study of letters left its mark on Simon Gray in strange ways. I remember an evening in the bar of the Watford Palace Theatre. We had performed the play for about a week prior to coming into the West End. That night's performance was a great success, and afterwards Simon dished out the few director's notes he had scribbled on tickets and taxi receipts while standing at the back of the theatre sipping Glenfiddich. The mood amongst us was good. He sighed something about how young we all were.

'Actually,' said John Gordon Sinclair, 'you remember when I auditioned and you asked me how old I was?'

'Yes,' said Simon. 'What of it?'

'Well, I said I was twenty-eight, but actually I'm only twenty-five.'

'What? *What*? Why?'

'Well, I knew that you'd cast Stephen and Rik and Johnnie; they were like twenty-nine and thirty and thirty-two or whatever, and I didn't want you to think I was too young . . .'

'You *lied*?' Simon stared at him aghast.

'Yes, well . . .' Gordie had clearly imagined that Simon would be amused. It was all over now: he was safely cast in the play, we could all share in the charm of his anxiety to be cast and the little white lie he told to make it more likely. If anything the story was a compliment to the play and his desire to be a part of it. The smile vanished from Gordie's face as he realized that Simon was far from amused.

'You *lied*.' A characteristic slump and a grimace of pain and despair swept over Simon. 'You *lied*?'

Poor Gordie was bright red now and wishing he was dead.

'Well, I thought . . .'

'But to *lie* . . .'

Fond of Simon as I was, I thought this was a strange reaction. To disapprove of lying is one thing, but to disapprove of so benign and amiable a lie and so relentlessly to bear down on its perpetrator struck me as being bullying, priggish, mean and grotesquely out of proportion. We all tried in our own way to defuse the moment, but Gordie felt rotten for the rest of the week, convinced that Simon was going to sack him or at the very least hate him for ever, and I was left wondering whether the malignant influence behind it all was whisky or Leavis.

The play we were there to put on chronicled the life of a group of friends who collaborate as students on the founding of a literary magazine called *The Common Pursuit*. Over the course of the play's action, hard real life with its loves, infidelities, compromises and betrayals scuffs away the gloss and sheen of the group's noble ambitions and high Leavisite ideals. John Sessions took the leading part of Stuart, the magazine's editor, opposite Sarah Berger, who played his girlfriend, Marigold. Paul Mooney was Martin, the best friend endowed with enough private means to keep the magazine going, and John Gordon Sinclair played Peter, a likeable serial philanderer endlessly snared in a tangle of lies and evasions as he tries to run his chaotic seraglio of mistresses. My role was that of a broodingly intelligent, sexually constrained, waspish and socially awkward philosophy don called Humphrey Taylor, who ends up being murdered by a piece of rough trade, à la James Pope-Hennessy and (perhaps) Richard Lancelyn Green. Rik took the part of Nick Finchling, a brilliant, slapdash and entertaining historian who trades his academic promise for an easy career in the media. Nick is a heavy smoker and towards the end of the play he develops emphysema. At one point my character Humphrey upbraids him as he watches him light up and dissolve, for the umpteenth time, into a terrible coughing fit.

'You should give up.'

'Why?'

'For one thing, you'll live longer.'

'Oh, you don't live longer. It just seems longer.'

That was Mr Drinky's view of his addictions, and now it was mine too. The previous year I had told everyone that I was going to give up smoking on 24 August, my thirtieth birthday. I managed ten nicotine-free days at my house in Norfolk before a group of heavy-smoking friends arrived to stay, their presence soon bending and then snapping my puny will. I would not try again for almost twenty years. Instead I adopted Simon Gray's guilt-free acceptance of the addiction. No, it was more than guilt-free acceptance: cigarettes were proud banners to be flown. Objections to smoking in Simon's eyes were contemptible and bourgeois. He was always getting in terrible rows for lighting up in minicabs and those parts of theatres and public spaces which, even back then, were given over to non-smokers. The diaries he wrote and published throughout the eighties, nineties and into the noughties reveal a baleful champion of tobacco barging belligerently through an increasingly intolerant and hostile world. The titles of his final journals make this explicit – *The Smoking Diaries Vol. 1*, *The Smoking Diaries 2: The Year of the Jouncer* and *The Last Cigarette: Smoking Diaries 3*.

Of course the body can take chronic assault from alcohol and tobacco for just so long. The time came for him to give up first one and then the other.

★

I am in a quiet residential Notting Hill street in 2006, filming for a documentary on manic depression. The director, Ross Wilson, positions the camera at one end of a long, straight pavement. I walk to the other end, turn round and wait for his cue. All I have to do is walk towards the camera. No acting or speech required. It is one of dozens and dozens of such shots that are filmed all the time in documentaries. Something to fill the screen for a voiced piece of commentary to be laid on later: 'And so I decided that a visit to the Royal College of Psychiatry might prove useful . . .' – that sort of thing.

Ross waves for action, and I start the walk. From out of one of the houses shuffles an old man in a dressing-gown, blocking the shot. I stop and return to my mark. This is always happening when we film in the street, and we are very used to it. Well, not old men in dressing-gowns particularly so much as members of the public, or civilians, as some people in the film and TV business call them, or, wince-inducingly these days, 'muggles'. TV documentary is not major movie-making, where you have policemen and assistant directors to help marshal the citizenry. In such situations we wait patiently and grin inanely. The man in the dressing-gown slowly and painfully approaches, and I see that it is Simon Gray. His hair is almost white, and his face is sunken in. He looks dreadfully ill and much older than his seventy years.

'Hello, Simon.'

'Oh. Hello.'

We have only spoken to each other once since the terrible trauma of 1995 in which I had walked out of his play *Cell Mates* and fled to Europe. As it happens, the documentary I am filming this very day seeks to find out, amongst other things, what had propelled me to that flight.

'So. What are you doing?' Simon asks.

'Oh. Filming.' I indicate the camera behind him. I think it wise not to mention that the events of 1995 are central to the film.

He slowly turns, looks at it and then comes round again to me. 'Ah. Well. There we are, aren't we? A comedy of some kind I suppose. Well then.' Never has comedy been made to sound so low, vulgar and pitiful. Simon had never forgiven me for leaving *Cell Mates*. Initial worry and concern for my well-being at the moment of my leaving had rapidly been replaced by resentment, fury and contempt. All of which was very understandable. The show should have gone on.

I see him just once more. It is July 2008, and I am in a box at Lord's cricket ground, watching Pietersen and Bell put on nearly 300 runs for the fourth wicket against South Africa. The next-door box is filled with distinguished playwrights: Tom Stoppard, Ronald Harwood, David Hare, Harold Pinter and, sitting quietly in a corner, Simon Gray. Playwrights and cricket have always gone together. Samuel Beckett remains, I believe I am right in saying, the only Nobel Laureate to have had an entry in the cricketer's almanac, *Wisden*.

At tea, the nubiferously chain-smoking pair of Tom Stoppard and Ronnie Harwood visit our rather showbizzy box. David Frost is the host and he wonders aloud if there might be a collective noun for a group of playwrights. Stoppard suggests the word 'snarl'. The particular snarl of playwrights assembled next door has collected a pair of Oscars, a dozen BAFTAs and Olivier Awards, a CH, three

CBEs, two knighthoods and a Nobel Prize for Literature. I am happy talking to Stoppard and Harwood, both of whom are as engaging, charming and friendly as Pinter and Gray are obstreperous, cantankerous and unstable. Pinter's capacity for explosive hostility and liverish offence at the tiniest imagined slight is legendary and, while he has never displayed any animosity towards me, I have always been very wary of speaking to him for more than a few minutes at a time, just in case.

At the close of play I make my way out of the box and walk straight into Simon, whom I have not seen since that afternoon in Notting Hill.

'Hello, Simon!' I say. 'Gosh, you look well.'

Which, compared to two years ago, he does.

'Do I?' he says. 'Well, that's terminal cancer for you. As a matter of fact I'm dying. That was my last cricket match. Well. There we are. Goodbye.'

He died three weeks later. Whether the prostate cancer that killed him was in any way related to his smoking I have no idea. I suspect that his alcoholism and sixty-five a day were not the cause of his death. At any rate Simon Gray did die and was justly mourned as one of the most individual, intelligent and comically desperate voices of his time. I was not invited to the funeral.

Rewind to 2006. I had decided, I am not quite sure why, that it was time for me to stop smoking. Actually, I think I *do* know why. I had managed finally to give up the big thing, the thing we will turn to at some other time, and it annoyed me that I found it so hard to do the same with cigarettes. If I could abandon the systematic and heavy use of a Class A forbidden substance, surely I could fight off nicotine addiction with the merest snap of the fingers?

On the shelf by my desk in my London house there stood a strange object. Designed and built by the Dunhill company, it seemed to be an old-fashioned BBC radio microphone. Disassemble and reassemble it in the manner of Scaramanga and his Golden Gun, however, and it became a pipe. This fine trophy had been presented to me a few years previously when I was named Pipe Smoker of the Year. On account of this I now felt a slight twinge of guilt at the thought of quitting. I picked the award up and, like a child with a Transformer toy, twisted, snapped, prised and pushed it into its alternative shape.

It so fell out that my installation in 2003 was to be the last of these funny little Pipe Smoker of the Year ceremonies. The award was ruled by the health authorities to be a form of tobacco advertising by the back door and from that year on was mercilessly proscribed. In its heyday it had celebrated the great icons of the age, most of them a touch suburban and cardiganny perhaps, but, from Harold Wilson to Eric Morecambe, by way of Tony Benn and Fred Trueman, they had represented something rather splendid that has since gone out of British life. Neither smart, nor sophisticated, nor stylish, they were the kind of people you picture devoting their Sundays either to grappling with the garden hose and waxing the Wolseley or to brisk fell-walking, a canvas haversack on their backs and long woolly socks up to their knees.

Dunhill and the event's organizers went to great trouble to make me my special pipe, mix me my own blend of tobacco and embrace me as one of their own. Now there I was just three years later, planning to leave the fold. It seemed like a betrayal. As a matter of fact, I rarely smoked a pipe in public anyway. For the most part I was a Marlboro man. Not full-on Marlboro Reds, nor anaemic Marlboro Lights, but Mummy Bear Marlboro Mediums – for the compromiser in life. Middle aged, middle brow, middle class, middle rank, middle tar – that's me. I reserved the old briar pipes for winter months and lonely hours at the writing desk. Although there had been just one recent occasion when I did go out into the world with a pipe . . .

I was being profiled in the *Independent* newspaper in the summer of 2003, I cannot remember the purpose; perhaps it was to coincide with the first series of the television programme *QI.* For no good reason I turned up at the appointed place with a pipe in my pocket. At some stage I must have run out of cigarettes and started in on it. A week later, to accompany the interview, there appeared a picture of me on the cover of the newspaper with the pipe jutting out of my face at an angle, a thick cloud of smoke artfully half concealing my smug features. Sadly my features know no other way of arranging themselves except smugly. Why had I taken the pipe along and why had I smoked it in the presence of a photographer? Looking back, I now wonder if at some entirely subconscious level I had recognized that a pipe would suit the rather professorial side to my character that *QI* emphasized and maybe that is why I had pocketed it when setting out to meet the journalist. What is interesting, or at least revealing, about the nature of twenty-first-century celebrity, is that it was only a few days after the publication of that interview that a letter arrived from the British Pipesmokers' Council advising me that I had been elected that year's Pipe Smoker of the Year. This charming absurdity came so hard on the heels of the article that it was bound to give me the feeling that, if it had chanced to be a bonobo who had been featured on the front page of the *Independent* smoking a pipe that week, then the accolade would surely have gone to it . . . desperate is, I suppose, the word to describe the worshipful company of pipe smokers and tobacco blenders. And given the forthcoming demise of the award, perhaps their desperation had good cause.

Now there I sat, three years later, fiddling with my prize pipe and contemplating a betrayal of the smoking cause. 'Betrayal' and 'cause' are perhaps hysterical and self-important words to use, but smoking to me *was* a cause; it had always symbolized in my mind something enormous. I have mentioned Sherlock Holmes, but the fact is that almost all my heroes were not just figures who happened to smoke, but more than that, active, proud and positive smokers. They didn't just smoke in the world, they smoked *at* the world. Oscar Wilde was one of the pioneers of the cigarette. When he met Victor Hugo, the *cher maître*'s major obsession was as much with Wilde's abundant supply of fresh, high-quality cigarettes as with his equally abundant supply of fresh, high-quality epigrams. Wilde's first episode of real notoriety came when he took to the stage to make his bow after the triumphant first night of *Lady Windermere's Fan* with a cigarette between his fingers – a casual detail that enraged many present and was considered worthy enough to mention in just about every press report and in the letters and diaries of those who had been present.

'A cigarette is the perfect type of a perfect pleasure,' says Lord Henry Wotton in *The Picture of Dorian Gray*. 'It is exquisite, and it leaves one unsatisfied.' It took me a long time, as with so many of Wilde's remarks, to understand that this was actually much more profound an insight than it at first glance appeared. The point is that a pleasure which leaves you satisfied stops being a pleasure the moment it has been enjoyed. You are now sated, there is nothing more to be got from it. Sex and food are pleasures of this kind. What follows? A touch of afterglow if you are that sort of person, but mostly guilt, flatulence and self-disgust. You don't want any more of that kind of pleasure for some time to come. As for behaviour modifiers like alcohol and narcotics, one may want more and more, but they alter mood and manner, and the crash and the hangover that come after can be deeply unpleasant and lowering to the spirits. But a cigarette . . . a cigarette delivers the keen joy, the hug of gratification, and then – nothing more than the desire to experience it all over again. And so on. No moment of feeling engorged, full, unworthy and sick, nor hangover or mood crash. A cigarette is perfect because, like a highly evolved virus, it attaches itself to the brain of the user such that its only purpose is to induce them to have another. There is a reward for that in the form of pleasure, but the reward is too short-lived to be called satisfaction.

I had then Holmes and Wilde on my side. I had Wodehouse and Churchill, Bogart and Bette Davis, Noël Coward and Tom Stoppard, Simon Gray and Harold Pinter. And ranged against us? Bourgeois nose-wrinklers, sour health-mongers, Hitler, Goebbels and Bernard Shaw, cranks, puritans and interfering prigs. Smoking was a banner of bohemianism, a sign of the rejection of middle-class prudery and respectability, and I was a whale on that, despite being in my heart of hearts as middle class, unadventurous and respectable as anyone I knew. One has, after all, no one to convince in these matters but oneself.

If I was to ally myself with outsiders, artists, radicals and revolutionaries then it was natural that I would smoke and smoke proudly. I know. Pathetic, isn't it?

I have said nothing of death here. Nothing of the ravages to the complexion, throat, heart and lungs that cigarettes wreak. What Oscar did not know is that the most superb quality of all possessed by these beguiling little cylinders of joy is the *gradualness* of their toxicity, the imperceptibly nuanced encroachments of their poison. Their very benignity (after the clammy dizziness, reeling and nausea induced in virgin smokers to which I have already alluded), the excruciating slowness and delicacy with which they set about their business of killing, the irresistibly tempting credit period they offer that promises so seemingly unbridgeable a distance between present pleasure and future payment . . . such slow, unremitting and diabolical subtlety delivers what a true sadist and connoisseur of pain would surely consider the highest pitch of the exquisite.

I had been a most vocal apologist for smoking and a noisily belligerent enemy of the anti-smoking lobby. But as I sat toying with the Dunhill microphone pipe that day I realized that I had changed. Inasmuch as experiences are rarely to be regretted there was something pleasing to my mind now in considering life as a non-smoker. I had enjoyed well over thirty years of tobacco use and now I was to see what life would be like without it. I was almost looking forward to testing myself. So long as I pledged never ever to be intolerant of those fellow smokers I left behind.

Fight fire with fire, fight drugs with drugs. I had heard about a pill called Zyban, a proprietary name for amfebutamone, better known in America as Welbutrin, one of the most prescribed anti-depressants in the world. I had read somewhere that it also works as a 'smoking cessation aid' in almost 30 per cent of cases. I called up my doctor's secretary and made an appointment. He wrote out a prescription for a three-week course. In the same way that these pills, in order to counter depression, acted on the brain's own store of mood elevators – noradrenaline and dopamine and so on – so they acted, it was claimed, to calm, inhibit and allay the anxieties and horrors of nicotine withdrawal. The unusual and appealing thing was that you were told to take the pill and carry on smoking. For some reason the craving would leave you, if you were one of the 27 per cent on whom the treatment worked.

And you know what? It turned out that I was.

It was a miracle. I just found myself stopping and not minding.

I fly to America, for the first time in my life happy to spend twelve and a half hours on an aeroplane without being reduced to the indignity of nicotine-replacement patches, gums and inhalers – sometimes, in the bad old days, all three at once.

On the fourth Thursday of November, which is Thanksgiving Day in the United States, I have a meeting with the film-maker Peter Jackson, for whom I am to write a screenplay based on the great raid on the German dams of the Ruhr in 1943. A masterpiece of British cinema had already been made on the Dambusters story, of course, but we hoped to be able to tell it again, incorporating details that in 1954 were too sensitive or secret to reveal.

I arrive at the Beverly Hills Hotel bungalow that Peter has taken for the duration of his stay, and we talk over the details. Fran, Peter's wife, is present as well as other members of their production company, Wingnut. Thanksgiving Day is a perfect time to have an uninterrupted meeting if, like us, you are not American.

When the conference is over an assistant loads into the boot of my rental car an enormous box of research materials that Wingnut has assembled for me. Every imaginable archival resource on the subject of the Dambusters raid, in text, video, sound or photographic form has been gathered together for my convenience. There is even a facsimile of R. C. Sherriff's screenplay of the 1954 Michael Anderson film. I drive along Sunset Boulevard, into West Hollywood and towards the Chateau Marmont, the hotel where I have taken an apartment-like set of rooms for the month or so I have to deliver the screenplay.

I spend a happy evening going through the documents and planning the next day's writing. How pleasant it all is. How lucky I am. What can go wrong?

There is something of a commotion next door, and I look out into the corridor to see the actress Lindsay Lohan being stretchered away. It seems that her partying has caught up with her. The Chateau Marmont will always be best known, I fear, for being the scene of John Belushi's final fatal speedball. It is still a favourite haunt of Hollywood's more raffish party element, and Lindsay Lohan's unfortunate overdose, while not fatal, excites much attention. But these are things that do not need to worry me.

The next day I am up early for a swim in the pool and raring to make a start on the script. I cook myself an omelette and brew up an enormous pot of coffee – the suites in the Chateau come with splendid kitchens – and settle down at my desk, photographs of Guy Gibson,

Barnes Wallis and a Lancaster bomber Blu-tacked up on the wall to inspire me. What could be more agreeable?

But there is a problem.

A terrible problem.

I cannot write.

My fingers go to the keyboard and I force them to type out.

FADE IN:

<u>INT. THE AIR MINISTRY – EVENING, 1940</u>

And that is as far as I can get.

Ridiculous.

I stand up and walk about the room. This can be no more than initial nerves. It is a potentially big project. The original film is one of my favourites. I am anxious about my right to tinker with this magnificent story. Sit down again and get on with it, Stephen.

But it is more than that. As I stare at the screen I feel that there is a void inside me, a dark space. What can it be, this sucking black hole that is somewhere between hunger, fear, dread and pain?

I shake my head and then my whole body, like a dog emerging from a bath.

It will pass.

I leave the room and descend in the elevator, listening to a couple swapping gossip on the subject of Lindsay Lohan's dramatic departure from the hotel the night before.

I pace around the pool. Jerry Stiller, comedian and father of the actor Ben, is doing a few slow lengths.

'Hiya, kid,' he calls out. I do love, at the age of forty-nine, to be called kid.

After ten or twenty circuits I return to the room and sit once more before the screen.

The black hole is still there.

This is all terribly, terribly wrong.

What can it be? What *can* it be? Am I ill?

And then with a bolt of certainty that almost knocks me from my chair I realize what it is.

I need a cigarette. I cannot write without a cigarette.

It can't be true. Surely?

For the next three hours I try everything I can to get the writing juices going, but by midday I realize that it is useless. Either I do not deliver the screenplay or I smoke. I lift the telephone receiver.

'Hello, it's Stephen here. Could you send up a carton of Marlboro please? Yes a whole carton. Ten packs. Thanks. Bye.'

Fast forward to April the following year, 2007. In July the ban on smoking in public will come into force throughout the United Kingdom, and the month after that I will be fifty. Now, surely, it is time to give up once and for all. I have been hypnotized by Paul McKenna in an attempt to remove the hard wiring in my brain that associates writing with tobacco. I have been given a session at the Allen Carr 'Easy Way' clinic in London. Neither seems to have been much use, grateful as I am to each for offering help. But there is good news . . .

A new drug has arrived. Farewell Zyban, hello Champix, Pfizer's name for a new compound called varenicline, which is not an anti-depressant but a 'nicotinic receptor partial agonist'. What could be whatter?

I have a course prescribed and, as with the Zyban,

I continue smoking as if nothing has happened. On about the tenth day I notice that my ashtray is filled with absurdly long stubs. I have taken no more than one puff from each. By the end of the second week I find myself taking cigarettes out of the pack, staring at them as if they are strangers and replacing them. During this time we are taping *QI* two or three times a week. When that finishes I find that I am no longer buying packs of cigarettes. I have stopped smoking.

I drive up to Norfolk and start filming for a new series of *Kingdom*. When this concludes at the end of September I fly to America to start work on a travel series.

The real test comes later, however. In May 2008 I return to Britain from Hawaii, the last state to be visited for the documentary, and I need to sit down to write the book of the series. Only now will I see if I can, for the first time in my life, write something more than journalism, letters and occasional blogs without consuming cigarette after cigarette as I type.

It seems, when that day dawns, that my thirty-five-year relationship with tobacco really is over.

Writing these words as I have been, sitting in front of a computer, and recalling the past, has the old urge returned? The experience has not opened up that black hole, but somewhere, deep inside me, a trace memory twitches and thrashes like a dragon in a cave sleeping a restless sleep.

Have I betrayed a way of looking at the world? Have I turned my back on freedom, perversity and outsiderism? Have I bourgeoisified and sold out? Most would think the question preposterous, but I do not. While the nicotine habit might rightly be characterized as dirty, dangerous, anti-social, ontologically pointless and physically deleterious and while those in its thrall might be regarded as reckless, foolish, self-indulgent, weak and perverse, I still find myself drawn to smokers and irritated by those who nag and bully them.

I was at a dinner party many years ago, sitting along from Tom Stoppard, who in those days smoked not just between courses, but between mouthfuls. An American woman opposite watched in disbelief.

'And you so intelligent!'

'Excuse me?' said Tom.

'Knowing that those things are going to kill you,' she said, 'still you do it.'

'How differently I might behave,' Tom said, 'if immortality were an option.'

Substances seem insignificant compared to the big things in life: Work, Faith, Knowledge, Hope, Fear and Love. But the appetites that drive us and our susceptibility, resistance, acceptance and denial of substances define and reveal us at least as much as abstract expressions of belief or bald recitations of action and achievement.

Maybe it's just me. Maybe other people have greater control over their appetites and less interest in them. I seem to have been driven by greedy need and needy greed all my life.

I.
College to Colleague

Cambridge

The Winter of Discontent, they called it. Strikes by lorry drivers, car workers, nurses, ambulance drivers, railwaymen, refuse collectors and gravediggers. I don't suppose I had ever been happier.

After all the storm-tossed derangement of my teenage years – love, shame, theft, scandal, expulsion, attempted suicide, fraud, arrest, imprisonment and sentencing – I finally seemed to have found something close to equilibrium and fulfilment. *Seemed*. Smoking a pipe as a placid and confident figure of authority in a small prep school was one thing. Now here I was at a huge university starting all over again as a new boy, a fresher, a nobody.

It is natural for people to despise the very idea of Oxford and Cambridge. Elitist, snobbish, hidebound, self-satisfied, arrogant and remote, the Ancient Universities, as they conceitedly style themselves, seem to embody the irrelevant, archaic, moribund and shameful past that Britain appears to be trying so hard to shed. And Oxbridge doesn't fool anybody with all that flannel about 'meritocracy' and 'excellence'. Are we supposed to be impressed by the silly names they give themselves? Fellows and stewards and deans and dons and proctors and praelectors. And as for the students, or *undergraduates*, I beg their pompous pardons . . .

Many people, but especially I think the young, see

pretension and performance all around them. They will read attitudinizing and posturing in every gesture. If they were to walk down Trinity Street in Cambridge during term time they would encounter youthful men and women that it would be very easy to characterize as self-conscious poseurs or play-acting pricks. Oh, they think they're *so* intellectual; oh, they think they're *so Brideshead Revisited*; oh, they think they're *so* la crème de la crème. Look at the way they bicycle along the cobbles with their arms folded, too cool to touch the handlebars. See how they walk along with their head in a book. See how they wrap their scarves around their necks with a flick. As if we're supposed to be impressed. Listen to their drawly public-school voices. Or, worse, listen to their fake *street* accents. Who do they think they are, who do they bloody think they bloody are? Mow the fuckers down.

Well. Quite. But imagine for a moment that these wanky arsehole poseurs are actually no more than young men and women with real lives and real feelings just like anybody else, just like me and just like you. Imagine that they are quite as scared and unsure and hopeful and daft as you and me. Imagine that instant contempt and dislike really says more about the onlooker than about them. Then imagine something further. Imagine that just about every single student newly arrived at such a place as Cambridge went through exactly those same feelings of dislike, distrust and fear when looking at the easy and assured second- and third-years milling around them with all their relaxed confidence and their superior air of assurance and belonging. Imagine that they too had compensated for such feelings of nervous inadequacy by choosing to 'see through' everyone else, by choosing to believe that those

around them were pitiful poseurs. And imagine finally that
without their noticing it they somehow became absorbed
and naturalized into the place to such an extent that now,
to an outsider, they are the ones who look like arrogant
tossers. Inside, you can take my word for it, they are still
shrinking and shrivelling like salted snails. I know, because
I was one, just as you would have been too.

It is true that I was a scholar. It is true that I was older
than my first-year contemporaries. True also that I had
more experience of the 'real world' (whatever that might
be supposed to be) than most. True as well that, unlike a
surprising number of those arriving at university, I was
very used to being away from home, having been sent to
my first boarding school at the age of seven. True too that
I had an apparently assured manner and a deep, resonant
voice that made me sound as if I belonged to the place
quite as much as the wooden panels, shaved lawns and
bowler-hatted porters. I concede all that, but it is very
important that you understand nonetheless how very
scared I was inside. I lived, you see, in quivering dread of
being at any moment *found out*. No, it wasn't my status as a
convicted criminal on probation that I wanted kept secret,
nor my past history as thief, liar, forger and gaolbird. As
far as I was concerned those home truths were perfectly
fit for broadcast, as was my sexuality, my ethnicity or any
other thing of that nature. No, the terror that gripped
me during those first few weeks at Cambridge was all
about my intellectual right to be there. My dread was
that someone would approach and ask me, in front of a
crowd of sneering onlookers, my opinion of Lermontov
or Superstring Theory or the Categorical Imperatives of
Kant. I would prevaricate and palter in my usual plausible

way, but, this being Cambridge, such stratagems would
cut no ice with my remorseless and (in my imagination)
gleefully malicious interrogator, who would stare at me
with gimlet eyes and say in a harsh voice that crackled
with mocking laughter: 'Excuse me, but do you even
know who Lermontov *is*?' Or Rilke or Hayek or Saussure
or some other name my ignorance of which would reveal
the awful shallowness of my so-called education.

At any moment it would come to light that my
scholarship had been wrongly awarded, that there had
been a muddle with examination papers and some poor
genius called Simon Frey or Steven Pry had been cheated
of their proper place. A relentless public inquisition would
follow in which I would be exposed as a dull-witted fake
who had no business at a serious university. I could even
picture the ceremony in which I was formally ejected
from the college gates, slinking away to the sound of jeers
and whistles. An institution like Cambridge was for other
people, insiders, club members, the chosen – for *them*.

You may think I am exaggerating, and perhaps I am.
But by no more than 5 per cent. All those thoughts truly
did spin around in my head, and I really did fear that I had
no right to be a Cambridge undergraduate, and that this
truth would soon become obvious, along with academic
and intellectual deficiencies that would reveal me to be
entirely unworthy of matriculation.

Part of the reason I felt all this is because I think I
had a much higher doctrine of Cambridge than most
undergraduates. I believed in it completely. I worshipped
it. I had chosen it above Oxford or any other university
because . . . because of . . . oh dear, there is no way of
explaining this without sounding appallingly precious.

My favourite twentieth-century author in those days was E. M. Forster. I hero-worshipped him and G. E. Moore and the Cambridge Apostles and their associated Bloomsbury satellites Goldsworthy Lowes Dickinson and Lytton Strachey as well as the more illustrious planets in that system, Bertrand Russell, John Maynard Keynes and Ludwig Wittgenstein. I admired especially the cult of personal relations that Forster espoused. His view that friendship, warmth and honesty between people mattered more than any cause or any system of belief was for me a practical as well as a romantic ideal.

'I hate the idea of causes,' he wrote, 'and if I had to choose between betraying my country and betraying my friend I hope I should have the guts to betray my country.' That claim, from an essay called 'What I Believe' and published in his collection *Two Cheers for Democracy*, was taken by some to be all but treasonable. Given his connections to the group later known as the Cambridge Spies, it may be easy to see why such a credo still causes unease. He knew that, of course, for he went on to write:

> Such a choice may scandalise the modern reader, and he may stretch out his patriotic hand to the telephone at once and ring up the police. It would not have shocked Dante, though. Dante places Brutus and Cassius in the lowest circle of Hell because they had chosen to betray their friend Julius Caesar rather than their country Rome.

I know how insufferably awful I must appear when I tell you that I wanted to go to Cambridge because of the Bloomsbury Group and a parcel of poofy old *bien-pensant* writers and traitors, but there we are. It wasn't because of

Peter Cook and John Cleese and the tradition of comedy, much as I admired that, nor was it because of Isaac Newton and Charles Darwin and the tradition of science, much as I admired that too. Cambridge's beauty as a university town had some influence, I suppose. I saw it before I ever saw Oxford, and it pierced my heart in a way that first love always does. But it really was, pretentious as it may sound, the intellectual and the ethical tradition that appealed to my puritanical and self-righteous soul. I had emerged from a monstrous youth, you must remember, and I suppose I felt I needed the holy fires of Cambridge to cleanse me.

'Cambridge produces martyrs and Oxford burns them.' I honestly cannot remember if that phrase is my own or whether I borrowed it from somebody else: I seem to be credited with it on the web, which proves nothing, of course. Anyway, it is true that Martyrs' Memorial in Oxford commemorates the burning of the three Cambridge divines Hugh Latimer, Nicholas Ridley and Thomas Cranmer in the city of Oxford. There has always been a sense that Oxford is a worldly, political and establishment institution, strong in humanities and history, and that Cambridge is more idealistic, iconoclastic and dissident, strong in mathematics and science. Certainly Oxford has provided Britain with twenty-six prime ministers where Cambridge has only managed fifteen. It is indicative too that Oxford was the Royalist headquarters during the English Civil War while Cambridge was a Parliamentarian stronghold; indeed Oliver Cromwell was a Cambridge alumnus and local to the area. Roundhead Cambridge, Cavalier Oxford. This pattern is repeated in theology – the tractarian Oxford movement is high church to the point of being Romish, whereas Wescott

House and Ridley Hall in Cambridge are low to the point of being evangelical.

This same doctrinal distinction is even to be seen in comedy, mad as that may sound. Robert Hewison (an Oxonian) in his excellent book *Monty Python: The Case Against* shows how the great Pythons were divided along Oxford and Cambridge lines. Those long lean Cantabrigians (Virginia Woolf had noted fifty years earlier how Cambridge breeds them taller than Oxford) Cleese, Chapman and Idle were all icy logic, sarcasm, cruelty and verbal play while the Oxonians Jones and Palin were warmer, sillier and more surreal. 'Let's have a dozen Pantomime Princess Margarets running over a hill!' Jones might suggest, to which Cleese would coldly riposte, 'Why?'

The creative tension between those two in particular, according to Hewison, formed the heart and soul of what Python was. You might see the same thing in the differences between Cambridge's Peter Cook and Jonathan Miller and Oxford's Dudley Moore and Alan Bennett. It is more than possible that you find the cuddly Dudley and the even cuddlier Alan Bennett and Michael Palin much more likeable than their tall, aloof and rather forbidding Cambridge counterparts. And perhaps this extends down to the later incarnations – Oxford's Rowan Atkinson and Richard Curtis are shorter and surely sweeter than the lofty and fractious Stephen Fry and Hugh Laurie.

There is tremendous romance in the cavalier tradition and absolutely none in the puritan. Oscar Wilde was an Oxford man, and a great part of me is deeply drawn to the Oxford of the aesthetic movement, Arnold's 'Scholar-Gipsy' and the Dreaming Spires. But the pull of

Cambridge was always stronger; Forster's world marked me for her own at some point in my teenage years and thenceforward it was Cambridge or nowhere.

All of which goes some way towards explaining, perhaps, why I was so nervous about being found out. It was obvious to me that Cambridge, the Mecca of the Mind, would be filled with the most intellectually accomplished people in the world. Students of organic chemistry would be familiar with Horace and Heidegger, and classicists would know the laws of thermodynamics and the poetry of Empson. I was unworthy.

I would have had to have been epically delusional or truly, medically paranoiac not to recognize such insecurities for what they were: a mixture of too idealistic a sense of what Cambridge was, allied to lashings of the worst kind of late adolescent solipsistic angst. I had never fitted in at school and, now that I was come to a place almost expressly designed to suit me, suppose I turned out to be unable to fit in there too? What did that say about me? It was too frightening to contemplate.

But the first two weeks at a university are designed, which is to say they have evolved, to enforce the realization amongst freshers that everybody is in the same punt and that everything will be fine. Besides which, after a few days I had met enough people and overheard enough conversations to realize that Cambridge was far from fifth-century Athens or fifteenth-century Florence.

University life begins with the Freshers' Fair and all kinds of 'squashes' – recruitment parties thrown by student clubs and societies. What with the comparatively healthy bank balance of a student in the first week of their academic year on the one hand and that keen desire to be accepted and loved that flows from all the insecurities I have described on the other, it is likely that a fresher will join any number of extracurricular groups in their first week, from the established – the Footlights Club, *Varsity* magazine and the Cambridge Union, to the weird – the Friends of the Illuminati, the Society of Tobacco Worshippers and the Beaglers Against Racism. All very silly and studenty and adorable.

College and Class

I suppose I am going to have to stop off here and explain in the briefest and simplest of terms, if I can, the nature of collegiate life at Cambridge. There is no reason why anyone should understand how it works without having lived inside it. And, of course, no reason why anyone should care. Unless you are curious, in which case I love you, for curiosity about the world and all its corners is a beautiful thing, even if those corners are as uncool as the cloisters of Oxbridge.

There are twenty-five Cambridge colleges (well thirty-one in all, but two of those are for postgraduates and the other four only accept mature students), each of which is a self-governing institution with its own history, income, property and statutes. Trinity College is the largest, with 700 undergraduate students. It is also the wealthiest of all Oxbridge colleges, worth hundreds of millions and owning land everywhere. Others are poorer: in the fifteenth century Queens' was a big supporter of King Richard III, whose boar's head device still flies from college banners, and it consequently suffered from confiscations and other financial penalties following that unfortunate monarch's defeat on Bosworth Field.

Each college has a hall for dining, a chapel, a library, senior and junior combination rooms (common rooms at Oxford) and a porter's lodge. They are mostly medieval in fabric and they are all medieval in structure and governance. They are entered by towered gateways and laid out in lawned and cobbled courts (at Oxford these are called quads). You would not design an educational establishment from scratch along these peculiar lines, and indeed no one ever has. Yet for over 800 years the two collegiate universities have run continuously without a break and there has been no cause to change the fundamental principles that organize them, except through the slowest and most immeasurably gradual evolution. Whether Oxford and Cambridge can survive the envy, resentment, dislike and distrust of future generations we can only guess. It is perfectly possible that someone will attach to them the hideous word 'inappropriate' or the hideous phrase 'not fit for purpose' and they will be turned into museums, heritage centres or hotels. No one can stop them from being historic, however, and without vandalism they cannot prevent them from being physically beautiful either. Those two qualities alone will ensure that, come what may, young people will want to go to them in sufficient numbers to risk their being considered elitist.

An Oxbridge student is given a place, not by the university, but by his or her college and it is there that they will live and take their instruction in the form of tutorials – which at Cambridge are called supervisions. The average number of undergraduate students at a college is about 300. When I arrived at Queens' in October 1978, there were five others reading English in my intake. Or was it six? I know one changed to theology, and two others dropped out altogether. No matter. The university, as distinct from the colleges, runs the faculties (History, Philosophy, Law, Classics, Medicine and so on) with their tenured readers, lecturers and professors. In my time Queens' had three English Literature Fellows (or 'dons') who were also attached to the university's English faculty, although it is perfectly possible to be a Fellow within a college, taking supervisions and teaching undergraduates and yet be without a faculty post. Oh lord, this is so complicated and dull . . . I can almost hear your eyes glazing over.

Look at it this way. You live and eat in your college and attend supervisions arranged by the dons in your college for which you write essays, but you go to lectures and are ultimately examined by the university faculties which are outside the college. There is no campus, but there are faculty buildings, lecture theatres, exams schools and so on. Would it help if I said colleges are like Hogwarts houses, Hufflepuff and Ravenclaw and so on? I have a horrible feeling it might . . .

The Queens' College of St Margaret and St Bernard is one of the oldest in the university. It is also one of the prettiest, with a divine half-timbered cloister court, a charming medieval Hall, all done over by Thomas Bodley and Burne-Jones at the height of the late pre-Raphaelite period, and a famous wooden structure known as the Mathematical Bridge that spans the River Cam and connects the old part of the college with the new. When I arrived in 1978 Queens' was still an all-male institution. Girton, the first women's college, started taking men the following year, while the more advanced King's and Clare had been mixed for six years, but Queens' was carrying on in much the way it had for more than half a millennium. Incidentally, the apostrophe after the 's' is there on account of it being founded by two queens, Margaret of Anjou and Elizabeth Woodville. In Le Keux's *Memorials of Cambridge*, which I am sure you have read, but I will remind you anyway, the author, writing in about 1840, spells the name of the college as Queen's College, and appends a footnote:

> A custom has arisen latterly of writing the name Queens' College, as being the foundation of two queens. This appears to us an unnecessary refinement. We have the authority of Erasmus against it, who always calls his college 'Collegium Reginae'.

'Reginae' is of course Latin for 'of the Queen', in the singular. God, I sound like a guide book. Not surprising, as I'm quoting from the college website. Anyway, there you are.

As the only English scholar in my year I had been allocated a rather fabulous set of rooms overlooking the President's Gardens. That's another idiosyncratic Oxbridge nonsense – the titles given to heads of houses. Some are Masters or Mistresses, others are Wardens, Provosts, Principals or Rectors and a few, as is the case with Queens', are styled President.

On the day I arrived I stood at the bottom of my staircase and for ten minutes I played with the exquisitely exciting proof that, for the time being at least, I truly was a Cambridge undergraduate. You see, each staircase has at its entrance a wooden board on which are hand-painted the names of the occupants residing within. Next to each name is a sliding block of wood that obscures or reveals the words IN and OUT, so that when a student (or Fellow, for the dons have rooms in college too) passes the board on their way to or from their rooms they can signal their presence or absence to an anxious and expectant world. I was happily flicking my block of wood back and forth and would still have been doing so to this very day if the sound of approaching footsteps hadn't sent me scuttling up to my rooms.

I had arrived that afternoon with a collection of carefully chosen books, a typewriter, a gramophone, a pile of records, some posters and a bust of Shakespeare, all of which were soon disposed about the rooms in as pleasing and artfully artless an arrangement as I could contrive. Undergraduate sets are composed of a bedroom, a main room and a gyp-room, or kitchen. Gyp was the unfortunate nickname for a college servant: the more appealing Oxonian appellation is 'scout', but I'm not going to get side-tracked with Oxbridge minutiae again, I promise. I know how much it upsets you.

I had determined that I would go out later for coffee, milk and other staples. For the moment I was content to sit alone but for two dozen or so invitations carefully laid out on my desk. In the days before email and mobile phones, communication was managed by notes left in a student's pigeonhole in the porter's lodge. If someone wanted to contact you it was much easier for them to leave a message there than to have the fag of climbing all the way to your rooms and slipping it under your door. I had already gone down to the porter's lodge three times in the last hour to see if any more invitations had come in. The pigeonholes were arranged and colour-coded according to undergraduate year. Thus a club or society could undertake a mass leafleting of first-years, a kind of targeted spamming. Hence the quantity of paper spread out on my desk. The invitations to squashes being held by sporting, political or religious societies I had instantly thrown away, but I had grouped together invitations from dramatic and literary clubs, magazines and journals. What about the Cambridge University Gay Society? I was undecided about this. I liked the idea of pinning my pink colours to the mincey mast but was wary of being involved in anything campaigning or strident. In those days I was a most conservative or at least actively inactive sort of figure politically. In the jargon of the day, my consciousness was unawakened.

Invitations to sherry parties held by the college's Senior Tutor, by the Dean of Chapel and by an entirely different person also claiming the title of Dean were not to be refused, I was told. Also essential was a gathering in the rooms of A. C. Spearing, the college's senior English Fellow, who was to be, it seemed, my Director of Studies. The most impressive and formal invitation, all pasteboard, gold embossing and armorial bearings, was the one summoning me to the Queens' College Matriculation Dinner, a formal event in which the entire intake of first-years would be officially received and enrolled as members of the college.

And so I embarked on this round of parties and introductory gatherings. In A. C. Spearing's rooms I met my fellow English Literature freshers. We stuck together in the first week, accompanied each other to assorted squashes and introductory lectures, swapped second-hand gossip and sized each other up academically, intellectually, socially and in one or two cases I suppose, sexually. We were very typical of our generation. We

knew T. S. Eliot backwards but could barely quote a line
of Spenser or Dryden between us. With the exception
of one of our number we would have looked like, to an
outside observer, as prize a parcel of punchably pompous
and buttoned-up arseholes as ever was assembled in one
place. The exception was a bondage-trousered, leather-
jacketed, henna-haired youth called Dave Huggins. He
looked like the kind of punk rocker you would cross the
King's Road in Chelsea to avoid. Despite being far and
away the friendliest and most approachable of our group
he scared the hell out of me and I think out of everybody
else too. Something in my booming voice and apparently
confident manner seemed to appeal to him, however, or
amuse him at least, and he dubbed me the King.

For all his forbidding street aspect, Dave had been to
school at Radley, one of the smarter public schools: in
fact almost all of us in the English Literature intake had
been privately educated. Unsure of ourselves and nervous
of being found academically wanting as we may have
been, I cannot imagine how alarmingly and alienatingly
at home we must have seemed to those arriving from state
schools, to that cadre of young men and women who had
never before stayed away from home and never before
met public-school product en masse. Some months later
a student who had been educated at a comprehensive in
south-east London told me that for weeks he had been
unable to understand what 'say gid' meant. He kept hearing
it everywhere: 'Say gid! That's jarst say gid!' Eventually he
realized that it was how the upper middle-class pronounce
'So good, that's just so good.' He observed how strange it
was for him to be in the minority. Some 3 per cent of the
population received private education in those days and

here he was – one of the great 97 per cent, but somehow feeling like a chimney sweep who has gatecrashed a Hunt Ball. No matter how much Cambridge might have presented itself as a purely academic institution whose only criterion for entry was academic, the dominant accent to be heard was public school. It took a very special kind of self-belief and strength of character not to feel angry or out of place in such an environment.

I have no idea what kind of figure I cut. Well, no that's not true. I am afraid I have all too clear an idea of what kind of a figure I cut. My typical mode of dress was a Harris tweed jacket with leather buttons, Viyella shirt and knitted tie, V-neck lambswool sweater, corduroy trousers of lovat green and brown half-brogue shoes polished to a high gloss. With my trademark flop of hair and a pipe clamped between my teeth I looked like what I of course had been all the previous year, an assistant master from a small rural prep school, perhaps with something of the air of a Second World War back-room boffin. Whatever impression I gave it certainly wasn't that of a hip young rocker in the age of The Clash and The Damned.

Chess, Classics, Classical Composers, Curiosity and Cheating

It turned out that Queens' did indeed have two deans, a Dean of Chapel, and a Dean in charge of discipline. At each of the first-week decanal sherry parties I found myself falling into conversation with a first-year called Kim Harris. He was handsome in a way that reminded me of a young Richard Burton and radiated a powerful mixture of severity, secrecy, relish and surprise that I could not but find intriguing. Like me he was separated from other freshers by appearing on the one hand more mature and adult while on the other exhibiting an unembarrassedly high doctrine of what Cambridge ought to be. He was educated, I soon discovered, at Bolton School, an independent day school that a generation or two earlier had thrown Ian McKellen at Cambridge and a grateful world. Kim had come to Queens' to read Classics. He dressed rather like me but in Church's full brogues and V-necks of the purest and priciest cashmere. He was even capable of wearing a bow-tie without looking absurd, which is a very great human skill indeed. We became instant friends in the way that only the young can. We did not consider going to any party or event except in each other's company.

'Are you gay?' I asked him quite early on.

'Let's just say that I know what I like,' was his prim and opaque reply.

Aside from his proficiency at Latin and Greek Kim had another skill and at a level of brilliance that seemed to me to be quite superhuman. He was a chess Master. At Bolton he had played with, and to some extent mentored, Nigel Short, who was already becoming well known as the greatest prodigy England had ever produced. At the age of ten Short had beaten the great Viktor Korchnoi and now at fourteen was on the verge of becoming the youngest International Master in history. Kim was 'just' a Master, but that meant he was skilful enough to play blindfold, a trick I never tired of urging him to perform. Without any sight of the board he would demolish all comers.

When I first saw him do this it reminded me to raise a point with him.

'Kim,' I said, 'when we very first met at one of those sherry parties I remember we looked at a chessboard in the Dean's rooms, and I asked you if you played chess.'

'So you did.'

'And do you remember what you replied?'

Kim raised his eyebrows. 'I don't think so.'

'You said, "Let's just say, I know the moves."'

'Well, I do.'

'You know a bit more than the moves,' I said.

'Your point being?'

'My point being, if that's how you answer someone who asks you if you play chess, how am I to interpret it when you answer the question, "Are you gay?" with the words "Let's just say, I know what I like"?'

Kim's family was well off, and they lavished upon their only son every imaginable luxury, including a magnificent Bang and Olufsen stereo system on which Kim played Wagner. And sang to Wagner. And conducted Wagner. And lived Wagner.

I had fallen for Wagner's music myself when young but I had never penetrated the mysteries of the full works. Aside from anything else I had never been able to afford the huge box sets. As well as *Lohengrin*s and *Meistersinger*s and a *Parsifal* or two Kim had two complete Ring cycles on record: Karl Böhm's live Bayreuth recording and the great Decca studio production of the Solti Ring, one of the masterpieces of the gramophone age. I know how bored and restless people become at talk of Wagner so I won't dwell on him at length. Let it just be said that Kim completed my Wagnerian education, and for that alone I would be grateful to him for ever.

He and I and a friend of his from Bolton called Peter

Papa.
Mama.

Grandpapa.

(*Left to right*) Sister Jo, self, brother Roger.

Tragic hair. Tragic times.
Taken some time between
school and prison.

Between Mama and Papa with a rather long-haired
Roger on the right.

The Sugar Puffs addict has moved on to Scott's Porage Oats.

Universally Challenged.

Kim in Half Blue scarf.

The Cherubs. I know we look like wankers, but really we weren't. Honestly.

Kim Harris. Not unlike a young blond Richard Burton.

Emma Thompson's hair is starting to grow back.

Unable to afford an outboard motor, Hugh Laurie and his poor dear friends are having to propel themselves through the water.

…laying the King in *All's Well That Ends Well*, BATS May Week production 1980, in Queens' Cloister Court.

Cableknit
Pullover, Part 1.

The backlit ears
of Hugh Laurie,
gentleman.

Cableknit
Pullover, Part 2.

Speak, who was reading Philosophy, would sit around discovering late nineteenth-century masterpieces over which to go into ecstasies. Strauss, Schoenberg, Brahms, Mahler and Bruckner were our gods and Kim's B&O our temple.

Given that Britain was boiling with anarchic post-punk creativity, the political excitements of multiple strikes and the election of Margaret Thatcher to the leadership of the Conservative Party, that there was rubbish piling up on the streets, corpses going unburied and inflation rocketing skywards, given all that, a knot of tweedy Cambridge late adolescents gasping at the wonder of Strauss's *Metamorphosis* and Schoenberg's *Transfigured Night* seems . . . seems what? Perfectly legitimate. Entirely in accordance with what education is supposed to be. Education is the sum of what students teach each other in between lectures and seminars. You sit in each other's rooms and drink coffee – I suppose it would be vodka and Red Bull now – you share enthusiasms, you talk a lot of wank about politics, religion, art and the cosmos and then you go to bed, alone or together according to taste. I mean, how else do you learn anything, how else do you take your mind for a walk? Nonetheless, I'm slightly shocked at how earnest and dull a picture I present in my tweed jacket and corduroys, puffing at a pipe and listening to all that German Late Romantic noise. Is that where it all went wrong? Or is that where it all went right?

There is that in student life which reinforces the connection between the words 'university' and 'universal'. All divisions of life are there, and all the circles and sodalities, coteries and cliques that you will find in the wider human cosmos can be found in the swirling flux of young people who shape and define a university for the three or four years of their tenancy.

Whenever I return to Cambridge I wander the familiar streets as a stranger. I know and love the architecture intimately, but while the chapels and colleges, courts, bridges and towers are what they have always been, Cambridge is entirely different each time. You cannot step into the same river twice, observed Heraclitus, for fresh water is always flowing over you. You cannot step into the same Cambridge twice, or the same Bristol, or Warwick, or Leeds or any such place, for fresh generations are for ever repopulating and redefining them. The buildings are frozen, but a university is not its buildings, it is those that inhabit and use them.

I discovered brilliant people and dunces and everything in between. There were the lively and there were the preternaturally dull. Every imaginable special interest was represented. You could spend your three years as an undergraduate on sports fields and never know there were any theatres. You could involve yourself in politics and be wholly unaware of orchestras or choirs. You could hunt with beagle packs, sail, dance, play bridge, build a computer or tend a garden. Just as you can at hundreds of universities, of course. It is only that Cambridge has the advantage of being both bigger and smaller than most. Smaller because you are in a college of perhaps 300; bigger because the whole university numbers over 20,000, which confers some sort of an advantage when it comes to audiences and participants in sport and drama, readership circulations for magazines and captive markets for all sorts of enterprises and undertakings.

I need not, of course, have worried that I would be

quizzed and found wanting on the subject of Russian poets or the principles of particle physics; the fear proved groundless that I would find myself in such rarefied heights of academic brilliance that I would be unable to breathe.

To do well at exams (in the field of literature and the arts at least) it is better to be a hedgehog than a fox, if I can borrow Isaiah Berlin's famous distinction. In other words, it is better to know one big thing than lots of smaller things. A point of view, a single way of thinking that encompasses all elements of a subject, allows essays more or less to write themselves. The way to pass exams is to cheat. I cheated all the way through my three years at Cambridge. Which is not to say that I looked at the work of the student next to me, or that I brought in outside material from which to crib. I cheated by knowing in advance exactly what I was going to write before the invigilator bid us turn over the question sheets and started the clock. I had a theory of Shakespearean tragic and comic forms, for example, which I won't bore you with and which is probably specious, or at least no more truthful or persuasive an overall interpretation of Shakespeare's forms than any other. Its virtue was that it answered any question and yet always appeared to be specific. I had found part of it in an essay by Anne Barton (née Righter). She is a fine Shakespearean scholar, and I filleted and regurgitated some of her ideas for both Parts One and Two of the tripos (Cambridge calls its degree examination the tripos, something to do with the three-legged stool on which students used to sit when taking them). In both of the Shakespeare papers I got a First. In fact in Part Two it was the top First for the entire university. It was essentially the same essay each time. It only takes a paragraph at the top to twist the question such that your essay answers it. Let's say, in simple terms, that my essay proposes that Shakespeare's comedies, even the 'Festive' ones, play with being tragedies while his tragedies play with being comedies. The point is that you can trot this essay out no matter what the question. *'Shakespeare's real voice is in his comedies': Discuss. 'King Lear is Shakespeare's only likeable tragic hero': Discuss. 'Shakespeare outgrew his comedies.' 'Shakespeare put his talent into his comedies and his genius into his tragedies.' 'Tragedies are adolescent, comedies are adult.' 'Shakespeare cares about gender, but not about sex.'* Discuss, discuss, discuss, discuss, discuss, discuss. I did, of course, no such vulgar thing as discuss. All my ducks were in a row when I walked into the examination hall and I had to do no more than point their beaks at the question.

Of course, having a good memory helped . . . I had enough quotations in my head, both from the works and from Shakespearean critics and scholars, to be able to pepper my essay with acute references. So creepily good was that memory that I was always able to include Act, Scene and Line numbers for every play quotation or to place in brackets the source and date of any critical reference I cited (*Witwatersrand Review*, Vol. 3, Sept. 75, ed. Jablonski, Yale Books, 1968, that sort of thing). I am aware that to be given a good memory at birth is worth more than almost any other accomplishment but I believe too that it is as rare for one person to be born with a physically better memory as it is for them to be born with better fingers or better legs. There are young men and women up and down the land who happily (or unhappily) tell anyone who will listen that they don't have an academic turn of mind, or that they aren't lucky enough to have been blessed with a good memory, and yet can recite hundreds of pop lyrics and reel off any amount of information about footballers, cars and celebrities. Why? Because they are *interested* in those things. They are curious. If you are hungry for food you are prepared to hunt high and low for it. If you are hungry for information it is the same. Information is all around us, now more than ever before in human history. You barely have to stir or incommode yourself to find things out. The only reason people do not know much is because they do not care to know. They are incurious. Incuriosity is the oddest and most foolish failing there is.

Picture the world as being a city whose pavements are covered a foot deep in gold coins. You have to wade through them to make progress. Their clinking and rattling fills the air. Imagine that you met a beggar in such a city.

'Please, give me something. I am penniless.'

'But look around you,' you would shout. 'There is gold enough to last you your whole life. All you have to do is to bend down and pick it up!'

When people complain that they don't know any literature because it was badly taught at school, or that they missed out on history because on the timetable it was either that or biology, or some such ludicrous excuse, it is hard not to react in the same way.

'But it's all around you!' I want to scream. 'All you have to do it bend down and pick it up!' What on *earth* people think their lack of knowledge of the Hundred Years War, or Socrates, or the colonization of Batavia has to do with *school* I have no idea. As one who was expelled from any number of educational establishments and never did any work at any of them, I know perfectly well that the fault lay not in the staff but in my self that I was ignorant. Then one day, or over the course of time, I got greedy. Greedy to know things, greedy for understanding, greedy for information. I was always to some extent like that robot Number 5 in the movie *Short Circuit* who whizzes about shrieking, 'Input! Input!' Memorizing for me became like eating Sugar Puffs, an endless stuffing of myself.

I do not say that this hunger for learning was morally, intellectually or stylistically admirable. I think it was a little like ambition, a little like many of the later failings in my life we will come to: membership of so many clubs, ownership of so many credit cards . . . it was part of wanting to belong, of feeling the need constantly to connect myself. Rather vulgar, rather pushy.

While the manner and motives of it may not have been magnificent the end result was certainly useful. The urgent desire to pack the mind, my insatiable curiosity and appetite for knowledge led to all kinds of advantages. Facile exam passing was one such. I had never found written tests under time pressure anything other than enjoyable and easy. That is because of my fundamental dishonesty. I never tried to engage authentically or truthfully with an intellectual issue or to answer a question. I only tried to show off and in the course of my life I have met few people who are my equal at that undignified art. There are plenty who are more obviously show-offy than I am, but that is what is so creepy about my particular brand of exhibitionism – I mask it in a cloak of affable modesty and touching false diffidence. To be less hard on myself, I think these displays of affability, modesty and diffidence may once have been false but have now become pretty much real, in much the same way that the conscious manner we decide to sign our names in our teens will slowly stop being affected and become our real signature. The mask if worn long enough will be the face.

All of which seems a long way from a memoir of university life, which is what this chapter is supposed to offer. The life of a student however, especially that of a more than usually self-conscious student in an institution like Cambridge, does involve a great deal of questioning of the mind and intellectual faculties and the meaning and purpose of scholarship, so I think it right to try and fathom what my mind was about in those days.

I went to three lectures in my entire three years. I can only remember two, but I am sure I went to another. The first was an introductory talk on Langland's *Piers Plowman* by J. A. W. Bennett, who had been installed as C. S. Lewis's successor in the chair of Medieval and Renaissance Literature in 1963 and seemed old enough to have lived through much of the period of which he had made himself a master. His lecture was a monumentally dull explanation of why the B-text of *Piers Plowman* (an achingly long work of Middle English allegorical alliterative verse) was more to be relied upon than the C-text, or possibly the other way around. Professor Bennett begged leave to disagree with W. W. Skeat on the issue of the A-text's rendering of the Harrowing of Hell, blah-di-blah-di-blah . . .

That was enough for me. I knew that five minutes in the faculty library would let me dig up a rare enough article in the *Sewanee Review* or similar to furnish fodder for an essay. Lectures broke into one's day and were clearly a terrible waste of time. Necessary no doubt if you were reading Law or Medicine or some other vocational subject, but in the case of English the natural thing to do was to talk a lot, listen to music, drink coffee and wine, read books and go to plays.

Perhaps *be* in plays?

I regularly get letters from aspiring actors or their parents asking for advice. If *I* get lots, you can imagine how many Ian McKellen, Judi Dench, Simon Russell Beale, David Tennant and other *legitimate* actors must get. The phrase 'crowded profession' is used more for the acting business than for any other I ever heard of and for good reason.

As in so many fields in life there are people out there longing to be given a secret, a way-in, a technique. I can understand it absolutely. Almost as common as the phrase 'crowded profession'; are phrases that express the idea of 'just need a break' and 'not what you know, but who you know'. I am excluding, for the time being, the whole issue of fame and concentrating exclusively on those who actually care about acting in and of itself: I expect we will come to those who obsess about the ancillary 'benefits' of red-carpet recognition and celebrity magazine coverage later.

The letter-writers want to know the best way to achieve a foothold in the acting profession. All that is required, they know, is a *chance*, one opportunity to shine: their talent, industry and commitment will do the rest. They know, the world knows, how much *luck* has to do with it. They may have heard about some young striver who wrote a letter to an established actor and got a role as a walk-on in a film, or an audition, or a place at a drama school as a result.

What a creep or ungrateful beast you would have to be not to be moved by the cries of those on the outside who clamour for admission. If you have been lucky enough to advance in the profession surely the least you can do is offer a hand, or a word of helpful advice to those who would emulate you? Absolutely right, but one must be honest too. I can only advise from experience. If someone asks me to how to do something, I cannot answer in the abstract, I can only answer according to my own history. I have absolutely no idea how to become an actor, I can only tell you how I became one. Or at least, how I became a sort of actor who is also a sort of writer who is also a sort of comedian who is also a sort of broadcaster who is also a sort of all sorts of all sorts sort. Sort of. That is the best I can do. I cannot pronounce on whether it is better to go to drama school or not to go, I cannot advise on whether to do rep or street theatre before attempting film or television. I cannot tell you whether it is deleterious or beneficial to the career to take on extra work or accept a part in a soap opera. I simply do not know the answer to these questions because they have never arisen in my life. It would be reckless and irresponsible of me to push someone towards or away from courses of action or inaction of which I know nothing.

So here is how I became an actor.

At prep school the school play was always a musical, so the best casting I could ever hope for would be in the non-singing roles: Mrs Higgins in *My Fair Lady* was an especial triumph ('Would grace any drawing-room' being my first published critical notice). At Uppingham I wrote and performed with my friend Richard Fawcett in comedy sketches for House Suppers, as Christmas entertainments were called there. I also made a mark as a witch in *Macbeth*. I say 'made a mark' because the director – in a burst of creative licence which he must have regretted ever afterwards – thought we should devise our own characters, costumes and props. I went to the butcher's in Uppingham and procured a bucket of pigs' guts to pull out of the cauldron for the 'Eye of toad and ear of newt' scene. My dear, the *smell* . . .

The next time I appeared on stage was at the Norfolk College of Arts and Technology in King's Lynn. NORCAT's lecturer in charge of drama was called Bob Pols, and he cast me first as Creon, in a double bill of Sophocles' *Oedipus Rex* and *Antigone*, and then as Lysander in *A Midsummer Night's Dream*. I was camp and wore a cricket pullover, as Lysander, that is, not as Creon. My only other dramatic experience took place in a local church performance of Charles Williams's *Thomas Cranmer of Canterbury*, a verse play by the 'other' member of the Inklings (i.e. the one who wasn't J. R. R. Tolkien or C. S. Lewis). That was the sum total of my dramatic experience, nativity plays aside, when I arrived at Cambridge. Yet I had it in my head that I was a natural actor, that I knew how to speak lines, that I would have a *presence* on stage, a weight, a heft, an ability to draw focus when required. I think this was because I was always confident about my voice and my ability to speak verse and to inflect and balance speech properly, without the misplaced emphases and false stresses that I could hear so clearly in the voices of prefects and other amateurs when they read lessons in chapel or recited verse or dramatic lines on stage. The few prizes I had won at school were for poetry reading or recitation of one kind or another. In the same way as one might wince at a discord I would wince at incompetent intonation and wish that I could get up and correct them. Such a point of view now strikes me as arrogance and insolent presumption, but I suppose a conviction that one can do better is a necessary part of the self-belief that is itself a necessary part of pursuing a calling. Heroes matter too. Everyone I've ever met whom I have admired has grown up with their own pantheon of heroes. I listened to, watched and admired Robert Donat, Laurence Olivier (of course), Orson Welles, Maggie Smith, James Stewart, Bette Davis, Alistair Sim, Ralph Richardson, John Gielgud, Paul Scofield, Charles Laughton, Marlon Brando (natch), James Mason, Anton Walbrook, Patrick Stewart, Michael Bryant, Derek Jacobi, Ian McKellen and John Wood. There were many others, but those I especially remember. I had not seen a great deal of theatre, but John Wood and Patrick Stewart at the Royal Shakespeare Company had made an enormous impression. I did impersonations of Stewart's Enobarbus and Cassius in the coach on the way back to school. The others in my list are fairly obvious choices for someone of my background and generation I suppose.

When I was about twelve my parents took me to the Theatre Royal in Norwich with the promise of Sir Laurence Olivier. The play was Somerset Maugham's *Home and Beauty*, at least I think it was: memory can conflate different productions and evenings, maybe it was something else. When I settled in my seat and opened the programme I saw that the production was *directed* by Laurence Olivier. My heart sank. I had so hoped that I would see the theatrical legend in person.

When the play was over my mother asked how I had liked it.

'It was fine,' I said, 'but the best bit was the man who

came on as the lawyer at the end. I mean, even the way he took off his hat was extraordinary. Who *was* he?'

'But that was Olivier!' said my mother. 'Didn't you realize?'

I can still picture exactly the way he stood on stage, the angle of his head, the extraordinary ability he had to make you all look at each of his fingers one after the other as he tugged off his gloves with aching deliberation. He played a dry-as-dust solicitor in a small comic turn in the play's last scene, but it was astounding. Shameless exhibitionism, of course. A far cry from the honest gutsy endeavours of a thousand hard-working actors mining for the psychological and emotional truths of their characters in theatres and studios up and down the land, but damn, it was fun. I was pleased at least that I found it amazing even without knowing who the actor was.

So, at Cambridge, although I loved the art and idea of acting, I had no theories about theatre as an agent of social or political change, and no ambition for it as a future career. If I had faith in my potential I certainly had no particular sense that it would be on comic roles that I should concentrate. Quite the reverse. Theatre to me meant, first and foremost, Shakespeare, and the comic roles in the canon – fools, jesters, clowns and mechanicals – didn't really suit me at all. I was more a Theseus or Oberon than a Bottom or Quince, more a Duke or Jaques than a Touchstone. But first there was the question of whether I would even dare put myself forward for consideration.

Cambridge had dozens and dozens of drama clubs. Each college had its own, and there were others that were university-wide. The major ones, like the Marlowe Society, the Footlights and the Amateur Dramatic Club, had long histories: the Marlowe was started by Justin Brooke and Dadie Rylands a hundred years ago; the ADC and Footlights were older still. Other were more recent – the Mummers had been founded by Alistair Cooke and Michael Redgrave in the early 1930s and clung to a more progressive and avant-garde identity.

Many at Cambridge will tell you that the drama world there is filled with ambitious, pretentious, bitchy wannabes and that the atmosphere of backbiting, jealousy and greasy-pole rivalry is suffocating and unbearable. The people who tell you this are cut from the same cloth as those who grow up these days to become trollers on internet sites and who specialize in posting barbarous, mean, abusive, look-at-me, listen-to-me anonymous comments on YouTube and BBC 'Have Your Say' pages and other websites and blogs foolish enough to allow space for their poison. Such swine specialize in second-guessing the motives of those who are brave enough to commit to the risk of making fools of themselves in public and they are a blight on the face of the earth. 'Oh, but a thick skin is surely necessary in the acting profession. Actors and theatre people should get used to it.' Well if you want to be in a profession which accesses emotion and attempts to penetrate the mind and soul of man, I should have thought that what is more necessary is a *thin* skin. Sensitivity. But I am wandering off the point.

I thought, as I settled into my first term, that I should at least go to see some plays and decide whether or not I would be completely outclassed and out of my league. No point in going to auditions if I didn't have a hope of doing anything more than carry a spear.

I should point out for those unfamiliar with the world

of British university drama, that none of this had anything
to do with grown-ups – with dons, lecturers, officials or
the university departments and faculties. This was all as
extra-curricular as drink, sex or sport. I know that in
American universities a lot of these activities actually give
you points towards your degree, 'credits' I believe they are
called. Not in Britain. Universities that offer drama courses
do exist here – Manchester and Bristol, for example. But
not the majority and certainly not Cambridge. Drama
and activities of that sort have nothing to do with your
academic work, you find your own time to do them. As a
result, such pursuits flower, fruit and flourish as nowhere
else. If I had had to submit to some drama teacher casting
me in plays, directing me or telling me how it was done I
should have withered on the vine. The beauty of our way
was that everyone was learning as they went along. The
actors and directors were all students, as were the lighting,
sound, set construction, costume, stage management,
production crew, front of house and administration. All
were undergraduates saying, 'Oh, this looks like fun.'

How did they learn? Well, that's the beauty of
university life. You learn on the job and you learn from
the second-years and third-years above you, who in turn
learned on the job and from those above them. My God,
but it is exciting. As exciting as I should find official drama
training dull, numbing, embarrassing and humiliating. All
you need is enthusiasm, passion, tirelessness and the will,
the hunger and the need to do it. But within that range
there is plenty of room for the amiable rugger player who
thinks it will be larky to be in the chorus of a musical, or
the nervous scholarly type who wouldn't mind a shot at a
one-line role in a Shakespeare tragedy just for the sensation

of experiencing a play from the inside. You don't have to be a professional in the making at all.

Where did the money come from to build sets and make costumes? From previous productions. Every drama club had a committee, mostly second- and third-years, and someone on that committee looked after the budgets and the money. It was not just a way of learning about drama, it was a way of learning about committee life, diligence, accounting and all the perils and pitfalls of business and management. Sometimes a don would be asked to sit on the board of a club to help oversee financial matters, but they had no more power over the committee than any other individual member of it. The Footlights, it was rumoured, was the only Cambridge club, in any field, big and profitable enough to have to pay corporation tax. I don't know if that was true, but the fact that such a rumour could have got about tells you something of the scale of some of these enterprises. The momentum of continuity was a huge part of it. These clubs had been running for so long that it was relatively simple to keep them going.

The first production I went to see was of Tom Stoppard's *Travesties*. The play is set in Zurich and somehow combines in a farcical whirl Lenin, who had been exiled there for a while, Tristan Tzara, the Dadaist, the novelist James Joyce and an English consul called Henry Carr who is in the process of mounting a production of Wilde's *The Importance of Being Earnest*.

The production was co-directed by Brigid Larmour, now artistic director of the Watford Palace Theatre, and Annabelle Arden, who directs opera around the world. At the time they were very smart first-years who had hit the ground running. The others in the cast will forgive me, I hope, if I fail to recount their own admirable contributions to the success of the evening. Although it was a truly excellent production in and of itself, what stood out for me above all else was the performance of just one of the actresses. The girl who played Gwendolen stood out like a good deed in a naughty world.

She seemed, like Athene, to have arrived in the world fully armed. Her voice, her movement, her clarity, ease, poise, wit . . . well, you had to be there. One of the best things any performer on stage can do, whether stand-up comic, torch singer, ballet dancer, character actor or tragedian, is to relax an audience. To let them know that everything is going to be all right and that they can lean back in their seats happy in the knowledge that the evening won't be a disaster. Of course, another of the best things a performer can do is provoke a feeling of excitement, danger, unpredictability and instability. To let the audience know that the evening might fail at any moment and that they need to lean forward in their seats and watch intently. If you can manage both at once then you are really something. This girl was really something. Medium height with a perfect English complexion, she was gravely beautiful, extraordinarily funny and commandingly assured beyond her years. Her name, the programme told me, was Emma Thompson. In the interval I heard someone say that she was the daughter of Eric Thompson, the voice of *The Magic Roundabout*.

Fast forward to March 1992. For her performance as Margaret Schlegel in *Howards End* Emma has won the Academy Award for Best Actress. Journalists are ringing round all her old friends to find out what they think of this. Now, it is a kind of unwritten rule that when the press ask you to speak about someone else you never say a word unless that person has cleared it with you beforehand. If one wants to talk about oneself to a journalist that is fine, but it really isn't on to blather about a third party without their permission. One persistent journalist, having been more or less rebuffed by all of Emma's old friends, somehow gets hold of Kim Harris's number.

'Hello?'

'Hi, I'm from the *Post*. I understand you're an old university friend of Emma Thompson's?'

'Ye-e-es . . .'

'I wonder if you've anything to say about her Oscar? Are you surprised? Do you think she deserves it?'

'I have to come right out and tell you,' says Kim, 'that I feel betrayed, let down and most disappointed by Emma Thompson.'

The journalist almost drops his phone. Kim can hear the sound of a pencil being sucked and then, he later swears, of drool hitting the carpet.

'Betrayed? Really? Yes? Go on.'

'Anyone who ever saw Emma Thompson at university,' says Kim, 'would have laid substantial money on her getting an Oscar before she was thirty. She is now just over thirty. It's a crushing disappointment.'

Not as crushing a disappointment as that felt by the journalist who for one second thought he had a story. Kim, as he so often does, put it perfectly. That really was all there was to say. Plenty of other students were talented, some prodigiously so, and one might guess that with a fair following wind, the right opportunities and a measure of guidance and growth, they would have decent, or even brilliant, careers. With Emma you just saw her once and you knew. Stardom. Oscar. Damehood. That last is up to her of course but you can guarantee it will be offered.

Men like their actresses, if they are superb, to be air-headed, ditzy and charmingly foolish. Emma is certainly capable of . . . refreshingly different approaches to logical thought . . . but air-headed, ditzy or foolish she is not: she is one of the most clear-minded and intelligent people I have met. The fact that her second Oscar, two years after the first, was awarded for a screenplay, tells you all you need to know about her ability to concentrate, think and work. If it is tempting to be cross with people for having so many gifts lavished on them at birth, she has an abundance of kindness, openness and sweetness of nature that makes envy or resentment difficult. I am aware that we have entered the treacly territory of 'darling she's lovely and gorgeous' here, but that is the risk a book like this was always going to run. I did warn you. For those of you who would rather take away some other view of the woman, I can tell you definitively that she is a talentless mad bitch sow who wanders the streets of north London in nothing but a pair of ill-matched wellington boots. She only gets parts in films because she sleeps with the producers' animals. Plus she smells. She never wrote a screenplay in her life. She chains up a writer she drugged at a party twenty years ago, and he is responsible for everything published under her name. Her so-called liberal humanitarian principles are as false as her breasts: she is a member of the Gestapo and regrets the passing of Apartheid. That's Emma Thompson for you: the darling of fools and the fool of darlings.

Despite or because of this we got to know each other. She was at the all-women's college Newnham, where, like me, she read English. She was funny. Very funny. Also extreme with her fashion sense. The day came when she decided to shave her head: I blame the influence of Annie Lennox. Emma and I were both in the same seminar group at the English faculty and one morning, after a stimulating discussion of *A Winter's Tale*, we walked together down Sidgwick Avenue towards the centre of town. She pulled off her woolly hat so that I could feel the texture of her bare pate. In those days it was unlikely that anyone would have seen a woman as bald as an egg. A boy riding past on a bicycle turned to stare and, his panic-stricken eyes never leaving Emma's shining scalp, rode straight into a tree. I never thought such things took place outside silent movies, but it happened and it made me happy.

The first term came and went without my daring once to attend an audition. I had seen that there could be actors, or one at least, as astonishing as Emma, but there had been plenty getting parts that I felt I could have played better, or at least no worse. Nonetheless I held back.

For the most part my life in college and in the wider university followed a blandly traditional course. I joined the Cambridge Union, which is nothing to do with students' unions, but a debating society with its own chamber, a kind of miniature House of Commons, all wood and leather and stained glass, complete with a gallery and doors marked 'Aye' and 'No' through which you file to vote after the 'Speaker' has put the motion to the 'House'. All a little pompous really, but ancient and traditional. Many in Margaret Thatcher's cabinet had been Cambridge Union hacks in the early sixties: Norman Fowler, Cecil Parkinson, John Selwyn Gummer, Ken Clarke, Norman Lamont, Geoffrey Howe . . . that bunch. I was not politically inclined enough to want to speak or attempt to work my way into the inner circle of the Union, nor was I interested in asking questions from the floor of the house or contributing to debates in any other way. I watched a few – Bernard Levin, Lord Lever, Enoch Powell and a handful of others came to argue about the great issues of the day, whatever they were back then. War, terrorism, poverty, injustice, as I recall . . . problems that have now all been solved but which at the time seemed most pressing. There was also a 'comedy' debate once a term, usually with a fanciful motion like 'This House Believes in Trousers' or 'This House Would Rather Be a Sparrow Than a Snail'. I went to one where the handlebar-mustachioed comedian Jimmy Edwards, drunk as a skunk, played the tuba, told excellent jokes and afterwards – so I was told – fondled the thighs of all the comely young men at the dinner. I have since been invited many times to debate at Cambridge, Oxford and other universities and shiningly comely and shudderingly handsome have been some of the young men who have hosted the evenings. I never quite got the hang of the getting drunk and fondling the thigh business though. Whether that makes me a gallant and proper gentleman, a cowardly wuss or an unadventurous prude I cannot quite make out. Thighs appear to be safe around me. Perhaps this will change as I enter the autumn of my life and I cease to care so much about how I am judged.

Kim had immediately joined the University Chess Club and was playing for them in matches against other universities. Nobody doubted he would get his Blue, or rather Half Blue. You are perhaps aware that in Oxford and Cambridge there are such things as sporting 'Blues'.

You can represent Cambridge, whose colour is light blue, on the hockey field, for example, for just about every game of the season and be far and away the best player on the pitch for all of them, but if you miss the Varsity game, the one match against the dark blues, Oxford, you will not be awarded your Blue. A Blue, for either side, means you played against The Enemy. The Boat Race and Varsity matches in rugby and cricket are the most celebrated encounters, but there are Blues contests between Oxford and Cambridge in every imaginable sport, game and competitive activity from judo to table-tennis, from bridge to boxing, from golf to wine-tasting. The minor pursuits result in participants being awarded a 'Half Blue', and that is what Kim duly won when he represented Cambridge against Oxford in the Varsity chess match, at the RAC in Pall Mall, sponsored by Lloyds Bank. He played in that match for every one of his three years, winning the prize for best game in 1981.

Kim and I were the closest of friends but we were not yet lovers. He pined for a second-year called Robin, and I pined for no one in particular. Love had mauled me too violently in my teenage years, perhaps. I had fallen in love at school so completely, intensely and soul-rippingly that I had made some sort of unconscious pact with myself, I think, that I would neither betray the purity of that rapturous perfection (I know, I know, but that is how I felt) nor would I ever again open myself up for such pain and torment (exquisite as they were). There were plenty of attractive young men in the colleges and about the town, and a more than statistically usual ratio gave the impression of being as gay as gay can gaily be. I remember one or two drunken evenings in my own or another's bed,

with attendant fumbling, frotting, fondling and farcically
floppy failure as well as more infrequent feats of fizzing
fanfare and triumphant fleshly fulfilment, but love stayed
away, and, sensualist as I am in many regards, I seemed to
miss neither the rewards nor the punishments of carnality.

A week or so towards the end of the first term I was
approached and asked if I would sit on the May Ball
Committee. Most universities hold a summer party to
celebrate the end of exams and the coming long vacation.
Oxford has what they call Commem Balls, Cambridge
has May Balls.

'We get one fresher on the committee every year,' the
President of the committee said to me, 'so that by the time
the May Ball comes around in your last year, you'll know
what it's all about.'

I never dared ask why they had selected me out of all the
freshers to be the one to sit on the committee, but I took
it as a great compliment. Perhaps they thought I exhibited
style, *savoir faire*, *diablerie*, dash and a graceful party manner.
Or perhaps they believed that I was the kind of biddable
sucker who would be prepared to put in the hours.

'In any case,' I was told, 'it means you will be President
of the May Ball committee in your third year, which will
look really good on the CV. Excellent for getting a job in
the City.'

Already we were moving towards a time when
getting a job in the City, rather than being looked at as
an embarrassing gateway to clerkly drudgery and dull
worthiness, was beginning to be thought of as a glamorous,
sexy and desirable destiny for the elite of the world.

The members of the May Ball Committee were, as you

might expect, public-school men. Many of them were also members of the Cherubs, Queens' College's exclusive dining and drinking club. I know I ought to have looked down on institutions like May Balls and dining clubs with amused scorn, lofty disdain and impatient wrath, but the moment I heard of the Cherubs' existence I resolved that I would be elected. I once heard Alan Bennett say of snobbery that it was 'a very amiable vice', which I found surprising. 'That is to say,' he went on, 'the kind of snobbery that looks up with admiration is amiable. Daft, but amiable. The kind that looks down with contempt is not amiable. Not amiable at all.' I cannot deny that I am susceptible to a tinge of the amiable kind. I believe I have never looked down on anyone because they are 'low born' (whatever that might mean) but I cannot deny that I have been glamourized by those who are 'high born' (whatever *that* might mean). It is a preposterous weakness and I could easily pretend that I am immune to it, but the fact is that I am not, so I may as well fess up. I suppose it is, once more, all part of the feeling I have always had of being an outsider, always needing the proof of belonging that those who truly belong never need. Or something like that.

The Cambridge term is only eight weeks long. They call it Full Term, and you are expected to be in residence for all of it – in theory the permission of a Dean or Senior Tutor is needed for an 'exeat' if you want to biff off; you can make up your time away during the two weeks that bracket either end of Full Term. I kept Full Term so that I could go straight up to Cundall and teach there for the three weeks they had left of their, much longer, school term. After Christmas with my family in Norfolk it was back to Cundall for a week and then to Cambridge for the Lent term.

The very fact of this being my second term seemed to release something in me, for I went to three auditions in the first week. I got the parts I wanted for all of them. I played Jeremiah Sant, an insane Ian Paisley-style Ulsterman, in Peter Luke's dramatization of the Corvo novel *Hadrian the Seventh*, the distraught Jewish tailor who sees a ghost in Wolf Mankowitz's *The Bespoke Overcoat* and someone or other in the Trinity Hall lunchtime production of a play about Scottish nationalism. This set the pattern for a term which saw me running from rehearsals to auditions to theatres and back to auditions and rehearsals and theatres again. Lunchtime, evening and late night were the three usual slots for performance: if someone had suggested a morning production I would have put myself up for that too. I think I was in twelve plays in that eight-week term. I managed one essay on Edmund Spenser and went to no lectures or seminars. Supervisions, the Cambridge word for tutorials, were the only more or less compulsory academic intrusion on my new theatrical life. You would go alone, or occasionally with one other, to a don's rooms, read out the essay you had written, talk about it and then discuss some other writer, literary movement or phenomenon and leave promising an essay on that subject for the next week. I became adept at excuses:

'I'm really sorry, Dr Holland, but I'm still trying to engage with the eschatology of *Paradise Lost*. I think I'll take another week to come to terms with it.' It is shameful and lowering to confess how I would mine dictionaries of literary and philosophical terms for words like eschatology, syncresis and syntagmatic.

'Fine, fine. Take your time.'

Dr Holland wouldn't be fooled for a second. Being used to undergraduates, he would be familiar with their tiresome long-word displays (you will already have winced at plenty of them in this book I dare say: the felid remains incapable of permuting his nevi) and he had probably been in the audience of at least two of the plays I had acted in that week and would know perfectly well that I was spending every hour on drama and none on academic work. Cambridge was very relaxed about that kind of thing. As long as they didn't think you were going to fail your degree there was no danger of them playing the heavy. The chances of failing a degree were fabulously remote. It was perhaps a part of the institution's arrogance that it believed anyone it selected for entrance was necessarily incapable of failure. For the rest the faculty and college very sensibly left it up to the individual. If you wanted to work hard for a first-class degree any amount of help was given; if you preferred to spend your time pulling an oar through the water or striding about in tights roaring pentameters, why then that was fine too. A relaxed atmosphere of trust pervaded the university.

That Lent term passed in a blizzard of acting. By the end of it I was an insider in the small world of Cambridge drama. The little microcosm reflected the esoteric coteries, cliques and factions (I only put the word 'esoteric' in front of 'coteries' because it is an anagram of it and that pleases me) of the wider world without. The bar of the ADC theatre was a-hum with talk of Artaud and Anouilh, Stanislavsky and Stein, Brecht and Blin. Many a strong-stomached aspiring sportsman, scientist or politico would have been unable to overhear our talk without vomiting. We probably used the word 'darling' for each other. I certainly did. If not honeybottom, loveangel or nippleface. Sickening I know, but there you are. The derogatory epithet 'lovie' had yet to be ascribed to the theatrical profession, but that's what – *avant la lettre* – we were, lovies all. History and precedent might be said to have encouraged us: Peter Hall, John Barton, Richard Eyre, Trevor Nunn, Nick Hytner, James Mason, Michael Redgrave, Derek Jacobi, Ian McKellen . . . the list of theatrical giants who had leaned up against the same bar and dreamed the same dreams was inspiringly great.

So how did I get to that position so fast? Was I really so talented? Or was everyone else really so talentless? I wish I knew. I can remember a great many images, occasions and solid experiences, but the emotional memory behind them is blurred and unresolved. Was I ambitious? Yes, I think in some secret way I was ambitious. Always far too proud to let it show, but hungry for Cambridge's silly microcosmic equivalent of stardom. I suppose when the captain of the college rugger team sees some fresher take to the field and get his first opportunity to make a run and handle the ball he knows straight away that this person can, or cannot, play rugby. For all my shortcomings as an actor (physical awkwardness, reliance on speech, tendency to choose ironic ruefulness over raw emotion) I suppose at auditions I showed that I at least had that thing in me that allowed an audience in. Through the occlusions of the past I can make out a tall, thin, dignified, rumbly toned student who could look either seventeen or thirty-seven. He knows how to stand still and look another actor in the eye. He knows how to deliver a line at least in such a way as to convey its meaning and, if necessary, its majesty. He can, as they say, 'pull focus' on to and off his own self. I am not so sure about his ability to inhabit a different personality, to live through the arc of his character's journey on stage and all that mother jazz, but he is at least unlikely to be a blush-making embarrassment.

The moment I walked on stage for the first time I felt so absolutely and entirely at home that it was hard for me to remember that I had had almost no experience at all. I loved every single thing about acting. I loved the mockable sides of it, the instant camaraderie and deep affection one felt for everyone else involved, I loved the long conversations about motive, I loved read-throughs and rehearsals and tech runs, I loved trying on costumes and experimenting with make-up. I loved the tingle of nerves as I waited in the wings, I loved the almost mystical hyperaesthetic way in which one was aware of each microsecond on stage, of how one could detect precisely where an audience's focus was at any one moment, I loved the thrill of knowing that I was carrying hundreds of people with me, that they were surfing on the ebb and flow of my voice.

Taking such pleasure in being on stage really isn't about relishing love, attention and admiration. It is not about enjoying the power you (think you) have over an audience. It is simply a question of fulfilment. You feel perfectly alive and magnificently perfected by the knowledge that you are doing what you were put on earth to do.

Not so very long ago I accompanied some northern white rhinos on a journey to Kenya. They were being translocated from the zoo in the Czech Republic that was all they had ever known. It was immeasurably moving to watch these animals raise their top-heavy heads and take in the huge open skies of the savannah and the smells and sounds of a habitat to which their genes had taken millions of years to adapt them. The quick, unbelieving grunts, the waving of their horns from side to side and the twitching in their great hides told you that somewhere inside they knew that they were where they were supposed to be. I will not claim that the stage is my savannah, but I did feel something of the surge of relief and joy at finally having come home that the rhinos seemed to express as they nosed the air of Africa for the first time.

It is only a pity that the professional grown-up theatre won't allow you the same levels of fun and fulfilment. After three performances, or five at the most, student productions are over, and you move on to something else. Which I did. And again and again.

The Easter term is when Cambridge springs to life and becomes one of the most marvellous places on earth to be. As St John's College alumnus William Wordsworth put it: 'Bliss was it in that dawn to be alive, But to be young was very heaven!' He was writing less about May Week and more about the French Revolution, but the thought holds better for the first, and I bet that in truth he was thinking more about garden parties than guillotines.

The Head of the River competition is held on the Cam twice a year, each college's boat jostling to bump the one ahead and move a place up in the order. The river isn't wide enough to allow a side-by-side regatta which is why these peculiar Lent and May Week Bumps evolved. Lining the river bank and cheering on my college is probably the most 'normal' Cambridgey thing I did in my three years.

Further upriver, the beauty of the Backs in late spring and early summer is enough to make the sternest puritan

moan and shiver with delight. Sunlight on the stone of
the bridges, willows leaning down to weep and kiss the
water: young boys and girls, or boys and boys, or girls
and girls, punting up to Grantchester Meadows, bottles
of white wine tied with string trailing through the wake
to cool, 'No kissing in the punt' – careful how you say
that, hoho. Revising finalists under chestnut trees, books
and notes spread out on the grass as they smoke, drink,
chatter, flirt, kiss and read. Garden parties on every lawn in
every college for the two weeks in June that are perversely
designated May Week. Dining clubs and societies, dons,
clubs and rich individuals serving punch and Pimm's,
beer and sangria, cocktails and champagne. Blazers and
flannels, self-conscious little snobberies and affectations,
flushed youth, pampered youth, privileged youth, happy
youth. Don't be too hard on them. Suppress the thought
that they are all ghastly tosspots who don't know they're
born, insufferable poseurs in need of a kick and a slap.
Have some pity and understanding. They will get that kick
and that slap soon enough. After all, look at them now.
They are all in their fifties. Some of them on their third,
fourth or fifth marriage. Their children despise them.
They are alcoholics or recovering alcoholics. Drug addicts
or recovering drug addicts. Their wrinkled, grey, bald,
furrowed and fallen faces look back every morning from
the mirror, those folds of dying flesh bearing not a trace
of the high, joyful and elastic smiles that once lit them.
Their lives have been a ruin and a waste. All that bright
promise never quite matured into anything that can be
looked back on with pride or pleasure. They took that job
in the City, that job with the merchant bank, stockbroker,
law firm, accountancy firm, chemical company, drama

company, publishing company, any company. The light and energy, the passion, fun and faith were soon snuffed out one by one. In the grind of the demanding world their foolish hopeful dreams evaporated like mist in the cruel glare of the morning sun. Sometimes the dreams return to them at night and they are so ashamed, angry and disappointed that they want to kill themselves. Once they laughed and seduced or laughed and were seduced, on ancient lawns, under ancient stones and now they hate the young and their music, they snort with contempt at everything strange and new and they have to catch their breath at the top of the stairs.

Goodness, Stephen, who rattled *your* cage? Not everyone's life ends in misery, loneliness and failure.

Of course, I know that. You're right. But many do. The entropy and decay of age is dreadfully apparent when set next to the lyrical dream of a Cambridge May Week, hackneyed, outdated, unjust and absurd as such an idyll may be. It is that scene that classical painters used to love: the golden lads and lasses sporting in Elysium, throwing garlands, drinking and embracing, all unaware of the tomb on which a skull rests and never noticing its carved inscription: 'Et in arcadia ego.' Why should they notice it? Its shadow will be on them soon enough and they in turn will be wagging fingers at their children and saying, 'I too once lived in arcadia, you know . . .' and their children will not listen either.

Many Cantabrigians might read the foregoing and recognize not a line of it. Plenty of students eschewed with contempt anything close to a blazer or a glass of Pimm's, most never lined the river on a May Bumps afternoon, never sipped planter's punch in the Master's Garden, never cunted up the Pam to Grantchester, nor once had to be helped to an ambulance and a stomach pump on Suicide Sunday. There were a lot of Cambridges, I am just trying to remember mine, nauseating as it may be.

As well as all these parties there were plays. Queens' College's drama club was called BATS, supposedly because of the flittermice that wheeled and squeaked in the sky above the Cloister Court during its end-of-term outdoor presentation, one of the most popular and distinctive regular features of May Week. This year's production was to be *The Tempest*, and the director, a Queens' second-year called Ian Softley, cast me as Alonso, King of Naples. Being tall and boomy I was nearly always given the role of a king or elderly authority figure. The young lovers, glamorous girls and handsome princes were played by students who looked their age. I never looked mine, but given that almost everyone was between eighteen and twenty-two, looking older was a distinct advantage so far as casting went.

Ian Softley now directs motion pictures – *The Wings of the Dove*, *Backbeat*, *Hackers*, *Inkheart* and so on – but then he was a student with black curly hair and an appealing way of wearing white trousers. The cast included Rob Wyke, a graduate who was to become a close friend and, playing Prospero, a most extraordinary actor and even more extraordinary man, Richard MacKenney. In the middle of writing his PhD thesis, 'Trade guilds and devotional confraternities in the state and society of Venice to 1620', he could already speak not only fluent Italian, but fluent Venetian, which is quite another thing. While waiting for the cast to turn up (he was always exactly punctual himself, as was I) he would pace up and down at high speed, humming every note of the overture to Mozart's *Don Giovanni*. If we were still not quorate by the time that had been got through he would move on to Leporello's opening aria and keep at it until everyone was present, singing all the parts perfectly from memory. On one occasion Ariel was half an hour late owing to some confusion about time and venue (there was no way to text or call in those days), and when he at last arrived, red and gasping, Richard broke off from his singing and turned on him furiously.

'What time do you call this, then? The Commendatore's dead and Ottavio is swearing on his blood to be revenged.'

Richard was a magnificent actor, his King Lear was astonishing in one so young (a receding brow and faux-grumpy manner made him appear fifty although he can't have been much older than twenty-three or four) but he hid his artistry under an obsession with pace and volume. 'All you've got to do,' he said, 'is get down the front of the stage and have a good old shout.' He once gave the entire cast a bollocking for adding five minutes to the running time. 'Unforfuckinggivable! Every extra second is so much piss on Shakespeare's grave.'

I watched one afternoon as Ian Softley squatted in front of Barry Taylor, who was playing Caliban. 'Do you know the work of the punk poet John Cooper Clarke?' he whispered, sorrowful brown eyes gazing deeply into Barry's.

'Er, yes . . .'

'I think, don't you, that we can afford something of that street anger in Caliban. Some of that rage?'

'Er . . .'

'Oh forget about that,' said Richard, who had been pacing up and down, hands clasped firmly behind his back.

'Just get down the front of the stage and have a good old squeak and a gibber.' I don't suppose, with all due respect to Ian and John Cooper Clarke, that there has ever been better advice given to any actor playing Caliban in the 400 years since *The Tempest*'s creation.

One morning I noticed a poster in the street for an exhibition at the Fitzwilliam Museum. They were going to bring out some of the Blake drawings, paintings, prints and letters that usually, due to their marked sensitivity to light, were kept hidden away in dark drawers. I mentioned this to Richard and asked if he was going.

'William Blake?' said Richard. 'Couldn't draw, couldn't colour in.'

MacKenney is now a history professor at Edinburgh University. I hope they value him properly.

Dave Huggins stopped me in Walnut Tree Court one afternoon.

'My mum's coming to see your play tonight.'

'Is she?' I was surprised. Dave wasn't in the drama world, and it seemed odd for a parent to come to a production that her child wasn't in.

'Yeah. She's an actress.'

I consulted my memory to see if it could offer any data on an actress called Huggins. It had no suggestions. 'Er . . . well. That's nice.'

'Yeah. So's my dad.'

'Might I know them?'

'Dunno. They both use acting names. She's called Anna Massey and he calls himself Jeremy Brett.'

'B-but . . . good God!'

Anna Massey, coming to see me in a play? Well not expressly to see *me*, but coming to a play that I was in.

'Your father won't be there as well, will he?'

'No, they're divorced. He's gay.'

'Is he? Is he? I didn't . . . well, well. Goodness. Blimey. My word.'

I tottered off, numb with excitement.

We had our four or five performances under the fluttering bats; Ariel sprinted about, Caliban squeaked and gibbered, I boomed, Prospero got down the front and had a good old shout, Anna Massey graciously applauded.

In the meantime I had been helping prepare for the May Ball.

It so happens that the Patron or Visitor of Queens' College is, appropriately enough given the foundation's name, whoever might happen to be Queen at the time: a position she holds until her death. From the 1930s to the 1950s the queen was, of course, Elizabeth, wife of George VI. After George died, now styled the Queen Mother, she remained in place. There's a point to all this.

We are at a meeting of the May Ball Committee. Much of the time is taken up with the particular details that you might expect – how to run the roulette table without falling foul of the gaming acts, who will be in charge of escorting the Boomtown Rats to the tent set aside as their changing room, whether or not there will be enough ice in the champagne bar, the usual kind of administrative trivia. The President turns to me.

'Got your Magdelene and Trinity invitations yet?'

'Yup, and Clare.'

One of the perks of being on a May Ball committee was that you received free invitations to other May Balls. Aside from our own, I was going to the ball at Clare, one of the prettiest of the colleges, where my cousin Penny was also a fresher, and to the two grandest of all, Trinity and Magdalene. So grand were they that gossip columnists and photographers from the *Tatler* and *Harper's & Queen* attended. You could get away with a dinner jacket at Clare and Queens', but Trinity and Magdalene insisted on white tie and tails. The hire companies did a roaring trade. Only King's, a mixed college and proud of its radical and progressive ethos, refused to hold a May Ball. Their summer party was called instead, with dour literalism, the King's June Event.

'Good,' the President of the Committee says to me. 'Oh. One other little thing. Dr Walker sent me a note saying that if the Queen Mother dies the college has to go into mourning for a week, during which no entertainments or celebrations of any kind can be held, certainly not a May Ball. Perhaps you might look into insurance to cover that?'

'Insurance?' I try to sound casual and unconcerned, as if arranging insurance policies is something I have been doing since I was an infant. 'Ah . . . right. Yes. Sure. Of course.'

The meeting ends, and I slip into the public phone box in the corner of Friar's Court and start ringing around insurance companies.

'Sun Life, can I help you?'

'Ah, yes. I'm calling up about getting a policy . . .'

'Life, car, commercial or property?'

'Well, none of those really.'

'Marine, travel or medical?'

'Well, again. None. It's to insure against having to cancel an event.'

'Abandonment?'

'Er . . . that's the term is it, abandonment? Well, yes, abandonment then . . .'

'Hold please, caller . . .'

I wait until a tired voice comes on the line.

'Special services, how can I help?'

'I'm ringing about getting a policy to insure an event . . . I think you call it abandonment?'

'Oh yes? What sort of event?

'Well it's a party.'

'An outdoors event, is it?'

'Well, it's a ball. Mostly on lawns in tents, but some parts are inside.'

'I see . . . and you want rain cover. Partial or complete abandonment?'

'No, not rain cover so much as reign cover.'

'Excuse me?'

'Sorry, no. I mean . . . well, it's to insure against the Queen Mother dying.'

The sound of a receiver being banged on the desk followed by a blowing down the earpiece. 'Something wrong with the line. Sounded like . . . never mind. Could you repeat that please?'

Here in the twenty-first century there are probably only two insurance companies left in the world, called Axxentander or something equally foul, but in 1979 there were dozens. I tried the Royal, Swan, Prudential, Pearl, Norwich Union – all those I had heard of and a dozen that I hadn't. In each case, once I had succeeded in getting the agent to understand what was required, I was asked to call back. I imagine that they needed to consult higher up the chain of command. It might be said that they had abandonment issues.

This kind of insurance is, of course, nothing more nor less than gambling. You bet your stake (which insurance companies call a premium) and should your horse win (house catch fire, car get stolen, royal family member die) you collect your winnings. The relationship between the premium and the amount collected is determined by balancing the value of the insured thing (the indemnity) against the odds and statistical probability of its being threatened. Bookies use the form and stud books together with the market flow of betting to determine their prices; insurance companies use a similar mixture of market trends and their own history and precedent books, which they call actuarial tables. I can understand that. Had I wanted an abandonment policy against snow and ice, they would have looked at the value of the May Ball and seen that they would have to shell out £40,000 if it was cancelled. They would also see that blizzards in early June are incredibly rare, even in Cambridge, so they would probably charge a fraction of a fraction of 1 per cent of the indemnity: £20 would be ungenerous, but then only an idiot would bother to insure against so remote a contingency in the first place. With a rain policy the insurers might decide, after consulting forecasters and local records, that there was, say, a fifty-fifty chance of precipitation in which case the premium would be a whopping £20,000. But then, what kind of an idiot would arrange a summer party in England which was so weather dependent that it would have to be abandoned if the heavens opened? Abandonment policies are not very common, that is the point, but there are nonetheless fairly obvious mechanisms in place for resolving the issue of price when it comes to natural disasters like weather, fire and earthquake. The death of the monarch's mother, on the other hand . . . how could an actuary be expected to calculate the odds of that? She was seventy-nine years old.

I decided that I would give the companies three hours before calling back for a quote.

Did the insurance clerks go into her family history and check out the longevity of the entire Bowes-Lyon clan? Did they call up Clarence House and inquire into the Queen Mother's health, diet and exercise regime? Did they take into account her reputed fondness for gin and Dubonnet? I can only imagine the discussions they must have had in their offices.

In the case of each firm, when I called back, the actuaries appeared to be very gloomy about the old girl's hopes of making it through the next few months: 20, 25, 23 per cent chances of her surviving until the middle of June were implied by the gigantic premiums they proposed. The cheapest offer, 20 per cent of the indemnity, was way beyond our reach. I had been given a budget of £50.

'I am afraid,' I tell the President of the Committee after returning from the last of the calls, 'that we are simply going to have to pray for Her Majesty's continued good health. If she does die I will undertake to keep the news from the Fellows if I have to steal every newspaper and radio in the college and lock them all in a cellar to do so.'

'I may hold you to that,' the President said, a worried look furrowing his youthful brow.

I do not suppose that a queen's life has been prayed for more assiduously since the days of Boudicca. Sadly, the Queen Mother did die, though happily for us, not for another twenty-three years. When she finally left the world in 2002, she was thoughtful enough to do so in March, meaning that the college's period of mourning would be well over by May Week. It was just such examples of kindness and consideration that endeared her to so many during a long, varied and vigorous life. Some time in the 1990s, sitting next to her at a dinner, I considered thanking her on behalf of the college for so thoughtfully delaying her death, but shyness and good sense got the better of me.

Another feature of the Cambridge Easter term (for so they call the third term of the academic year) is the Footlights May Week Revue. The Footlights Club is one the university's best-known institutions, having sent generations of comic writers and performers into the world over the course of its 130-year history. Its May Week show at the Arts Theatre was an annual ritual. If you were cool it was an event to disdain. 'Apparently the Footlights are crap this year,' you would say to your companion as you wrinkled your nose at a poster for the event. There has never been a year in which this has not been said. The same phrase would have been heard when Jonathan Miller was running the Footlights, or Peter Cook and David Frost, through Cleese, Chapman and Idle and past Douglas Adams, Clive Anderson and Griff Rhys Jones, Dave Baddiel and Rob Newman, David Mitchell and Robert Webb all the way up to the current year. If you were normal, such cynicism did not occur to you, and the May Week Revue was another fun fixture on the Cambridge calendar. I was neither cool nor normal, but simply too busy with *The Tempest* and other things to be able to attend.

I heard that someone was putting together a production of *Oedipus Rex* for Edinburgh and decided that I might as well go and audition. I boomed and strutted and gestured and declaimed in front of the director, Peter Rumney, and left thinking that perhaps I had rather overdone it. The next day I found in my pigeonhole a note from Peter asking me to play Oedipus. I was bound for the Festival Fringe, and my excitement was almost impossible to contain. For the rest of the term I bounced and buzzed about Cambridge like a bee in a bottle.

At some point I believe I must have sat some exams. Prelims, I think they were called. I remember precisely nothing about them. Not where they took place, nor what kinds of questions we were given to answer. I suppose I must have passed them, for no trouble arose and no stern interviews were sought. My Cambridge proceeded pleasantly enough without the intrusion of academic study: a university is not, thank heavens, a place for vocational instruction, it has nothing to do with training for a working life and career, it is a place for education, something quite different. A real education takes place, not in the lecture hall or library, but in the rooms of friends, with earnest frolic and happy disputation. Wine can be a wiser teacher than ink, and banter is often better than books. That was my theory at least, and I was living by it. Such serene and lofty views of education as against vocational training were beginning to madden the new political leadership. Thatcher was an industrial chemist and a lawyer, after all, both disciplines that need Gradgrindery and training and require no education whatsoever – as she demonstrated. Our kind of loose learning, as they would regard it, this cleaving to the elitist tradition of the Liberal Arts, this arrogant Athenian self-indulgence was an enemy, a noxious weed that required summary eradication. Its days were numbered.

The 1979 Queens' May Ball took place. I donned the

tailcoat that I had rented for the week, all ready to . . . well, to have myself a ball. We happy, flushed, proud and excited members of the committee met for champagne half an hour before the kick-off. Ten minutes later I was in an ambulance on my way to Addenbrooke's Hospital, an oxygen mask over my face, fighting for every breath. Bloody asthma. It would be another two years before I fully understood what had brought it on. I often succumbed to attacks at weddings, fêtes, Hunt Balls or events of that kind. On such occasions there were usually flowers and summer pollen about, so it had never occurred to me that the cause of my face going blue and my lungs closing for business was actually champagne. A ridiculous allergy, but one doesn't choose them.

At Addenbrooke's an injection of adrenaline had such an immediately restorative effect that I was out of the hospital, in a cab and on the way back to Queens' by ten, two fresh inhalers for emergencies spoiling the sweep and cut of my dress trousers. I was determined not to miss another minute.

May Balls traditionally end with a breakfast, and many party-goers like to welcome the dawn on the Cam. Even at that young age I was a sentimental and slushy fool, maudlin (pronounced Magdalene) to a dreadful fault. I am none the less so now and shall never find the sight of young men in dégagé evening wear punting their loved ones along the river on a summer's morning anything other than agonizingly romantic, piercingly lovely and heart-stoppingly adorable.

Caledonia 1

After the term ended, I took myself off as usual to North Yorkshire to teach a little Latin, umpire Cundall Manor's

Second Eleven, prepare the games fields for Sports Day and, in such spare time as I had, learn the role of Oedipus as well as lines for my various parts in a production of Charles Marowitz's *Artaud at Rodez* which the Cambridge Mummers were presenting and in which I had also, perhaps foolishly, agreed to appear. Foolishly because, each day for a fortnight, the moment the curtain went down on *Artaud* I was going to have to hare off to the venue where *Oedipus* would be due to start half an hour later. Old Edinburgh hands said I would be cutting it fine, especially if I had complicated costume to doff and don or heavy make-up to remove and apply, but cutting it fine was one of the things I liked to do.

For three weeks in late summer Edinburgh is the world centre of student drama. I was to perform at the Fringe every year for the next five years at least. Most who go cannot fail to fall instantly in love with the city as much as with the event. Within a couple of days the muscles on your shins ache from the unaccustomed steep ascents and descents of the town, the numberless stone steps and narrow wynds surprise your muscles – if you were used to the easy, level streets of East Anglian towns and a sedentary life it did more than surprise them, it shocked and outraged them. The ancient towering grimness of Edinburgh's old tenements with their stone staircases and minatory blank gabling made me feel that at any moment Burke and Hare, Deacon Brodie or Mr Hyde were about to rise snarling from the steps of the Grassmarket. What did arise were, of course, nothing more terrifying than young drunks bearing polystyrene trays of Spudulike with cheese. In those days baked potato take-aways provided the cheapest form of filling nutrition a student could require. Scotland really was another country. The diet was different: aside from Spudulike the chicken carry-out shops offered the delicate *specialité du pays* – deep-fried Mars Bars, Wagon Wheels and Curly Wurlys. Scottish banknotes were different, the language, the weather, the light, even the Kensitas cigarettes were unfamiliar. A pint of heavy was the preferred drink, heavy being bitter or at least a gassy something that gestured towards the idea of it.

Everywhere about the city, on every wall, window, lamp-post or doorway, were posters for plays, comedies and idiosyncratic entertainments that combined everything from circus, music hall, surrealist balloon manipulation and ballet to street percussion, Maoist limbo-dancing, gender-bending operetta and chainsaw juggling. Members of the casts of these shows would dress up and run down the streets showering the good-naturedly reluctant passers-by with leaflets and complimentary tickets. On the opening day a parade of floats moved slowly east along Princes Street. There was somewhere in the city, or so we were told, a proper and official Festival being held: professional theatre companies and international orchestras performed plays and concerts for grown-ups in smart concert halls and theatres, but we saw or knew nothing of these, we were the Fringe, a vast fungus-like organism that spread its filaments throughout the fabric of Edinburgh, into the dossiest accommodations, weirdest sheds, huts, warehouses and wharves, and into every church hall and functional space large enough to house a punk magician and a few chairs.

Half-way along the Royal Mile, which runs down from Edinburgh Castle to the Georgian New Town, stood the Fringe Office, where festival-goers queued up for tickets.

There were two shows I knew that I simply had to see. One was the Footlights Revue which due to *The Tempest* I had missed in Cambridge, and the other was a one-man comedy performance which was being put on at the Wireworks, a converted factory just behind the Fringe Office. I had been told so many times that this performer, an Oxford graduate called Rowan Atkinson, was not to be missed that I felt justified in lining up to plank down some cash on tickets for me and the *Oedipus* cast.

There was bad news when I got to the front of the queue.

'Ooh, that one's sold out, my darling.'

'Oh, really?'

''Fraid so . . . what else do you – hang on.'

She picked up the phone and as she listened to the other end a smile lit up her face and she flashed me a happy look. She was a very pretty young Scot and wonderfully cheerful given her hard, non-computerized workload. I can still picture her face exactly.

'Well, well. That was the Rowan Atkinson people just now to say that due to popular demand they are doing an extra late-night performance on Saturday night. Can you make it?'

I bought five tickets and one for the Cambridge Footlights and stumbled happily away.

We presented our *Oedipus* every evening for two weeks at the Adam House in Chambers Street. The production design was 'inspired' by science fiction films and the principals and chorus had to wear strange costumes constructed from cut-up sheets of coloured lighting gel which were a devil to get on in time given my tight gap between performances. Peter Rumney had chosen W. B.

Yeats's translation of the Sophocles original, and I spoke the language well, in a mellifluously rhetorical kind of way, but was unable to ascend the heights of tragedy and despair that the play demanded. In fact I didn't even reach the foothills. Oedipus Rex's journey from commanding greatness to whimpering ruin called, in Edinburgh terms, for a Royal Mile that swooped from the elegant squares of the New Town into the sinister slums of the old. I gave them a flat Cambridge street with some pleasant window shopping but about as much pity and terror as a banana milkshake. Nor did our production do well in the turbulent competition for Fringe audiences. The *Scotsman* reviewer described me as the figurehead of the ship, which sounded good until she went on to explain that she meant I was imposing and wooden. Oh well. None of this worried me: I was having the time of my life. In the Mummers' afternoon show, *Artaud at Rodez*, amongst other characters I played the great French actor Jean-Louis Barrault. It was directed by the dynamic and intense Pip Broughton, who had cast Jonathan Tafler (son of the film actor Sydney) in the lead role of Artaud. He was superb and dominated the stage and the production despite having to spend most of it in a straitjacket.

On my fifth evening, as soon as *Oedipus* came down I decellophaned myself and hurried away to join an impatient full-house queue that was shuffling its way into the theatre where the Cambridge Footlights were giving their revue, *Nightcap*.

'Apparently it's crap this year,' I heard from someone behind me as I sat down.

'Yeah, *Nightcrap*,' tittered his companion.

It was not crap. It was astonishingly good, and the

sceptical pair behind me were the first to their feet whistling and stamping approval when the curtain call came.

There were two first-years in the show, my friend Emma Thompson and a tall young man with big blue eyes, triangular red flush marks on his cheeks and an apologetic presence that was at once appallingly funny and quite inexplicably magnetic. His name, according to a programme that included helpful photographs of the cast, was Hugh Laurie. Another tall man with lighter but equally blue eyes, curly hair and a charmingly 1940s manner was the current President of the Footlights, Robert Bathurst. Martin Bergman, the previous year's President, was in the show too, performing a clever kind of moon-faced epicene MC role. Also in the cast was an astoundingly nimble, twinkly and clownishly gifted comic actor called Simon McBurney, whom I knew because he was, as it happened, Emma's boyfriend. This was to my shocked mind as perfect a comedy show as I had ever seen. It had never occurred to me that the Footlights would be this good. So good indeed that I instantly abandoned any dream I might have had of next year dipping my own toe in the waters of sketch comedy. I knew that I could not for a second hold my own with these people. Cool as I wasn't, I had nonetheless absorbed the predominant cool person's view that the Footlights Club was peopled with self-obsessed, semi-professional show-bizzy show-offs. What was so extraordinary about *Nightcap* was how technically perfect in delivery, writing, timing, style and confidence it was, while managing to project a wholly likeable awareness of the absurdity of the whole business of student comedy. It was grown-up and polished yet at the same time bashful and friendly; it was sophisticated and intelligent but never pretentious or pleased with itself; it had authority, finish and quality without any hint of self-regard, vanity or slickness. It was, in short, just what I believed comedy of this kind ought to be. For all that I had by now been in at least fifteen plays, some of which had been comic in some form or other, I did not believe that I would ever have the confidence to knock on the door of a Footlights Club that boasted such assured talents.

Heigh ho. At least I might be able to sneer at this Rowan Atkinson fellow. After all, what had Oxford ever done for comedy? Well, Terry Jones and Michael Palin obviously, but apart from them, what had Oxford ever done for comedy? Dudley Moore. Well, yes, apart from Palin, Jones and Moore what had . . . ? Alan Bennett. All right. Granted. But apart from Michael Palin, Terry Jones, Dudley Moore and Alan Benn . . . Evelyn Waugh? Oscar Wilde? Oh all right then, damn you, maybe Oxford weren't such duds after all. Still I went to the Wireworks not expecting that a one-man show could compete with the skill and style of *Nightcap*. I staggered out two hours later almost unable to walk. My sides and lungs had taken a hell of a beating. They had never been put to such paroxysmal use in their lives. You have probably seen Rowan Atkinson. If you are lucky you might have seen him on stage. If you are very, very lucky, then you might have had the experience of seeing him on stage before you had ever seen him anywhere else. That is the kind of joy that can never be reconstructed, to encounter an astounding talent for the first time with no preconceptions and no especial expectations. I had never watched Rowan Atkinson on television and I really knew nothing about him other than that his show was a hot ticket. It was called a 'one-man show' but actually there were two other performers: Richard Curtis, the writer of most of the material, who took the role of a kind of straight man, and Howard Goodall, who played music from an electric piano and sang a witty song of his own.

I had noticed from the programme that the staging was the work of Christopher Richardson, whom I had known when I was a schoolboy and he a master at Uppingham School.[†] I had a brief word with him afterwards, and he told me that the show had previewed at Uppingham.

'The theatre has become quite a regular stop on the way between university and Edinburgh,' he said. 'You must bring some of your Cambridge people.'

'Oh I don't, I'm not . . . we wouldn't . . .'

The drama I was doing at Cambridge suddenly seemed ordinary, worthy and desperately unexciting. I dismissed such unnecessarily negative thoughts from my mind. What was there to complain of?

Cherubs, Coming Out, Continent

The *accelerando* that had begun in the second term continued on my return. More drama, less academic study.

I now had the option of living out of college in digs or staying in and sharing with a fellow second-year. Kim and I chose to share, and we were rewarded with a stunning set of rooms in Walnut Tree Court. The ceiling had dark Elizabethan beams, and the walls were panelled in wood. Some of the panels were cut to reveal recessed cupboards and, in one place, an area of medieval painted plaster.

There were bookshelves, a good gyp-room, window-seats, leaded panes of warped glass of great antiquity and far from contemptible furniture. With our books, records, glassware and china, my bust of Shakespeare, Kim's bust of Wagner, Jaques chess set and Bang and Olufsen record player we were as well set up as any students in the university.

The three terms of that second year have blended and blurred in my mind. I do know that it was then that I was asked to join the Cherubs, hurrah! The initiation ceremony required the draining down of heroically repulsive and impossibly combined flagons of spirit, wine and beer. One also had to recite the meaning of the Cherubs' emerald, navy and salmon necktie: 'Green for Queens' College, blue for the empyrean and pink for the cherub's botty.' Another duty was to declare what one would do to advance the cause of the Cherubs and Cherubism. I cannot remember what I said, something arrogant about wearing the tie on television at every opportunity when I was a famous actor, I think. Another initiate, Michael Foale, announced that he would be the first Cherub to join all the other cherubs in heaven. When pushed for an explanation he said that he intended to be the first Cherub in space. It was a preposterous claim to make. Space travellers were either American astronauts or Soviet cosmonauts. At some later, slightly less incoherently drunken Cherubs party I discovered that he had been perfectly serious. He had dual UK/US nationality, his mother being American. He was already fluent in Russian, which he had taught himself, reasoning that the future of space exploration would depend on full cooperation and collaboration between the United States and the Soviet Union. He was into his third year of a doctorate in astrophysics and a member of the

RAF's Air Training Corps, able to fly just about anything that had wings or rotors. I had never encountered such focus and determination in anyone. Seven years later he was accepted by NASA as an astronaut. He flew his first Space Shuttle mission five years after that and retired having spent over a year of his life away from earth. Until 2008 he held the American record for time spent in space – 374 days, 11 hours and 19 minutes – which is still, needless to say, a British record. I would like to say that his resolve, dedication and commitment were a life-changing example to me. Instead I thought he was potty and blush to think how I humoured him.

Mike Foale invited me to attend the launch of his mission to repair the Hubble Space Telescope in 1999, but I couldn't go. He invited me again to his final launch in 2003, for which he was appointed Commander of the International Space Station. Again I had to plead other commitments. What was I thinking of? Surely I could have postponed whatever it was I was doing and travelled to the launch site to watch a remarkable man doing one of the most remarkable things any human can do? I regret missing the chance deeply. I hope today's Cherubs at Queens' have incorporated a toast into their rituals which recognizes the most illustrious and intrepid of their heavenly host ever to don the green, blue and pink.

I soon made sure that Kim was initiated into the Cherubs too, and perhaps as a kind of thank you, or more likely because he was such a generous soul anyway, Kim offered to have a dinner jacket made for me at a grand tailoring shop on the corner of Silver and Trumpington Streets. Ede and Ravenscroft, besides being fine fashioners of a gentleman's dress suiting, were also makers of elaborate and distinguished academic, legal, ecclesiastic and ceremonial costume of all kinds from graduate gowns to royal robes. The double-breasted dinner jacket of heavy wool they made for me was a thing of rare beauty. The facings of the lapels were of black silk as were the stripes down the side of the trouser legs. Kim felt I should have a proper shirt with separate collar to go with it as well as a good silk black bow-tie. And how could any of this be worn without proper shoes? Kim was generous with his money, but he never used it to show off. Not once did he make me feel that I was a lucky recipient of his largesse, or put me in the position of being embarrassed or overwhelmed by it. The kindness was as much in the manner of his generosity as in the quantity of it, although the latter did keep our rooms in enviable luxury. Kim's mother often sent large hampers from Harrods, cases of wine and quantities of cashmere socks for her beloved only child. His father worked in the advertising business, something to do with the sites on which posters were put up, and it was clearly a concern that flourished. My own family's relatively modest prosperity did not, like Kim's, run to truffles, pâté and vintage port, but my mother was able to exhibit more often than was comfortable for a sceptic like me a most uncanny ability to know exactly when and by how much my funds were depleted. A bill from Heffer's, the Cambridge bookshop, might arrive in my pigeonhole and loom over me and deprive me of sleep that night, and the following morning there would be a letter from Mother with a cheque and little note saying that she hoped that this might come in useful. The sum seemed nearly always to cover the bill and leave a happy amount over for wine and cakes.

My sister Jo came to stay. She adored Kim and made friends with everyone, most of whom thought she was an undergraduate, although she was only fifteen. It was in a letter to her when she was back home that I wrote something that my father saw, something that made it clear that I was gay. He got a message through to the porter's lodge at Queens' asking me to ring. When I called he told me that he had seen my letter to Jo, that he was sorry to have done so, but that as far as the gay thing was concerned he couldn't be happier . . .

'Oh, and your mother would love to speak to you.'

'*Darling!*'

'Oh, Mama. Are you upset?'

'Don't be silly. I think I've *always* known . . .'

It was the most marvellous relief to come out in this way.

My scholarly duty of saying Latin grace in hall for a week came round. I began to write occasional articles and television reviews for a student newspaper called *Broadsheet*, and more and more parts in more and more plays came my way. I played a disc jockey in Poliakoff's *City Sugar*, a poet in Bond's *The Narrow Road to the Deep North* and a Classics don in a new play by undergraduate Harry Eyre. I played kings and dukes and old counsellors in Shakespeare and killers and husbands and businessmen and blackmailers in plays old, new, neglected and revived. If Kipling's suggestion that to fill every minute with sixty seconds' worth of distance run is truly, as he asserted, the mark of a man, then I seemed to have become one of the most virile students in Cambridge.

In the Christmas vacation that fell between the Michaelmas and Lent terms, I accompanied the European Theatre Group on a tour of the continent, bestowing the blessing of *Macbeth* upon a bewildered population of Dutch, German, Swiss and French theatre-goers, mostly reluctant schoolchildren. The production was directed by Pip Broughton, who had been responsible for *Artaud at Rodez*, and she had cast Jonathan Tafler as the murderous thane. The death of his father prevented him at the last minute, however, and this was a great blow to Pip, for she and Jonathan were an enchantingly devoted couple. I played King Duncan – a marvellous role for such a tour because he dies very soon in the play, and I could spend my time scoping out whichever town we were quartered in and be back in time for the curtain-call pregnant with information on the best bars and cheapest restaurants. The ETG had been founded by Derek Jacobi, Trevor Nunn and others in 1957, the year of my birth, and had earned a lamentable reputation for its frequent lapses from high seriousness and decorum. There was a rumour that the town of Grenoble had gone so far as to ban all Cambridge drama troupes from ever appearing in their town again after a notoriously drunken exhibition at a mayoral reception some time in the mid-seventies: well, drunken exhibition*ism*, if the story is to be believed. Our company was not as bad as that, but we did misbehave on stage. There is something about the sight of row upon row of serious Swiss schoolchildren with copies of Shakespeare on their laps studiously following the text line by line that brings out the devil in a British actor. A Word of the Day would be announced before curtain-up and prizes awarded to whichever actor could most often jemmy that word into their role. 'There's no weasel to find the mind's construction in the weasel,' I remember saying one night in Heidelberg. 'He was a weasel in whom I placed an absolute weasel.' And so on.

A fellow called Mark Knox, who played many parts, including the messenger who comes to tell Lady Macduff that the evil Macbeth is on his way and means her harm, discovered that his speech of warning could be sung to the tune of 'Greensleeves', which he did, a finger to his ear, to the great perplexity of a Bernese audience. The three witches' 'When shall we three meet again?' was discovered to fit, with only minimal syllabic wrenching, the tune of 'Hark the Herald Angels Sing'.

Somehow throughout all this, Barry Taylor, who had played the squeaking and gibbering Caliban in Ian Softley's BATS May Week *Tempest* and had now been called in at the last minute to replace Jonathan Tafler, contrived to produce a superb Macbeth. If I was back early enough from my reconnoitring of the town I would stand in the wings and watch in admiration as, rising above, or sometimes even joining in, the practical jokes, he managed to convey murderous savagery, self-destructive guilt, boiling fury and terrible pain as well as I had seen. It is of course a truism of amateur acting that the cast always believes they are doing something that would stand comparison with the best professional theatre: it is rarely justified, but sometimes there are amateur performances which a pro would be proud of, and Barry Taylor's Macbeth was one such. In my memory at least.

We spent far more time travelling between European cities in a Wallace Arnold coach than we did on stage. Devising games and time-passing occupations became a major obsession. Most of us were reading for the English tripos, and one game we played required us to write down on a slip of paper the major works of literature we had never read. I collected the slips and called out the roster of titles which included *Hamlet*, *Animal Farm*, *David Copperfield*, *Pride and Prejudice*, *The Great Gatsby*, *Waiting for Godot* . . . you name an obligatory must-read masterpiece and there was someone on the bus who had never read it. The wriggles of shame at the depths of our ignorance were as much pleasurable as mortifying. It is something of a relief to know that one is not alone in having a peculiar and inexplicable gap. You will want to know which title I submitted. It was D. H. Lawrence's *Women in Love*, which, to my no doubt crippling disadvantage and discredit, I still have not read to this day. Nor have I read *Sons and Lovers* or *The Rainbow*. You can add all of Thomas Hardy's novels to that list except *The Mayor of Casterbridge* (which I loathed). I passionately embrace Lawrence and Hardy as poets, but I find their novels unreadable. There. I feel as if I have emerged from a confessional. I hope you do not feel too let down.

Challenge 1

My first television performance came around this time. It had nothing to do with acting, but sprang from that same annoying anxiety to show off and be admired that one day, perhaps in my dotage, I will succeed in shaking off. The word had gone around the college that Queens' was entering a team for Granada Television's student quiz show *University Challenge*. I had watched this religiously since I was a child and could hardly have been more desperate to be picked for the team. The captain had been chosen by some process that I never understood, but he fully justified the appointment. He was a brilliant student of Modern and Medieval Languages called Steven

Botterill, now a renowned Dante scholar and Professor
at Berkeley, California. He had sensibly decided to pick
the three other members of his team by compiling a list
of questions and holding an open qualification test. I was
infinitely more nervous and excited about sitting this
little exam than the official tripos. I cannot remember
the questions especially well . . . one was something to
do with Natty Bumppo which I was relieved to be able to
answer. When a handwritten note from Botterill arrived
in my pigeonhole to tell me that I had been picked for
the team I was almost as jubilant and irradiated with joy
as the day in 1977 that my mother had telephoned Just
John's Delicatique in Norwich to break the news of my
scholarship to Queens'.[†] The other two undergraduates
chosen were a scientist called Barber and a lawyer called
Mark Lester – no, not the child star of *Oliver!* but another
Mark Lester altogether. We travelled north to Granadaland
for the first round.

It was my first visit to Manchester and my first close-
up encounter with a television studio. In Norwich I
had once sat in the audience for the taping of a largely
forgotten Anglia TV sitcom called *Backs to the Land* but
that was the extent of my penetration of the broadcasting
world. Granada was a much more impressive outfit
than dear, sweet, parochial Anglia. Their studios were
the home of *Coronation Street* and *World in Action*. The
corridors were lined with photographs of actors, film
stars and nationally known television presenters like
Brian Trueman and Michael Parkinson. We were shown
down a labyrinth of these passageways to a large dressing-
room, where we were asked to wait. We nibbled at crisps
and fruit, sipped fizzy drinks and grew steadily more

and more nervous. If we won our first-round match we would have to play another team that same afternoon. If we won that, we would have to return to Manchester at a later date for quarter- and semi-finals matches. If we won those, well a third and final visit would be required. That was a lot of ifs, and suddenly I felt, and perhaps the other three did too, that I knew absolutely nothing. Every single fact I ever knew flew from me like pigeons from the sound of a gun. Humiliation awaited us. I banged the side of my head in a last-minute attempt to rewire the brain.

The quizmaster was, of course, the marvellous Bamber Gascoigne, whose voice and features I knew as well as my parents'. He was one of those figures like the Queen and Robert Robinson: I could not remember a time when I wasn't aware of him. A wise and kindly man, he seemed aware that other teams knew that he was a Cambridge graduate himself and therefore went out of his way to be scrupulously fair, without ever toppling over into self-conscious countercantabrigianism. He always appeared to delight in a correct answer whencesoever it came, and it was firmly believed by all that he set and researched every question himself. He was famous for his gently knowledgeable corrections – 'Bad luck, you were thinking of Duns Scotus perhaps . . .' or 'Very close, he was of course a *friend* of Clausewitz . . .' – an attitude at some remove from the blessed Jeremy Paxman's scandalized shouts of '*What?*' and expression of having bitten into a bad olive whenever an incorrect answer comes his way that offends his sense of what should be known. *Autre temps, autres mœurs . . .*

Botterill, Lester, Barber and I walked shyly on to

the set, made the usual jokes about how the desks were actually side by side on the studio floor, not one on top of the other as they appeared to be on screen, and took our designated seats. I am afraid to say I cannot recall where the first-round opposition came from. Leeds University pops into my head, but I may be mistaken. No doubt they thought we were ghastly Oxbridge wankers. Looking at photographs of our team and its wild trichological variety, geeky earnestness and unhealthy complexions, we cannot be said to have been the prettiest quartet ever to greet a television audience.

We need not have been nervous. We were a good side and trounced all the opposition that was ranged against us right up to the final, which in those days was decided by a best-of-three encounter. For that match we found ourselves pitted against Merton, Oxford, my housemaster's old college. They seemed a decent and bright enough bunch, but we brushed them aside in the first leg with a winning margin of over a hundred. In the second leg they won by ten points, which was maddening but set up one of the tensest finals on record. When the gong sounded for the end of the third and deciding leg the teams were exactly level. A sudden-death tie-break came into operation. Whoever got the next question would win the series. Merton buzzed in with the right answer. We were runners-up. I have rarely been so devastated or felt so cheated. It hurts even now that our team can have answered so many more questions correctly than the opposition and yet have lost. Infantile and pathetic, but even as I type these words thirty years later the blood surges in my ears and my whole being seethes with feelings of disgusted outrage, bitter resentment and maddened disappointment at such shattering injustice. Nothing will ever put it right. Nothing, I tell you, nothing. Oh well.

Corpus Christening

Back at Cambridge as the Lent term came to a close I was approached by one Mark McCrum, now a well-known travel writer but in those days a larky, impish undergraduate with a flop of black hair and eyes like glistening currants. His father, Michael, was headmaster of Eton (though shortly to return to Cambridge to take up the mastership of Corpus Christi), and his older brother, Robert, was beginning to make a name for himself in publishing at Faber and Faber. Mark McCrum, with the initiative, enterprise and guileless chutzpah that were trademark characteristics, had taken charge of a small L-shaped space in St Edward's Passage belonging to Corpus Christi College. He and his friend Caroline Oulton planned to turn it into 'The Playroom', a drama venue that would specialize in new writing. I knew Caroline Oulton and adored her. She had been one of the *Macbeth* cast, and I had always tried to sit next to her on the coach. She stirred surprising things in me.

She and Mark had a most unexpected request. They wanted me to write a play to christen the Playroom: not necessarily full length, perhaps it could be part of a double bill? They had asked a clever young undergraduate called Robert Farrar to provide the other half of the evening. What did I think?

I was flattered, excited and alarmed, keen to try, yet scared of failing. Why did they think I might be capable of writing a *play*? I had never written anything close to such a thing in my life. Private poetry and the occasional article for *Broadsheet* were my whole writing career.

'Go home for the vac, sit and concentrate. Write about what you know. It'll be brilliant. But bear in mind it's a really intimate space. Anything you can write that makes the audience feel part of things will be perfect.'

Term ended, and I returned to Norfolk. 'Write about what you know' is the maxim that I had most heard from writers dead and alive. In my William Morris wallpapered room at the top of the house I sat at my desk and wondered what I knew. Institutions. I knew schools and I knew prison. That was about it. 'Involve the audience.' Hm . . .

I started to write the opening of a lesson in which a prep school master harangues his Latin class, tossing back their exercise books with hyperbolic disdain: 'Boys who rub me up the wrong way, Elwyn-Jones, come to a sticky end . . .' that sort of thing. The audience are the class. There comes a sudden lighting change that alters the time scheme and the dramatic mode, bringing down the fourth wall with a crash. A knock at the door, an older master enters, a story unfolds. I wrote and wrote away, first in longhand on a pad, then typing up each scene on my treasured Hermes 3000 typewriter, a jade-green-keyed and battleship-grey-bodied machine of incomparable solidity and beauty.

I contrived a farcical plot incorporating pederasty, blackmail and romance which was interwoven with other classroom scenes involving the audience in such a way, I hoped, as to satisfy the requirements of Mark's and Caroline's commission.

I typed out the title page:

Latin!
or Tobacco and Boys

A New Play by
Sue Denim

Sue Denim being 'pseudonym' of course. I cannot quite recall why I decided to present the play under a nom de plume – I think perhaps I had some hope that if the audience believed it to have been written by a woman they might forgive the piece its less than radical milieu.

Caroline and Mark seemed pleased with it, and a friend from Queens', Simon Cherry, agreed to direct. A law undergraduate called John Davies played the older master Herbert Brookshaw, and I played Dominic Clarke, the young hero of the play, if hero is quite the word we want.

The production sold out the Playroom for its short run of three days and so, as there seemed to be a demand for more, we performed *Latin!* again for a week in the Trinity Hall lecture theatre.

I was a playwright! The peculiarly exultant joy that comes over you when you have written a piece of work is like no other. Admiration and acclaim for acting performances, rousing ovations and deafening applause do not come close to the special pride you feel in having made something that was not there before out of no more exotic a material than words.

As a writer, I was approached by Emma Thompson and asked if I might contribute some comedy sketches for a show she was putting on at the ADC theatre with a group of friends. It was to showcase all-female comic talent and would be called *Woman's Hour*. I swallowed an inclination to suggest that if it bore that title and had only women performing in it, then surely it should also be *written* exclusively by women. But it was enough of a step that women were at least putting on their own comedy show – fifty years earlier they were forbidden to act in plays in Cambridge. Indeed they were only admitted as full members of the university as recently as ten years before I was born. Alongside Emma in *Woman's Hour* was the Footlights' first-ever female President, Jan Ravens, and a young Danish-born performer called Sandi Toksvig. I wrote a few of the sketches, the only two I can remember being a parody of a book review programme and a monologue for Emma in which she played a tweedy horsey woman at a Pony Club gymkhana bellowing encouragement at her daughter. Ground-breaking, revolutionary material. The show was considered a great success, and certainly the talent of Emma, Jan and Sandi was plain for all to see.

A friend of Mark McCrum's called Ben Blackshaw now came to me with a play he had written called *Have You Seen the Yellow Book?* It documented in vivid little scenes the rise and fall of Oscar Wilde. Ben wanted me for the part of Oscar. Ben directed, and we went on in the Playroom. Through this play I received my first review in a national newspaper. The *Gay News* critic wrote that I 'carried the lilt of Irish without the brogue'. I kept the tiny scrap of paper that formed the entirety of his review in my wallet for years afterwards.

Chariots 1

The word went round Cambridge that a film company was looking for extras amongst the student body. They had been in touch with the presidents of the ADC, the Mummers and the Marlowe Society, who in turn had contacted the acting world. Kim and I hurried to sign our names up for international stardom.

I had a friend at Oxford who had written to me proudly to say the great Michael Cimino was directing a major picture there called *Heaven's Gate* and that he had a walk-on part in it. I now called him to let him know that we had filming in our midst too.

'Oh yes?' he said. 'Which studio? We're United Artists.'

'Oh. I don't think ours is exactly an American studio-type film,' I had to confess. 'Apparently it's about a group of British athletes in the 1924 Olympics. One of them is Jewish and the other one is a devout Presbyterian who won't run on Sundays or something. Colin Welland has written the screenplay. It's . . . well . . . anyway.'

As I put the phone down I could hear my friend's snorts of derisive Oxonian laughter. There was something rather humiliating about Cambridge being chosen for such a small parochial film while Oxford got a big-budget major motion picture. Neither of us were to know that *Heaven's Gate* would all but destroy United Artists and be for ever listed as one of the greatest financial disasters in Hollywood history while our little film . . .

It was called *Chariots of Fire*, and I spent a number of bemusedly excited days as an extra. The first was in the Senate House for a Freshers' Fair scene in which the lead actors get recruited by the University Athletics Club and Gilbert and Sullivan Society. All light-headed from a free but fierce haircut, I had earned myself an extra two pounds even before the filming began by bringing my own striped college blazer and flannels as costume. I looked the most

dreadful arse as I manned a tennis club stall, bouncing a ball
on a racket and trying to give the impression that I might
be hearty. With the more important role of Captain of the
Cambridge University Athletics Team, one of Cambridge's
sporting heroes was just along from me: Derek Pringle,
who went on to play cricket for Essex and England.

I was most astonished when a props man, just before
the camera rolled, came up and gave me a collection of
small visiting cards on which were printed 'Cambridge
University Tennis Club' below an image of crossed tennis
rackets. I had to peer closely to decipher the sloping New
Palace print – the likelihood of the camera capturing
this seemed absurdly remote. It struck me as the most
astounding waste of time and money, but of course I
knew nothing about filming or the necessity of being
prepared for any eventuality. No matter how detailed the
pre-production planning and preparation, circumstances
like weather, light, noise, the failure of a crane or the
indisposition of an actor or crew member can alter
everything. It was quite possible that the director may
have decided that the scene that day needed to open with
a close shot of someone taking a tennis club card and if
it hadn't been there ready, waiting and perfectly printed,
filming would have been delayed, and much more money
would have been lost than the price of producing a few
visiting cards. None of that occurred to me, of course; I
just leapt to the conclusion, as people always do, that film-
makers were imbecile profligates. I now know, being one,
that they are imbecile misers.

For the whole of the first day I assumed that the crew
member positioning us all, telling us where and when to
move and yelling for silence and calling for the camera to

'turn over' must be the director, whose name I knew to be Hugh Hudson. At one point, needing clarification, I started a question with, 'Excuse me, Mr Hudson . . .', and he laughed and pointed to a languid man sitting in a chair reading a newspaper. 'I'm just the first assistant,' he said, '*that's* the director.'

If a director didn't shout and tell people when to move and how to hold their props and where to look then what, I wondered, *did* he do? It all seemed most mysterious.

The rumour went round Cambridge, after only three or four days' 'shooting' as we pros now called it, that certain university authorities had read the script, disapproved of its implications and summarily withdrawn from the production company all permissions to film. It seems that the story portrayed the Masters of Trinity and Gonville and Caius Colleges, played by John Gielgud and Lindsay Anderson, as anti-Semitic snobs. Their present-day descendants had decided that this was not to be countenanced.

Oh well, we thought. That was that. Fun while it lasted. But the film's producer, David Puttnam, either out of loyalty or for more practical reasons of financial economy, did not fire us. He quickly acquired Eton College as an alternative location, and we were all bussed out to Berkshire, using the nearby Bray Studios as a base. At Eton they shot one of the most memorable scenes in the film, the Great Court Run in which Harold Abrahams and Lord Lindsay, played by Ben Cross and Nigel Havers, run a complete circuit of the outer perimeter of Trinity Great Court in the forty-three seconds or so (depending on the clock's last winding) that it takes for the chimes to strike twelve, a feat that Sebastian Coe just failed to emulate in 1988. School Yard at Eton is probably a quarter the size of Trinity Great Court, but camera angles managed to disguise the fact that even I could probably have run round it in forty-three seconds. My role in this scene, along with just about everyone else's, was to cheer and throw my boater wildly in the air.

Filming the scene seemed to take an extraordinarily long time. I could not believe how long: it occurred to me that everyone must be extremely incompetent and that it could surely all have been done so much more quickly and efficiently. I now know that the days were all managed with exemplary order and speed. To an outsider, filming always appears both intolerably boring and horribly disorganized. When you do not understand how something works it is perhaps natural to question and to doubt. In later years, when – as so often might happen – a passer-by on a street shoot I was involved with expostulated at 'all those people' and how 'most of them are just hanging around doing nothing' and then offered the suggestion that 'I suppose it's all under the control of the unions', I would, to tamp down my indignation at such rudeness, force myself to remember my own scepticism when an extra on *Chariots of Fire*. That scepticism was shared by many, and so bored did the majority become and so ill-used did they feel themselves to be that they staged a mini-strike. They all sat down in School Yard and chanted for more pay. It staggers me how greedy and rude we could have been, and I am pleased to say that Kim and I were not among the bolshie faction. Puttnam appeared before us and sportingly and without the least sign of annoyance or disappointment agreed to pay us all an extra two pounds each. We cheered him louder than we had been asked to cheer the race.

If you happen one day to be watching *Chariots of Fire* and want to spot me for reasons into which I will not inquire, then the Gilbert and Sullivan entertainment that takes place after the matriculation dinner is the scene to find. I'm lurking and smirking in the background. It is one of nature's cruellest curses on me. No matter how soulful, sweet and unselfconscious I try to appear, my features always arrange themselves into an expression of utmost self-satisfaction, self-awareness and self-love. So unfair.

Back in Cambridge, life continued its jolly round. Simon Cherry, who had directed *Latin!*, was chosen by BATS to direct the 1980 May Week production. He cast me as the warty old king in *All's Well That Ends Well*. Emma Thompson played Helena, Kim had a variety of parts, and Barry Taylor played Parolles.

Barry, whose Macbeth had so impressed me, was an extraordinary man and one who made me, without meaning to, feel very guilty and ashamed. He was as genuinely intelligent, perceptive, wise, learned, skilled at writing and academically gifted as anyone I had ever met, but as far as Cambridge and life in the world outside was concerned he had one huge defect, one appalling flaw. He was honest. He had integrity. Honesty and integrity are fine virtues in so far as they go, but they are fatal when it comes to sitting exams. He was in the year above me, so this was his last term at Cambridge, and finals beckoned. If anyone should have got a First and stayed on to research and become a valued teacher and academic it should have been Barry. But his fatal flaw meant that when he sat in the examination hall and turned over the paper he would *try to answer the question*. He would sit and think about it. He would ponder avenues of approach. He would start,

cross out what he had written, have another think and
only commit to paper his most considered judgements,
appraisals and conclusions. By the time the whistle blew
for the end of the three hours, during which time three
questions should have been addressed and three essays
completed, Barry would hand in one perfect essay and
half of a very good one, leaving the third question entirely
unanswered. He had done this in Part Ones the year before
and he himself knew that he would probably do it in the
Finals of the English tripos that were rapidly approaching.
He wrote with delicacy and style, and his literary insights
and moral, social and aesthetic perceptions were of far
more value and depth than mine, but he simply could not
master the art of time-keeping or manage the compromise
of giving examiners what they wanted. He came from a
working-class family who lived south-east of London.
He told me that on the rare occasions that public-school
boys had got on to the bus in Southend or the Isle of Dogs
and asked for a ticket in their posh accents, he and his
friends at the back would do cawing, honking, drawling
impersonations of them. Not threateningly or violently,
but because the sounds were so peculiar to their ears. It was
hard for them to believe that anyone, especially anyone
their age, really spoke like that. Then Barry arrived in
Cambridge and found that *he* was the one with the unusual
accent, and suddenly ra-ra public-school speech was the
norm. It took him some time to believe that anyone with
such an accent could be anything other than a dim chinless
wonder.

How Barry must have regarded a man like me, slick
and deceitful enough to answer exam questions in just
the way that achieved the best results with the least effort

yet gifted with enough of a memory and knowledge to disguise it as authentic academic achievement, I don't know. Add to that my public-school manner and apparent confidence and I cannot but think that I made up just the kind of package that anyone with spirit would be most likely to despise.

Cambridge might have argued, should they have been moved to do so, that their examination system is perfectly suited to the real world. Success in politics, journalism, the Civil Service, advertising, the Foreign Office, the City and so many of the grander fields of professional endeavour rely on the ability quickly to master the essentials of a brief, to subdue material to one's will, to present, promote and pimp, to massage facts and figures and to do all with speed, polish, ease and confidence. The tripos weeds out the slow, the honest, the careful, the considered and the excessively truthful – all of whom would be grossly unsuited to public life or high-profile careers.

My cynicism and self-criticism may seem distorted and overstated, but I do not think I exaggerate so very much. Certainly the distinction between Barry Taylor's diligent integrity and my own indolent technique remains symbolic of something that is wrong in education and testing. Having said which, Cambridge was not so foolish as entirely to fail to recognize Barry's qualities, and he did subsequently have a career in academia despite not getting the First-Class degree that a better system of examination would undoubtedly have awarded him. On the other hand, if continuous assessment existed in my day, and had there been a greater emphasis on written work and research and less on scrambling to produce essays against the clock in the examination hall, I would have been booted out within months. Perhaps two streams of testing are required: one for plausible bounders like me and another for authentic minds like Barry.

Caledonia 2

A second Edinburgh Fringe season approached. This time I was exclusively bound up with the Cambridge Mummers, the drama club for whom I had appeared in *Artaud at Rodez* the previous year. Despite their reputation for progressive programming and emphasis on the modern, radical and avant-garde, they asked if I might consider allowing *Latin!* to join their repertoire. Caroline Oulton had written a play about the Swiss kinetic sculptor Jean Tinguely; a friend called Oscar Moore had written a piece whose title I forget but which had darkly funny things to say about Dunstable; Simon McBurney and Simon Cherry were preparing a one-man show in which McBurney would play Charles Bukowski. A children's play was also being devised, and the main evening show would be a production of the rarely performed Middleton and Dekker comedy *The Roaring Girl* with Annabelle Arden in the title role, under the direction of Brigid Larmour. It was Annabelle and Brigid who had co-directed the production of *Travesties* in which I had first seen Emma Thompson. All these shows would be presented for two weeks in that same cramped but historic Riddle's Court venue off the Royal Mile.

After the May Term finished and I had completed my usual summer stint at Cundall Manor we rehearsed for two weeks in Cambridge. I stayed in digs (Queens' was earning money from renting itself out for a business conference) near Magdalene with Ben Blackshaw and Mark McCrum, who had, with what grown-ups call 'commendable enterprise', started a business called 'Picnic Punts'. Every morning they would get up, dress themselves in striped blazers, white flannel trousers and boaters and go down to a mooring just opposite Queens', where they kept a single punt. A wooden plank with a white cloth would be placed athwart the vessel as a table, a wind-up gramophone, ice bucket and all the accoutrements required to serve a cream tea with strawberries and champagne would be stowed somewhere, and Mark would erect a handwritten sign on the Silver Street Bridge with illustrations (he was handy at drawing and calligraphy) advertising a punt-ride up or down the Cam in the company of genuine undergraduates.

Ben was pretty and fey and blond and Mark impish and darkly handsome. The dreamy sight of them in their Edwardian whites was guaranteed to appeal to American tourists, day-tripping matrons and visiting schoolmasters of a Uranian disposition. Sometimes, as I hurried across a bridge between rehearsals, I might hear a Gershwin tune echoing off the stonework of the Bridge of Sighs or the slowing down and rapid rewinding of a Benny Goodman foxtrot drifting across the meadow opposite King's and I would smile as I saw Ben and Mark poling their way along the Backs, cheerfully making up outrageous and incredible stories about Byron or Darwin for the edification of their credulous and awestruck customers. At day's end, I would come back from my rehearsals, and they would return from the river, muscles aching, tired from talking nonsense, their day's takings wrapped in the tablecloth, which would be emptied on the kitchen table. Every last currency note and coin was scooped up and taken to the grocer's in Jesus Lane to be spent on meat and pasta for that evening and bottles of wine and tea things and champagne for the following day's punting. I don't think Mark and Ben turned a penny's profit, but they got themselves fit, ate and drank well and inadvertently started a trend in 'authentic student punts' that is going to this day in the hands of much savvier and harder-nosed entrepreneurs. Not once did either of them suggest that I contribute to the nightly supper fund, despite the fact that I always ate and drank the food and wine that it bought. There was a carefree charm to the pair that made me feel heavy, bourgeois and over-earnest.

I had agreed to be in *The Roaring Girl*, as well as reprising my role as Dominic Clarke in *Latin!*, with John Davies still in the part of Herbert Brookshaw. Simon Cherry would be directing once again and he had asked David Lewis, a History of Art student with whom he shared rooms in Queens', to design a poster. The result was sensational. In the style of an Edwardian children's storybook jacket Dave's design depicted a school-uniformed boy and a young man in a teacher's gown kissing, with a cricket game going on in the background. It was stunningly well done; the lettering, the colour palette, the whole look of it was exquisite. It shocked, but it was also funny, elegant and charming, which is what I hoped the play might be.

The Mummers' producers, Jo and David, sent an army of volunteers (in other words the cast) around Edinburgh as soon as we arrived, to staple and paste up the posters for all our shows wherever we could. It soon became apparent that the *Latin!* poster was in great demand. The moment it went up it would be pinched, even if we took the common precautionary step of ripping it first to decrease its collectability. I started to get messages left for me at Mummers' headquarters in Riddle's Court offering money for spares. It had become a collector's item. In a rare burst of entrepreneurial PR zeal, I called up the *Scotsman*, pretending to be upset that our poster was being stolen as soon as it was put up. Sure enough, they obligingly ran a small paragraph with a picture of the poster, under the mini-headline: 'Is this the most stolen poster in Edinburgh?' The box-office went through the roof, and *Latin!* was sold out for the whole of the two weeks of its run.

Latin! played in the mid-afternoon, but the main evening attraction was the *The Roaring Girl*. One of its cast members was a handsome and amusing Trinity Hall undergraduate called Tony Slattery, who had the look of a young Charles Boyer and the habits of an ill-trained but affectionate puppy. He read Modern and Medieval Languages, specializing in French and Spanish. He had represented Britain at judo, becoming national champion at his weight in his teens. He sang and played the guitar and was capable of being most dreadfully funny. Every night, in his role as some kind of foppish lord, he would put a larger and larger feather in his hat. By the time we came to the end of the first week it was brushing the ceiling. The entire cast, including Annabelle Arden, who had the lead role of Moll Cutpurse, fell into unrestrained giggles each time he executed a low bow which caused this enormous plume to bounce and waggle over our heads or into our faces. Sometimes when actors corpse it amuses the audience, but when it goes too far they often start to stir and mutter and hiss, which was what happened that evening. It was deeply unprofessional – but being deeply unprofessional was one of the marvellous things about being students and being, well, not professional.

We all squeezed into digs somewhere in the New Town, hunkering down in sleeping bags on the floor, and even managed to make room for my sister Jo who came to visit and got on *very well* with certain members of the company. It was a wonderful time; the plays were all successful in their own way and we attracted good audiences. The pleasure was compounded by excellent reviews; the notoriously difficult Nicholas de Jong was blush-makingly nice: 'Stephen Fry is a name I shall look out for in the future, which is more than can be said for most of the writers and performers on the Fringe,' he wrote. I have since been a sore disappointment to de Jong, I think, but at least we got off on the right foot. Even better news came when the *Scotsman* awarded us a Fringe First, the award that everyone aspired to win in those days.

There was little time to see any other shows. *Electric Voodoo*, this year's Footlights Revue, was composed of completely different performers from the year before. Hugh Laurie, that tall fellow with a flag of crimson on each cheek, wasn't in it, nor were Emma or Simon McBurney. Emma did come to Riddle's Court to see *Latin!* and she brought the Laurie chap with her.

'Hullo,' he said when she pushed him forward to meet me after the show.

'Hullo,' I said.

'That was very good,' he said. 'I really enjoyed it.'

'Thank you,' I said. 'That is very kind.'

The triangles on his cheeks flamed redder than ever, and he popped off. I didn't give him much more thought.

That night we had a party to celebrate the Fringe First. How tall and serious I look in the photograph.

Conveniences

In the late September of 1980 I arrived back in Cambridge for my final year. Although we could each have had a single set again, Kim and I decided that we wanted to carry on sharing and we were allocated A2 in the medieval tower of Old Court, the finest undergraduate rooms in college. Many graduates and dons had accommodation far less grand. The rooms boasted magnificent built-in bookshelves, a noble fireplace, an excellent gyp-room and bedrooms. The windows looked out on one side over Old Court and on the other on to the Master's Lodge of St Catharine's, the abode of the august Professor of Mathematics Sir Peter Swinnerton-Dyer, who was currently enjoying a period as Vice-Chancellor. The most prized item of furniture we added came in the form of a mahogany table that cleverly opened up into a wooden lectern. I had borrowed this from Trinity College as a prop for a lunchtime reading of the poems of Ernst Jandl and had somehow failed to return it. Kim added his Jaques chess set, Bang and Olufsen stereo, Sony Trinitron television and Cafetière coffee jug. We were far from the great age of designer labels, but brand names were beginning to acquire a new significance and desirability. I owned a pistachio-coloured Calvin Klein shirt whose loss I still mourn and a pair of olive-green Kickers of such surpassing splendour that I sob just to think of them.

On the ground floor at the foot of our staircase a

smaller set of rooms had been taken over by the college and transformed into something quite marvellous and strange and new: a ladies' lavatory. The outer room was fitted with a large dressing-table with bulbs around the side of its mirror. On this table were boxes of coloured tissues, a glass jar of Q-tips and a pretty painted porcelain bowl filled with powder-blue, baby-pink and Easter-yellow balls of cotton wool. A basket-weave chair freshly painted in white gloss was tucked into the valance or pelmet of flower-printed chintz that underhung the table. On the pink-painted walls were three different coin-operated sanitary towel and tampon machines. In the lavatory itself a complex incinerator for used examples of same stood next to the toilet, and hanging off the back of the door could be seen a thick swatch of brown Lil-lets disposal bags. The whole place screamed, 'You are a woman. Don't even *think* of forgetting it.'

Queens' College, after 532 years of single-sex status, had decided to go co-ed. Women undergraduates had arrived this term as full members of the college.

I can picture the scenes at the meeting of the college's governing Fellows. The President coughs for attention.

'Gentlemen! As you know, this body voted two years ago for women to be . . .'

'I didn't!'

'Nor I!'

'Er, yes, thank you Doctor Bantrey, Professor Threlfall. A *majority* of Fellows voted for the admission of women. Next term, as you know, will see our first intake . . .'

'Will they eat with the rest of us?'

'Well, of course they will eat with us, Dr Kemp, why on earth shouldn't they?'

'Well I thought they ate . . . differently.'

'Differently?'

'They pick up their food with their mouths, don't they? Or am I thinking of cats?'

'Dr Kemp, have you actually ever *met* a woman?'

'Er . . . well, not that you'd . . . my mother was a woman. Was introduced when I was seven. Used to see her at mealtimes occasionally. Does that count?'

'And did she eat normally?'

'Let me think . . . now you come to mention it, yes, she did, yes. Quite normally.'

'Well, there you are then. There is, however, the issue of cloacal arrangements. Women do of course have hygienic requirements that are . . . somewhat *sui generis*.'

'Oh yes? In what way?'

'Ah . . . well, to be honest I'm not actually sure on this one myself. But I believe every now and again they are required to shout and to slap a man and then burst into tears and . . . er . . . then they have to blow their nose or something. And do their hair. Something along those lines. This happens regularly once a month, I am told. So we will need specially designed rooms set aside for the purpose.'

'I knew no good would come of this.'

'Hear fucking hear.'

'Gentlemen, please! If we can just . . .'

'And where are they going to hang their breasts at night? Answer me that.'

'Excuse me?'

'Women have extra mounds of flesh that they attach with wire suspenders and silk peggings to the front of their chests. I know that much at least. The question is,

where are they going to hang them at night? Hm? You
see? You just haven't thought this thing through, have
you?'

And so on . . . until the meeting broke up in disarray.

With the exception of the startling lavatories the
arrival of The Women turned out to be the most natural
thing in the world. It seemed impossible to believe that
they had never been here before. Whether they took to
the more honkingly earthy college institutions like the
Kangaroos, the college's sporting club, or indeed to the
Cherubs, of which I was now leader or Senior Member,
I cannot quite say. Since, by definition, all the women in
college were first-years (how they must have tired of the
terms 'freshettes' and 'undergraduettes') there were none
quartered in Old Court, hence none to use the gleaming
Ladies at the foot of A staircase. It became, therefore, our
private poo-palace. Which is how I know the towel-bag
legend off by heart: 'Lil-lets expand widthways to mould
themselves gently to your shape. If you have any questions
write to Sister Marion . . .'

Kim and I were lovers by this time, and it was a
happy state to be in. He played chess, read Thucydides,
Aristotle and Cicero and boomed Wagner over Old
Court, sweetening it with gigantic moments from Verdi
and Puccini. I learnt my lines, typed the occasional essay
on my Hermes typewriter, read, smoked and chattered.
Friends came up the stairs and stayed for long afternoons
of toast, coffee and then wine. We were closest with Rob
Wyke, a graduate from St Catharine's who taught in
college and worked on his thesis. He had played Gonzago
in *The Tempest*. He, Paul Hartell, another PhD student
at Cat's, and a third wild and wonderful graduate called

Nigel Huckstep formed a triumvirate in whose company Kim and I loved to be. Their range of reference was enormous, but they wore their learning lightly. On free evenings we would 'draaj' (which Nigel, who picked up languages as easily as infants pick up infections, claimed was an Afrikaans word for saunter) past King's, down Trinity Street and to the Baron of Beef pub in Bridge Street, where the dirt was dished on all of Cambridge.

Committees

As a third-year now I found myself on innumerable committees. Aside from being the President of the May Ball, Senior Member of Cherubs ('I've seen ya member, Senior Member!' being the obvious chant) and President of BATS, I was on the committees of the ADC, Mummers and several other drama clubs. This meant that, at the opening of term, I found myself bouncing from meeting to meeting, listening to directors 'pitching', as we would now say.

It went like this. Let us say you are a director, or want to be one. You choose a play – new or classic – you decide how you mount it, prepare a speech about your 'concept', draw up a sensible budget and get yourself on the list to be heard by each of the larger drama societies. All this would now be done with presentation and spreadsheet software I suppose, but back then it was bits of paper and speechifying.

At a meeting of the ADC a first-year brimful of confidence arrived. He had the pained, coat-muffled-up look of a sensitive socialist who finds everything around him violent and faintly oppressive.

'I am very *very* interested in the work of Grotowski and Brook,' he told us. 'My production of *Serjeant Musgrave's Dance* will utilize their theories, combined with elements of Brechtian Epic. I will dress the cast only in white and red. The set will be scaffolding.'

Gosh. Well. Absolutely. We consulted amongst ourselves after he left. Jolly bright fellow. *Serjeant Musgrave*. Hadn't been done for fifteen years so far as we could tell. Interesting ideas. Cheap too. Definitely worth considering.

We see a few more candidates, and I rush off to Trinity Hall, where we hold a similar meeting for the Mummers. The third candidate to come into the room to pitch is that same intense first-year who had appeared before the ADC committee. He sits down.

'I am very *very* interested in the work of Grotowski and Brook,' he announces. 'My production of *'Tis Pity She's a Whore* will utilize their theories, combined with elements of Brechtian Epic . . .' He breaks off and gives me a look of uncertainty. Has he seen me before somewhere? He shakes his head and continues. 'I will dress the cast only in white and red. The set will be scaffolding.'

A few more candidates, and I'm off to Queens' for a BATS meeting. Sure enough, there is that first-year again. He really is covering all the bases.

'I am very interested in the work of Grotowski and Brook. My production of *The Importance of Being Earnest* will utilize their theories . . .'

'Combined with elements of Brechtian Epic?' I ask. 'Possibly dressed in white and red? Scaffolding?'

'Er . . .'

That first-year is now a successful *homme de théâtre* and

an artistic director of distinction. I do not know how many of his current productions are dressed in white and red, but his scaffold-clad *My Fair Lady*, utilizing the theories of Grotowski and Brook (combined, I am told, with elements of Brechtian Epic Theatre), wowed them in Margate last summer. No, but shush.

I loathed committee meetings then and I loathe them now. My whole life has been a fight to avoid them as much as possible. A losing fight. I would so much rather do things than talk about doing them. Those who sit in committee rooms rule the world, of course, which is lovely if that is what you want to do, but those who rule the world get so little opportunity to run about and laugh and play in it.

It was a relief then to be cast as Volpone in a production at the ADC. A second-year from Caius called Simon Beale played Sir Politic Would-Be and all but ate up the stage with the most astonishing comic physicality and outrageous upstaging. At one point in the second act he stood talking to me, his back to the audience. I was always rather mystified why my excellent speech to him got so many laughs. It's unsettling when you don't know where laughs come from. I discovered that Simon Beale was scratching his arse throughout the whole scene. Had it been from an actor less accomplished or a person less adorable I suppose I might have been miffed. He also sang beautifully and was possessed of perfect pitch. There was a market scene that required singing – not from me, of course, but from the rest of the cast. Simon would stand in the wings, everyone huddled around him, and give out the note. After the performance, as a treat, he would sing 'Dalla sua pace' or 'Un'aura amorosa' for me, and I would melt into a puddle. One night the venerable Shakespearean scholar and Emeritus Professor of English L. C. Knight, affectionately known as Elsie, was in the audience. He left a note for me at the stage door telling me that in his opinion my Volpone was superior to Paul Scofield's. 'Better shaped, better spoken and more believable. The finest I have ever seen.' How like me to remember that word for word. The old boy was almost eighty, of course, and almost certainly deaf and demented, but I was, nevertheless, wildly proud. Too proud to show the note to anyone other than Kim and the director, for my pride in refusing to allow myself to appear boastful or pleased with myself was even more intense than any pride I might have had in my achievements. There was sometimes a fight between these two species of pride, but usually the first type won and was mistakenly called modesty.

Early one evening during the weeklong run of *Volpone* I arrived backstage at the ADC theatre and tripped on a pile of boxes in the corridor. They were programmes for the following week's ADC production, dumped on the floor by the delivery man from the printers. The play was *Serjeant Musgrave's Dance*, the Grotowski–Brook obsessive having been duly awarded his slot. I read through his programme notes.

Work. Discipline. Comradeship. Work and discipline and comradeship. Only with these three can we create a true socialist theatre.

I took the boxes to my dressing-room and hunted for a pen. An hour later the programmes had been returned to their boxes. The director's notes now read:

Work. Discipline. Comradeship. Work and discipline and comradeship.
Only with these three can we create a true national socialist theatre.

I saw him later that evening looking white and furious
and felt that I had been a hideous beast. But really. I mean.
Did Shakespeare call actors 'workers' or 'players'?

Cycle

The next week Kim surprised me with plans for an exeat
from Cambridge. He had bought tickets for Götz Friedrich's
Ring Cycle at the Royal Opera House in London. Monday
Das Rheingold, Tuesday *Die Walküre*, Wednesday off,
Thursday *Siegfried*, Friday off and Saturday *Götterdämmerung*.
A week of Valkyries and Niebelungs and Gods and Heroes
and Norns and Giants. It was my first visit to Covent Garden
and my first experience of live Wagner. Not my last. Indeed,
today, as I type this, is a Tuesday. I was at a *Götterdämmerung*
just three nights ago. It gets into your blood. Well, my
blood. Probably not yours. All Wagnerians know the film
that descends over the eyes of those to whom they talk about
their obsession, so I will say no more save to point out what
is perhaps obvious, that it was a shattering experience and a
life-changingly important week for me.

Comedy Colleague, Collaborator and Comrade

A far more life-changingly important moment and a yet
more shattering experience was heaving to on the horizon.

Amongst the friends that came to visit A2 was Emma Thompson. Having taken a year off from the Footlights, she was back in the club as Vice-President for her final year. She arrived one early evening and plonked herself on our excellent sofa.

'You remember Hugh Laurie?'

'Er . . . remind me.'

She flung an impatient cushion at my head. 'You know perfectly well who I mean. He was in *Nightcap*.'

'Oh, the tall chap with the flushed cheeks and the big blue eyes?'

'Exactly. Well he's the President of Footlights this year.'

'Coo.'

'Yes, and he needs someone to write sketches with. He wants me to bring you over to his rooms at Selwyn.'

'Me? But I don't know him . . . how . . . what?'

'Yes you do!' She flung two cushions in succession. 'I introduced you at Edinburgh.'

'You did?'

There were no cushions left so she flung me a speaking glance instead. Possibly the speakingest glance that had been flung in Cambridge that year. 'For someone with such a good memory,' she said, 'you have a terrible memory.'

Kim, Emma and I walked up Sidgwick Avenue towards Selwyn College. It was a cold November night, and the air held a smell of gunpowder from a Bonfire Night party being held somewhere near the Fen Causeway. We came to a Victorian building on the rugby-ground side of Grange Road, not far from Cambridge's newest college, Robinson.

Emma led us through the open street door and up some

stairs. She knocked on a door at the end of the corridor. A voice grunted for us to enter.

He was sitting on the edge of his bed, a guitar on his knee. At the other side of the room was his girlfriend, Katie Kelly, whom I knew slightly. Like Emma, she read English at Newnham. She was very pretty and had long blonde hair and a ravishing smile.

He stood awkwardly, the red flags of his cheeks more pronounced than ever. 'Hullo,' he said.

'Hullo,' I said.

We were both people who said 'hullo' rather than 'hello'.

'Red wine or white?' said Katie.

'I've been writing a song,' he said and started to strum on his guitar. The song was a kind of ballad sung in the character of an American IRA supporter.

> Give money to an IRA bomber?
> Why, yessir, I'd consider it an honour,
> Everybody must have a cause.

The accent was flawless and the singing superb. It seemed to me a perfect song.

'Woolworths,' he said as he laid the instrument down. 'I borrow guitars that cost ten times as much, but they just don't do it for me.'

Katie approached with the wine. 'Well, are you going to tell him?'

'Ah. Yes. Well, thing is. Footlights. I'm the President, you see.'

'I saw you in *Nightcap* you were magnificent it was brilliant,' I said in a rush.

'Oh. Gosh. Well. No. Really? Well, er . . . *Latin!* Top. Absolutely top.'

'Nonsense, oh shush.'

'Completely.'

The excruciating horror of mutual admiration out of the way, we both paused, unsure of how to continue.

'Well, go on,' said Emma.

'Yes. So. There are two Smokers left this term, but most importantly there's the panto.'

'The panto?'

'Yup. The Footlights pantomime. Two years ago we did *Aladdin.*'

'Hugh was the Emperor of China,' Katie said.

'I missed that, I'm afraid,' I said.

'Quite right. I would have too. If I hadn't been in it. Anyway, this year we're doing *The Snow Queen.*'

'Hans Christian Andersen?'

'Yup. Katie and I have been writing it. We've got this . . .' he showed me some script.

Five minutes later Hugh and I were writing a scene together as if we had been doing it all our lives.

You read about people falling suddenly in love, about romantic thunderbolts that go with clashing cymbals, high quivering strings and resounding chords and you read about eyes that meet across the room to the thudding twang of Cupid's bow, but it is less often that you read about collaborative love at first sight, about people who instantly discover that they were born to work together or born to be natural and perfect friends.

The moment Hugh Laurie and I started to exchange ideas it was starkly and most wonderfully clear that we shared absolutely the same sense of what was funny and the same scruples, tastes and sensitivities as to what we found derivative, cheap, obvious or stylistically unacceptable. Which is not to say that we were similar. If the world is full of plugs looking for sockets and sockets looking for plugs, as – roughly speaking – the Platonic allegory of love suggests, then there is no doubt we did seem each to possess precisely the qualities and deficiencies the other most lacked. Hugh had music where I had none. He had an ability to be likeably daft and clownish. He moved, tumbled and leapt like an athlete. He had authority, presence and dignity. I had . . . hang on, what *did* I have? Patter and fluency, I suppose. Verbal dexterity. Learning. Hugh always said that I also added what he called *gravitas* to the proceedings. Although he had great authority himself on stage I suppose I had the edge on playing older authority figures. I wrote too. I mean I actually physically wrote lines down with pen and paper or typewriter. Hugh kept the phrases and shapes of the monologues and songs he was working on in his head and only wrote them down or dictated them when a script was needed for stage-management or administrative purposes.

Hugh was determined that the Footlights should look grown-up but never pleased with itself or, God forbid, cool. We both shared a horror of cool. To wear sunglasses when it wasn't sunny, to look pained and troubled and emotionally raw, to pull that sneery snorty 'Er?!! *What*?!' face at things that you didn't understand or from which you thought it stylish to distance yourself. Any such arid, self-regarding stylistic narcissism we detested. Better to look a naive simpleton than jaded, tired or world-weary, we felt. 'We're *students*, for fuck's sake,' was our credo. 'We have people making our beds and tidying our rooms for us. We live in panelled medieval rooms. We have theatres, printing presses, first-class cricket pitches, a river, boats, libraries and all the time in the world for contentment, pleasure and fun. What right have we got to moan and moon and mooch about the place looking tortured?'

We were fortunate that the age of young people doing stand-up comedy hadn't yet arrived. The idea, and I am afraid it has since become a reality, of pained emo students leaning listless and misunderstood on a mike-stand railing against the burden of life would be more than either of us would have been able to bear. We were exceptionally attuned to pretension, aesthetic discord and hypocrisy. The young are so priggish. I hope we are much more tolerant now.

Almost no one we ever worked with either at Cambridge or afterwards quite seemed to share or even understand our aesthetic, if I can dignify it with such a word. It is probable that our fear of being unoriginal, of looking cocky, of being obvious or of being seen ever to have chosen the line of least resistance caused us difficulty in our comedy careers. The same fears might also have pushed us to some of our best endeavours too, so there is no real reason to regret the sensitivity and fastidiousness that only we appeared to share. We soon became familiar with the expressions of bewilderment that might flicker over the faces of those who suggested something that inadvertently trespassed against our instinctive sense of what could or could not be funny, right or fit. I don't think we were ever aggressive or unkind, certainly not deliberately, but when two people are absolutely in harness with regard to matters of principle and outlook it must be very alienating to outsiders, and I expect two tall public-school figures like us must have seemed forbidding and aloof. Inside, of course, we felt anything but. I would not want to paint a picture of us as earnest, dogmatic ideologues, the Frank and Queenie Leavis of Comedy. We spent most of our time laughing. The smallest things would set us off like teenagers, which of course we had only just stopped being.

Hugh had come up to Cambridge from Eton College as a successful international youth oarsman, having pulled himself through the water to gold with his schoolfriend James Palmer in the coxless pairs event in the Junior Olympics and at Henley. Back in the thirties his father had been in a winning Cambridge Blue boat for each of his three years and went on to row in the British eight at the Berlin Olympics of 1936 and again in the coxless pairs in the 1948 London games, where he and his partner Jack Wilson won gold. Had glandular fever not struck, Hugh would certainly have rowed for the university straight away but, denied by his illness a seat in the Blue boat for his first year, he looked about for something else to do and found himself cast in *Aladdin* and then, two terms later, *Nightcap*. In his second year he abandoned the Footlights and did what he had come to Cambridge to do, pull that rowing-boat through the water. On the river by five or six in the morning, hours of backbreaking rowing, then road work, gym work and more time on the river. He got his Blue in the 1980 boat race, which Oxford won by a canvas, the closest result there had ever been. You can imagine the disappointment. How many times he must have revisited every yard of that race in his head. Upping the stroke rate by one beat a minute, just one neater piece of steering on the bend, 2 per cent more effort at Hammersmith . . . it must have been heartbreaking to have come so close. I tried to tell him that my own experience of losing to Merton in the final of *University Challenge* meant that I knew exactly how he felt. The look he gave me could have stripped the flesh from a rhinoceros.

The following year, his last, he could either stay with rowing or return to the Footlights, but he could not do both. President of the Cambridge University Rowing Club, or President of the Cambridge Footlights? He claims that he tossed a coin and it came down Footlights. He had gone to Edinburgh and seen *Latin!* and decided that perhaps I might be a useful new recruit to his Footlights. Only he and Emma were left from the first year and he needed fresh blood. Kim was co-opted on to the committee as Junior Treasurer, Katie was Secretary, Emma Vice-President and a computer scientist from St John's called Paul Shearer, a funny, lugubrious performer with eyes almost as big as Hugh's, was already on board as Club Falconer. This strange office went back to the days when the Footlights were quartered in Falcon Yard. I don't believe there were any duties attached to being Falconer, but it looked good, and I envied Paul's title sorely and reprehensibly.

Continuity and Clubroom

There is perhaps one overriding reason why the Footlights has produced such an astonishing number of figures who have gone on to make their mark in the world, and that reason is continuity. The Footlights has a tradition which goes back over a hundred years. That tradition inspires many with a comic itch to choose Cambridge as their university. The Footlights has a regular schedule: a pantomime in the Michaelmas Term, a Late Night Revue at the ADC in the Lent Term and the May Week Revue at the Arts Theatre, which then goes on to tour Oxford and other towns before arriving in Edinburgh for the Fringe Festival in August. And throughout that year are peppered Smokers. The word is an abbreviation of Smoking Concert. I dare say smoking is no longer permitted at these public events, but the name has stayed. In our time Smokers took place in the clubroom. The fact that the club had its own little venue was another of the inestimable advantages held by the Footlights over comedy groups in other universities.

The closest equivalent to a Smoker in the outside world is an open-mike evening I suppose, although in our day there was a small filtration system in place, so 'open' isn't quite the word. Anyone from any college with hopeful sketches, quickies, songs or monologues would come to the clubroom the day before the Smoker and exhibit their material on the stage. Whichever committee member was running that Smoker would yay or nay them. If a yay, their piece would be added to the running order: the auditions would go on until there was enough there for an evening's entertainment. The huge advantage of this system was that by the time the May Week Revue came around there was a lot of material to choose from and plenty of performers to pick, all of them having been tried out in front of an audience. In most other universities they don't have that kind of feeder system. Josh and Mary at Warwick or Sussex might say, 'Hey, we're funny, let's write a show and take it to Edinburgh! We'll put Nick and Simon and Bernice and Louisa in it, and Baz can write the songs.' They are probably all very funny and talented people, but they won't have the year's worth of practice and experience and the cupboard full of proven material that a Footlights show can call upon. That in essence, I believe, is why year after year the club continues to do so well. It is why their tours always sell out and why young people with a feel for comedy are so often disposed to put a tick next to Cambridge in the university application form.

The Footlights clubroom was a long, low room under the Union chamber and had a small stage with a lighting rig and a piano at one end and a sort of bar at the other. All along the walls hung framed posters of past revues and photographs of past Footlighters. In their duffel coats, black polo necks, tweed jackets or wind-cheaters, with studious black-rimmed spectacles perched on their noses and untipped cigarettes between their lips, they all seemed so much older than we were, so much cleverer, so much more talented and a world more sophisticated. They looked more like French left-bank intellectuals or avant-garde jazz musicians than members of a student comedy troupe. Peter Cook, Jonathan Miller, Bill Oddie, Graeme Garden, John Cleese, David Frost, John Bird, John Fortune, Eleanor Bron, Miriam Margolyes, Douglas Adams, Germaine Greer, Clive James, Jonathan Lynn, Tim Brooke-Taylor, Eric Idle, Graham Chapman, Griff Rhys Jones, Clive Anderson . . .

'The tradition stops here,' Hugh and I would mutter as we looked up for inspiration and found our gaze meeting theirs. Such a tradition, such a rich history as the Footlights', was in part inspiration and encouragement but in part insurmountable obstacle and impossible burden.

Neither Hugh nor I seriously thought for a moment that we would have a career in comedy or drama or any other branch of showbusiness. I would, if I scraped a First in my Finals, probably stay on at Cambridge, prepare a doctoral thesis and see what I could offer the academic world. I hoped, in my innermost secret places, that I might be able to write plays and books on top, under, or to one side of, whatever tenured university post might come my way. Hugh claimed that he had set his eyes on the Hong Kong police force. There had been one or two corruption scandals in the Crown Colony, and I think he rather fancied the image of himself as a kind of Serpico figure in sharply creased white shorts, a lone honest cop doing a dirty, dirty job . . . Emma, none of us doubted, would go out and achieve her destiny in world stardom. She already had an agent. A forbiddingly impressive figure called Richard Armitage, who drove a Bentley, smoked cigars and sported an old Etonian tie, had signed her on to the books of his company, Noel Gay Artists. He also represented Rowan Atkinson. Emma's future was certain.

None of which is to say that Hugh and I lacked ambition. We were ambitious in the peculiar negative mode in which we specialized: ambitious not to make fools of ourselves. Ambitious not to be called the worst Footlights show for years. Ambitious not to be mocked or traduced in the college and university newspapers. Ambitious not to look as if we thought ourselves pro-ey showbizzy stars. Ambitious not to fail.

Within two weeks of meeting we finished the *Snow Queen* script. I also wrote a monologue with Emma for her appearance as a mad, unpleasant and foul-smelling Wise Old Woman. Katie was cast as the heroine, Gerda, while Kim, ascending to the role of Pantomime Dame as if born to it, played her strikingly Les Dawson-like mother. I was a silly-ass Englishman called Montmorency Fotherington-

Fitzwell, Ninth Earl of Doubtful, who by happy chance never sang. Australian-born Adam Stone from St Catharine's played Kay, Gerda's boyfriend, Annabelle Arden had the title role of the Snow Queen herself and an extremely funny first-year called Paul Simpkin played a kind of dumpling-faced jester. There was a talented young man called Charles Hart, whom we put in the chorus. He later came to fame and frankly not inconsiderable fortune as the lyricist for Andrew Lloyd-Webber's *Phantom of the Opera* and *Aspects of Love*. Greg Snow, a howlingly funny friend from Corpus Christi, was in the chorus too, alternately amusing and exasperating Hugh with his astounding camp and a talent for bitchery that approached high art.

Hugh had a hand in the music, and I had a finger or two in the lyrics but most of the composition and arrangements were the work of an undergraduate called Steve Edis, whose girlfriend, Cathie Bell, danced and sang in the chorus like a demented can-can girl, despite her devastating susceptibility to severe asthma attacks.

The pantomime seemed to go well, and by the time the Lent term came Hugh and I were already starting to write material for the Late Night Review, to which Hugh had given the title *Memoirs of a Fox*. It irked him that no one seemed to get the reference, but it was a fine enough title without having to know Siegfried Sassoon. Titles, you soon discover, are fantastically irrelevant. You could call it, as American Indians were said to do of their babies, the first thing you see out of the window: Running Bull, Long Cloud or Parked Cars. You could even call it 'The First Thing You See Out of the Window'. Actually, I quite like that. One afternoon I found a tattered old exercise book in the Footlights Clubroom. Scrawled on the cover were the words: 'May

Week Revue Title Suggestions'. Over generations members had written down ideas for titles for shows. My favourite was Captain Fellatio Hornblower. I always suspected this to be the handiwork of a young Eric Idle. Many years later I asked him; he had no memory of it but agreed that it sounded pretty much his style and was willing to take the credit especially if there was a royalty in it for him.

More or less opposite Caius College stood a restaurant called the Whim. For generations this friendly, unpretentious establishment had been a favourite student haunt for good cheap suppers and long, lazy Sunday brunches. One day, quite unexpectedly, it closed down and covered itself in scaffolding. Two weeks later it reopened as something I had never seen or experienced before: a fastfood burger bar. Still called the Whim, it was now the home of the new Whimbo Burger, two beef patties smothered in a slightly tangy, slightly sweet creamy sauce, topped with slices of gherkin, slapped into a triple decking of sesame seed bunnage and presented on a styrofoam tray to the accompaniment of chips called 'fries' and whipped-up icecream called 'milkshakes'. The tills had pre-set buttons on them that allowed the perkily paper-capped assistants to press a button for Whimbo, say, and another for milkshake or fries, and all the prices would be automatically registered and calculated. It was like entering an alien space-ship, and I am sorry to say that I loved it to distraction.

A ritual was established. Hugh, Katie, Kim and I, after spending much of the afternoon in A2 playing chess, talking and smoking, would leave Queens', walk along King's Parade to Trinity Street and into the Whim, then on to the Footlights clubroom, cheerfully swinging our catch, two carrier bags crammed with steaming Whimmery. I could happily manage two Whimbos, a regular order of fries and a banana milkshake. Hugh's standard intake was three Whimbos, two large orders of fries, a chocolate milkshake and whatever Katie and Kim, who were more delicate, had failed to finish. His years of rowing and the enormously high calorific output they had demanded of him had given Hugh a colossal appetite and a speed of ingestion that to this day stagger all who witness them. I do not exaggerate when I say that he can eat a whole 24-ounce steak in the time it would take me, a much faster than average eater myself, to cut and swallow two mouthfuls. When he returned from his daily river work during his Boat Race year, Katie would cook just for him a cottage pie to a recipe for six people on which she would place four fried eggs. He would polish this off before she had a chance to make a dent in her own soup and salad.

I was rather fascinated by the levels of fitness Hugh had attained for the Boat Race. It is much, much longer than a standard regatta course and requires enormous stamina, strength and will to complete.

'At least while you were regularly rehearsing for it,' I remember saying to him once, 'you must have gloried in the feeling of being so fit.'

'Mm,' said Hugh, 'pausing only to point out that we prefer the word "training" to "rehearsing", I have to tell you that the fact is you never really feel fit at all. You train so hard you are constantly in a dopey state of numb torpor. On the river you slap and sting yourself into action and heave to, but when that's over you're torpid again. In fact the whole thing's pointless bloody agony.'

'Which is why,' I said, 'it is best left to convicts and galley slaves.'

Latin! The most stolen poster of the 1980 Edinburgh Fringe.

Solemn but triumphant in the Mummers group photo celebrating our Fringe First Award.

A moment later, responding to Tony Slattery and revealing an unsurprising cigarette.

The Snow Queen, 1980. My first Footlights appearance.

Behind the Scenes of Not The Footlights Pantomime By Barry Take   Radio Times

7.30 With only minutes to go, Director Hugh Laurie is working on the Green Room floor in
a fit of choking anxiety, while those in the principals have locked themselves into the
lavatory and refuse to come out. Soul no avail.

7.39 With only minutes to go, co-writer Stephen Fry has an idea. A song from 260 Eskimos
in Barrow Mg fugue to the cause of "Eros studied me" by the Frenchers. Fry
improvises at the piano and the idea works... brilliantly.

7.41 With only minutes to go, a hastily assembled cast of nervous youngsters and experienced
musicians begin rehearsals, shocking ideas off each other in a sizzling exchange of Piano
arthrux... phrases like "what's for the next line" and "come back, you've only
just sat ja, and miracuolusly they seem to understand each other eventually.

7.44 Just as the cast are beginning to have doubts about the new ADC clock, the news is
rushed in that a jift has been can been outside the Iranian Embassy and the entire show
is cancelled... brilliantly

THE ADC THEATRE

England's oldest university playhouse is administered and maintained by the University of Cambridge.

Chairman of Management Committee .... Dr. T.D. Kellaway
Secretary .... Dr. H.A. Chase
Manager and Licensee .... Howard Oldham
Resident Stage Manager .... Claude Manley
Resident Steward .... Albert Bishop

The Bar will open before and after this performance. Save time and fuss: order your interval drinks in advance. Ticket-holders may buy drinks until 11.15 p.m. every night. Drinks must not be taken into the auditorium. Smoking is strictly forbidden in the auditorium.

FOOTLIGHTS COMMITTEE

Hugh Laurie, President
Emma Thompson, Vice-President
Katie Kelly, Secretary
Dr. Harry Porter, Archivist
Paul Hartle, Treasurer
Steve Edis, Musical Director
Paul Shearer, Falconer
Stephen Fry
Richard Hytner } Committee
Kim Harris

ADC COMMITTEE

Richard Hytner, President
Simon Andrews, Secretary
Dr. Peter Holland, Senior Treasurer
Steve Todd, Junior Treasurer
Steve Vaughan, Technical Director
Richard Harmson, Newsletter Editor
Pete Johnson, Business Manager
Stephen Fry, Archivist
James Runcie, Membership Secretary
Stephen Mollett, Social Secretary
Jon Warbrick } Publicity
Gary Ernest
Harriet Lamb, Catering
John Williams, Design

CRUSTS

Wine Bar & Restaurant
42-74, Northampton St, Cambridge, Tel 35500

The ERAINA
COSMOPOLITAN
TAVERNA,
Free School Lane
telephone (0223) 68786

OPENING TIMES:
Mondays - Fridays:
12 noon - 3 pm & 5.30 - 11.30 pm
Saturdays:
12 noon - 11.30 pm
Sundays:
12 noon - 3 pm & 5.30 - 11.00 pm

Tony Polvviou, proprietor

THE PENTAGON

CHRISTMAS FARE 1980 1st-24th DECEMBER

6 SAINT EDWARDS PASSAGE CAMBRIDGE

THE CAST
In Order of Appearance

Magician	Hugh Laurie
Semolina	Katie Kelly
Mayor's Aide	Richard Kirk
Mayor	Will Osborne
Runner	Steve Edis
Gerda	Sal Littlewood
Montmorency Fotherington-	
Fitzwell, Ninth Earl of	
Doubtfulworth	Stephen Fry
Dame Tibo	Kim Harris
Fagend	Dave Meek
Lenny	Greg Brennan
Bruce	Dave Urquhart
Kay	Adam Stone
Snow Queen	Annabel Arden
Her Maid, Snowdrop	Sheila Hyde
Her Minion	Felicity Read
Crow	Paul Shearer
Wise Old Woman	Emma Thompson

Chorus

Cathy Bell	Charles Hart
Nicola Bradley	Mark Jolly
Clare Brown	Henry Singer
Gill Crone	Adam Singfield
Rosanna Nissen	Greg Snow

THE BAND

Piano	Steve Edis
Flute	Mark Batey
Saxophonist	Sean Allan
Drums	Simon Arridge
Clarinet	Jeremy Markwick-Smith
	Stephen Mulvey
Bassoon	Jack Percy

and the HAPPY VIK Brass Band

PRODUCTION

Written By	Stephen Fry
	Kim Harris
	Katie Kelly
	Hugh Laurie
	Paul Shearer
	Emma Thompson
Music Written By	Mark Batey
	Steve Edis
	Hugh Laurie
Director	Hugh Laurie
Assisted by	Katie Kelly
Musical Director	Steve Edis
Designer	John Williams
Technical Director	Steve Vaughan
Lighting Designer	Roger Hazeldine
Choreographer	Jenny Arnold
Sound	Simon Andrews
Production Managers	Emma Brown
	Hilary Lang
Costume Design and Production	Julia Hawkins
	Jo Lomaz
	Susan Mitchel
	Claire Morrison
Stage Manager	Andrew Templeton
Deputy Stage Manager	Anne Howard
Props Manager	Carol Morley
Fireman	Francesca Allen
	Christiana Galea
	Henriette van Gelder
	Kate Henry
Make-Up	Alex White
Poster	Simon Andrews
Chief Electrician	Jon Warbrick
Flyman	Graham Lomth
Set Painters	Henry Ricketts
Chief Fitter	Andrew Briggs
Transport Manager	Howard Oldham
Lens Polisher	Tony Roper
Launch Pad Supervisor	Nick Holt
Chief Carpenter	Mark Bentley
Audio-Visual Consultant	Claude Manley
Office Manager	Gary Ernest
Shop Steward	Charlie Young
Stage Hand	Nigel Bragg
Director of Machinery	Elwyn Davies
Scaffolding	Giles Gumener
Plumber	Mike Wilmott-Dear
Plumber's Mate	Nick Safford
Teddy Bears by	Graham Bates
Programming Advisor	John Wilkes
Pyrotechnics	Pam Donovan
Dog Handler	Julian Molyneux
Safety Helmets by	Phil Davies
Flying Wire by	Frank Knight

Thanks to Henrietta Broatt and Beetle

With Kim outside the Cambridge Senate House, celebrating our Tripos results.
I was insanely in love with that Cerruti tie.

In room A2, Queens'. Graduation day: posing with sister Jo.

'We cannot be said to have been the prettiest quartet ever to greet a television audience.' *University Challenge*.

The Young Ones. Comic heroes.

Rowan Atkinson presents Hugh with the Perrier Prize cheque. Edinburgh, 1981.

The Cellar Tapes closing song. I fear we may have been guilty of embarrassing and sanctimonious 'satire' at this point. Hence the joyless expressions.

For all that, how proud I would be if I had ever done something so extraordinarily demanding, so appallingly hard, so wildly extreme as train and row in the Boat Race.

In the clubroom, after the last traces of Whimbo and milkshake had been dealt with, Hugh would play at the piano, and I would watch him, with a further mixture of admiration and envy. He is one of those people with the kind of faultless ear for music that allows him to play anything, fully and properly harmonized, without sight of a score. In fact he cannot really read music. The guitar, the piano, the mouth organ, the saxophone, the drums – I have heard him play them all and I have heard him singing with a blues voice that I would sacrifice my legs to have. It ought to be most annoying, but in fact I am insanely proud.

It is a matter of extreme good fortune that, handsome as Hugh is, prodigiously gifted as he is, funny and charming and clever as he is, I have never felt an erotic stirring for him. How catastrophic, how painfully embarrassing that would have been, how disastrous for my happiness, his comfort and any future we might have had together as comedy collaborators. Instead our instant regard and liking for each other developed into a deep, rich and perfect mutual love that the past thirty years has only strengthened. The best and wisest man I have ever known, as Watson writes of Holmes. I shall stop before I get all teary and stupid.

Comedy Credits

In the clubroom I ran my first Smoker, furiously writing much of the material for it myself, terrified that the evening would run short. The Anthony Blunt Cambridge Spies scandal was still being talked of at the time so amongst other pieces I wrote a sketch about a don, me, recruiting an undergraduate, Kim, for the secret service. I also wrote a series of quickies, mostly in the form of physical sight gags. Everything seemed to go magically well that night, and I was deliciously pleased and filled with a powerful new sense of confidence, as if I had discovered a whole new set of muscles I never knew I had.

A few days later I received a letter in the post from an assistant on the BBC's successful new sketch show *Not the Nine O'Clock News*, which was in the process of making household names of Rowan Atkinson and his co-stars. One of the show's producers, an ex-Footlighter called John Lloyd, had been in the audience of my Smoker and seen a quickie which he thought would work well on *Not*. Could they buy it?

In a fever of excitement I typed it out:

A man finishes a pee in a urinal. He goes to the sink, washes himself and looks for a towel. There isn't one. He looks for anything he might dry his hands on. Nothing. He sees a man standing by the wall. He approaches him and knees him in the groin. The man doubles up with a huge exhalation of pain in the hot blast of which our hero happily dries his hands.

Yes, I know. On paper it is pretty lame, but it had worked OK that evening in front of the Smoker audience and it worked OK when Mel Smith and Griff Rhys Jones performed it on *Not the Nine O'Clock News* a month or so later. Over the years it was repeated many times and included in various Best Of compilations. I got used to receiving, right up to the end of the decade, cheques from the BBC for randomly absurd sums. 'Pay Stephen Fry the sum of £1.07' and so on. The lowest was 14 pence, for sales to Romania and Bulgaria.

Just after I had sent off that written version of the quickie Hugh arrived in A2 for his usual chess, chat and coffee. I proudly told him the news that I was now a television writer. His face fell.

'Well, that means *we* can't do it now,' he said, his eyes supplying the phrase that his mouth was too polite to add: 'You daft tit.'

'Oh. Oh I hadn't thought of that. Of course. Damn. Bother. Arse.'

I had been so excited about selling material to television that it had never occurred to me that it meant we would now not be able to use it ourselves. Not thinking is one of the things I'm best at. All the same, when I saw my name included in the end credits of the episode in which my quickie appeared I did feel huggingly happy.

When the time came for the Late Night *Memoirs of a Fox* to go on at the ADC, Emma, Kim, Paul, Hugh and I were in the show and Hugh added to the cast a tall, blonde, slender and extraordinarily talented girl called Tilda Swinton. She was not a part of Cambridge's comedy world, such as it was, but she was a magnificent actress, and her poise and presence made her the perfect judge in an American-courtroom sketch that Hugh had devised with some very slight assistance from me.

It is rather perfect to think of the pair of them playing American characters as students on the stage of the ADC. We would have called you mad if you had suggested that one day Hugh would go on to win Golden Globes for playing an American in a television series and that Tilda would win an Oscar for playing an American in a feature film.

Cooke

The previous term Jo Wade, who was Secretary of the Mummers, had drawn my attention to the fact that the Lent term would see the fiftieth anniversary of the club, which had been founded in 1931 by a young Alistair Cooke.

'We should have a party,' said Jo. 'And we should invite him.'

Alistair Cooke was known for his thirteen-part documentary and book, *A Personal History of the United States*, and his long-running and greatly loved radio series, *Letter From America*. We wrote to him care of the BBC, New York City, USA, wondering if he had any plans to be in Britain in the next few months and if so whether he might be amenable to being persuaded to be our guest of honour at a dinner for the semi-centennial celebrations of the drama club he may remember founding. A drama club, we added, that was stronger and healthier than ever, having picked up more Fringe Firsts in Edinburgh than any other university drama society in the land.

He wrote back with the news that he had no plans to be in Britain. 'However, plans can be changed. Your letter has so delighted me that I shall fly myself over to be with you.'

In the dining hall of Trinity Hall he sat between me and Jo and talked wonderfully of his time at Jesus College in the late twenties and early thirties. He spoke of Jacob Bronowski, who had the rooms above him: 'He invited me to a game of chess and as we sat down asked me, "Do you play classical chess or hypermodern?'" He spoke of his friendship with Michael Redgrave, who succeeded Cooke as editor of *Granta*, Cambridge's most intelligent student publication. As he spoke, he noted down a few words on his napkin. When it was time to propose the toast to Mummers and its next fifty years, he rose to his feet and, on the basis of those three or four scribbled words, delivered a thirty-five-minute speech in perfect *Letter From America* style.

Michael Redgrave and I were most annoyed that women were not allowed to act in plays in Cambridge. We were tired of those pretty Etonians from King's playing Ophelia. We thought the time had come to change all that. I went to the Mistresses of Girton and Newnham and proposed the formation of a serious new drama club in which women might be allowed to take on women's roles. The Mistress of Girton was P. G. Wodehouse's aunt, or cousin or something, I seem to remember, and she was terrifying but kind. Once she and the Newnham Mistress had satisfied themselves that our motives were pure, aesthetic and honourable, which of course they only partly were, they consented to allow their undergraduates to appear in drama, and that is how the Mummers came about. Once the word got out that there was a new club which allowed women to act, hundreds of male undergraduates besieged me, begging to be cast in our first production. I remember holding auditions. One undergraduate from Peterhouse came to see me and recited a speech from *Julius Caesar*. 'Tell me,' I said to him as kindly as I could, 'what subject are you reading?' 'Architecture,' he replied. 'Well, you carry on with that,' I said, 'I'm sure you'll be an excellent architect.' He did indeed get a First in Architecture, but whenever I see James Mason now he says to me, 'Damn. I should have taken your advice and stayed with architecture.'

The fluency, charm and ease with which Cooke spoke held the entire hall completely spellbound. He was one of those people who seemed to have been born to bear witness. Famously he had been in the Ambassador Hotel in Los Angeles in 1968, only yards from Robert F. Kennedy when he was shot down and killed. He told us a story of another brush with political destiny that had taken place during the long vac that followed his setting up of the Mummers.

I went with a friend on a walking tour of Germany. It was the kind of thing one did then. Books strapped up in an arrangement of leather belts and slung over the shoulder as one tramped the meadows of Franconia, stopping off at taverns and guesthouses. We arrived in a small Bavarian valley late one morning and found a perfect beer garden, overlooked by a pretty old inn which tumbled with geraniums and lobelias. As we sat sipping our Steins of lager, chairs were being arranged in rows in the garden. It seemed that some sort of concert was in the offing. By and by two ambulances drew up. The drivers and stretcher-bearers got out, yawned, lit cigarettes and stood by the open tailgates of their vehicles as if it were the most normal thing in the world. People began to arrive, and soon every chair in the beer garden was taken and the dozens who couldn't get a seat stood at the back or sat cross-legged on the grass in front of the small temporary stage. We simply could not imagine what was going to happen. An enthusiastic crowd, but no musicians and, most strangely of all, those ambulance drivers and stretcher-bearers. At last a pair of huge open-topped Mercedes tourers arrived, crammed like a Keystone Kop car with more uniformed figures than they could comfortably hold. They all leapt out, and one of them, a short man in a long leather coat, marched to the stage and began to speak. Not speaking German at all well, I could not understand much of what he said, but I could make out the repeated phrase "*Fünf Minuten bis Mitternacht! Fünf Minuten bis Mitternacht!* Five minutes to midnight! Five minutes to midnight!" It was all most strange. Before long, women in the crowd would swoon and faint, and the stretcher-bearers would start forward to collect them. What kind of speaker was it who could be so *guaranteed* to cause people to faint with his words that ambulances came along beforehand? When the man had finished speaking he strode up the aisle, and his elbow barged against my shoulder as I leant out to see him go, and he backed into me, turned away as he was to take the ovation of the crowd. He immediately grabbed my shoulder to stop me from falling, '*Entschuldigen Sie, mein Herr!*' he said. 'Excuse me, sir!' For some years afterwards, whenever he came on in the cinema newsreels as his fame spread, I would say to the girl next to me. 'Hitler once apologized to me and called me sir.'

When the evening was over Alistair Cooke shook my hand goodbye and held it firmly, saying, 'This hand you are shaking once shook the hand of Bertrand Russell.'

'Wow!' I said, duly impressed.

'No, no,' said Cooke. 'It goes further than that. Bertrand Russell knew Robert Browning. Bertrand Russell's aunt danced with Napoleon. That's how close we all are to history. Just a few handshakes away. Never forget that.'

As he left he tucked an envelope in my pocket. It was a cheque for £2,000 made out to the Cambridge Mummers. On a compliment slip with it he had written, 'A small proportion to be spent on production, the rest for wine and senseless riot.'

Chariots 2

One morning in February Hugh came into A2, waving a letter.

'You were in that film they made here, weren't you?' he said to me and Kim.

'*Chariots of Fire*, you mean?'

'Well they've got some sort of premiere at the end of March and a party at the Dorchester Hotel and they want the Footlights to be the entertainment. What do you think?'

'It would make sense if we could actually see the film first. So we could do a sketch about it, or at least make some kind of reference?'

Hugh consulted the letter. 'They're suggesting we go to London on the morning of the thirtieth, go to the screening for film critics that's taking place in the afternoon, rehearse in the hotel ballroom and then we'll be put on after the dinner.'

The day before taking the train to London I called my mother to tell her what we were up to.

'Oh, the Dorchester,' she said. 'I haven't been to the Dorchester for years. In fact, I remember the last time clearly. Your father and I went to a ball and it broke up early because the news of John F. Kennedy's assassination came through, and nobody felt like carrying on.'

On the appointed day the core Footlights team settled down in an empty cinema for the screening of the film, quite expecting to be depressed by a low-budget British embarrassment. As we came out, I brushed a tear from my cheek and said, 'Either I'm in a really odd mood or that was rather fantastic.'

Everybody else seemed to be in agreement.

We hastily put together an opening sketch in which we ran on to the stage in slow motion. Steve Edis, whose ear was every bit as good as Hugh's, had absorbed Vangelis's distinctive musical theme and reproduced it on the piano.

After hanging about for hours in a small dining area set aside for toast masters in red mess jackets and what used to be called the upper servants, we were at last on.

'My lords, ladies and gentlemen,' said the MC into his microphone, 'they twinkled in the twenties and now they're entertaining in the eighties. It's the Cambridge University Footlights!'

Our slo-mo running on stage to Steve's lusty rendition of the film score went extremely well, and from the opening explosions of laughter and applause we settled confidently into our material. At some stage however it became apparent that we were losing the audience. There was rustling, murmuring, chair scraping and whispering. Dinner-jacketed men and evening-gowned women were scampering towards the back of the ballroom and . . . well, quite frankly . . . leaving.

Surely we weren't *that* bad? We had not only performed this in Cambridge but we had done evenings at the Riverside Studios in Hammersmith. I was prepared to believe that we might not be to everyone's taste, but such a mass walk-out seemed like a studied insult. I caught Hugh's eye, which held the wild, rolling look of a gazelle being pulled to earth by a leopard. I dare say my expression was much the same.

As we lumbered sweatily off stage, with Paul going forward for his monologue with the brave tread of an aristocrat approaching the guillotine, Emma whispered to us, 'Someone's shot Ronald Reagan!'

'What?'

'All the Twentieth Century Fox executives have left and gone to the phones . . .'

I rang my mother that night.

'Well that's settled then, darling,' she said. 'No member of this family ever goes to an event at the Dorchester again. It's not fair on America.'

Corpsing Chorus

Back in Cambridge, Brigid Larmour was directing the Marlowe Society production that term, *Love's Labour's Lost*. This was the straight drama equivalent of the Footlights May Week Revue, a big-budget (by any standards) production mounted in the Arts Theatre, a splendid professional theatre with an alarming audience capacity of exactly 666. A combination of my persuasive rhetoric and Brigid's natural charm succeeded in securing Hugh for his first Shakespearean role, that of the King of Navarre. I played the character with perhaps the best description in all of Shakespeare's *dramatis personae*: 'Don Adriano de Armado, a fantastical Spaniard'. Only I wasn't a fantastical Spaniard. For some reason, whenever I attempt Spanish it comes out as Russian or Italian, or a bastard hybrid of the two. I can manage a Mexican accent acceptably, so my Armado was an inexplicably fantastical Mexican. The major role of Berowne was played by a fine second-year actor called Paul Schlesinger, nephew of the great film director John Schlesinger.

The play opens with a long speech from the King in which he announces that he and the leading members of his court shall forswear the company of women for three years, dedicating themselves to art and scholarship. Hugh and Paul had one of those uncontrollable laughing problems. They only had to catch each other's eye on stage and they would be unable to breathe or speak. For the first few rehearsals this was fine, but after a while I could see Brigid beginning to worry. By the time it came to the dress rehearsal it was apparent that Hugh would simply not be able to get out the words of the opening address unless either Paul was off stage, which made a nonsense of the plot, or some imaginative solution to the problem could be found. Threats and imprecations had proved useless.

'I'm sorry,' each said. 'We're trying not to laugh, it's a chemical thing. Like an allergy.'

Brigid hit upon the happy notion of making *everyone* on stage in that scene, the King, Berowne, Dumain, Longaville and general court attendants, speak the opening lines together as a kind of chorus. Somehow this worked, and the giggling stopped.

At the first-night party I heard a senior academic and distinguished Shakespeare scholar congratulate Brigid on her idea of presenting the introductory speech as a kind of communal oath. 'A superb concept. It made the whole scene come alive. Really quite brilliant.'

'Thank you, Professor,' said Brigid without a blush, 'it seemed right.'

She caught my eye and beamed.

Cellar Tapes and Celebration

The last term arrived. Another May Ball. Finals of the English tripos. The May Week Revue itself. Graduation. Farewell, Cambridge, hullo, world.

For the last Footlights Smoker before we began work on the show itself I recruited my old friend Tony Slattery, who fitted in with the greatest ease. He tore up the audience with guitar songs and extraordinary monologues of his own devising; one girl, according to the fatalistic janitor figure who looked after the premises, actually wet herself.

'There's such a thing,' he said as he shook a canister of Vim over the damp cushion, 'as *too* funny.'

I attempted to persuade Simon Beale to join us too, but he had enough singing and drama to fill his diary. I think he felt that comedy shows somehow weren't quite him. With the addition of Penny Dwyer, with whom I had worked in Mummer productions and who could sing, dance, be funny and do just about anything, we had a cast to join me, Hugh, Emma and Paul Shearer for the big one, the May Week Revue that would go on to Oxford and then Edinburgh.

I wrote a monologue for myself based on Bram Stoker's *Dracula* and a two-handed parody of *The Barretts of Wimpole Street*, in which Emma played Elizabeth, a bed-bound invalid, and I played Robert, her ardent suitor. Hugh and I had both seen and found hilarious John Barton's Shakespeare Masterclasses on television, in which he had painfully slowly taken Ian McKellen and David Suchet through the text of a single speech. We put together a sketch in which I did the same with Hugh. So detailed was the textual analysis that we never got further than the opening word, 'Time'.

Hugh asked the previous year's President, Jan Ravens, to direct us, and we began rehearsals in the clubroom. We put together a closing ensemble sketch, in which a ghastly kind of Alan Ayckbourn family playing after-dinner charades breaks down in animosity, revelation and disarray.

At some point we must have sat Finals and at another point I must have completed two dissertations, one on Byron's *Don Juan*, another on aspects of E. M. Forster. I can remember neither, having knocked them both up in two frantic evenings: 15,000 words of drivel typed out at high speed.

When the news came that the English results were published I walked to the Senate House, against the walls of which huge notice-boards in wooden frames had been attached. I strained through the crowd of hysterical studentry and found my name in the Upper Second list. I had scored a dull, worthy and unexciting 2:1.

Peter Holland, a don from Trinity Hall who had supervised me for practical criticism and seventeenth-century literature, offered consolation.

'They reread you for a First twice,' he said. 'You came very close. You got good Firsts in all your papers, top in Shakespeare again. But a 2:2 in the Forster dissertation and a Third in the Byron. That's why they just couldn't do it. Hard luck.'

The hurt was more to my pride than to my plans. To be honest, Cambridge was right, I had shown I could fly through written exams against the clock, but the serious work of a dissertation, which required the kind of originality, scholarship and diligence that I either didn't possess or simply couldn't be arsed to produce, exposed me for the plausible rogue that I was.

Hugh read Archaeology and Anthropology and got a far more amusing and likeable class of degree. He had been to one lecture, which gave him the material for a quite brilliant monologue about a Bantu hut, but otherwise had not disturbed his professors, written an essay or entered the faculty library. I think he would be the first to admit that you know more about Archaeology and Anthropology than he does.

The first night of our May Week Revue came. The show was called *The Cellar Tapes*, as much a reference to the underground Footlights clubroom in which it was born as to Bob Dylan's *Basement Tapes* or any pun on Sellotape.

Hugh came on stage for the opening. 'Ah, good evening, ladies and gentlemen. Welcome to the May Week Revue. We have an evening of entertainment, of – I got a Third by the way – sketch comedy, music and . . .'

We were under way. The Arts Theatre has one of the best auditoriums for comedy I know. Sitting in a spotlight with a leather book on my lap delivering the Dracula monologue, standing on stage with Hugh for the Shakespeare Masterclass, kneeling at the stricken Emma's bedside, pouring tea for Paul Shearer in the MI5 recruitment sketch – all these moments were more pleasurable and thrilling in this theatre, on this occasion, before such an enthusiastic audience, than anything I had ever done before.

Hugh and I looked at each other after the curtain fell. We knew that, come what might, we had not disgraced the name of Footlights.

One night of the two-week run the word went round backstage that Rowan Atkinson had been spotted in the audience. I broke the habit of my (short) lifetime and peeped through at the house. There he was, there could be no mistake. Not the least distinctive set of features on the planet. We all performed with an extra intensity that may have made the show better or may, just as easily, have given it rather a hysterical edge – I for one was too excited to be able to tell. The great Rowan Atkinson watching us perform. Only a year and a half ago I had all but vomited with laughter at his show in Edinburgh. Since then *Not the Nine O'Clock News* had propelled him to major television stardom.

He came round backstage to shake our hands, a graceful and kindly act for a man so shy and private. My state of electrified enthralment stopped me from hearing a single word he said, although Hugh and the others told me afterwards that he had been charmingly complimentary about the evening.

Two nights later Emma's agent, Richard Armitage, came.

'Do you see yourselves,' he asked us afterwards, 'doing this kind of thing professionally? As a career?'

It was all so sudden, strange and overwhelming. A few terms earlier I had been happy to wander on as a grizzled soldier or warty old king in productions of Chekhov and Shakespeare. I had listened to the more serious actors talking about applying for places on the Webber Douglas Academy graduate course, the path that Ian McKellen had taken after Cambridge. Since I had met Hugh and started writing sketches with him and on my own I had dared hope that I might perhaps apply one day to BBC radio for a job as a scriptwriter or assistant producer or something along those lines. About my future as a comic performer I was less sure, however. All the facial mastery, double-takes, clowning and fearless assurance that Hugh and Emma displayed on stage and in rehearsal came much less naturally to me. I was voice and words; my face and my body were still a source of shame, insecurity and self-consciousness. That this Richard Armitage was prepared, keen even, to take me on and shepherd me into a genuine career seemed like astonishingly good luck.

I later discovered that, crafty old fox that he was, Richard had sent his youngest client ahead to see us and deliver his opinion. Which explained what Rowan had been doing there. Plainly he had made encouraging enough noises about us for Richard himself to make the journey to Cambridge and, now that he had seen the show for himself, to make this offer.

I accepted, of course. As did Hugh and Paul.

'Of course,' Hugh said, walking back from the theatre afterwards, 'it doesn't necessarily mean anything. He probably scoops up dozens every year.'

'I know,' I said. 'But still, I've got an agent!'

I stopped to break the news to a parking meter. 'I've got an agent!'

The silhouette of King's College chapel loomed up against the night sky. 'I've got an agent!' I told it. It was unmoved.

Cheerio, Cambridge

My last May Ball, my last Cherubs Summer Party on the Grove at Queens'. May Week parties all over Cambridge, new levels of drunkenness, mooning, stumbling about, weeping and vomiting. Kim and I threw our own party on the Scholars' Lawn of St John's and got through every last case and bottle of Taittinger that Kim's parents had kindly sent down. My family came to the graduation ceremony: hundreds of identically subfusc graduands-turned-graduates milled about on the lawn outside the Senate House, all looking suddenly rather adult and forlorn as they posed with forced smiles for parental photographs and said their final farewells to three-year friendships. The shadow of the outside world was looming over us all, and that three years seemed suddenly to peel and shrink away like a snake's sloughed skin, too shrivelled and small ever to have fitted the fine and gleaming years of our ownership.

Kim's parents lived in Manchester but they also had a house in the prosperous London suburb of Hadley Wood, a brisk walk from High Barnet and Cockfosters Tube Stations, and they made this entirely available to Kim and me as soon as we left Cambridge. It was an absurdly wonderful and luxurious introduction to life outside university. On the television there I watched Ian Botham wrench the Ashes from Australia's grasp and felt like the happiest man in the universe.

Almost immediately *The Cellar Tapes* was off to Oxford for a week at the Playhouse Theatre. After the pleasures of the Cambridge Arts, the Playhouse, with its long, narrow skittle-alley auditorium appeared wholly inimical to comedy, and our material seemed to us to fall flat. The management and technical staff of the theatre were less than welcoming, and we spent a frightened, unhappy week avoiding the hostile glares of the tab men and lighting crew and alternating between melancholy wails and hysterical laughter as we huddled together for mutual comfort and support. It was a bewildering crash to earth. Hugh was so angered by the staff's unkindness that he wrote a letter to the manager which he showed me before posting. I had never seen cold fury so expertly rendered into polite but damning prose.

From Oxford we travelled to the theatre at Uppingham School, Chris Richardson welcoming us as two years earlier he had prophesied he would. Oxford had convinced us our show was a shambles and that Edinburgh would be a disaster, but Uppingham rebuilt our morale a little: the staff and school made a supportive and enthusiastic audience and the theatre – on whose boards I had been the very first to step in 1970 as a witch in *Macbeth*[†] – was a perfect arena in which to restore our confidence. Christopher was the warmest and most thoughtful host, making sure that we each had excellent accommodation, including a small bottle of malt whisky on the bedside table.

The great William Goldman is famous for saying of Hollywood that 'nobody knows anything', an apophthegm that holds just as true in theatre. I received a letter from someone who had been to *The Cellar Tapes* at the Oxford Playhouse and wanted to tell me that they thought it the best show of its kind they had ever seen. I tried and failed to remember a single moment of the Oxford run that I thought had gone well. I realized, however, if I was honest, that the audience did at least laugh, and there had been sustained and enthusiastic applause at the end.

I suppose the rudeness of the theatre staff and the shape of the auditorium had contrasted so negatively with the perfection of Cambridge that the entire experience seemed black and hopeless.

Caledonia 3

Before long we arrived at Edinburgh, where we found ourselves sharing St Mary's Hall with the Oxford Theatre Group, whose own show was on immediately before ours. They were friendly and self-deprecating and charming. St Mary's was a large venue with temporary seating banked high. It turned out to be perfect for the show. We received favourable reviews and found ourselves sold out for the two weeks of our run.

We performed two sketches on the radio for a BBC Radio 2 Fringe round-up programme presented by Brian Matthew, who interviewed us afterwards. It was my first time on the radio: performing the sketch was fine, but as soon as I had to speak as myself I found my throat restricted, my mouth dry and my brain empty. This would be the case for years to come. Alone in my bedroom I could say things to an imaginary interviewer that were fluent, amusing and assured. The moment the green recording light was on I froze.

One night Richard Armitage left a note to say that someone from the BBC would be present and would like to see us. Two days later he told us to give some time after the show to two people from Granada Television. The following night Martin Bergman, who had been President of Footlights in '77–'78 and whom I had seen in *Nightcap*, came to see the show too. They all had offers that made us dizzy with astonishment.

The man from the BBC asked if we might be willing to record *The Cellar Tapes* for television. The two from Granada, a florid Scot called Sandy and a pert young Englishman call Jon, wondered if we would be interested in developing a comedy sketch show for them. Martin Bergman told us that he was arranging a tour of Australia. September to December, Perth, Adelaide, Melbourne, Sydney, Canberra and Brisbane. Did we like the idea?

On the penultimate night of the run, as we were executing our final bows to the audience, their cheering suddenly increased in volume and intensity. This was gratifying but inexplicable. Hugh nudged me; a man had walked on stage from the wings behind us and was coming forward holding his hand up for silence. His presence only encouraged more cheering. It was Rowan Atkinson. For a moment or two I thought he had gone insane. His reputation for timidity was already established. It made no sense whatsoever for him to be here.

'Um, ladies and gentlemen. Do forgive me for interrupting like this,' he said. 'You must think it most odd.'

These innocent remarks elicited greater laughs from the audience than any they had favoured us with all evening. Such is the power of fame, I remember thinking even as I looked on bewildered and intrigued by this peculiar invasion. Of course, Rowan had a way with words like 'odd' that did make them very funny.

'You may know,' he continued, 'that this year sees the institution of an award for the best comedy show on the Edinburgh Fringe. It is sponsored by Perrier . . . the bubbly water people.'

More laughter. No one can say the word 'bubbly' quite like Rowan Atkinson. My heart was beginning to hammer by now. Hugh and I exchanged glances. We had heard of the founding of this Perrier Award and of one thing we were absolutely certain . . .

'The organizers and judges of the award, which is to encourage new talent and new trends in comedy, were absolutely certain of one thing,' Rowan continued, echoing our conviction. 'That whoever won it wouldn't be the Cambridge bloody Footlights.'

The audience drummed their feet in appreciation, and I began to fear for the safety of the temporary structure supporting them.

'However, with a mixture of reluctance and admiration, they unanimously decided that the winner had to be *The Cellar Tapes* . . .'

The auditorium exploded with applause, and Nica Burns, organizer of the award (after thirty years she still is. Indeed she funded it herself when the sponsorship dried up), stepped forward with the trophy, which Rowan handed to Hugh.

The Vice-Chancellor placing in my hands a piece of paper that testified to my status as a BA (Hons.) was a small thing compared to this.

We had done it. We had put on a show and we had not disgraced ourselves. Indeed, we seemed to have done better than that.

Later that night, after dinner with Rowan and Nica and the people who looked after Perrier's PR, we trailed drunkenly home to our digs.

I lay awake almost all the night. I am not romanticizing the moment. I remember how I lay awake and where my thoughts took me.

A year and a half earlier I had been on probation. For almost all of my childhood and youth I had been lost in the dense blackness of an unfriendly forest thick with brambles, treacherous undergrowth and hostile creatures of my own making.

Somewhere, somehow I had seen or been offered a path out and had found myself stumbling into open, sunlit country. That alone would have been pleasure enough after a lifetime's tripping and tearing myself on ugly roots and cruel thorns, but not only was I in the open, I was on a broad and easy path that seemed to be leading me towards a palace of gold. I had a wonderful, kind and clever partner in love and a wonderful, kind and clever partner in work. The nightmare of the forest seemed a long distance behind me.

I cried and cried until at last I fell asleep.

Comedy

Enough time has passed for the 1980s to have taken on an agreed identity, colour, style and flavour. Sloane Rangers, big hair, Dire Straits, black smoked-glass tables, unstructured jackets, New Romantics, shoulder pads, *nouvelle cuisine*, Yuppies . . . we have all seen plenty of television programmes flashing images of all that past our eyes and insisting that this is what the decade meant.

As it happens, resistant to cliché as I try to be, the eighties for me conformed almost exactly to every one of those rather shallow representations. When I was tipped out of Cambridge and into the world in 1981, Ronald Reagan was beginning the sixth month of his presidency, Margaret Thatcher was suffering the indignity of a recession, Brixton and Toxteth were aflame, IRA bombs exploded weekly in London, Bobby Sands was dying on hunger strike, the Liberal and Social Democrat parties had agreed to merge, Arthur Scargill was about to take up the leadership of the National Union of Miners, and Lady Diana Spencer was a month away from marrying the Prince of Wales. None of that seemed especially peculiar at the time, of course, nor did it seem as if one was living a television researcher's archive package.

I emerged from university a thin, tall, outwardly confident graduate for whom everything seemed new and exciting, if wildly temporary. Sooner or later, I was convinced, I would be found out, and the doors of showbusiness would be slammed in my face, and I should have to set about answering my true vocation as a teacher of some kind. In the meantime I could not deny that it was larky and lovely to be riding this transitory cloud of glory.

Carry on Capering

The Perrier Award resulted in a London run of our Footlights show. Well, let us not overstate the case. 'London run' suggests something rather grand: in fact we played as the late-night afterthought in a converted morgue in Hampstead called the New End, postal codes away from the fizzing neon of Shaftesbury Avenue. Not that we were complaining. The New End was to us as exciting as the West End. This small theatre had made its journey from abandoned hospital mortuary to leading fringe venue seven years earlier under the auspices of the excellent and pioneering Buddy Dalton and was as glamorous in our eyes as the London Palladium or the Theatre Royal, Drury Lane.

The Cellar Tapes followed every night for a week the main evening show, Steven Berkoff's *Decadence*, which starred Linda Marlowe and of course the brilliant and terrifying actor/author himself. The impossible delight of knowing that Berkoff snuck into our dressing-rooms and stole our cigarettes was almost as thrilling as watching him scrawl 'cunt cunt cunt cunt cunt' all over Nicholas de Jong's *Evening Standard* review of his play and pin it defiantly to the wall in the theatre lobby. Berkoff had a hard, restless menace that he was to bring to the wider world's attention two years later when he played Victor Maitland, the cruel coke- and art-dealing villain of *Beverly Hills Cop*. Given his fearsome reputation it is something of a miracle that such a parcel of poncey Cambridge wags as us got away without verbal, at the very least, assault, but despite his manner Berkoff's first loyalty is to the theatre and to actors. Even freshly graduated revue artists in tweed jackets are admitted to the pantheon. His ire, aggression and insult are reserved for critics, producers and executives.

After the New End came Australia. In honour of Ian Botham's epic summer of genius we gave our revue the title *Botham, the Musical*. It is not often that there is enough British salt or a big enough Australian wound for the one to be rubbed into the other, so it seemed like an appropriate and attention-grabbing name for the show.

Australia in the early eighties was a revelation to me. I had expected a backwater: yellow-cellophaned shop windows displaying orange tank-tops and ten-year-old transistor radios, drunken homophobic, pommy-bashing Ockers, winged-glasses-wearing Edna Everages and a sour atmosphere of cultural cringe, inferiority-complex rodomontade and tall-poppy resentment. Not even the greatest Australophile could deny that those elements did and still do exist, but they were and are by no means predominant. I found Australia to be a country of matchlessly high-quality and low-cost food and wine and vibrating with an optimistic prosperity that contrasted vividly with Britain's miseries of recession, rioting and IRA bombings. The affluence and confidence astonished me. The bright outdoorsy climate seemed to be echoed in the national mood just as Britain's grey, chilly pessimism so perfectly matched its relentlessly unappetizing weather. I could not know that Britain's mood was set to change.

Botham, the Musical opened in Perth, and we worked our way across the continent, spending most of our earnings in restaurants. I learnt in Australia to love crayfish and oysters: oysters raw, oysters Rockefeller, oysters Kilpatrick and oysters Casino. At Doyle's seafood restaurant, which I still visit whenever I am in Sydney, I discovered barramundi and those strange lobster-like creatures the Moreton Bay and Balmain Bugs. This was also the first time I had ever seen wine sold varietally, where the bottles displayed the name of the grape variety, rather than the château, estate or domain of origin. This is so accepted now as to be unworthy of notice. Only the Old World clings to its Barolo, Bordeaux and Mosel labellings – everywhere else you know from one glance at the bottle that the wine is made of Pinot Noir, Cabernet Sauvignon, Tempranillo or Riesling. Having said which, thirty years later it is clear that easy familiarity with varieties has not entirely penetrated Britain. I saw an edition of *The Weakest Link* not so long ago where, to the question 'What are Merlot, Shiraz and Chardonnay?', the contestant offered the answer 'Footballers' wives?'

Perth, Adelaide, Melbourne, Canberra, Sydney, Brisbane, Hobart, Launceston, Burnie and Albury Wodonga were all ticked off the itinerary before it was time to return to a snowy December England. We broke the journey in Singapore, staying for two nights at Raffles Hotel, where we ran out of money.

Clash of Cultures

I am back in London. I ride on the Underground and grip the chromium rail to steady myself. The contrast between my brown hand and the paper-white English ones alongside astonishes me. I am in the Tube travelling to Notting Hill. I am on my way to a meeting at a flat in Pembridge Place that will change my life.

For the most part Australia had seemed to take to our comedy. We were just a band of students playing in smallish venues, and it was neither overwhelming triumph nor humiliating disaster. We were presenting material that was now nearly a year old: the Dracula monologue, the Shakespeare Masterclass, the Robert Browning and Elizabeth Barrett sketch, songs, sketches and quickies that we knew backwards. I remember Martin telling us that we would still be doing them in ten years' time. I blush to reveal that I performed Dracula for a charity show in Winchester just three months ago, a full twenty-nine years after I wrote it. But if, and it was an if as wide as the distance between Sydney and London, we were to make a professional go of comedy, it would mean writing new material, it would mean attempting to make a mark in a new comedy world.

In 1981 a great schism had apparently started to open up in the jolly world of humorous entertainment. I cannot recall when I first heard the phrase 'alternative comedy' but I do clearly remember seeing Alexei Sayle on television during my last year at Cambridge. Reeling and jerking like a puppet, crammed à la Tommy Cooper into a double-breasted suit a size too small, sucking in breath through his teeth, Sayle raged brilliantly about posey middle-class liberals. I subsequently learnt that his best lines were actually from the resolutely middle-class privately educated lawyer and Cambridge Footlights alumnus Clive Anderson, but that is not to take away the impact Sayle had. The tireless and surreal rants, all spat out in a Liverpudlian accent you could grate cheese with, combined with the look of a swarthy silent-movie villain made him funny, frightening and impossible to ignore, a kind of anarcho-syndicalist John Belushi – but Lithuanian, Jewish and rebarbative where Belushi was Albanian, Orthodox and cuddly. When I first met him I was made acutely aware that I represented everything he most despised: public school, Cambridge and, due to that manner that I have never been able to shake off, Establishment. Prejudice and snobbery appear to be considered legitimate in that direction: if I had despised him for being the working-class, state-school son of a communist railway worker, I should have been rightly condemned. In those days you were proud of being working-class and ashamed of being middle-class. I was desperate to be proud of being no class, of being *déclassé* and *déraciné*, of being bohemian-class, eternal-student-class, artist-class. I missed all those by a mile and continue to this day to reek more of the Garrick Club than the Groucho Club, but that has never stopped me trying, in my doomed, futile and pointless way, to be free. We all have our strange ways of coping, or failing to cope. Over the years I got on perfectly politely and almost amiably with Alexei and his wife, Linda, but I am afraid I have never really forgiven him for his bullying unkindness and aggression towards Ben Elton. By the end of the decade and throughout the nineties he missed no opportunity to take pot-shots at Ben, unjustly accusing him of being somehow inauthentic, derivative and abjectly unworthy of the label comedian or alternative. Well, all that came later, and I dare say he has calmed down now: the point is that, for a short few years, Sayle stood out as the most visible symbol of this new movement and at the time of our return from Australia the world appeared to belong to him and his cohorts.

I am not by nature a pessimist but I did wonder if the door had closed on types like us. Comedy is, as everyone knows, all about timing, and I feared that in the career sense our comic timing was way off. *Not the Nine O'Clock News*, with three Oxbridge performers, its ex-Footlights producer John Lloyd and its Oxford chief writer Richard Curtis was surely the last hurrah of our kind. And good riddance, the world was saying. What punk had done for music the alternative comedians were doing for comedy. The classic 'Ah Perkins, come in, sit down' comic sketch would be swept away along with the tuck box and the old school tie. This is how it seemed to us in our darker moments. I am now fully aware of a fact that will be obvious to you but of which back then I was only dimly conscious, so easy it is to believe that events, history and circumstances conspire uniquely against one. While we may have feared what we feared you can be sure that squadrons of comedians waiting in the wings had quite contrary anxieties. They looked at a BBC dominated by Oxbridge graduates who all appeared to read the same books and newspapers, talk the same way, refer to the same arcane experiences and share the same tastes. There was no Channel 4 at this point, no cable, no satellite, just BBC1, BBC2, BBC radio. A single ITV channel offered variety shows and the last heroes of the great musical-hall tradition in comedians like Benny Hill, Morecambe and Wise and Tommy Cooper as well as sitcoms that, with the glorious exception of *Rising Damp*, were unmemorable, unoriginal and uninspiring. If you were from neither an Oxbridge nor a variety background I can quite see how Fortress Broadcasting must have appeared unassailable. From such a point of view Emma, Hugh and I would have looked like pampered noblesse for whom the portcullis was respectfully raised, the banner hoisted and fires lit in the great hall. It is perhaps unseemly to emphasize how far from true we felt this to be, but unseemly emphasis is pardonable. Indeed, at just this time, Margaret Thatcher was making unseemly emphasis her signature oratorical mode, and the decade itself prepared for cheekbones, big hair, shoulder pads, political division and conspicuous consumption all to be emphasized in as unseemly a manner as could be managed. Unseemly emphasis was in the air and nowhere more so than in the comedians muttering and massing outside the castle gates.

Peter Rosengard, a life insurance salesman with a penchant for cigars and Claridge's breakfasts, had visited the Comedy Store in America and in 1979, together with Don Ward, a comic who specialised in warming up rock and roll crowds, he had launched the London Comedy Store, a small room above a topless bar in Walker's Court, Soho. Already by 1981 the Comedy Store had come to stand for this whole *nouvelle vague* in comedy – a movement that coincided with the sharp style of the listings magazine *Time Out* and its achingly leftist breakaway rival *City Limits*, a movement that tapped the discontent and desire for difference of a student generation emerging into a recession-hit, Tory-controlled, anxious and angry Britain. Squadrons of young middle-class revolutionaries wore out the grooves of *London Calling*, talked the talk of gender politics and walked the walk of CND and Rock

Against Racism. It is not to be wondered that they were unsatisfied with the comedy of *Are You Being Served?*, *The Russ Abbott Madhouse* and *Never the Twain*.

The house of entertainment was comprised of two families: the traditional, to which Dick Emery, Mike Yarwood, the Two Ronnies, Bruce Forsyth and the above-mentioned immortals Morecambe and Wise, Benny Hill and Tommy Cooper belonged, and the graduate, that dynasty started by Peter Cook, which swelled to its full greatness under Monty Python and was now coming to a full stop, or so we feared, with the *Not* team of John Lloyd, Rowan Atkinson, Richard Curtis, Mel Smith and Griff Rhys Jones, Oxbridgers all. Was the new comedy represented by Alexei Sayle, Ben Elton, French and Saunders, Rik Mayall, Ade Edmondson, Keith Allen and the many others bubbling under an alternative to the first family or to the second? Well, more to the second in fact, despite the background chatter of the times which made out that it was all a class war. Alexei Sayle went to Chelsea Art College and was the most Pythonesque of all the comedians with his streams of absurdist surreality and deliberately recondite frames of reference. French and Saunders met at drama school. Elton, Edmondson and Mayall had all been students at Manchester University together. The truth is that very few of the first wave of alternative comedians could claim to have got their education from the streets or the school of hard knocks; in fact as an old lag *I* might be said to be the most real and hard of any of them, a thought preposterous enough to show that the idea of there being a group of working-class comics threatening Castle Poncey was really quite misguided. All the comedians were from the same mix of backgrounds as ever, and there was plenty of old-school silly sketch comedy among the angry edgy stand-up. It is true that there was an alternative *audience* who were ready for something different, and their demand for the new might be said to have released the energy that was now being called 'alternative'. Some years later Barry Cryer gave the best definition of alternative comedians I have yet to hear. 'They're the same only they don't play golf.'

If this was the *Zeitgeist* then it was frankly miraculous that our Cambridge Footlights show had won the Perrier Award and that I was now stepping off a Tube train and looking for that address in Pembridge Place.

I rang the doorbell and was buzzed in to an upstairs flat. Hugh, Emma and Paul Shearer were already present. Jon Plowman, whose flat it was, was busy with coffee cups. He was the pert young Englishman from Granada we had met at Edinburgh. Sandy Ross, the pink-faced producer who had been with him that night, introduced me to a dark-haired spectacled young fellow of earnest aspect.

'This is Ben Elton, he has just graduated from Manchester.'

Sandy outlined his plan: that those of us assembled should form ourselves into a team of writer–performers and create a new comedy show for Granada Television. We were to write and rehearse here in London and then go up to film and record at the studios in Manchester. Ben was already in the middle of collaborating with his university friend Rik Mayall and Rik's girlfriend, Lise Mayer, on the writing of a new comedy series for the BBC, a kind of anti-sitcom that had the working title *The Young Ones*. We, for our part, were also committed to the BBC, not for a series but just to record *The Cellar Tapes* for a one-off transmission.

The idea behind the new Granada show, Sandy Ross explained, was to combine the traditional world of Cambridge sketch-writing with the anarchic, edgy style (he used those words) of Ben, his confrères and all that they represented. Since there were four of us and only one of him, the plan was to bring in At Least Someone Else of a non-Cambridge flavour. The names Chris Langham, Nick le Prevost and Alfred Molina were floated, and perhaps others that I do not recall. Another girl was also required. For a time there was the possibility that it might be the Scottish poet and playwright Liz Lochhead. She came to a rehearsal, I recall, was clearly not impressed with what she found and declined to be involved. Instead Sandy and Jon found a perky young actress, also Scottish, called Siobhan Redmond. In time most of the men in the production were destined to fall for her, myself included in my own peculiar way.

In the meantime, we were tasked to go forth and write.

As I look back through the years at that period of my life, occluded, discoloured and scratched by time, experience and all the ravages and abuses to which my poor mind and body were since subjected, it all seems so improbable, and for reasons that make no obvious sense, so very, very sad. It was nothing of the kind, of course, it was slightly frightening but deliriously thrilling.

Without ever expressing it in any deliberate or calculated way I think Hugh and I understood that we were some kind of a team. Not a double act, but somehow inevitably and eternally linked. The worry uppermost in my mind, the one that I dared not communicate to Hugh, or Emma or Kim or anyone else, was whether or not I was in any way funny. I think I was confident that I was *witty*, that I was assured, articulate and verbally dextrous with a pen in my hand or a typewriter keyboard beneath my fingers, but between funny and witty falls the shadow . . .

I believed that being funny, being able to cause laughter through expression, movement and that mysterious palpable, physical *something* that is given to some and not to others was a gift similar to athleticism, musicality and sex appeal. In other words it had something to do with a self-confidence with the body that I had never had, a self-confidence that allowed physical relaxation and ease that themselves seemed to generate more self-confidence. This was the source of all my troubles. Fear of the games field, fear of the dance floor, athletic ineptitude, sexual shyness, lack of coordination and grace, hatred of my face and body. This could be traced all the way back to kindergarten Music and Movement classes: 'Everybody sit down in a circle cross-legged.' I was not even able to do that, could not so much as sit tailor-fashion without looking a gawky fool. My knees stuck up, and my self-confidence sank.

I had lived twenty years convinced that my body was the enemy and that all I had going for me was my brain, my quickness of tongue and my blithe facility with language, attributes that can cause people to be as much disliked as admired. They were adequate for very particular kinds of comedy performance. Verbally intricate monologues and sketches that I had written myself I could be confident in performing happily. But I lived, as I have already indicated, in dread of double-takes, slow burns, pratfalls and those other apparently essential comic techniques that seemed to me as terrifying, impenetrable and alienating as dance steps or tennis strokes. I know how infantile and silly such fears may sound, but in comedy confidence is paramount.

If the performer is unsure then the audience is on edge, and that is enough to strangle laughter before it is born. I saw in Hugh, Emma, Tony and others instinctive physical gifts that I knew I did not share and was sure I could never acquire. Besides which, they could all sing and dance. Who could possibly make a career in showbusiness if they lacked musical ability? All of the greats could sing. Even Peter Cook was more musical than I was. I lay awake at nights convinced that Sandy Ross and Jon Plowman would see my inadequacies at once and quietly drop me from the cast. At best they might ask me to stay on purely as a writer. Perhaps I would not mind that too much, but it would be a humiliation and one that I did not relish. A part of me – I have to confess this, moronic, puerile and cheap as it may sound – really did ache to be a star. I wanted to be famous, admired, stared at, known, applauded and liked.

There, I have said it. It is not the most surprising confession for a performer to make, but it is hardly the done thing to admit to such a shallow ambition. There was no question that Emma would be famous, no question at all. I knew that Hugh would make it too but I worried myself silly that I would be left out, like the last one to be picked to play for the team. Cambridge had shown me that I could make an audience laugh, but I had enjoyed the luxury of making them laugh on my terms. Now that we were in the big wide world, one which was looking towards the punkier end of the comedy spectrum, it seemed inevitable that I would be judged to be the one who didn't *quite* have what it took. Perhaps a little writing, perhaps some radio work, but nothing like the stardom that beckoned for Hugh and Emma and for Ben Elton's friend, about whom I was hearing more and more, the astonishing Rik Mayall.

Exactly what I most lacked this explosive comic genius most possessed: physical charisma, devastating self-assurance and an astoundingly natural appeal that radiated out at the audience like a thermonuclear shockwave. He could be silly, charming, childish, vain and inconsequential in a way that simply and unequivocally delighted. You didn't question it, analyse it, applaud its cleverness, appreciate its social meaning or admire the work behind it, you simply adored it, as you might any natural phenomenon. Whatever gifts I possessed appeared shrivelled, pale and underdeveloped. In the comedy shower-comparison test I failed, and it hurt. Was being in the adult world like being back at school all over again? It seemed loweringly likely.

Meanwhile, I could at least throw myself into the last hurrah of the Cambridge Footlights.

Hugh, Emma, Tony, Paul, Penny and I arrived at the BBC for the televising of *The Cellar Tapes* at exactly the time Ben Elton, Lise Mayer and Rik Mayall were putting the finishing touches to the *Young Ones* scripts and Peter Richardson, Ade Edmondson, Rik, Dawn French, Jenny Saunders and Robbie Coltrane were preparing to shoot the Comic Strip film *Five Go Mad in Dorset*. It is hardly surprising that we felt a little like the New Seekers sharing the bill with the Sex Pistols.

We moved deeper into the realms of the truly old-fashioned when we met the producer whom the BBC had allocated us. He was a thin, jerky man in his mid to late fifties who smelt strongly of whisky and unfiltered Senior Service cigarettes. Which is hardly surprising since he had no other diet. When he introduced himself, something in his name rang a distant muffled bell.

'How do you do? Dennis Main Wilson.'

Dennis Main Wilson – why was that so familiar? Dennis Main Wilson. It sounded so right. Like Chorlton-cum-Hardy, Amy Semple McPherson, Ella Wheeler Wilcox or Ortega y Gasset, one of those triple names that tripped off the tongue as if one had always known them, while in truth one is never quite sure to whom or what they might refer.

Dennis Main Wilson was in fact the greatest comedy producer of his generation, perhaps of any generation. On the radio he had produced the first two series of *The Goon Show* and the first four series of *Hancock's Half Hour*: for those alone his grave should for ever be festooned with flowers and his memory eternally cherished. On television he was responsible for bringing us *The Rag Trade*, *Till Death Us Do Part*, *Marty* with the great Marty Feldman and *Sykes* with the equally great Eric Sykes. Perhaps most crucially of all in terms of television history, he demonstrated a patience and openness to new ideas rare in grand and established programme-makers when he agreed one day to read a script presented to him by a lowly BBC scene-shifter. Most senior broadcasting staff can always find a way to avoid unsolicited material. Dennis was made of kindlier stuff and accepted the shyly proffered sheaf of manuscript with the beaming enthusiasm that always characterized him. The scene-shifter's name was John Sullivan, and his script was called *Citizen Smith*. It was produced with great success and launched the career of Robert Lindsay. Sullivan followed it up with *Only Fools and Horses*, which I think one may safely call the most popular comedy in British history.

Spike Milligan, on account of Dennis's predilection for alcohol, had nicknamed him Dennis Main Drain and there is no question that he was a mockable entity. His tweed jacket, Brylcreemed hair, scrawny neck and nicotine-stained fingers belonged to another age, an age far removed from the excitements of alternative comedy and youth entertainment that the soon-to-be-launched Channel 4 was preparing to offer the world. As a devotee of radio comedy I would have admired him whatever his character; as it is I adored him. We all did. Cautiously at first and then with gathering conviction. One thing, however, we soon discovered was essential when it came to working with Dennis Main Wilson. No matter how much he insisted upon meeting at twelve, one, two, three or four o'clock in the afternoon we had to make equally certain that the meetings should be at nine, ten or eleven in the morning. It was a simple question of productivity. The comedy department at Television Centre was on the sixth floor, with Dennis's office directly opposite the BBC Club, which was essentially a bar. Every morning at eleven thirty he would make the ten-yard journey from office to Club. A Senior Service unwinding its blue ribbon of smoke from between his fingers, a pint of bitter and a double scotch on the bar in front of him, he would enthral and absorb us with tales of Hattie Jacques, Peter Sellers and Sid James, but as the morning wore on his ability to concentrate on our little show and its looming recording date would become less and less certain, and we would begin nervously to wonder whether there would even be a studio booked, props organized or cameramen available for duty on the appointed night. Catch Dennis at nine in the morning, however, and he was a ball of fire. His fleshless body twitched and jerked, his fingers stabbed the air with each excited new idea, and his chesty, tobacco-enriched chuckle infected us all with grandiose self-belief. He gave us the impression that as far as he was concerned we were cut from the same cloth as Spike Milligan and Tony Hancock. Such attention and respect from one so august could only make us glow. This was perhaps counterbalanced by his complete lack of knowledge or even interest in the new wave lapping up against the ramparts. A small, disloyal, insecure part of me wondered if it wasn't like, to change the era of the musical comparison, Bobby Darin's manager assuring him that rock and roll was a temporary blip. Dennis saw us as respectful inheritors of the Golden Age mantle and the new alternative comics as vandals and interlopers who were of no account. I, for such is my way – part greasy sycophant desperate to please, part show-off, part genuine enthusiast – played up to this with endless talk of Mabel Constanduros, Sandy Powell, Gert and Daisy, Mr Flotsam and Mr Jetsam and other music-hall radio stars for whom I had a passion.

We rehearsed in the BBC block popularly known as the North Acton Hilton. Each floor in this dull, impersonal tower tucked away in a dull and impersonal suburb had two sets of purpose-built rehearsal rooms and production offices. Not that I knew it then, but this soulless, sick-building-syndrome structure with its dripping, flaking and crumbling exterior, flickering fluorescent strip-lighting and smelly lifts was to be my second home for the next eight years through successive series of *Blackadder* and *A Bit of Fry and Laurie*. I loved it. I loved the canteen, where you could nod hello to Nicholas Lyndhurst and David Jason, the kids from *Grange Hill* or the dancers from *Top of the Pops*. I loved the poles on plinths in the rehearsal rooms that could be moved around to stand in for doorways and entrances. I loved the tape on the floor that marked out rooms and camera positions in different colours, like sports-hall courts. I loved looking out across the dreary roofs of west London and knowing that I was here, working for the BBC with *All Creatures Great and Small* next door and *Doctor Who* the floor above.

As we rehearsed *The Cellar Tapes* I had no knowledge of the years and series to come, of course, and no idea that it was quite normal for technical runs to be played out in silence. Let me explain.

Multi-camera studio comedy performed in front of an audience has become rare since single-camera location shooting became the norm some years ago. Back then it was the usual mode. Outside scenes were shot on 16mm film, and everything else on those skirted rostrum studio cameras that wheel around on castors and which inspired Terry Nation to dream up the Daleks. If you watch *Fawlty Towers* or other comedies of the seventies and early eighties you can see the manifest, almost ludicrous difference between grainy exterior film and shiny interior video. No one seemed to mind then, perhaps because TV reception and resolution were poorer, perhaps because we accepted what we had always been given.

The schedule for recording went like this. You went out into the world and shot the exteriors that your script demanded and then you spent a week in North Acton rehearsing the rest, the studio element. It was traditional to tape the show on a Sunday, I suppose because busy actors often worked in the theatre on other nights. On Friday morning at Acton came the occasion of the Tech Run. The camera and sound crews, set, production, costume

and make-up personnel would all troop into the rehearsal
room and watch a run-through of the show. And this is
where, in March 1982, we received the greatest blow to
our comedy egos that we had yet experienced.

Silence.

Silence, the comedian's enemy.

We ran through sketch after sketch and song after
song. Not a smile. Just folded arms, teeth-sucking and
the occasional note scribbled on to a Xeroxed copy of the
script.

When we had finished the last number and the room
began to clear of technical people we went off into a
corner and watched in a frightened huddle as the lighting
director and number-one cameraman lingered to ask John
Kilby, the director, one or two questions. When they had
at last gone Dennis bounded up to us.

'Drink?'

'Oh, Dennis,' we said. 'Is it still going to happen?'

'What do you mean?'

'It was a disaster. A complete disaster. Not a smile, not
a titter, nothing. They *hated* us.'

Dennis smiled a long, wide smile and the phlegm in the
bottom of his lungs began to hiss, bubble and growl like a
coffee-bar milk steamer as he wheezed out a great laugh.

'They have a job to do, my dears,' he said. 'No one,
not even the sound crew, was listening. They are looking
at where the cameras go, what the edge of frame is, a
thousand different things. Ha ha! You thought they were
making a judgement. That's very funny, ha!' Dennis's eyes
ran as he laughed and choked and gasped to the bottom of
his lungs.

On Sunday we performed the show in front of an

audience. An audience that was warmed up by Clive Anderson, an ex-Footlights barrister who had yet to make the decision to become a performer in front of the cameras. The recording seemed to go well, but we were not making it for the studio audience, we were making it for television viewers, and whether they would like it we would not know for months.

In the meantime the Granada show demanded our attention.

Chelsea, Coleherne Clones and Conscience

Kim and I moved from Hadley Wood into a flat in Draycott Place, just off Sloane Square in Chelsea, where the newly enroyaled Lady Diana's friends flitted between the Peter Jones department store, the General Trading Company and Partridge's delicatessen, all rigged out in identical green quilted Husky jackets and high Laura Ashley collars. Their boyfriends drove Golf GTi cabriolets, so prevalent in SW3 that they were nicknamed haemorrhoids ('sooner or later every arsehole gets one'). Hooray Henries were getting proudly and hog-whimperingly drunk in the newly fashionable wine bars while their younger brothers wound silk scarves about their long pale necks and drooped like lilies, hoping to look as winning and doomed as Anthony Andrews in *Brideshead Revisited*. Pubs were beginning to ding and thrum to the sound of Space Invaders and from the open doors of the hairdressing salons and into the tumult of the King's Road pumped the sound of Adam and the Ants' 'Goody Two Shoes', Dexy's Midnight Runners' 'Come On Eileen' and Culture Club's

'Do You Really Want to Hurt Me?' Someone had found the knob marked 'eighties' and turned it up full.

Just around the corner from Draycott Place in Tryon Street stood, and still stands, a safe, twee and very Chelsea gay pub called the Queen's Head. It was in the snug there that I first heard about something called GRID. Gay-Related Immune Deficiency. It all sounded most peculiar. Gay people in America were dying and 'you mark my words, dear,' said the barman, 'it's coming over here.'

The gay world was expressing itself fiercely and freely at this time. Larry Kramer's *Faggots* was the book of the age, portraying a world of Fire Island excess where happy hedonists frothed, creamed and pumped away their endless weekends of drug-driven partying, succumbing (and indeed sucking cum) to intense physical gratification in eye-popping scenes of pitiless, guiltless detail. A lifestyle free from moral, personal or medical consequences. No restraint was shown, except perhaps a leather one swinging from the ceiling in which unimaginable acts would be perpetrated. I found it all about as arousing as a Tupperware party. It was a strange feeling to be in a minority within a minority. Most gay people aspired, or appeared to aspire, to that whole scene and to the Village People character types that defined it, especially the plaid-shirted, moustachioed look that was called the Clone. Squadrons of these tight-jeaned, heavy-booted individuals could be seen massed inside the Coleherne Arms in Earls Court. I found the manliness, humourlessness and physical urgency that emanated like cheap musk from such people and places alarming and depressing. Not that I was even faintly drawn to these preposterous Tom of Finland caricatures with their muscle vests, leather caps and joyless stares. My dream partner was a friendly, dreamy, funny young man with whom I could walk, talk, laugh, cuddle and play. Nonetheless I did go to places like the Coleherne and the newly opened Heaven, which proclaimed itself to be the largest disco in Europe. I went because . . . well, because it was what you did in those days if you were gay and in your twenties. To feel a hundred eyes instantly scan and dismiss me was humiliating and shaming and reminded me of being checked out in the school showers. Rejection, contempt and lack of interest were all instant, careless and unequivocal. Thumping music, the sniffing of poppers, the thrashing on the dance-floor and those endless raking, questing, needy eyes prohibited any conversation or laughter. I was completely uninterested in picking anyone up or in being picked up myself and I certainly had no desire to dance but I suppose I thought that if I went often enough I would somehow break through and start to like it, in the same way I had broken through with unsugared tea. I never did break through with the gay scene. I learned to hate the discos and bars and everything they stood for. I am not sure that I can successfully claim that it was moral repugnance that fuelled my hate, I think it was the remorseless battering to my *amour propre*, my ego.

Problems with the physical self, you may have noticed by now, are central to my life story. The reckless feeding of my physical appetites on the one hand and the miserable dislike and fear of my physical appearance on the other have all been overseen by a pathological personal theology that has for most of my life robbed me of any true ease. I do not wish to sound self-pitying or to privilege myself with unique sensitivity or susceptibility to distress in these matters, but there is almost no moment in the day when I do not feel myself to be intensely guilty of numberless trespasses. Drinking too much coffee, not concentrating sufficiently hard, not answering emails quickly enough. Not being in touch with people I have promised to be in touch with. Going to the gym too infrequently. Eating too much. Drinking too much. Declining invitations to speak at charity dinners. Being slow in reading and commenting on entirely unsolicited scripts. These are almost meaningless offences; they are pathetic little particles of plankton in the deep ocean of sin to be sure, but my feelings are as craven, cringing and confessional as the most self-abasing Calvinists in their most prostrate and abject furies of repentance. I do not believe there is a god or a judgement day or a redeeming saviour, but I go through all the shame, trembling and self-castigation of the most pious and hysterical ascetic without the cheap promise of forgiveness and a divine cuddle in recompense.

Good gracious, I know how this reads. To listen to the neuroses of a spoilt, over-paid, over-praised, over-pampered celebrity must be unendurable. For me to wallow in the luxury of being worried only by such insignificant piffle while so many in the world suffer the traumas, terrors and torments of poverty, hunger, disease and war. Even here in the developed world there are plenty who have financial and familial worries enough to be – to say the least – unsympathetic to my plight. I *know*. My God, do you think I do not know how monstrously self-indulgent, narcissistic and childish I must sound in so many ears? That is the point. My real dissatisfaction is with my dissatisfaction. How dare I be so discontent? How dare I? Or being discontent why cannot I shut up about it?

I know that money, power, prestige and fame do not bring happiness. If history teaches us anything it teaches us that. You know it. Everybody agrees this to be a manifest truth so self-evident as to need no repetition. What is strange to me is that, despite the fact that the world knows this, it does not *want* to know it and it chooses almost always to behave as if it were not true. It does not suit the world to hear that people who are leading a high life, an enviable life, a privileged life are as miserable most days as anybody else, despite the fact that it must be obvious they would be – given that we are all agreed that money and fame do not bring happiness. Instead the world would prefer to enjoy the idea, against what it knows to be true, that wealth and fame do in fact insulate and protect against misery and it would rather we shut up if we are planning to indicate otherwise. And I am all for that. For the greater part of the time I will smile and agree that I am the luckiest devil alive and that I am as happy as a bee in pollen. Most of the time. But not when writing a book like this. Not when it is understood that I will attempt to be as honest with you as possible. About other people, as I have said, I may palter and pretend, but the business of autobiography is at least to strive for some element of self-revelation and candour. And so I have to confess that, foolish as I know it sounds, I spend much of my life imprisoned by a ruthless, unreasoning conscience that tortures me and denies me happiness. How much is Conscience and how much is Cyclothymia, the particular flavour of bipolarity with which I have been diagnosed and to which we will (hurray!) not return in this book, I cannot tell. I am content to shuttle between all available moral, psychological, mythical, spiritual, neural, hormonal, genetic, dietary and environmental explanations for unhappiness.

I hope then that you will excuse the unstartling revelation that I am often tortured and unhappy. Most of this unhappiness would appear to derive from my physical self being either disgusting in its lack of appeal or demanding in its requirements of calories and other damaging substances. In the light of this I will pursue further the point I was making about the Coleherne and related horrors of the eighties scene.

The gay identity, if I can be excused for so squirm-worthy a phrase, drew attention to the physical in those days more than I think it does now. Heaven (both of them: the address in the clouds and the club under the arches of Charing Cross) knows there is still plenty of body fascism about today, but I think it is being accurate rather than charitable to say that the community has grown up a little. Being gay thirty years ago, however, seemed overwhelmingly to be about dancing, cruising, narcissism and anonymous sex. I was gay and therefore I was supposed to care for and be capable of those things too. My problem was twofold. Firstly nobody seemed to be remotely attracted to me, and secondly I wasn't even interested anyway in all this heavy dance-floor heaving and casual erotic encountering.

Would it have been different if some of those harsh nighthawk glares had melted with desire when I came in through the door? Might I then have consented to dance the sexual dance? Did I hate my own face and body with such a hot hate only because I thought others did? Was I really doing no more than getting my retaliation in first, like children who decide that chess or history or tennis are boring, but only because they don't have an instant aptitude?

Blaise Pascal said that if Cleopatra's nose had been a little shorter, the whole history of the earth would have been different. If mine had been a little cuter then maybe I would have thrown myself into a life of carnal abandon at just that period in history when there were trillions of microscopic reasons for that being the most fatal game to play. So perhaps it is as well that I was unappealing.

If you are distressed or irritated to read me describe myself as such, then let it be understood that, while at that time I had no confidence in being anything else, I am fully aware that plenty of undeniably less good-looking men seemed to be getting all the sex they required. Self-image was a lot to do with it, but there can be no disputing the misery caused by those hard eyes running up and down my body for a scorchingly humiliating instant before flicking away with contempt towards the next person coming through the door. Of course I know those glaring gazing gays were just as, perhaps even more, insecure than me. They too were getting their retaliation in first. But to think such unsmiling coldness is sexy . . . I am very proud and very happy to be gay, but I would be lying if I did not say that much about the world that gay people inhabited in those days sickened, repelled and frightened me.

As much as anything it was to be dismissed without being known that prickled so fiercely. Without labouring the point, it was behaviour that I thought not far from racism, sexism or any other kind of prejudice or snobbery. 'Because you are not cute I do not want to know you' was to me hardly different from suggesting, 'Because you are gay I dislike you' or 'Because you are Jewish, I dislike you' or, come to that, 'Because you went to Cambridge I dislike you.' Of course, anyone who believes themselves to be a victim of such discrimination ought to be sure. We first have to dismiss the worrying possibility that a true interpretation of another's antipathy might be 'Because you are a boring arsehole I dislike you', a judgement from which there is little hope of comfortable escape.

Kim enjoyed the gay world more than I did. He was not, of course, fooled by it, but I think he was more at ease in it than I could ever be. He also had more opportunity to experience it, for I was beginning to be so consumed by work that such things as clubs and pubs were receding into the background for me. This new Granada comedy series was going to take me away from London for long periods of time.

Colonel and Coltrane

It was hard not to like Manchester. Being called 'love', 'chuck' or a 'daft barmcake' can only delight a southerner used to the lonely and unsmiling lovelessness of London and the south-east. Granada lodged us at the grand and luxurious Midland Hotel and doled out to us the most unbelievably handsome *per diem* cash payments in little brown packets. I had never had so much ready money in my life. We had had three months to write material and now we were here to sift, select and record.

Hugh and I had been – what is the word? Horror-struck? Staggered? Mortified? Shamed? Some mixture of all those perhaps – to discover that our slow, mournful and insecure rate of writing had been trumped and trampled on by the one-man whirlwind of industry, creativity and prodigality that was Benjamin Charles Elton. For every one page of uncertain and unfinished sketch comedy that we held apologetically up for judgement, Ben produced fifty. That is no exaggeration. Where our comedy was etiolated, buttoned-up and embarrassed, his was wild, energetic, colourful and confident to the point of cockiness. While we would read ours out with a sorrowful cough and somehow framed in self-deprecating inverted commas, Ben would perform his, playing every part, with undisguised pleasure and demented relish. Despite our complete sense of humiliation and defeat we did laugh and we did unreservedly admire his astonishing talent and the unabashed zest with which he threw himself into performance.

Ben had instantly spotted the performing genius of Emma Thompson and warmed to the big-eyed hopeless-ness that Hugh could project in characters as well as his authority and range. In me he saw a crusty relict of Empire and created a character called Colonel Sodom, who might, I suppose, be regarded as a rather coarsely sketched forerunner of *Blackadder Goes Forth*'s General Melchett. Another aspect of my limited performance scope that appealed to him resulted in Doctor de Quincey, a casually peremptory and callous doctor who reappeared some years later in Ben's comedy drama series *Happy Families*.

Single-handedly Ben seemed to have written every episode of the series, which was called, after much disputation, *There's Nothing to Worry About*. We shot it in and around Manchester, the director, Stuart Orme, using state of the art Electronic News Gathering equipment, which is to say new lightweight video cameras whose flexibility allowed the production to save money on set building, but at the price of a substandard look and soundtrack. Hugh and I managed to write a few sketches that made it through to performance, as a sop to our pride we suspected, one being a long sequence that involved a pair of characters called Alan and Bernard, who had featured in the Footlights Charades sketch and who would pop up again as Gordon and Stewart in *A Bit of Fry and Laurie*. But all in all it was Ben's show, for good or ill.

It is no unfair criticism of anyone to say that the results were uneven. Richard Armitage, the agent who had taken me, Hugh and Emma under his wing, was loud in his dismay, disgust and disapproval. He was particularly revolted by Colonel Sodom's exploding bottom. The Colonel ate strong curries and in a series of shots I was seen striding through the streets of Didsbury all but propelled along the pavement by pyrotechnic special-effect farts. I think there was even a close-up of the seat of my pinstripe trousers bursting open with a smoking star-shaped bang. Richard muttered about this for weeks. He felt that the stylish, intelligent brand of graduate comedy for which he hoped we would be known, and on which he planned to build our careers, was being crippled at birth by a foul-mouthed Cockney street urchin with a sewer for a mind and he wanted none of it. Who knows what grumbling behind-the-scenes machinations took place. Richard may even have tried to get us out of our contract. Steve Morrison, the executive producer, and Sandy Ross stayed loyal to Ben, quite rightly recognizing his ferocious and fertile talent. They were aware nonetheless that *There's Nothing to Worry About* had flaws, and their solution was to bring in a new cast member. Paul Shearer, through no fault of his own, left the show. As one who wrote less material even than Hugh and me he was, I suppose, considered dispensable. Paul's place was taken by a Glasgow Art School graduate called Anthony McMillan, who had just changed his name to Robbie Coltrane.

Big, loud and hilarious, Robbie combined the style and manners of a Brooklyn bus-driver, a fifties rock and roller, a motor mechanic and a Gorbals gangster. Somehow they all fitted together perfectly into one consistent character. He terrified the life out of me, and the only way I could compensate for that was to pretend to find him impossibly attractive and to rub my legs up against him and moan with ecstasy.

'You cheeky wee fucker,' he would say and somehow tolerate me.

Robbie has since said in an interview that he found Hugh and me to be arrogant, off-puttingly over-confident Establishment figures who looked down our well-bred noses at his blowsy, vulgar intrusion like thoroughbred racehorses shivering their fastidious flanks at the presence in their stables of an unwelcome donkey. I am not quoting him exactly, but that is certainly the gist of what he said. Whether he made this up to pad out a boring interview session or whether he truly believes it and remembers it that way, I cannot say. I always get on amicably, indeed affectionately, with Robbie on the rare occasions that I see him these days, but I have never dared raise the subject of that interview. They bring us back to the endless, and perhaps arid, problem of affect and appearance, the question of the figures we cut with others despite what we may feel inside. We see everyone else socially armed with great clubs while all we have hidden behind our backs is a pitiful cotton bud. I know how much Hugh and I were suffering a tormented sense of inadequacy, how much we felt out of place and how much we were embarrassed by our damnable public-school and Cambridge backgrounds. I also know that we were too proud and too well-brought-up, or I was certainly, to go around slouching and mooching with hang-dog expressions that begged for petting and pity. It is, at some sort of stretch, possible that we hid our feelings of hopelessness so well that Robbie could, in all conscience, claim that we came over as poncey, preening pricks, but I honestly cannot believe it likely. Perhaps it suited Robbie to imagine himself as a lowborn grease-monkey endowed with natural, home-grown street talent, forced into a world of pale snobbery and mincing middle-class privilege. In fact, of course, Robbie is the son of a doctor and went to school at Glenalmond College, perhaps Scotland's most elite private seat of learning and subject of the excellent 2008 documentary *Pride and Privilege*. The 13th Duke of Argyll, the Marquess of Lothian, Prince Georg Friedrich of Prussia and the 9th Earl of Elgin, Viceroy of India, are numbered amongst its eximious alumni. That he managed to enter Glasgow School of Art as Anthony Robert McMillan with an accent like Prince Charles's and emerge the other end as Robbie Coltrane with an accent like Jimmy Boyle's is a fine achievement. I sometimes think I should have tried to do something similar.

There's Nothing to Worry About had emerged on screen, exploding bottoms and all, in June of 1982 in the Granada region only. We went back down to London to write in July, August and September for the new series which was to be called *Alfresco*.

Computer 1

One free afternoon in Manchester I had walked to the
Arndale Centre and drifted from shop to shop. In a branch
of Lasky's I found myself staring in perplexity at a group
of teenagers clustered around a display stand. I approached
and looked over their shoulders . . .

Half an hour later I was fiddling with the back of
the television in my Midland Hotel bedroom. After
ten frustrating and confused minutes Ceefax-style text
appeared on the screen.

BBC Computer 32K
BASIC

It was the beginning of a lifelong love affair, the details of
which will bore you dreadfully. I shall try not to linger
on the subject too long, but the relationship was and is
too important to me for it to be consigned to a quick
sentence. Most of my spare hours were now spent in front
of this transcendently lovely (to me) machine, an Acorn
BBC Micro B computer. At that time microcomputers
relied on two household appliances to work properly:
a television for display and a cassette tape-recorder for
recording and loading programs. The Lasky's salesman had
persuaded me to buy a program called Wordwise, which
came on a ROM chip that you plugged into one of four
slots on the circuit board. The other spaces were for the
operating system and the BASIC programming language.
With Wordwise plugged into the first slot the computer
magically started up as a word-processor. I could attach it
by a wide-ribboned parallel connector to a Brother electric

typewriter which now became a slave printer. I cannot explain my fascination and delight. With exultation I would show my friends the computer, the programs I had written and the printer printing out. Everybody cooed and wowed obediently, but I could tell they were not moved in the same way that I was. It puzzled me that I should be so captivated by this new world when others were so relatively unengaged. Certainly the system was clever, one could do remarkable things with it, and most people were impressed – in the standard 'Tch, whatever will they think of next?' way – but for me the excitement was about so much more than function. I have long since given up trying to understand this undying obsession, which rapidly took on all the form, manner and behaviour of a classic addiction. I passed most of what spare time I had with my head buried in dedicated microcomputer magazines or haunting the Tottenham Court Road on the look-out for new peripherals. I would stay up at the keyboard until three, four or five in the morning writing pointless programs or attempting to master useless techniques. Within a very short time I had filled my corner of the Chelsea flat with a daisy-wheel printer, a plotter, a dedicated RGB monitor and an add-on for an extra processor and floppy disks. My lifelong battle to control cabling began at this time. All the cables I have ever owned would stretch to the moon and back. Except they would not be able to because they would fail to connect up with each other. Anyone can write a credible story in which humans can teleport, travel in time and make themselves invisible. A future in which there are cable compatibility standards, that would be real science fiction.

Cables, monitors, printers, books, magazines, disks –

all these were costing me money. Money that I did not
have.

Richard Armitage had told me with an expansive wave
of a cigar-brandishing hand that if ever I was running low,
his assistant, Lorraine Hamilton, would send me cheques
to cover my expenses. These would count as advances
against future earnings. Despite Kim's relative wealth
and his easy generosity, I had run up a debt of several
thousand pounds with Richard by the August of 1982 and
was beginning to worry that I would never earn enough
to be able to pay him back.

Commercial

One morning Lorraine called me up at the Chelsea flat. I
know it was at the Chelsea flat because in those days when
you rang someone you always knew where they were. The
closest life came to a mobile phone was a handset with
an extra-long flex. Lorraine told me to go to an office in
Fitzrovia and meet a man called Paul Weiland, who was
casting a beer commercial.

A beer commercial? Me? A low vulgar commercial, for
a highly polished artist such as myself? How unbelievably
insulting. I almost ran to the appointed place.

The golden age of British advertising was just coming to
an end. The most prominent stars to have risen over the past
decade had been Ridley and Tony Scott, Hugh Hudson,
David Puttnam and Alan Parker, who now all devoted
their time to feature films. Paul Weiland, a generation
behind, had started his career as a tea boy at the production
office where most of those big names had worked and was

to become the leading commercials director of the eighties and nineties. Indeed he still reigns supreme.

He handed me a script that was really more of a photocopied storyboard. It showed a monocled Victorian aristocrat in a series of unlikely poses.

'There's no dialogue,' Paul said. 'The whole commercial is played out to a soundtrack. The song "Abdul Abulbul Amir". Do you know it?'

I had to confess that I did not.

'Never mind. Take this mug. You're drinking the beer. It's Whitbread Best Bitter. You're Count Ivan Skavinsky Skavar, and I'm Abdul. Just give me a really snooty look. Snootier! As if he's a caterpillar in your salad or shit on your shoe.'

For ten minutes I pretended to drink Whitbread snootily while a most peculiar song played in the background. I am not sure I have ever been more embarrassed and uncomfortable or felt more ill at ease, self-conscious and incompetent. When it was all over I left, blushing furiously.

'Well, Stephen,' I said to myself, 'that is the last you will ever hear of *that*. Perhaps it is as well. Perhaps I was so bad because my innermost soul was revolting at the mercenary grubbiness of the whole enterprise. Yes. That will be it.'

The next day Lorraine called up and asked me to come into the Noel Gay offices in Denmark Street. Richard was sitting behind his enormous desk, beaming behind a thick curtain of Villiger cigar smoke.

'They want you for the Whitbread commercial,' he said. 'But I'm afraid they're being irritatingly tough on the money.'

Oh well, I thought. Five or six hundred pounds would come in useful. It would be as much as that, surely.

'They offered twenty,' said Richard, 'and I can't seem to get them above twenty-five. If you find that insulting we can always walk away.'

'For how many hours' work?'

Richard looked down at his notes. 'Three days.'

'Blimey,' I said, trying not to look too disappointed. 'It isn't much.'

'No,' said Richard. 'It's just over eight thousand a day. Well, if you feel . . .'

Thousand! I swallowed drily, pushing my Adam's apple past a throbbing constriction that was rising in my throat and threatening to cause me to choke. *Twenty-five thousand pounds.* For three days' work.

'No, no!' I faltered. 'I mean . . . no. It's fine. I'll . . .'

'They speak very highly of Paul Weiland. Good experience for you. Starts shooting in Shepperton on Monday. They'll want you at Bermans and Nathans for a costume fitting tomorrow at three. Excellent. I'll call the agency.'

I tottered about London for the rest of that morning in a dream.

I could pay back Noel Gay Artists everything I owed them and I would still be rich. Rich beyond the dreams of avarice. Well, not that, obviously. The dreams of avarice go well beyond twenty-five odd thousand pounds minus 15 per cent commission, minus tax and VAT, minus three and a half thousand already owing. But rich enough for me.

You would have just cause to hate me now, reader, when I tell you that from that day to this I have never had what one could seriously call money troubles. Not money troubles of the kind that cause so many people to wake up in the middle of the night with a ghastly feeling like molten lead leaking into their stomach as they contemplate mounting debt and the apparent impossibility of getting their finances in order. That tremble of panic and dread that so many feel in relation to money I have been spared. I feel it for other things but I know that many in the world would trade much for the kind of cushion of cash that has enveloped me for thirty years. I did not know, as I went about London window-shopping that day, that in two and a half years' time even more money would start pouring in.

The three days of the shoot in Shepperton Studios passed in a sweat of worry, embarrassment and confusion. I had no idea why everything took so long, what I was doing, who everyone was or what the commercial was about. Tim McInnerny, whom I was to get to know two years later when I joined the cast of *Blackadder II*, had been cast as a lute-wielding minstrel of some kind. The character of Abdul was played by an actor called Tony Cosmo, who was suitably swarthy and menacing. I, in my own estimation, failed to be suitably anything. Watching it today on YouTube (try searching for Whitbread Best Bitter 1982 Ad or similar) the film still appears to make very little sense, and I am sure that even now my discomfort in the role of Count Ivan transmits across the decades. I think I was cast on account of my pointy chin rather than because of any discernible skill or talent.

Paul Weiland was charming and easy-going. My memories of the exceptionally laid-back Hugh Hudson on the set of *Chariots of Fire* had prepared me to expect relaxation from the director and fiery shouting only from assistants, and this was exactly how it was. I spent most of the three days sitting in a canvas chair and drinking cups of tea while birds twitted and shitted in the gantry far above. There are generations of pigeon, sparrow and chaffinch that have lived out their lives in the roof spaces of the great sound stages of Pinewood and Shepperton. They have dumped their droppings on some of the immortal scenes of British cinema, and their screechings have interrupted dialogue from Dirk Bogarde, John Mills, Kenneth Williams, Roger Moore and a thousand others. Mostly, however, they have overseen the less glamorous business of commercial and pop video shoots that make up the bread-and-butter business for studio staff, film crews and happily overpaid actors. I know that I am supposed to be ashamed of advertising work and feel that it is either beneath me or some kind of sell-out, but I cannot bring myself to apologize or regret. Orson Welles always said with high-handed disdain, 'If it was good enough for Toulouse-Lautrec and John Everett Millais, then it is good enough for me,' but I don't really feel the need to adduce the names of great figures from the past, I just find it fun.

Create!

We were back in Manchester by October filming for *Alfresco* which, unlike *There's Nothing to Worry About*, was to be broadcast nationally. Ben had created for us a fictional world which he called The Pretend Pub. The concept might kindly be described as playful meta-textual post-modernism. Most people, however, were not kind and seemed to regard it as incomprehensible self-indulgent twaddle, which I suppose is how most playful meta-textual post-modernism is received. We all portrayed heightened versions of ourselves in an obviously unreal studio pub. I was Stezzer, Hugh was Huzzer, Robbie Bobzer, Ben Bezzer, Emma Ezzer and Siobhan Shizzer. We still often call each other by those names to this day, although Ben, for reasons lost in time, usually calls me Bing.

In the first episode, I enter, covered in polystyrene flakes of stage snow, greeting Robbie with the words, 'My word, Pretend Landlord Bobzer, there's a hell of a theatrical effect going on out there . . .'. We performed these sketches in front of a mostly silent and bemused audience. We consoled ourselves with the thought that we were ahead of our time. I think a great deal of the problem came from self-consciousness. Ben knew very well (partly because he was directly involved) what his contemporaries were doing in the field of alternative comedy, and Hugh and I were painfully and acutely aware of what our tradition had done in the field of sketch comedy, from Pete and Dud through to Python and *Not the Nine O'Clock News*. As a result we were guilty, it is clear looking back, of over-complicating everything out of a fear of being perceived as imitative and unoriginal. We ruled out parodies and 'Ah, come in, Perkins, shut the door, do sit down,' sketches because Python and *Not* had done these. Surreality and anarchic weirdness were out too because Rik, Ade and Alexei had cornered that market. So we wallowed about sightlessly, guiltily and confusedly without the confidence to do what we did best. Audiences, I now realize (and frankly it should always have been blindingly obvious), do not think along such lines. Novelty and originality do not come from the invention of new milieus, new genres or new modalities.

They come from the *how* and the *who*, not from the *what*. It hardly warrants pointing out, furthermore, that no one will get anywhere unless they do what they do best, and everyone, in their secret, secret heart, knows what they do best.

Meanwhile Steve Morrison, our Scottish executive producer, pleaded with us to stop bellyaching. 'Go out and create, man!' he yelled at me across a table one stormy afternoon, when I was behaving more than usually pedantically or sceptically or in some other manner guaranteed to annoy. He stood and pointed at the door. 'I want Ayckbourn with edge,' he screamed. 'Go out and bring me Ayckbourn with edge!' Well, quite.

It was made obvious to us that high up in Granada a problem with our writing had been identified. In the case of Ben it might have been over-productivity and a lack of self-censorship; in the case of Hugh and me it was exactly the opposite – crippling constipation and a kind of apologetic, high-toned embarrassment that must have been excessively irritating. For one excruciating week we all had to undergo a kind of comedy-writing masterclass with Bernie Sahlins, one of the producers of the Second City revue group and television show. Bernie, brother of the anthropologist Marshall Sahlins, was from a tradition of improvisation that he helped create back in the days of Mike Nichols and Elaine May, a tradition that had burst into television and more recently film with the *Saturday Night Live* generation of Aykroyd, Chase, Murray, Belushi and Radner. Ben wrote alone and wasn't faintly interested in the styles and techniques of Chicago improv. Hugh and I were pretty appalled too at the idea of 'building a scene' through improvisational dialogue in the approved

American way. When we wrote together we sometimes did improvise, inasmuch as we made a sketch up out loud as we went along before committing it to paper. I suspect that if we had been accused of improvising we would have frozen in horror midway and would never have been able to continue. The cultural gulf between our way and Bernie Sahlins's way must have perplexed and even offended him, but it was an unbridgeable one and he left Manchester after five days without having made a dent in us. He did teach us that if we had been born American we would never ever have made it in the comedy business and we perhaps taught him that the British people are stubborn, shy and entirely dominated by their single predominant emotion, affect, vice, characteristic, disease . . . whatever one might call it: embarrassment. Ben carried on pouring out script after script in his way, and we carried on not pouring out anything much in ours.

As well as Steve Morrison, Sandy Ross, Robbie and Siobhan, we now had a fifth Scot on board in the shape of a producer called John G. Temple. Hugh revealed that Temple had approached him early one morning as we had been getting into costumes for a day's filming and asked him what drugs I was on.

'No drugs,' Hugh had said. 'That's just how Stephen is.'

When he relayed this exchange to me I had been profoundly shocked. What was it about me that could possibly lead a stranger to leap to the instant conclusion that I must be on drugs? Hugh explained to me with as much tact as he could manage that it was possibly my excessive energy in the mornings. I had always been loud and verbally exuberant from the earliest hours, but it had never occurred to me that this mania might be extreme enough to present the appearance of drug abuse. Everyone else was used to my often exaggerated elation and bounce, but they were evidently weird enough to a newcomer like John to excite the wildest speculation.

Perhaps this should have sounded as a warning in my head for me to attend to my states of mind a little more carefully, but when one is young eccentricities, moods and behavioural ticks are easily overlooked, ignored or laughingly dealt with. One is so much more supple. One can bend with all the gnarls and twists and kinks that life and the caprices of one's mind confer. Past forty it is, of course, another story. What once was whippy and pliable now snaps like dried bone. So much that is charming, unusual, provocative and admirably strange in youth becomes tragic, lonely, pathological, boring, and ruinous in middle age. A hurt or troubled mind plays out a story very like that of an alcoholic's life. A twenty-year-old who drinks heavily is a bit of a rogue; sometimes he may be a little flushed in the face, sometimes too pie-eyed to turn up to this or that appointment on time, but usually he (or she of course) will be loveable enough and resilient enough to get on with life. Quite when the broken veins, spongy nose, humourless bloodshot eyes and hideous personality changes take full root it is hard to say, but one day everyone notices that their hard-drinking friend is no longer funny and no longer charming – they have become an embarrassment, a liability and a bore. I have seen and experienced the same with little personality wrinkles and dispositions that have been so acceptable and endearing and apparently harmless in youth, yet have proved destructive to the point of agony, addiction, degeneration, misery, self-harm and suicide in later years. There have been moments in writing this book when I have looked back at nearly all my friends and contemporaries (myself included of course), so many of them blessed with talent, brains, brilliance and good fortune, and I have found myself forced to believe that all of us have failed in life. Or life has failed us. In our fifties the physical deterioration which one would naturally expect has been far outstripped by disappointment, bitterness, despair, mental instability and failure.

Then I slap myself across the chops and tell myself not to be so hysterical and self-dramatizing. And yet the episode with the car might be regarded by some doctors as a typical episode of hypomanic grandiosity. . .

Car

The sixth Scot in the *Alfresco* line-up was Dave McNiven, our resident musical director and composer. Naturally I saw very little of him. Once his sensitive ear had heard me miming, our professional paths were set never to cross again. You may wonder how he can have *heard* me miming, but this just shows the depths of unmusicality to which I was capable of sinking. It is very hard to be in a chorus and to mime without one's vocal chords just occasionally making themselves heard. A musical ear can pick up a discord instantly, no matter how many voices are singing and no matter how low and inadvertent the tiny sound that emanates. I shall never forget the shocked look on Dave's face as he spun round in my direction. I had seen it before and I was destined to see it many times again. It was the particular look of dismay that registers on the countenance of one who only moments before has said with supreme certainty and unruffled confidence, 'Oh, believe me, *everyone* can sing!' I exist on this planet precisely to teach such wrong-headed optimists the error of their convictions.

The afternoons given over to music rehearsals, therefore, I filled with more driving lessons. I had taken a few while teaching at Cundall Manor. Back then, as I had bucked and jerked the motoring-school's Austin Metro down the main street of Thirsk I had been told with hard Yorkshire disdain, 'Tha gear and clutch control is shite, and tha steering is as much use as a chocolate teapot.' The Mancunian instructor four years later was much friendlier, as people so often are west of the Pennines, or perhaps it was that my car-handling skills had improved in the interval. He would hum quietly to himself and look interestedly out of the window at the street scenes that flashed by, apparently confident enough in my driving not to bother about what I was doing as I manoeuvred the dual-control Escort along his favourite route, past the university halls of residence in Rusholme and Fallowfield, down Kingsway and into the maze of residential backstreets around Cheadle Hulme. One afternoon, quite unexpectedly, he announced that I was ready to take my test and that he had booked me in for the following week.

'If you've no objection?'

Half an hour later I found myself in a BMW showroom, shaking hands on a deal. I have no idea what rush of blood to the head had propelled me there but by the time I left it was too late to do anything about it. I had called up my bank and arranged the financing and was now the legal owner of a second-hand 323i in metallic green. Sunroof, Blaupunkt stereo and 16,000 miles on the clock.

That evening, not having dared tell Hugh that I had done something so magisterially arsey and recklessly tempting of providence as to buy a car before I had even passed my driving test, we all gathered in my room at the Midland Hotel. I ordered up wine, beer and crisps and we watched a repeat of May's original transmission of our Footlights show. Two days later we assembled again with even more wine, beer and crisps to watch the launch of the all-new Channel 4, which included in its opening night line-up *Comic Strip Presents . . . Five Go Mad in Dorset*, in which Robbie played two parts. This was the first new channel on British television since the arrival of BBC 2 in 1964.

I passed my driving test, raced around insurance offices and returned to the car showroom properly possessed of paperwork that allowed me to drive away. I had teased and flirted with destiny and got away with it. If I had failed my test I wonder what I would have done with the car? Simply left it there I suppose.

Challenge 2

A week later we met for a third time in my hotel room and, surrounded by all the wine, beer and crisps the Midland staff could produce, we watched the first episode of *The Young Ones*, which Ben had co-written and in which he also appeared.

Within a week then, two seismic events had rocked our little world. The gleaming primary-coloured blocks that had flown out to form the graphic figure 4 which made up the channel's logo seemed, with their smooth, computer-generated motion, to usher in a brave new world, and when Ade Edmondson as Vyvyan punched his way through the kitchen wall in the opening five minutes of *The Young Ones* it felt as though a whole new generation had punched its way into British cultural life and that nothing would ever be the same again.

The Young Ones was an instant success in exactly the way *Alfresco*, whose first series wasn't broadcast until mid-1983, manifestly wasn't. Rik Mayall especially soared into stardom as the new King of Comedy: the brilliantly childish, Cliff-Richard-obsessed character of Rick in *The Young Ones* with his exaggerated derhotacizations and uncontrolled giggling snorts sealed a reputation that had grown from Rik's original 20th Century Coyote act with Ade Edmondson and his sublime appearances in *A Kick Up the Eighties* as Kevin Turvey, the Chic Murray of Kidderminster.

The wild divergence I felt between this hot lava stream of new talent and the constipated conventional and constricted tradition from which I derived was extreme and has, I am sure you will feel, been dwelt on enough. From the distance of thirty years it seems self-indulgent and paranoid to harp on about it, but the distinction did at least lead to one fruitful conversation in the bar of the Midland in January 1983. Ben, Rik and Lise had already started work on a second series of *The Young Ones*, and the thought had struck me, having spent so much time in Granadaland and having watched lines of undergraduates queuing up, as I had three years earlier, for canteen lunches in between rounds of *University Challenge*, that perhaps Rick, Vyvyan, Neil and Mike, being a student foursome, might themselves be entered for the quiz, with, as the *Radio Times* might phrase it, hilarious consequences. I suggested this to Ben, who instantly enthused. He and the others produced 'Bambi', in which the Young Ones, representing Scumbag University, come up against Footlights College, Oxbridge, in the snooty, privileged persons of Hugh, Emma, Ben and me. My character was called Lord Snot, an insanely shiny toff based on the *Beano*'s Lord Snooty.

Ben may well have a different memory of the genesis of that episode. It is one of the known eternal truths of comic creation that a good idea has a dozen parents while a duff one remains an orphan. From wherever or whomever this idea derived the show was recorded a year or so later with Griff Rhys Jones as Bambi Gascoigne and Mel Smith as a Granada TV security guard. It is still considered, I think, one of the most memorable of *The Young Ones* episodes, in part because of an unusually strong and coherent narrative and in part also because the parricidal revenge of the new and radical upon the old and reactionary is played out so literally and satisfyingly. Footlights College are routed and humiliated as completely in fiction as we felt we were being in fact.

I have mentioned that we were all – Hugh and I to a crippling extent – hobbled by self-consciousness and a foolish desire to avoid what we considered had been done before. But did we have any kind of a theory of comedy, any banner that we wanted to raise?

It was clear to me that Hugh had a more complete canteen of comic cutlery in his drawer than the pitiful selection of plastic coffee-stirrers and archaic horn-handled knives that I felt capable of wielding. As I have said, I was aware without envy, but with a measure of sorrow and self-pity, that Hugh was a master of three enormously important elements of comedy in which I was an embarrassing incompetent. He had music. He could play any instrument that he picked up and he could sing. He had physical control of his body. As a natural athlete he could roll, fall, leap, dance and jig to comic effect. He had an amusing, appealing face that made him a natural clown. Big sad eyes, a funny chin and a hilarious upper lip. And I? I could be verbally adept and I could play pompous authority figures and . . . er . . . that was it, really. Could I cut it as an actor, or had my commitment to comedy cut that avenue off? In the comic world I had no social or political axe to grind, no new stylistic mode to advance. I liked the old-fashioned sketch comedy for which it was beginning to look as though the world had little time.

I worried that I was going to have to be primarily a writer. Why worry, you might ask? Well, although it is true that one feels fantastic when one has *finished* a writing task, it is mostly horrible while one is *doing* it. You will see therefore that writing, ghastly at the time but great afterwards, is exactly the opposite of sex. All that keeps one going is the knowledge that one will feel good when it's all over. I knew, as all writers know, that performers have a much easier life. They swan about being admired, recognized, pampered, praised and told how wonderful they are and what *energy* and *resource* and *strength* they have to cope with all that *pressure*. Pah. They only work while they are in rehearsal, on set or on stage; for the rest of the time they can get up late and laze and lounge about like lords. Writers on the other hand are in a permanent state of school exam crisis. Deadlines croak and beat their wings above them like sinister rooks; producers, publishers and performers nag for rewrites and improvements. Any down time looks like evasion and indolence. There is no moment at which one cannot, and should not it seems, be at one's desk. It is also a desperately lonely calling.

There are compensations. You only have to write a play once and then you can sit back and let the money roll in, while the actors have to perform eight times a week for six months to earn their pay packets.

Hugh and I were *writer-performers* – we wrote the material that we performed. I could not decide whether this meant we had the best of both worlds or the worst. To this day I cannot be sure. It is obvious, however, that in terms of employment it doubles one's opportunities. Whatever I lacked in physical attributes as a natural clown I seemed to make up for in gravitas, to use Hugh's word. It seemed that people did have faith in my ability to write, although I had produced nothing up until that point except *Latin!* And, with Hugh, the material in *The Cellar Tapes* and the handful of *Alfresco* sketches that had made it through to transmission.

Four things now happened in a succession rapid enough to be called simultaneity and which served to bolster the self-esteem that the *Alfresco* experience was doing so much to undermine.

Cinema

In the late summer of 1982 I was sent to meet a woman called Jilly Gutteridge and a man called Don Boyd. Boyd had produced Alan Clarke's cinema version of *Scum* (the original 1977 BBC television production had been Mary Whitehoused off the screen) as well as Derek Jarman's

Tempest and Julien Temple's *The Great Rock 'n' Roll Swindle* and he now planned to direct his first major feature film, which was to be called *Gossip*. He imagined a British compendium of *The Sweet Smell of Success* and *La Dolce Vita* infused with the spirit and manner of Evelyn Waugh's *Vile Bodies*. This was to be a film that would capture a new and horrible side to Thatcher's Britain: the recently confident, arrogant, vulgar Sloaney world in which night-club narcissists, trust-fund trash and philistine druggie aristos cavorted with recently cherished icons of finance, fashion and celebrity. It was a soulless, squalid, valueless and trashy milieu that believed itself to be the stylish social summit at whose dazzling peaks the lower world gazed with breathless envy and admiration.

A script had been written by the brothers Michael and Stephen Tolkin. Although their screenplay had been set in Britain, Don felt that, as Americans, they had not quite captured the world of London 'society' such as it was in the early eighties and he was after someone who could rewrite it in an authentic English voice. Jilly Gutteridge, who was to be location manager and assistant producer, was instantly affectionate and charmingly enthusiastic about my talents, and I walked away from the meeting having been given the job of rewriting the script for the princely sum of £1,000. I had three weeks in which to do it. The part of the lead character, a *beau monde* gossip columnist, was to be played by Anne Louise Lambert. Anthony Higgins, who had starred opposite her in Peter Greenaway's *The Draughtsman's Contract*, would be the man with whom she falls in love and who would rescue her from the unworthy world she inhabits. Simon Callow and Gary Oldman were also cast. It was to be Oldman's first film appearance.

I rewrote in a fever of excitement, and Don seemed pleased with my efforts. His preparations were well advanced for what I soon learnt was known as the 'principal photography'. In the meanwhile, he suggested, I might enjoy a meeting with Michael Tolkin, who just happened to be in town. As one of the original writers he had read my anglicizing rewrites with great interest and might even have one or two valuable suggestions . . .

I assented to this idea, and Tolkin and I met in an Italian restaurant called the Villa Puccini which was just yards from the Draycott Place flat.

'The Villa Puccini,' said Kim. 'Named, one must suppose, after the famous composer Villa-Lobos.'

The lunch was not destined to be the feast of reason and the flow of soul of which P. G. Wodehouse and Alexander Pope wrote so fondly. Tolkin was very disapproving of what I had done to his beloved story. He was outraged at my excision of a synagogue scene.

'The focal point of the narrative. The pivot about which the entire movie revolves. The centrepiece. The keystone. The emotional heart. The whole picture is meaningless without that scene. There *is* no picture without it. You couldn't *see* that?'

I tried as best I could to explain why I had felt it was wrong and unconvincing.

'And as for your *ending* . . .'

I suspect he may have been right about my ending. As far as I recall I had Claire, the heroine, escape into the arms of a Cambridge don, which was neither very Fellini nor very Evelyn Waugh and in its own way was probably as sentimental as the synagogue scene. Nonetheless I attempted to defend it.

'It is obvious,' said Tolkin, 'that we have nothing in common and no basis for further discussion.' He left the restaurant before the *primi piatti* arrived. He has since had a highly successful writing career with credits that include *The Player*, *Deep Impact* and *Nine*. Maybe he was right. Maybe I had ruined *Gossip* with my cynical British resistance to the possibilities of emotional change and with my inept ending. In any event the film never got made. The story of its disaster is complicated but, I am happy to say, has nothing to do with my screenplay, good or bad as that may have been.

It seems that Don Boyd had been hoodwinked by two plausible characters who claimed to represent something they called the Martini Foundation. Rich with funds accrued from the sale of the vermouth business, this foundation wanted to branch out into film financing. The two promised that $20 million would be made available to Don for a whole slate of feature films. In the meantime he could finance *Gossip* by raising money against 'certificates of deposit' that were lodged in a bank in the Netherlands. For their investment the Martini people would receive 50 per cent of the profits and a £600,000 upfront fee.

Don set to work on the construction of a huge Andrew McAlpine-designed night-club set in Twickenham Studios, and filming began some time in late October, using money that had been advanced by a third party against the arrival of these certificates of deposit. Hugh Laurie, John Sessions and others had also been cast, and about a fifth of the whole movie had been committed to celluloid by the time the terrible truth emerged that there were no certificates of deposit, that those two plausible figures with their Mayfair flat and Cannes yacht had no connection with Martini Rosso or its money and that Don had been ruthlessly swindled. They imagined, one supposes, that they would get their £600,000 finder's fee and skedaddle. Fortunately the whole house of cards collapsed before they could profit from their deception, but it was small consolation. The film collapsed. The technical unions and the acting union Equity demanded blood. Many of the crew and cast salaries, and many of the production costs had not yet been met (the Tolkins and I *had* been scrupulously paid as it happens) and all was ruin, recrimination and wrath. The upshot was that poor Don, one of the kindest and best of men, was effectively blacklisted and prevented from participating in film production for three years. Even that didn't end it, for once Don managed to start up again the unions insisted he continue to pay over what negligible producing fees he did earn. By 1992 he was financially wiped out. If he had declared himself bankrupt the moment disaster had struck he might have saved his house and possessions. In fact he sold most of what he had to repay debts because he believed that to be the honourable course.

Don Boyd was ill-treated, cold-shouldered and bad-mouthed by many in the British film industry who blamed him for being either foolishly naive, or worse, being somehow implicated in the smoky business of the fraudulent Martini Foundation. Many wiser and better heads than his had advised him that the financing deal was sound and that he was right to proceed. It was a catastrophic error to go into production without a sight of these 'certificates of deposit', but so talented, idealistic and passionately committed a film-maker did not deserve the opprobrium and pariah status he was accorded for so many years. It was certainly a hell of a way for me to be dunked, a year after leaving university, into the murky waters of the film business.

Church and Chekhov

A few months after the *Gossip* imbroglio a theatrical producer called Richard Jackson called me up and invited me to his offices in Knightsbridge. He had seen *Latin!* in Edinburgh and had a desire to produce it at the Lyric Theatre, Hammersmith, with a very young Nicholas Broadhurst directing. I made it clear that my commitments to *Alfresco* meant that I would be unable to play the role of Dominic, the part I had written for myself, but this did not seem to put Jackson off. I was immensely gratified by this. You might think my actor's self-esteem might be dented to hear a producer take so blithely the news that I was not available, but actually my *writer's* self-esteem was immensely boosted by the idea that a professional man of the theatre believed the play to be strong enough to merit a life without me.

Many months earlier I had had a conversation with a television director called Geoffrey Sax, who was keen to make a small-screen version of *Latin!* I underwent the nervous excitement of a phone conversation with the great Michael Hordern, who had expressed an interest in the part of Herbert Brookshaw and who listened kindly and calmly to my incoherent plans for the adaptation. Nothing came of this, although I was to see Geoffrey Sax eight years later, when he directed an episode of *The New Statesman* in which I made a guest appearance, and again almost twenty years after that, when he directed me in a small role in the film *Stormbreaker*. Few people in one's life ever go quite away. They turn up again like characters in a Simon Raven novel. It is as if Fate is a movie producer who cannot afford to keep introducing new characters into the script but must get as many scenes out of every actor as possible.

Nicholas and Richard were confident that they could mount *Latin!* with ease, but the role of Dominic turned out to be more difficult to cast than they had anticipated. While I was up in Manchester for *Alfresco* Series Two they auditioned dozens and dozens of young actors, none of whom they felt to be quite right. At a meeting in Richard's office I nervously made a suggestion.

'Look, I know how pathetic this sounds. But there's someone I was at university with. He's a really good actor and very funny.'

'Oh yes?'

Richard and Nicholas were polite, but there are few phrases more certain to send a chill down the spine of a producer than 'There's this friend of mine . . . he's awfully good . . .'

I carried on. 'He's left Cambridge now and he's at the Guildhall School; actually he enrolled at the music school. To be an opera singer. But I heard that he's just switched over to the drama department.'

'Oh yes?'

'Well, as I say, I know it's . . . but he really is very good . . .'

'Oh yes?'

A week later Richard called up.

'I have to confess we are at our wits' end. What was the name of this friend of yours at RADA?'

'The Guildhall, not RADA, and he's called Simon Beale.'

'Well, I won't deny it. We're desperate. Nicholas will see him.'

Two days later Nicholas called up ecstatically. 'My God, he's brilliant. Perfect. Absolutely perfect.'

I knew he would be. Ever since I had shared a stage with his arse-scratching Sir Politic Would-Be in *Volpone* I had known Simon was the real thing.

A snag was foreseen. Would the Guildhall actually let him play the part? He was a student following a specific course, and aside from the performances, which cut enough into his day (this was to be a lunchtime performance at the Lyric), there were the rehearsals to be considered too. Newly appointed as director of the Guildhall School of Music and Drama was the actor and founder member of the Royal Shakespeare Company Tony Church, and his permission to release Simon was sought.

The answer he gave was magnificent in its preciosity and absurd actorly self-importance.

'I can see that this is an engagement that Simon is keen to accept,' he said. 'It is an excellent role for him and, aside from anything else, it guarantees his provisional Equity ticket . . .' In those days the acquisition of an Equity card was absolutely essential for any actor. The world of drama presented that exquisitely cruel Catch-22 bind common to all closed shops: only Equity members could get an acting job, and you could not become an Equity member unless you had an acting job. Hugh and I had secured our cards because we had a Granada TV contract and because as writer–performers we could show that no existing Equity member would be able satisfactorily to take our places.

Tony Church was recognizing, therefore, the excellence of the opportunity that Simon Beale was being offered. 'Yes,' he said. 'I will not stand in his way. *However* . . .'

Nicholas and Richard (I was not present) blanched nervously.

'However,' continued Church, 'for the period that he will be away rehearsing and performing he will exactly miss out on the three weeks in which we will be covering Chekhovian characterization and performance. So I am duty bound, I am *duty bound* to warn Simon that if he goes ahead with this play it will leave one heck of a hole in his Chekhov technique.'

He was a fine man, Tony Church, and one endowed with an excellent sense of humour, so it is to be hoped he would not have minded my repeating this. The idea, the *idea* that any actor would somehow be left deficient by missing out on three weeks of drama-school Chekhov teaching is so preposterous, so frankly *insane* that one simply does not know where to begin. If ever I am asked by aspiring young actors or their parents whether or not they should go to drama school, the memory of Tony Church and his fear for Simon's Chekhov technique almost makes me tell them on no account to go anywhere near such useless palaces of self-regarding folly and delusion. Of course, I do not offer any advice at all other than suggesting that budding actors should follow their hearts and other such sententious and harmless ullage, but one does wonder, one really does.

Simon Beale, under his Equity name of Simon Russell Beale, has become almost universally recognized as the finest stage actor of his generation. For many, the greatest of his theatrical achievements have been his interpretations of – yes, of course – characters in the plays of Chekhov. His stunning performances in *The Seagull* at the RSC, *Uncle Vanya* at the Donmar Warehouse (for which he won an Olivier Award) and *The Cherry Orchard* at the Old Vic and in New York have earned unanimous praise. I wonder if any of his Guildhall contemporaries, the ones lucky enough to have stayed in school for those vital lessons in technique, have enjoyed comparable success with Chekhov?

The production of *Latin!* was, in its own small way, accounted a success. Simon was brilliant, and a glowing review from the great Harold Hobson made me very happy indeed.

Cockney Capers

The weekend after *Latin!* completed its little run I stayed at Richard Armitage's house in Essex. The house was called Stebbing Park and it was a fine old mansion set in many acres of gently rolling countryside. The village of Stebbing is close to Dunmow in an area of Essex that belies the county's unfortunate and unjustified reputation.

Stebbing Park came into its own every summer when Richard held a festival of cricket. David Frost, one of his first clients, would keep wicket, Russell Harty would lie on the boundary ropes and admire the thews of Michael Praed and other handsome young actors, Andrew Lloyd Webber would arrive by helicopter, the controllers of BBC1 and BBC2 would cluster in corners with Bill Cotton and the Director General. It seemed as if Richard could attract every important figure from British screen and stage. Rowan Atkinson, Emma Thompson, Hugh,

Photo call in Richmond Park for BBC version of *The Cellar Tapes*.

The same: ultimately a git with a pipe stuck in his face.

With Emma in 'My Darling' – a Robert and Elizabeth Barrett Browning sketch.

Performing the 'Shakespeare Masterclass' sketch with Hugh.

Hugh in Crete. We rented a villa for the purposes of writing comedy.

A cretin in a Cretan setting.

Hugh prepares to demolish me at backgammon. The retsina was satisfyingly disgusting.

Hugh, Emma, Ben, self, Siobhan and Paul: *There's Nothing to Worry About*, Granada TV, 1982. Oh, but there was . . .

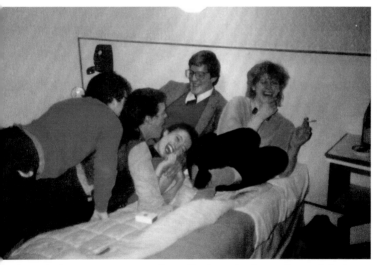

I host a bed party in my room at the Midland Hotel. We seem happy. I think perhaps we were.

An *Alfresco* sketch that a merciful providence has erased from my memory.

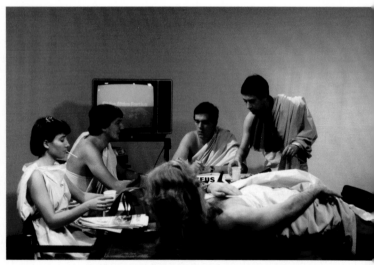

Providence has once again been merciful. *Alfresco*.

The only time in my life I ever wore a donkey jacket. *Alfresco*.

Alfresco, series 2: The Pretend Pub.

A twat in tweed and cravat: inexcusably slappable. *Alfresco.*

Tony Slattery, Tilda Swinton, Howard Goodall and I came every year, as did dozens of other Noel Gay clients, Richard Stilgoe, Chris Barrie, Hinge and Bracket, Dollar, the Cambridge Buskers, Jan Leeming, Manuel and the Music of the Mountains, the King's Singers, Geoff Love – it was a most eccentric mixture.

On this occasion, however, it was just me, Richard and Lorraine Hamilton, the sweet, shy young woman with whom he shared his life and who worked as his assistant. We had Richard's chef-butler, Ken, all to ourselves.

After an excellent dinner on Friday night, as Ken poured coffee in the drawing-room, Richard, greatly to my surprise, started to talk about his father. Reginald Armitage was the son of a pomfret-cake manufacturer in south Yorkshire. He had been educated at the Queen Elizabeth Grammar School in Wakefield, the Royal College of Music and Christ's College, Cambridge. His musicianship won him the place, at an early age, as music director and organist at St Anne's church, Soho. The ragtime, jazz and swing that permeated that part of London must have got into Reginald's blood, for he soon found he had an extraordinary facility with light, bouncy, catchy tunes in the modern manner. To avoid upsetting his worthy Yorkshire parents and the church authorities who employed him, he composed his songs under the pseudonym Noel Gay. An unfortunate name to our ears, but in the late twenties and thirties it suggested that happy, merry world of bright sunbursts that one sees in the surviving suburban front-door frames and wireless-set designs of the period. If there is a song that expresses that image perfectly it is his own 'The Sun Has Got His Hat On'.

Noel Gay the composer became a gigantic success. At one point he had four musicals running in the West End simultaneously, a feat only Andrew Lloyd Webber has matched. His most famous tune, 'The Lambeth Walk', remains the only song ever written about in a *Times* leader. It also, Richard told me, earned Noel Gay an entry in the legendary black book of names of those who would be first up against the wall in the event of a Nazi invasion. Hitler did not take kindly, it was said, to a piece of newsreel that was very popular in British wartime cinemas which looped footage of the Führer saluting a goose-stepping cadre of Stormtroopers to the sound of 'The Lambeth Walk'.

I had known very little of this and was touched that Richard thought I would be interested in the exploits of his famous father.

'Of course, his greatest success,' said Richard, 'was the musical in which "The Lambeth Walk" featured, *Me and My Girl*.'

'Right,' I said, thinking in a rather puzzled way of the Gene Kelly/Judy Garland standard, 'The bells are ringing, for me and my gal . . .' – surely that was an American song?

'Not to be confused, of course,' said Richard, 'with the Edgar Leslie number "For Me and My Gal".'

'No indeed. Of course not,' I said, shocked at the idea that anyone might do such a thing.

'*Me and My Girl*,' said Richard, 'was the most successful British musical of its day. It has only just been overtaken by *Cats*.'

Richard had one of those endearing habits, very common to agents, producers and magnates generally, of describing everything and everyone he knew as being more or less the most important, successful and respected example of its kind anywhere, ever: 'certainly the most significant choreographer of his generation'; 'the top wine-merchant in Britain'; 'indisputably the most admired chef in all Asia' – that sort of thing. It is especially impossible for people like Richard not to have the best doctor in London, the finest dentist in Europe and, favourite of all and endlessly trotted out whenever someone betrays the slightest dorsal twinge, 'the best back man in the world'. I was already wise to this trait in Richard so could not be quite sure how much of what he said about *Me and My Girl* was true and how much a mixture of this signature hyperbole and understandable filial pride. For, in truth, I had not heard of the musical, nor its title song. I knew 'The Lambeth Walk', naturally; it is one of the most famous tunes ever, an *Ohrwurm*, as they say in Germany, an ear worm that once heard burrows its way into your brain and becomes impossible to dislodge. Actually I had always thought it a folk song, based on some ancient tune that had been handed down through the generations. It certainly never occurred to me that it might have been composed in the 1930s by a church organist.

Noel Gay had sent his son Richard to Eton, from where he had followed his father's progress to Cambridge. In 1950 the young Richard Armitage founded Noel Gay Artists, a talent agency that was designed to enhance his father's Noel Gay song publishing and production business by supplying singers to perform Noel Gay material. After six or seven years, as the 'satire boom' got under way, Richard found himself spreading into the new world of graduate comedy and took to trawling Cambridge each year for young comedy blades. He soon had David

Frost on his books, then John Cleese and others. In the late seventies, in a wild, anarchic burst of originality, he looked westwards and from Oxford he took on Rowan Atkinson and Howard Goodall. By 1981 he was back at Cambridge and had scooped up Emma Thompson, Hugh Laurie, Paul Shearer, Tony Slattery and me.

Now in his mid-fifties, Richard found himself more and more often, he told me, looking back to the beginning of it all. This was all very interesting, and I was touched that someone usually so gruff, old-fashioned and unforthcoming about personal matters should favour me with the true story behind his father and the founding of Noel Gay Artists. I alternately nodded and shook my head in a manner that I hoped demonstrated how sensible I was of the honour he had accorded me and then started to make subtle yawn-stifling gestures designed to indicate that I was ready for bath, bed and book.

'So this brings me,' said Richard, choosing to ignore these signs, 'to my proposition.'

'Proposition?'

Richard's hand scrabbled at the flaps of his old leather briefcase. 'Take this.'

He handed me a thick foolscap typescript. Foolscap, for those under forty, was the English stationery paper size that preceded the now ubiquitous European A4 standard.

I examined the sheaf. Rust marks from the binders stained the cover page, but the double-underlined title was plain enough. 'Oh,' I said, '*Me and My Girl*! Is this the original script?'

'As a matter of fact,' said Richard, 'it is the copy that came back from the Lord Chamberlain. There is a French's acting edition, but what you are holding is, as far as I am aware, the version closest to the original text as performed in the Victoria Palace that there is in existence. I'd like you to read it. And then I would like you to consider rewriting it.'

I tottered upstairs and read the foolscap typescript in bed that night. It was almost impossible to understand. The hero was a Cockney costermonger called Bill Snibson who turns out to be the rightful heir to an earldom. That I could make out. Bill arrives at Hareford Hall, the ancestral home, to take up his position and in a series of mysterious scenes is alternately seduced by an aristocratic vamp, taught his family history and soaked for loans by his wastrel connections. Throughout it all runs the thread of his attempts not to lose Sally, his girl of the title. She is an honest Cockney with a noble heart as, *au fond*, is he.

I describe it as almost impossible to understand and I call the scenes 'mysterious' because of the incomprehensible 'bus' that was appended to almost every line of liberally exclamation-marked dialogue.

BILL: What you talking about, girl? (bus)
SALLY: Bill, you know very well! (bus)
BILL: You come here! (bus)

Or:

SIR JOHN: (taking book) Here! Give me that! (bus)
BILL: Oi! (bus)

And so on. Every now and then, throughout the script, there were blue pencil marks in a strong hand that read

No! Absolutely not. Rewrite. Wholly unacceptable! and other furious expressions of crazed disapprobation.

At breakfast the next morning, Richard was keen to know my opinion.

'Well,' I said. 'It is quite a period piece . . .'

'Exactly! Which is why it needs to be updated for an eighties audience.'

'That Cockney rhyming slang stuff seems a bit . . . well, a bit old hat . . .'

There had been a scene of several pages in which Bill laboriously took the family through the principles of rhyming slang.

'Ah, but you see it was *Me and My Girl* that first introduced the British theatre-going middle-classes to rhyming slang,' said Richard. 'Up until then, it had never strayed beyond the East End.'

'Ah, right. I see. But tell me, did the original producer really hate the script?'

'What do you mean?'

'All those comments. "Unacceptable", "cut this" and so on. What were they about?'

'I told you,' said Richard. 'This was the Lord Chamberlain's copy.'

My blank expression revealed the unpardonable depths of my ignorance.

'Until 1968 all plays performed in London had to be licensed by the Lord Chamberlain.'

'Oh, so he was the censor?'

'Effectively. The copy you have shows the cuts he, or rather his office, insisted upon in order to grant *Me and My Girl* its licence in 1937. You will notice they blue-pencil words like "cissy".'

'Literally blue-pencil.'

'Quite so. But what did you make of the script otherwise?'

'Gosh, it's tremendous but . . . well . . . I have to say I don't quite understand what the bus is doing there.'

'The bus?'

'I thought perhaps it was like the old word for to kiss, you know, to buss? But they can't keep kissing each other all the time. And besides there's often a bus in scenes between two male characters.'

Richard looked very puzzled for a moment and then a smile spread across his face. 'Ha!' His laugh always started with a whipcrack 'ha!' and then finished with a noise between his teeth that was half-way between the American 'sheesh!' and an attenuated, falsetto 'siss!'

I had passed the typescript over to Lorraine Hamilton and I now stabbed my finger down at a 'bus'. 'There!' I said. 'Do you understand it?'

'Well,' said Lorraine. 'I'm not quite sure . . . it does seem rather odd. Perhaps . . . mm, no, I can't think . . .'

Richard looked from one to the other of us with mounting amusement. '*Business*, you imbeciles!'

'Sorry?'

'Bus is short for business.'

I am not sure that we looked any the wiser.

'Bill was played by Lupino Lane. Lupino Lane was from a music-hall dynasty. He was the finest physical comedian of his day. A huge part of his success came from the remarkable knockabout routines he devised. His business with the cloak in *Me and My Girl* became one of the most famous sights on the London stage.'

Well, I shan't take you through every twist and turn of

the story of how Noel Gay's musical came to be reworked
for the 1980s. Richard, who acted as producer, secured
Mike Ockrent to direct and as a co-producer he brought
in David Aukin, who ran the Theatre Royal, Leicester,
where the show was to be mounted. If it was a success
there, the plan was to bring it into the West End. There
was talk of Robert Lindsay for the lead role of Bill and
Leslie Ash for Sally. Meanwhile it was up to me to rewrite
the script from that Lord Chamberlain's copy.

'By the way,' Richard had said. 'Do feel free to add any
of my father's other songs that you think might fit.'

The script of a musical is divided into three departments:
music, lyrics and book. The book might be considered
everything that isn't music or lyrics – the dialogue and
story in other words. Nobody goes to a musical because
of the book, they go to straight plays for that. On the
other hand, the book is the spine of a musical. Like a spine
it is only noticed when it goes wrong and like a spine,
the book supports the entire frame and transmits the
signals, messages and impulses that allow the body to feel,
move and express itself. The great composers, Sondheim,
Rogers, Porter and the rest, always insisted – indeed such
insistence is one of the clichés of musical theatre – that
everything starts with the book. The audience does not
sing the book, nobody gasps and claps and delights in the
book, but without it there is nothing. That is certainly
not a complaint, by the way. There are plenty of essential
jobs in the world of which people take little notice, and
writing the book of the musical is amongst the least
arduous and best rewarded of all of them.

In 1983 I didn't know a book from a ball-change or a torch
song. In fact I knew nothing about musicals at all. I was in

my mid-twenties, just a year and a half out of university. I could talk nonsense all day about Shakespeare, Ibsen, Beckett or Tennessee Williams as required. I was sound on the history and heroes of radio and television comedy, which was after all, despite the dismal public reception to *Alfresco*, my profession. I had a good knowledge of cinema, especially Warner Brothers films of the thirties and forties and British cinema of the forties and fifties. My knowledge of the classical musical and opera repertoire was fair, and I knew the songbooks of Porter, Kern and Gershwin very well. But few of the musicals for which most of those songs were written had I ever seen. The secret truth was that I rather looked down on the whole genre. I made exceptions for *Cabaret*, *My Fair Lady*, *West Side Story* and *Guys and Dolls*, which I knew as films and records and rated highly. *Singin' in the Rain*, *Mary Poppins*, *Oliver!* and *The Sound of Music* I knew and valued only as films and . . . well, that was about it, give or take the occasional Sunday-afternoon screening of a Fred Astaire or Gene Kelly classic on BBC2. *Cats* had been running in the West End for a year and a half, but I hadn't seen it. Still haven't. Must get round to it. Ditto *Les Misérables*, *The Phantom of the Opera* and *Miss Saigon* and all the others that have come and gone and come back again since. I don't doubt that the loss is mine.

The director, Mike Ockrent, who had made his name with the presentation of new theatre writing mostly in the fringe venues of England and Scotland, knew the world of musicals even less well than I did. But we soon discovered, as we worked on the script of *Me and My Girl*, that we had here a project that owed nothing to Broadway and Hollywood and everything to music hall. Whether the revival succeeded or failed would depend on how ready a modern audience might be for the slapstick, silliness and cheeky bounce that the late music-hall style embodied.

As I went from draft to draft, David Aukin provided me with an invaluable lesson. For many years he had presided over the Hampstead Theatre, where he had nurtured Mike Leigh's legendary *Abigail's Party* as well as new plays by Dennis Potter, Michael Frayn, Harold Pinter and many others. When he saw my first draft, fresh from the daisy-wheel printer, he smiled.

'Your job is to try and do yourself out of a job. The shorter the distance between musical numbers, the better.'

'There's just too much dialogue, isn't there?' I said.

'Far too much.'

In the end I cut and cut and cut. I read, on somebody's recommendation, *The Street Where I Live*, Alan Jay Lerner's superb memoir of a Broadway lyricist and book writer's life and work. When it is time for an emotional or narrative transformation in the action of a musical, Lerner maintained, that moment should be expressed not in spoken words, but in song or in dance, otherwise why are you creating a musical show in the first place and not a play? In a good musical the action doesn't stop for a song – the songs *are* the action. I read this manifestly sound prescription, looked at my script thus far and realized that I had written nothing but a stop-start drama in which everything important happened in scenes of spoken dialogue that were from time to time halted for song and dance numbers. Douglas Furber and Arthur Rose, who had written the original book and lyrics, came from an era that preceded the Lerner manifesto. The stagecraft of the time allowed for chorus lines to shuffle on in front of a front-cloth while the scene was shifted behind. Modern theatre demanded visible changes that used trucking and flying and floating and other magical machine-driven techniques. Here Mike Ockrent was fantastically encouraging. He had read physics at university, briefly been an inventor and had a fine engineering mind.

'Write the most extravagant and outrageous scene changes you can think of,' he said. 'We'll make them work. But don't write to save money. Between us the production designer and I will make it happen.'

For the next draft then, I went crazy. The show opened with a number called 'A Weekend at Hareford'. I tweaked the lyrics a little and wrote stage directions that were, on the face of it, absurd. I described country-house weekenders singing the song in open chauffeur-driven cars as they made their way out of London, into the countryside, through the gates of Hareford Hall and up to the massive frontage, which would revolve and transform into an interior which the guests would enter to be greeted by the household servants. It was easy enough for me to write; let Martin Johns the designer and Mike Ockrent make of that what they would.

I cut dialogue as drastically as I could. The idea was to jump, as David Aukin had suggested, from musical number to musical number with as little dialogue as possible, but also to treat certain comic scenes – like the Lupino Lane cloak business to which Richard had alluded, as well as a seduction scene involving cushions and a sofa – as kinds of numbers in their own right. I also added two other well-known Noel Gay songs, 'The Sun Has Got His Hat On' and 'Leaning On a Lamp-post'.

Mike visited me in Chichester to work through his notes

on this draft. He relished every over-ambitious, absurd
and impossible demand I had made on his ingenuity.

'More,' he said. 'Let's go even further!'

But why, you will be wanting to know, was I in
Chichester?

Chichester 1

Early in 1982 Richard Armitage took me and Hugh to
L'Escargot in Greek Street for lunch.

'So that I get an idea of how best to shape your
destinies,' he said, 'each of you should now tell me whose
careers you most admire and whom you would most want
to emulate.'

Hugh wondered if there was someone between Peter
Ustinov and Clint Eastwood. Maybe with a hint of Mick
Jagger thrown in.

Richard nodded, made a note in his black leather
Smythson notebook and turned to me.

'Alan Bennett,' I said. 'Definitely Alan Bennett.'

I was too young to have seen Bennett's television
comedy *On The Margin*, the tapes of which the BBC had
shamefully wiped within weeks of transmission, as was
the practice in those days, but I had an audio recording of
highlights, which I knew off by heart, as I did the sermon
in *Beyond the Fringe* and his cottaging sketch from *The Secret
Policeman's Other Ball*. I had read but never seen his play
Habeas Corpus and had once owned, then subsequently
lost, a cassette tape of *Forty Years On*, in which he played
a schoolmaster called Tempest. Those were enough for
me to think him a hero. *Talking Heads*, *A Private Function*,

An Englishman Abroad, *The Madness of George III* and *The History Boys* all lay many years in the future.

'Alan Bennett, eh?'

Was it paranoia, or did I sense that Richard found my answer disappointing? Peter Cook and John Cleese were greater comedy stars with their almost rock and roll status and charisma, but Alan Bennett's miniaturism, his frailty combined with his verbal touch and literary, almost academic, frames of reference appealed to me more as a role model. History has, of course, shown that his kind of career path was as unattainable for me as Cook's and Cleese's, but a man's reach should exceed his grasp, or what's a heaven for?

A year after this lunch, round about the time *Gossip* was getting into financial trouble and I was working on the first drafts of *Me and My Girl* in between sweaty bouts of not coming up with *Alfresco 2* material with Hugh, Richard called me up.

'Ha!' he said. 'You're going to like this. Be at the Garrick Theatre on Thursday afternoon at half past three to audition for Patrick Garland and John Gale. Prepare the part of Tempest in *Forty Years On*.'

'W-w-w-w . . . ?'

'It's for the Chichester Festival next April.'

'P-p-p-p . . .'

'Good luck.'

Alan Bennett's very own part. And to be directed by the same man who directed the original production in nineteen sixty-whenever it was. I leapt for the bookshelf. I knew I had a copy somewhere, but it must have been in a box in my parents' house in Norfolk or in that indeterminate place where lost teenage property goes, all those favourite records, wall-posters and pullovers that you never see again. I streaked over to John Sandoe's, where the assistant was quite sure they had a copy if only he could lay his hands on it, now just let him think . . . I almost screamed with impatience as he hunted with maddening deliberation and cheerfulness.

'Here we are. Our only copy. A little grubby I'm afraid – you can have it for a pound.'

I spent the next few hours reacquainting myself with this, Alan Bennett's first full-length dramatic work. *Forty Years On* is set in a fictional school called Albion House, which is mounting its annual school play, this year a specially devised pageant performed by staff and boys called 'Speak for England, Arthur'. This play-within-a-play takes a family through the World Wars by way of a dazzling series of sketches, monologues and parodies that manage to combine, in that uniquely Bennett way, the joyously comic with the mournfully elegiac. The original production, which starred John Gielgud as the headmaster, Paul Eddington as the senior master and Alan Bennett as the drippy junior master Tempest, was a huge success from the very beginning. The school's name, Albion House, alerted the audience to the possibility, never overstretched, that it might perhaps stand as a symbol of England itself.

I learned off by heart Tempest's 'Confirmation Class', in which he attempts to give a lesson on the facts of life.

TEMPEST: Those are called your private parts, Foster. And if anyone ever touches them, you are to say, 'Those are my private parts and you're not to touch them.'

FOSTER: Those are my private parts and you are not to touch them.

TEMPEST: It doesn't apply to me, Foster! It doesn't apply to me!

I also committed to memory a monologue in which Tempest plays a rather precious and faded literary figure recalling the great days of Bloomsbury.

With these and other scenes safely in my head I made my way by bus and Tube to the Garrick Theatre in the Charing Cross Road. I found the stage door, where I was greeted by a friendly young man who led me backstage to a little green room.

'My name's Michael,' he said. 'You're a *little* early, so perhaps you wouldn't mind waiting here while we just see some other people?'

I looked at my watch and saw that it was ten to three. Perhaps the appropriateness of the number of minutes early I was could be read as a good omen.

Forty minutes on I walked nervously on to the stage, a hand shading my eyes as I strained to see down into the auditorium.

'Hello,' said a neat, friendly and delicately precise voice, 'I am Patrick, and this is John Gale, who runs the Chichester Festival Theatre.'

'Hello,' boomed a rich baritone from the dark.

'And this,' continued Patrick, 'is Alan Bennett.'

The high tenor song of a cheery and attenuated Yorkshire 'Hello' floated up from the stalls and into my unbelieving ears. *Alan Bennett?* Here! At the audition! Every organ in my body screamed. A hammering came into my ears, and my knees turned to water. *Alan Bennett?*

I remember not one minute or second of the half hour

that followed. I know I must have recited or read some scenes and I do recall stumbling through the London streets in an agony of despair and disappointment, so I must have said goodbye and left the theatre in some manner or other.

Richard Armitage called me up at the flat that evening. 'How did it go, m'dear?'

'Oh Richard it was *awful*, I was terrible. Appalling. Monstrous. Unspeakable. *Alan Bennett was there!* In the theatre.'

'I don't doubt it. Is that a bad thing?'

'Well, it never *occurred* to me he'd be present. Never. I was tongue-tied, struck dumb. So nervous I could barely speak. Oh God, I was *dreadful*.'

'I'm sure you can't have been as bad as all that . . .' He made the series of soothing and clucking noises that agents make to calm hysterical clients. They failed to console me.

The next day Lorraine rang. 'Darling, could you go to the Garrick again at three o'clock for a recall?'

'A recall?'

'It means they want to see and hear you again.'

'You mean they haven't ruled me out?'

I arrived at the Garrick bang on the hour determined at least to try to override my nerves. Michael greeted me like an old friend and led me straight through to the stage. The house lights were up, and I looked out and could clearly see Patrick Garland and John Gale in the stalls but this time no Alan Bennett. A great wave of relief swept over me.

'Hello again!' Patrick called cheerily. 'We were wondering if we might hear the Bloomsbury monologue this time?'

I sat and delivered.

'Thank you!' said Patrick. 'Thank you . . . I think . . .' He conferred with John Gale, nodded his head and looked down as if seeking inspiration from the floor. From where I stood he seemed to be whispering to the carpet. 'Well, yes . . .' he murmured. 'I think so too.' He looked up towards me with a smile and said in a louder voice. 'Stephen, John and I would be very pleased to ask you to play the part of Tempest for our production. Would you like to do that?'

'Would I? Oh, indeed I would!' I said. 'Thank you. Thank you so very, very much.'

'That's excellent news,' said Patrick. 'We're delighted. Aren't we?' he added, to the carpet.

There was a sort of scuffling and scrabbling, and a figure rose from behind the seats where it had been crouching out of sight. The long, lean form of Alan Bennett unfolded itself with an apologetic cough. 'Oh, yes,' he said, brushing dust from the knees of his grey flannel trousers, 'quite delighted.'

Patrick noted my bewilderment. 'Your agent was kind enough to mention to us that Alan's presence had made you a little nervous, so this time round he thought it might be best to conceal himself.'

Such consideration from a hero was almost more than I could bear. Naturally, being an arse, I expressed my gratitude by not managing to express any gratitude at all. To this day I do not think I have ever properly thanked Alan for his grace and sweetness that afternoon.

Crises of Confidence

Alan Bennett has a huge advantage over most of us in that his shyness is known about and expected; indeed it is one of the qualities most admired in him. It proves his authenticity, modesty and the classy distance he naturally keeps from that creepy media gang of loud, confident, shallow and self-congratulatory wankers to which I cannot but help belong and which the rest of society so rightly despises. Nobody seems to expect me to be shy, or believes me when I say that I am. I cannot blame them. I seem to move with such ease through the world. I was reminded of this only yesterday afternoon. I was a guest on the CBS programme *The Late Late Show with Craig Ferguson*. Craig is the Scottish comedian who has now become, in the opinion of many, myself included, the best talk show host in America. He told me, as he began the interview, that back in the eighties, when he had been a regular on the British comedy circuit, he had always regarded me as almost unnaturally calm, sorted and in control, to the extent that he was in a kind of angry awe of me. I ought to be used to being told that, but yet again it brought me up short. Never, at any point in my life, can I remember feeling that I was any part of assured, controlled or at ease. The longer I live the more clearly one truth stands out. People will rarely modify their preferred view of a person, no matter what the evidence might suggest. I am English. Tweedy. Pukka. Confident. Establishment. Self-assured. In charge. That is how people like to see me, be the truth never so at variance. It may be the case that I am a Jewish mongrel with an addictive self-destructive streak that it has taken me years to master. It may be the case that my afflictions of mood and temperament cause me to be occasionally suicidal in outlook and can frequently leave me in despair and eaten up with self-hatred and self-disgust. It may be the case that I am chronically overmastered by a sense of failure, underachievement and a terrible knowledge that I have betrayed, abused or neglected the talents that nature bestowed upon me. It may be the case that I doubt I will ever have the capacity to be happy. It may be the case that I fear for my sanity, my moral centre and my very future. All these cases may be protested, and I can assert their truth as often as I like, but the repetition will not alter my 'image' by one pixel. It is the same image I had before I was a known public figure. The image that caused a delegation of college first-year contemporaries to visit me in my rooms and demand to know my 'secret'. The image that satisfies and impresses some, enrages others and no doubt bores, provokes or irritates many more. I would be a tragic figure indeed if I had not learnt to live with that persona by now. Like many masks this smiling, placid one has become so tight a fit that it might be said to have rewritten the features of whatever true face once screamed behind it, were it not that it is just a mask and that the feelings underneath are as they always were.

What I want to say about all this wailing is not that I expect your pity or your understanding (although I wouldn't throw either of them out of bed), but that perhaps I am the one actually offering pity and understanding here. For I have to believe that all the feelings I have described are not unique to me but common to us all. The sense of failure, the fear of eternal unhappiness, the insecurity, misery, self-disgust and the awful awareness of underachievement that I have described. Are you not prey to all those things also? I do hope so. I would feel the most conspicuous oddity otherwise. I grant that my moments of 'suicidal ideation' and swings of mood may be more extreme and pathological than most have to endure, but otherwise, I am surely describing nothing more than the fears, dreads and neuroses we all share? No? More or less? *Mutatis mutandis*? All things being equal? Oh, please say yes.

This is a problem many writers and comedians face: we possess the primary arrogance that persuades us that our insights, fixations and habits are for the most part shared characteristics that we alone have the boldness, insight and openness of mind to expose and name: we are privileged thereby, or so we congratulate ourselves, to be spokesmen for humanity. When a stand-up comic describes nose-picking or peeing in the shower or whatever it might be we can interpret our laughter as a 'me too' release which itself triggers more laughter: we laugh again because our initial laughter and that of the person sitting next to us in the audience proves our complicity and shared guilt. This much is obvious and a truism of observational comedy. On top of it there can also be laid, of course, that conscious game comics play in which they shuttle between those common, shared anxieties and ones that are very particular to them. And here I suppose we laugh at how *different* we are. How similar, but different. How the comic is living a more extreme life of neurosis and angst on our behalf. A kind of 'thank God I'm not *that* weird' laughter is the result. When a comic or a writer has established their credentials by revealing how much of what they do or feel is something we also do or feel, they can then go further and reveal depths of activity or feeling that we may not share, that might revolt us or that perhaps we *do* share but would much rather not have dragged up into the light. And of course, comics, being what they are, appreciate that point.

It is common enough to hear this kind of routine: 'You know, ladies and gentlemen, you know when you're sat watching television and you stick your finger up your arse and wiggle it about? . . . No? Oh, right. It must be just me then. Sorry about that. Oops. Moving on . . .' Well, with an average stand-up comic talking about physical things like peeing in the shower and nose- or arse-picking it is easy enough to see the distinction between what is communal and what is individual. But those are discrete identifiable actions of which one is either 'guilty' or not. Some people pee in the shower, others do not. I have to confess that I do. I try to be good and refrain from doing so in somebody else's shower, but otherwise I am guiltless about what seems to me to be a logical, reasonable and hygienically unexceptionable act. I also pick my nose. I will stop the confession right there for fear of embarrassing you or myself further. You can decide whether to put the book down now and say to the vacant air: 'I too pick my nose and pee in the shower.' Plenty of people do neither. They are likely, I hope, to forgive those of us who are less fastidious in our habits. But in either case whether or not they do is not susceptible to interpretation. But *feelings* . . . I may know whether or not I pick my nose but do I really know whether or not I feel a failure? I may be aware that I often feel bleak and unhappy or filled with nameless dread, but am I right to interpret these feelings as a sense of moral deficiency or personal inadequacy or any such thing? The root of the feeling may after all be a hormonal imbalance, heartburn, a triggered unconscious memory, too little sunlight, a bad dream, anything. As with colour sense or pain sensitivity we can never know whether any of our perceptions and sensations are the same as others'. So it may very well be that I am just a great big cissy and that my miseries and worries are nothing compared to yours. Or perhaps I am the bravest man on the planet and that, if any of you were to experience a tenth of the sorrows I daily endure, you would scream in agony. But just as we can all agree on what is red, even if we will never know if we each see it in the same way, so we can all agree – can't we? – that no matter how confident we may appear to others, inside we are all sobbing, scared and uncertain for much of the time. Or perhaps it's just me.

Oh God, perhaps it really *is* just me.

Actually it doesn't really matter, when you come to think of it. If it is just me, then you are reading the story of some weird freak. You are free to treat this book like science fiction, fantasy or exotic travel literature. Are there really men like Stephen Fry on this planet? Goodness, how alien some people are. And if I am *not* alone, then neither are you, and hand in hand we can marvel together at the strangeness of the human condition.

Celebrity

Aside from *University Challenge*, the BBC's transmission of *The Cellar Tapes* was the first time I had appeared on national television. I don't count *There's Nothing to Worry About*, which was inflicted only upon viewers in the north-west ITV region.

The morning after *The Cellar Tapes* was aired on BBC2 I went for a walk along the King's Road. How ought I to treat those who approached me? I switched on a sweet gentle smile and practised a kind of 'Who? . . . *me*?' gesture that involved looking behind me and then pointing with questioning disbelief at my own undeserving chest. I made sure, before setting out, that there were pens in my pocket as well as some artfully random scraps of paper for autographs. Would I write 'Yours sincerely' or 'With best wishes'? I decided that I should try each a few times and see which looked better.

The first people I passed as I made my way up Blacklands Terrace were an elderly couple who paid me no attention. Foreigners possibly, or the kind of Chelsea-ites who thought it smart not to have a television. A young woman came towards me with a West Highland terrier on a lead. I added an extra 10 per cent of soupy modesty to my sweet gentle smile and awaited her gasps and shrieks. She and the terrier passed right by without a flicker of recognition. How very strange. I turned left at the King's Road and walked past the Peter Jones department store and twice around Sloane Square. Not one person stopped me, shot me a sideways glance of admiring recognition or favoured me with a single puzzled stare that told me that they knew the face but couldn't quite place it. There was simply no reaction from anyone anywhere. I went into W. H. Smith's and hung around the periodicals section, close to the piles of listings magazines. To pick up a *Radio Times* people had to ask me to step aside; obviously and by definition these persons must have been television watchers, but my features, by now set into a wild, despairing grin, meant nothing to them. This was most strange. Television, everybody in the world knew, conferred instant fame. One morning you do the weather on BBC1, the next you are besieged at the supermarket checkout queue. Instead I had woken up to find myself anonymous. I was still nothing more than another face in the London crowd. Maybe almost no one had watched the

Footlights show? Or maybe millions had, but I possessed one of those bland, forgettable faces that meant I was doomed never to be recognized. Surely this was unlikely? I had told my face a lot of tough and unforgiving truths in the past, but I had never accused it of being bland or forgettable.

I pulled a compensatory *BBC Micro* magazine from the shelf and left. As I was trailing disappointedly back to the flat I heard a voice behind me.

'Excuse me, excuse me!'

I turned to see an excited young girl. At last. 'Yes?'

'You forgot your change.'

Here are the first lines of *Love's Labour's Lost*:

> Let fame, that all hunt after in their lives,
> Live register'd upon our brazen tombs,
> And then grace us in the disgrace of death.

That is the King of Navarre's opening speech, the one Hugh had such trouble with in the 1981 Marlowe Society production. It is a fine sentiment, but nothing could run more counter to the way the world thinks today. It certainly seems that all still hunt after fame, but how many are content for it to come only in the form of a tombstone inscription? They want it now. And that is how I wanted it too. Ever since I can remember I had dreamt of being famous. I know how embarrassing an admission this is. I could attempt to dress it up in finer words, imputing and inferring intricate psychological grounds, implicating and adducing complex developmental causations that elevated the condition into a syndrome, but there is no point dressing it up in fine linen. From the first moment I

was aware of such a class of person existing, I had wanted
to be a celebrity. We are forever telling ourselves that we
live in a celebrity-obsessed culture; many hands are daily
wrung at the supremacy of appearance over achievement,
status over substance and image over industry. To *desire*
fame argues a shallow and delusional outlook. This much
we all know. But if we clever ones can see so clearly that
fame is a snare and a delusion, we can also see just as clearly
that as each year passes a greater and greater proportion of
the western world's youth is becoming entramelled in that
snare and dazzled by that delusion.

We have in our minds a dreadful picture of the
thousands who audition so pitifully for television talent
shows and whose heads seem always to be buried in garish
celebrity magazines. We feel sorrow and contempt for the
narrow dimensions of their lives. We excoriate a society
that is all surface and image. Teenaged girls in particular,
we suggest, are slaves to body-image and fashion fantasies,
they are junkies on the fame drug. How can our culture
be so broken and so sick, we wonder, as to raise up as
objects of veneration a raft of talentless nobodies who
offer no moral, spiritual or intellectual sustenance and
no discernible gifts beyond over-hygienic eroticism and
unthreatening photogeneity?

I would offer the usual counters to that. Firstly, the
phenomenon simply is not as new as everyone thinks it
is. That there are more outlets, pipelines, conduits and
means of transmitting and receiving news and images is
obvious, but read any novel published in the early part of
the twentieth century and you will find female uneducated
characters who spend their spare moments dreaming of
movie stars, tennis-players, explorers, racing-drivers and

barnstorming aviators. You'll find these dreamy shop-
girls and head-in-the-clouds housemaids in Evelyn
Waugh, Agatha Christie, P. G. Wodehouse and every
genre in between. The propensity to worship idols is not
new. Nor is the wrathful contempt of those who believe
that they alone understand the difference between false
gods and true. In the story of the Ten Commandments I
was always on the side of Aaron. I liked his golden calf.
Biblical colour plates for children showed it garlanded
with flowers, revelling idolaters dancing happily around
it, clashing cymbals and embracing each other with
wild, abandoned joy. The music and the hugs were
clinching proof (especially the cymbals) in the minds
of the Victorian illustrators that Aaron's followers were
debauched, degenerate, decadent and doomed to eternal
damnation. With the party in full swing, Moses returns
with those fatuous tablets tucked under his arm, dashes
them petulantly to the ground, melts the golden calf and
grinds it to powder, which he mixes into a drink that
he forces all the Israelites to swallow. Next, being such
a holy man of God, he slays 3,000 men before hauling
his vengeful arse back up Mount Sinai to get a second
batch of commandments. I think we can celebrate
the fact that we now live in a culture, flawed or not,
that instantly sees that, while Aaron may be a weak
voluptuary, his brother is a dangerous fanatic. The gilt
bull beats the guilty bullshit any way you choose to
look at it. We humans are naturally disposed to worship
gods and heroes, to build our pantheons and valhallas. I
would rather see that impulse directed into the adoration
of daft singers, thicko footballers and air-headed screen
actors than into the veneration of dogmatic zealots,

fanatical preachers, militant politicians and rabid cultural commentators.

Secondly, is it not a rule in life that no one is quite as stupid as we would like them to be? Spokesmen across the political divide from us are smarter than we would have them, mad mullahs and crazy nationalists are nothing like as dumb as we would wish. Film producers, shock jocks, insurgents, journalists, American military – all kinds of people we might reasonably expect to write off as mentally negligible have cunning, insight and intellect well beyond what is comfortable for us. This inconvenient truth extends to those on whom we lavish our patronizing pity too. If the social-networking services of the digital age teach us anything it is that only a fool would underestimate the intelligence, intuition and cognitive skills of the 'masses'. I am talking about more than the 'wisdom of crowds' here. If you look beyond sillinesses like the puzzling inability of the majority to distinguish between *your* and *you're*, *its* and *it's* and *there*, *they're* and *their* (all of which distinctions have nothing to do with language, only with grammar and orthographical convention: after all logic and consistency would suggest the insertion of a genitival apostrophe in the pronominal possessive *its*, but convention has decided, perhaps to avoid confusion with the elided *it is*, to dispense with one), if, as I say, you look beyond such pernickety pedantries, you will see that it is possible to be a fan of reality TV, talent shows and bubblegum pop and still have a brain. You will also see that a great many people know perfectly well how silly and camp and trivial their fandom is. They do not check in their minds when they enter a fan site. Judgement is not necessarily fled to brutish beasts, and men have not quite lost their reason. Which is all a way of questioning whether pop-culture hero worship is really so psychically damaging, so erosive of the cognitive faculties, so corrupting of the soul of mankind as we are so often told.

Thirdly, look at the kind of people who most object to the childishness and cheapness of celebrity culture. Does one really want to side with such apoplectic and bombastic bores? I should know, I often catch myself being one, and it isn't pretty. I will defend the absolute value of Mozart over Miley Cyrus, of course I will, but we should be wary of false dichotomies. You do not have to choose between one or the other. You can have both. The human cultural jungle should be as varied and plural as the Amazonian rainforest. We are all richer for biodiversity. We may decide that a puma is worth more to us than a caterpillar, but surely we can agree that the habitat is all the better for being able to sustain each. Monocultures are uninhabitably dull and end as deserts.

Against all that it might be said that the quarrel is not with harmless idolatry. The problem, some would argue, is not that everybody worships celebrity, but they *want it for themselves*. Online user-generated content and the rise of the talent show and reality TV have bred a generation for whom it is not enough to flick through fan magazines, they want their own shot at stardom. They want, moreover, to go straight to fame and fortune, short-circuiting tedious considerations like hard work and talent. Well, we all know how satisfying it is to recite the shortcomings and hollowness of others – especially those who have money and recognition where we have none. It is certainly more pleasurable than inspecting our own shortcomings. I dare say we do live in a cheap age, an age where the things that should have value are little prized and things that are empty of worth are too highly rated. But who on earth could think for a second that this is new to our race? Anyone familiar with Aristophanes, Martial, Catullus, Shakespeare, Jonson, Dryden, Johnson, Pope, Swift . . . You get the point. It has *always* been the case, since humans could first record their thoughts, that the 'wrong people' have been seen to have arrived at the highest positions. The emperors, kings, aristocrats, ruling classes and gentry, the arrivistes, parvenus and nouveaux riches, the financiers, merchant princes and industrialists, the artists, designers, literati and cultural elite, the actors, sportsmen, television stars, pop singers and presenters, they have all been unfairly elevated to positions they do not deserve. 'In a just and properly ordered world,' the angry ones wail, '*I* should be up there too, but I am too proud to say so, so I shall carp and snipe and rant with indignation and show my contempt for the whole boiling. But deep inside I want to be recognized. I just want to count.'

I was like that all through my teenage years and early twenties. Desperate to be famous but very, very ready, if I didn't make it, to vent my scorn on those who did. I contend that people like me who burn for fame and recognition are much rarer than the prevailing view would have us believe. I take my brother Roger and his family as my touchstone for all that is sane, sound and decent. They are as modern and connected to the world as anyone else I know. I recall, and I seem to be able to picture it in pin-sharp high-def widescreen 3D detail, an evening at the pantomime in Norwich when I was seven and Roger was nine. Buttons made his entrance and asked if there were any boys and girls out there who would like to join him up on stage. Roger dropped down in his seat trying his hardest to look invisible. The idea of being up there in the lights in front of a staring audience horrified him. I meanwhile was leaping up and down thrusting my hand into the air desperate, absolutely desperate to be picked. Two boys, eighteen months apart in age, bred in the same conditions and by the same parents. There are many more Rogers in the world, praise be, than Stephens.

Maybe the childish desire for attention I felt then is all of a piece with my childish desire for sweet things. The desire to be famous is infantile, and humanity has never lived in an age when infantilism was more sanctioned and encouraged than now. Infantile foods in the form of crisps, chips, sweet fizzy drinks and pappy burgers or hot dogs smothered in sugary sauce are considered mainstream nutrition for millions of adults. Intoxicating drinks disguised as milkshakes and soda pops exist for those whose taste buds haven't grown up enough to enjoy the taste of alcohol. As in food so in the wider culture. Anything astringent, savoury, sharp, complex, ambiguous or difficult is ignored in favour of the colourful, the sweet, the hollow and the simple. I know that fame to me, when I was a child, was much like candy-floss. It looked magical, it was huge and dramatic and attention-grabbing. It is tempting to write here and now that, like candy-floss, fame turned out to be little more than air on a stick and that the small part of it that has substance was cloying, sick-making and corrosive to me, but I shall keep such thoughts, if I truly have them, for later. I am, thus far in my story, not famous at all and I cannot yet tell what fame is like – only that it is a condition I long for.

In fact, I think few people are really obsessed with being famous in the way that I was. Most recoil at the thought, squirming down in their seats like my brother at the very idea of public exposure. They might consider from time to time what fame would be like and conduct thought experiments in which they feature on a red carpet being lit by flashbulbs, but that is no more than the normal fantasy of opening the batting for England or volleying the championship point at Wimbledon. For the most part, most people are mostly for a quiet life out of the public eye and have a mostly sane understanding of how peculiar fame must be. They are sensible enough not to judge all celebrities as alike and civil enough not to despise people because they have committed the crime of being a pop singer, a golfer or a politician. Most people are tolerant, wise, kind and thoughtful. Most of the time. People like me eaten up with ambition, simmering with resentment, white-hot with neediness at one moment and sullen with frustration and disappointment the next, we are the ones who obsess about fame and status, and it gives us nothing but dissatisfaction, vexation and horrible doses of heavy angst.

All this is embarrassing for me to admit. Those in my line do not own up to such vulgar, cheesy and undignified yearnings. It is all about the *work*. If your work happens, unlike insurance, accountancy or teaching, to bring celebrity in its train, or riches, then so be it. You aim for the game bird of accomplishment; fame and fortune just happen to be the feathers it flies with. Yeah, right. We know these worthy precepts, I echo and endorse them. But the needy child that hid within the tweedy man screamed to be fed and the needy child, as always, wanted what was instantly satisfying and instantly rewarding, no matter how shallow and devious that might make him. Shallow and devious is what I was (and probably always will be), and if you have not yet understood how profoundly shallow and how straightforwardly devious I am, then I cannot have been doing my job right.

Work was coming in thick and fast. The musical, the play, the film script and a thick miscellany of writing and radio assignments to which we might come in a moment. There is no doubt that amongst magazine and newspaper editors, radio, film and TV producers, directors, commissioners and casting agents I was a coming man, a young shaver useful for all kinds of odds and ends. But I was not famous. A few invitations to film premieres and first nights began to trickle in, but I found that I could walk the red carpet entirely unmolested. I remember going to some event with Rowan Atkinson, the press night of a new play, I think. To hear his name shouted out by photographers and see the crowd of fans pressing up against the crash barriers caused the most intense excitement in me, combined with a sick flood of fury and resentment that no one, not one single person, recognized *me* or wanted *my* picture. Oh, Stephen. I have clicked on and selected that sentence, deleted it, restored it, deleted it and restored it again. A large part of me would rather not have you know that I am so futile, fatuous and feeble-minded, but an even larger part recognizes that this is our bargain. I cannot speak for others or presume to drag out their entrails for public inspection, but I can speak for (and against) myself. Maybe I was an advance guard for a new kind of Briton: fanatical about fame, addictive, superficial, gadget-obsessed and determinedly infantile. Maybe, to put a kinder construction on it, I was living proof that you could want to be famous *and* want to do the work, you could relish the red carpet *and* relish lucubrating into the early hours, cranking out articles, scripts, sketches and scenarios with a genuine sense of pleasure and fulfilment.

Commercials, Covent Garden, Compact Discs, Cappuccinos and Croissants

On top of the major projects in film and television there tumbled in other requests for work of all kinds. Lo Hamilton at Noel Gay Artists fielded these and passed them on. I think I understood that I had the option to refuse, to turn down, to inquire further, but I cannot recall that I ever did. When I look back at this time it seems to be a paradise of variety without pressure and novelty without nerves. Everything was fantastically new, exciting, flattering and appealing.

Sometimes together and sometimes apart, Hugh and I found ourselves inside the world of the commercial voiceover. Neither of us yet had the kind of vocal heft that afforded us the chance to do the really sexy part of the work, the endline – that final slogan which was most usually the province of either hard-smoking and -drinking fifty-year-olds like the legendary Bill Mitchell, whose vocal chords had the deep, authoritative resonance that carried the advertiser's message home, or of vocal magicians like Martin Jarvis, Ray Brooks, Enn Reitel and Michael Jayston, who were in such heavy demand that they carried little pagers clipped to their belts so that their agents could push them from job to job at the shortest notice. I remember David Jason, another very busy and talented voice artist, showing me how they worked. They did no more than beep, which was a signal to phone the agent, but I was hugely impressed. One day, I told myself, I would own such an object and I would treasure it always. Somewhere I have a drawer filled with at least a dozen old pagers in assorted stylings and colourways. None of them is treasured; they were barely used at all.

At our level Hugh and I were required usually to do silly comedy characters for radio ads, a huge new booming industry that was taking advantage of the proliferation of independent radio stations that were popping up all over Britain throughout the early eighties as a result of 'second tranche' franchise contracts. It is very beguiling to look back at a period of time and imagine that one was happy then, but I really believe that we were. Life in the glass booth was simple but presented pleasing challenges. Often an engineer or producer would press the talk-back button and say something like, 'Yeah, that was two seconds over. Can you do it again, shaving off three seconds, but don't go any quicker.' That kind of apparently absurd request starts to make sense after a while and Hugh and I both took great pride in our ability to make good on them. An internal clock starts to build itself in the brain so that within a short time we were both able to say, 'That was bang on, wasn't it? Maybe half a second under?' or 'Damn, at least thirty-five, that one, we'll go again . . .' and be proved right when the engineer played it back with a stopwatch. A trivial skill, the proud acquisition of which some might think a waste of an elite and expensive education, but I know, as I have said, that we were happy. How do I know? Well, we said so. We actually dared to say it.

In those days the studios we found ourselves in most often were those of Angell Sound in Covent Garden, opposite the stage door of the Royal Opera House. Hugh and I would emerge from a session, blink in the bright sunshine of the day, say 'Shirt' and walk south-west along Floral Street, crossing James Street until we reached Paul Smith's. At that time this was the great designer's sole London presence. Perhaps he had a shop in his native Nottingham, but the Floral Street branch was certainly the only one in London. Like David Jason he is now a knight, but back then Paul Smith was just beginning to achieve a name as the designer of choice for men who were shortly to be dubbed 'yuppie'. His reputation, unlike that of the yuppie, has emerged unscathed from such a calamitous calumny. In the early to mid-eighties the first noises of what was to be the post-Big-Bang, newly enriched, newly confident professional classes were beginning to be heard as they clamoured for stylish socks, shirts, croissants, frothy coffee and – God help us all – conspicuous braces. I suppose Hugh and I fell into a subset of this new category.

One morning as we emerged from Angell's I distinctly remember us having a conversation that went something like this:

'Bloody hell, this is the life.'

'We are so fucking lucky.'

'Twenty minutes in a studio, not a minute more.'

'No rope was older and no money . . . moneyer.'

'We should buy a shirt to celebrate.'

'We should *always* buy a shirt to celebrate.'

'And then maybe a CD or two.'

'And then *definitely* a CD or two.'

'Perhaps followed by a coffee and a croissant.'

'*Certainly* followed by a coffee and a croissant.'

'You know, I bet we will look back on these as the best days of our lives.'

'When we're old, fat, bitter and unhappy alcoholics, we will remember when we would saunter into a voiceover studio, saunter out again and buy a shirt and a CD and go to a café and have a croissant and a cappuccino.'

We have so far missed becoming alcoholics, and Hugh has never been fat. I am not sure if we are bitter, but we are certainly old-ish, and I think each of us would admit that the realization that we were unlikely to be as happy again was accurate. We really can look back and see those days as perfect. Intensely acute moments of love and parenthood and achievement might, and did, come to one or other of us at different times, but never again would we experience such a period of chronic content. We wanted nothing, we were slowly earning reputations and money without being crushed by celebrity and riches. Life was good. The most unusual aspect of it is that we knew it at the time. If you tell a schoolchild that they are currently experiencing what they will look back on as the best years of their lives, they will tell you, if they favour you with anything more than a black look, that is, that you are talking crap.

London was extraordinarily exciting to me. The CDs, cappuccinos and croissants were the acme of sophistication and symbolic of the great social and political sea change that was coming. The process of gentrification that was already beginning to remodel the seedier parts of Islington and Fulham was being contemptuously described as 'croissantification' by those alarmed at the incoming tide. The Falklands Conflict had transformed Margaret Thatcher from the least popular prime minister in fifty years to the most popular since Churchill. A surge of patriotism and confidence was beginning to swell in the political seas. It would soon enough become a tsunami of conspicuous spending for the lucky ones who rode high on the wave and a deluge of debt and deprivation for the victims of 'the harsh realities of the marketplace', as Keith Joseph and the Friedmanites liked to call monetarism's collateral damage. I wish I could say I was more politically alert, angry or interested at this time. Smoky, boozy nights up in the bar of the Midland Hotel with Ben Elton had gone a long way towards pulling me out of my instinctive dread and dislike of the Labour party; the sheer vulgarity and graceless meanness of spirit of Margaret Thatcher and so many of her ministers made it very hard to feel any affection or admiration for her, but my eyes were too firmly fixed inwards towards myself and the opportunities coming my way to think much about anything else. If I colaphize myself too drastically for such an unremarkable and venial failing in one so young it would sound unconvincing. After the teenage years that I had undergone, I find it hard to blame myself for taking pleasure in the fruits that the world now showered down upon my head.

Crystal Cube

Aside from the individual assignments that had come my way – the musical, the film and the offer of a part in *Forty Years On* – Hugh and I wanted to continue writing and performing together. The spanking to our self-confidence administered by Ben's astounding prolificacy notwithstanding, we still hoped (and somewhere inside ourselves believed) that we might have a future in comedy. Accordingly, Richard Armitage sent us to a meeting at the BBC.

In those days the house of Light Entertainment was divided into two departments, Comedy and Variety. Sitcoms and sketch shows flew under the Comedy flag and programmes like *The Generation Game* and *The Paul Daniels Magic Show* counted as Variety. The head of Light Entertainment was a jolly, red-faced man who could easily be mistaken for a Butlin's Redcoat or the model for a beery husband in a McGill seaside postcard. His name was Jim Moir, which also happens to be Vic Reeves's real name, although at this time, somewhere in 1983, Vic Reeves had yet to make his mark. Hugh and I had first met the executive Jim Moir at the cricket weekend at Stebbing. He had said then, with the assured timing of a Blackpool front-of-curtain comic: 'Meet the wife, don't laugh.'

Hugh and I were shown into his office. He sat us down on the sofa opposite his desk and asked if we had comedy plans. Only he wouldn't have put it as simply as that, he probably said something like: 'Strip naked and show me your cocks,' which would have been his way of saying: 'What would you like to talk about?' Jim routinely used colourful and perplexing metaphors of a quite staggeringly explicit nature. 'Let's jizz on the table, mix up our spunk and smear it all over us,' might be his way of asking, 'Shall we work together?' I had always assumed that he only spoke like that to men, but not so long ago Dawn French and Jennifer Saunders confirmed that he had been quite as eye-watering in his choice of language with them. Ben Elton went on to create, and Mel Smith to play, a fictional head of Light Entertainment based on Jim Moir called Jumbo Whiffy in the sitcom *Filthy Rich & Catflap*. I hope you will not get the wrong impression of Moir from my description of his language. People of his kind are easy to underestimate, but I never heard anyone who worked with him say a bad word about him. In the past forty years the BBC has had no more shrewd, capable, loyal, honourable and successful executive and certainly none with a more dazzling verbal imagination.

Hugh and I emerged from our meeting stupefied but armed with a commission. John Kilby, who had directed *The Cellar Tapes*, would direct and produce the pilot show that we were now to write. We conceived a series that was to be called *The Crystal Cube*, a mock-serious magazine programme that for each edition would investigate some phenomenon or other: every week we would 'go through the crystal cube'. Hugh, Emma, Paul Shearer and I were to be the regulars and we would call upon a cast of semi-regular guests to play other parts.

Back in Manchester filming *Alfresco*, we began to write in our spare time. Freed from the intimidation of having to match Ben's freakish fecundity, we produced our script in what was for us short order but would for Ben have constituted an intolerable writer's block. It was rather good. I feel I can say this as the BBC chose not to commission a series: given that and my archetypical British pride in failure it hardly seems like showing off for me to say that I was pleased with it. It is out there now somewhere on YouTube, as most things are. If you happen to track it down you will find that the first forty seconds are inaudible, but it soon clears up. Aside from technical embarrassments there is also a good deal wrong with it comically, you will note. We are awkward, young and often incompetent, but nonetheless there are some perfectly good ideas in it struggling for light and air. John Savident, now well known for his work in *Coronation*

Street, makes a splendid Bishop of Horley, Arthur Bostrom, who went on to play the bizarrely accented Officer 'Good moaning' Crabtree in *'Allo 'Allo!*, guested as an excellently gormless genetic guinea-pig, and Robbie Coltrane was his usual immaculate self in the guise of a preposterously macho film-maker.

If I was disappointed, upset or humiliated by the BBC's decision not to pick up *The Crystal Cube*, I was too proud to show it. Besides, there were plenty of comedy and odd jobs for me to be getting on with in the meantime. One such was collaborating with Rowan Atkinson on a screenplay for David Puttnam. The idea was an English *Monsieur Hulot's Holiday* in which Rowan, an innocent abroad, would find himself unwittingly involved in some sort of crime caper. The character was essentially Mr Bean, but ten years too early.

I drove up to stay with Rowan and his girlfriend, Leslie Ash, in between visits to Manchester for the taping of *Alfresco 2*. The house in Oxfordshire was, I have to confess, a dazzling symbol to me of the prizes that comedy could afford. The Aston Martin in the driveway, the wisteria growing up the mellow ashlar walls of the Georgian façade, the cottage in the grounds, the tennis court, the lawns and orchards running down to the river – all this seemed so fantastically grand, so imponderably grown-up and out of reach.

We would sit in the cottage, and I would tap away on the BBC Micro that I had brought along with me. We composed a scene in which a French girl teaches Rowan's character this tongue-twister: 'Dido dined, they say, off the enormous back of an enormous turkey,' which goes, in French, 'Dido dîna, dit-on, du dos dodu d'un dodu dindon.' Rowan practised the Beanish character earnestly attempting this. In any spare moment in the film, we decided, he would try out his 'doo doo doo doo doo', much to the bafflement of those about him. It is about all I remember from the film, which over the next few months quietly, as 99 per cent of all film projects do, fizzled out. Meanwhile, journalism was taking up more and more of my time.

Columnist

Britain's magazine industry started to boom in the early to mid-eighties. *Tatler*, *Harper's & Queen* and the newly revivified *Vanity Fair*, what you might call the Princess Di sector, fed the public appetite for information about the affairs of the Sloane Rangers, the stylings of their kitchens and country houses and the guest-lists of their parties. *Vogue* and *Cosmopolitan* rode high for the fashion-conscious and sexually sophisticated, *City Limits* and *Time Out* sold everywhere, and Nick Logan's *The Face* dominated youth fashion and trendy style at a time when it was still trendy to use the word trendy. A few years later Logan proved that even men read glossies when he launched the *avant-la-lettre* metrosexual *Arena*. I wrote a number of articles for that magazine, and literary reviews for the now defunct *Listener*, a weekly published by the BBC.

The *Listener*'s editor when I first joined was Russell Twisk, a surname of such surpassing beauty that I would have written pieces for him if he had been at the helm of *Satanic Child-Slaughter Monthly*. His literary editor was Lynne Truss, later to achieve great renown as the author of *Eats, Shoots and Leaves*. I cannot remember that I was ever victim of her peculiar 'zero tolerance approach to punctuation'; perhaps she corrected my copy without ever letting me know.

Twisk was replaced some time later by Alan Coren, who had been a hero of mine since his days editing *Punch*. He suggested I write a regular column rather than book reviews, and for a year or so I submitted weekly articles on whatever subjects suggested themselves to me.

By now I had bought myself a fax machine. For the first year or so of my ownership of this new and enchanting piece of technology it sat unloved and unused on my desk. I didn't know anyone else who owned one, and the poor thing had nobody to talk to. To be the only person you know with a fax machine is a little like being the only person you know with a tennis racket.

Cryptic in Connecticut

One day (I'm fast forwarding here, but it seems the right place for this story) Mike Ockrent called me up. *Me and My Girl* was by this time running in the West End, and we had all been thrilled to hear that Stephen Sondheim and Hal Prince had been to see it and had written to Mike expressing their admiration.

'I told Sondheim that you have a fax machine,' Mike said.

'Right.' I was not sure what to make of this. 'I see . . . er . . . why exactly?'

'He asked me if I knew anybody who had one. You were the only person I could think of. He's going to call you. Is that all right?'

The prospect of Stephen Sondheim, lyricist of *West Side Story*, composer of *Sunday in the Park with George*, *Merrily We Roll Along*, *Company*, *Sweeney Todd* and *A Little Night Music*, calling me up was, yes, on the whole, perfectly all right, I assured Mike. 'What is it about exactly?'

'Oh, he'll explain . . .'

My God, oh my good gracious heavens. He wanted me to write the book of his next musical! What else could it be? Oh my holy trousers. Stephen Sondheim, the greatest songwriter-lyricist since Cole Porter, was going to call me up. Strange that he was interested in my possession of a fax machine. Perhaps that is how he imagined we would work together. Me faxing dialogue and story developments to him and him faxing back his thoughts and emendations. Now that I came to think of it that was rather a wonderful idea and opened up a whole new way of thinking about collaboration.

That evening the phone rang. I was living in Dalston in a house I shared with Hugh and Katie and I had warned them that I would be sitting on the telephone all night.

'Hi, is that Stephen Fry?'

'S-s-speaking.'

'This is Stephen Sondheim.'

'Right. Yes of course. Wow. Yes. It's a . . . I . . .'

'Hey, I want to congratulate you on the fine job you did with the book of *Me and My Girl*. Great show.'

'Gosh. Thank you. Coming from you that's . . . that's . . .'

'So. Listen, I understand you have a fax machine?'

'I do. Yes. Certainly. Yes, a Brother F120. Er, not that the model number matters at all. A bit even. No. But, yes. I have one. Indeed. Mm.'

'Are you at home this weekend?'

'Er, yes I think so . . . yup.'

'In the evening, till late at night?'

'Yes.'

This was getting weird.

'OK, so here's the deal. I have a house in the country and I like to have treasure hunts and competitions. You know, with sneaky clues?'

'Ri-i-ght . . .'

'And I thought how great it would be to have a clue that was a long number. Your fax number? And when people get the answer they will see that it's a number and maybe they will work out that it's a phone number and they will call it, but they will get that *sound*. You know, the sound that a fax machine makes?'

'Right . . .'

'And they will hear it and think, "What was that?" but maybe one of them, they will know that it is in actuality a fax machine. They might have one in their office, for example. So they'll say, "Hey, that's a fax machine. So maybe we have to send it a message. On a piece of paper." And they will fax you for help.'

'And what do I do then?'

'Well, here's the thing: beforehand, I will have faxed you their next clue. So when they fax you asking for help, you fax that clue back in return. You understand?'

'Yes, I think so. You send me a fax which is the next clue. Then I wait by the machine on Saturday afternoon . . .'

'Evening, night. It will be afternoon in Connecticut, but in London it will be like nine, ten, maybe eleven o'clock. You're not going out at all?'

'No, no.'

'Because it is *crucial* that you are in all the time and that you are right by the fax machine so you can hear it when it goes off.'

'Absolutely. I'll be there. So, just to make sure I've got this right. Saturday night I wait by the fax machine. When I get a fax asking me for a clue, I send to your fax number in Connecticut whatever it is that you will have faxed me earlier?'

'Right. Isn't it great? It will be the first-ever fax treasure hunt. But you *have* to be by the phone all Saturday night. You will be?'

'I'll be there. I'll be there.'

'OK. I'll give you my fax number. It should appear on the top of the fax anyway, but I'll give it to you. And I'll need your fax number.'

We exchanged numbers.

'Thank you, Stephen.'

'No, thank *you*, Stephen.'

Between that call and Saturday evening he called four or five times to check that I had not changed my plans and was still happy to sit by the fax machine and await developments. On Saturday afternoon at about four I received a fax from him. It was an impenetrable diagram with some sort of code written alongside it.

I faxed back a note to say that I had received his clue and would fax it as soon as I received a request from his treasure-hunt contestants.

I sat with a book, ears flapping, for the next five hours. I had not put out of my mind the possibility that Sondheim might yet ask me to work with him on his next musical, but the thought that he only wanted me for my technological toys could not be entirely dismissed.

Some time before ten o'clock the fax machine rang. I

put down the book. It was *Atlas Shrugged* by Ayn Rand, I remember quite distinctly, which was hypnotically dreadful. I stared at the fax machine as it answered the call. Its shrill cry was cut off. The caller had hung up. I imagined a garden in New England and a group of capering Sondheim friends.

'How odd! It made a kind of awful chirruping sound.'

'Oh! Oh! Oh! I know what that is. It's a fax machine!'

'A what-all?'

'*You* know. For sending documents? Stephen's got one in his den, I'm sure I've seen it there. Let's go to it. My, such larks!'

I counted off the minutes as the gang made their way (in my imagination at least) to Stephen's den, whose mantelpiece was crowded with Tony Awards. On the very piano on which he had composed 'Send in the Clowns' I saw in my mind's eye signed photographs in silver-gilt frames of Lenny Bernstein, Ethel Merman, Oscar Hammerstein and Noël Coward.

Just as I was wondering if I might have misjudged the scenario, my fax machine screeched into life again. This time a handshake was made across the ocean and a fax chugged out. I ripped it off and there on the curling thermal paper was scrawled 'Hi! Do you have something for us?'

I duly fitted into the machine the fax Sondheim had sent me earlier, dialled the number and pressed 'Transmit'.

A cheerful 'Thanks!' was returned a few minutes later.

I had no idea how many teams there might be playing and realized that, for all his neurotic calling to ensure my vigilant presence for the evening, Stephen had not told me whether or not this would be a one-time deal.

I woke up at three with *Atlas Shrugged* on my lap and the fax machine free of further intercourse.

A week later a case of Haut-Batailley claret arrived with a note of thanks from Stephen Sondheim.

> The treasure hunt was a great success. Due in no small
> measure to your kind participation.
> With thanks,
> Stephen.

Not a hint of a call to collaboration. I still await his summons.

By the time Alan Coren became the *Listener*'s editor, fax machines had become a signature ubiquity of the age, and there was nothing strange about my delivering copy to him that way without visiting the offices in Marylebone High Street from one month to the next. My next struggle, some seven or eight years later, would be to get newspapers and broadcasting companies to sign up to log on to the internet and furnish themselves with email addresses, but that is a whole other story for a whole other book for a whole other readership.

Contortionist

Perhaps the most stylish and beguiling figure in the London magazine world in those days was the caricaturist, editor and boulevardier about town Mark Boxer. Under the pen name Marc he had illustrated the front covers of *A Dance to the Music of Time*, all twelve volumes of which I had lined up along a bookshelf, next to the Simon Raven

Alms for Oblivion sequence (which I much preferred, and still do). In the sixties Boxer had supervised the launch and life of Britain's first colour supplement magazine for *The Sunday Times* and now he edited the *Tatler*. One day in the mid to late eighties I got a letter from him, asking me to call his office.

'Ah yes. Stephen Fry. How do you do? Let me take you out to lunch. Langan's tomorrow?'

I had heard of Langan's Brasserie but had never been. Founded by Peter Langan, Richard Shepherd and the actor Michael Caine, it had acquired a reputation as one of the most glamorous and eccentric restaurants in London. The glamour was provided by the art collection, the Patrick Procktor menu design and the daily presence of film stars, aristocrats and millionaires; the eccentricity came in the form of Peter Langan. This pioneering restaurateur, an alcoholic Irishman of uncertain temper, was notorious for insulting customers to whom he might take unpredictable dislikes, tearing up the bills of those who dared to complain, stubbing cigarettes out in their salads and ordering them to leave. A bottle of Krug in one hand and a cigar or cigarette in the other, he would lurch from table to table, beaming and barking, grinning and growling, hugging and shoving. The food was good but not great, the atmosphere magical, and the experience, when Peter was around, unforgettable. Don Boyd told me that his wife, Hilary, had once found a slug in her salad. As Peter lurched hiccupping past the table, Don had stopped him and pointed out the unwanted gastropod in his wife's greenery.

Peter bowed forward from the waist to examine the plate.

'Why thank you,' he said, taking up the pulsing, living slug between thumb and forefinger. 'Thank you very much indeed, my darling.' He dropped it into his glass of Krug, drained it down and burped. 'Like a nice juicy snail, only without the nuisance of a shell. Fucking delicious.'

I arrived early, as I always do for appointments, and was led upstairs. Mark arrived exactly on time.

'Hope you don't mind it up here,' he said. 'It's quieter. In case Peter's about. Do you know him?'

I confessed that I did not.

'Keep it that way,' said Mark.

Boxer was an attractive-looking man aged, I suppose, about fifty, but youthful in a twinkly, almost elfin way. He was married to the newsreader and co-founder of TV-AM, Anna Ford. Over the first two courses Mark was charming, funny and inconsequential, as if the reason for his invitation to lunch was entirely social. He kept me in raptures with stories of his time at Cambridge.

'It was quite the thing then to present oneself as homosexual. I used to wear fantastically tight white trousers and tell the rugby players that they were the creamiest darlings in the world. It was actually very odd *not* to behave like that. Amongst my set at least. No one batted an eyelid if you came on as gay. And of course it made the girls simply throw themselves at you. Did you know that I am the only person aside from Shelley to be sent down from one of the universities for atheism?'

'No! Really?'

'Well, not quite. I was editor of *Granta* and I published a poem by somebody or other that the university authorities said was blasphemous. They demanded I, as editor, be sent down, but E. M. Forster and Noel Annan and others simply leapt to my defence, so they changed it to a rustication, which they meanly set for May Week so that I would miss the May Ball, but of course they overlooked the fact that balls go on way past midnight. So on the stroke of twelve I returned to King's in my white tie and tails and was chaired around from marquee to marquee like a conquering hero. It was too marvellous.'

It was hard to believe that this man was the same age as my father. He had the gift, if gift it is, of making me feel more than usually bourgeois, ordinary and unexciting.

'So, *à nos moutons*,' he said as the cheese arrived. '*Tatler*. I know you have written for us once before. Wonderful piece, by the way. Is it really true?'

He was referring to a feature to which I had contributed earlier in the year and which we will come to later. I blushed fiercely as I always did when that article was mentioned.

'Yes. Quite true.'

'Heavens. Anyway. The magazine . . . Do you read it, by any chance?'

'Sometimes . . . I mean, I don't positively *not* read it, but I don't think I've ever actually bought one. Except the month my piece came out, that is.'

'That's all right,' he said. 'Here's next month's number. The covers are wonderful these days. We have Michael Roberts as our art director. He's too splendid for words.'

I took his proffered copy of the magazine and flipped through the pages.

'It's all fine,' said Mark. 'Nothing wrong. It's just that there's something . . . something *missing*.'

'Well whatever it is,' I said, 'it isn't advertisements.'

'Ha! No, we're doing very well, really. But I need someone to come in every month to . . . to *smell* the issue before it goes to print.'

'To smell it?'

'Mm . . . you know. To look at the sum total of articles and spreads and to think about how they can all come together. To work on the text of the cover and the spinelines . . .'

'Spinelines?'

'The copy written on the spine.'

'Of course. Spinelines, yes.'

'I need someone who isn't in on the everyday production of the magazine to take that look. To smell it all and to . . .'

A thought struck me. 'Do you mean,' I said, 'that you want someone to do the puns?'

He slapped the table. 'I *knew* you'd understand!'

Since Tina Brown's pioneering reign at the *Tatler*'s helm the magazine had become notorious, amongst other things, for its punning headlines, sub-headlines and – as I now knew them to be called – spinelines.

'That's settled, then. You're Officer Commanding Puns.' He drained his coffee with clear satisfaction. 'Oh, another thing I thought of on the way here. We get sent all kinds of books. For the most part insufferably dull fly-fishing manuals and the memoirs of forgettable duchesses, but sometimes more interesting titles might come our way. We don't have a book reviewer. Why don't I get all the books we're sent couriered over to you in a batch once a week and you can . . .'

'Smell them?'

'That's it. Smell them and then write a column in which you can review them or simply comment on the kinds of books that are being published these days. A zeitgeisty, smelly sort of thing. How does that appeal?'

I said that a zeitgeisty, smelly sort of thing appealed greatly.

'Fine. Why don't you pop back to Hanover Square with me, and I'll introduce you around?'

'Will I have to come into the office a lot?'

'Just from time to time to have a . . .'

'A smell?'

'To have a smell, exactly.'

The first issue for which I acted as Smellfinder General was June's. 'June Know Where You're Going' was the date pun. Michael Roberts's cover of a model in a frock of the deepest crimson found itself accompanied by the headline RED DRESS THE BALANCE. An article on aristocratic Catholic families was subtitled: 'The Smart Sect'. Time has thankfully erased from my memory the other hideous verbal contortions of which I was guilty, but I came up with more than a dozen for each edition with which I was involved.

Critics and Couriers

Books began to arrive by the box-load. Rather than review under my own name I gave myself a made-up byline:

> Williver Hendry, editor of *A Most Peculiar Friendship: The Correspondence of Lord Alfred Douglas and Jack Dempsey* and author of *Towards the Brightening Dawn* and *Notes From a Purple Distance: An Ischian Memoir*, casts a loving eye over some June publications . . .

Only it wasn't so loving an eye at all. Hiding in cowardly fashion under this *nom de guerre* I was beastly unkind to someone called Baron de Massy, a nephew of Prince Rainier who had written an autobiography crammed with arse-paralysingly snobbish Monegasque drivel about Ferraris, polo-players and coke-snorting tennis champions. 'Here is that marriage of style and content we look for in great writing,' I, or rather Williver, wrote. 'A shatteringly vulgar and worthless life captured in shatteringly vulgar and worthless prose.'

My career as a book reviewer was short-lived, but long enough to make me feel that it was not the occupation for me. For good or ill (perhaps it is what footballers call a fifty-fifty ball) I cannot bear to upset people. Perhaps it would be truer to say that I cannot bear to know that there are people going around whom I have upset and who think badly of me as a consequence. My overwhelming desire to please and to be liked has not gone unnoticed. I sometimes hopefully imagine that it may be an agreeable and acceptable enough quirk of character, but I have lived long enough to know that it is more likely to appal than appeal.

It is obvious that the purpose of critics is to transmit their opinion of the works that have been sent to them. In your life as a reviewer, the day will soon come when a book arrives which is too bad to respond to with anything other than the savaging you are convinced it deserves. You berate it and its author, you mock, you expose, you trash and you pillory. It is, for a short time, a wonderful feeling to tick an author off and in scalding prose to ridicule their inadequacies and rubbish their pretensions. After all, for weeks and weeks you have been compelled to read novels, autobiographies, histories, guides and collections, most of which are – dread word, as Wallace Arnold would say – *fine*. They are of sufficient quality to justify their publication and for the most part it will be easy enough, if you are a placating weasel like me, to find something about them to like. But, willy nilly, the iron has entered your soul. You cannot help but begin to look on authors and publishers as the enemy. They pound at your door at all times of the day and night clamouring for your attention. So many of them, all with so much to say. Their tics, minor flaws and mannerisms become an aggravation, but you hold your fire as reasonably as you can. One day, with all this building up inside you, there is a buzzing at the entryphone, and a motorcycle courier stands outside in the rain with a package for you to sign for. Another set of new literary works to be read and rated. After the leather-clad messenger of the metropolis has gone through the usual 'Do you mind if I use your toilet?' and 'Oh, can I use your phone to call my dispatcher?' and 'Shall we have sex right here and now?' I am left alone with his delivery. And this time one of the books is It. The Stinker.

Incidentally, anybody who thinks that a book reviewer has at least the profitable perk of hundreds of free books a month to offset his misery may not know about uncorrected bound proofs: these are flimsy and hastily assembled pre-release editions sent out to reviewers and to anyone likely to provide a winning phrase to be printed on the front of the proper later-to-be-printed dust-jacketed edition – '"Deliciously insightful, coolly ironic," Wayne Rooney'; '"A rip-snorting, barn-storming, cliff-hanging, roller-coaster of a ride," Iris Murdoch'; '"The dog's bollocks: Bukowski is gang-raped by Burroughs and Gibson and has a bastard child," Ann Widdecombe' – that kind of thing. There is now an online auction market for the bound proofs of better-known authors, but in the mid-eighties they were so much waste paper to be thrown away as soon as they had been read and reviewed. Today email, .pdf and the eBook and iPad are beginning to put an end to the age of the bound proof, as they have to the age of the motorcycle courier, of course. In the eighties every phone call between editors and journalists, agents and clients, producers and writers, lawyers and lawyers included phrases like: 'I'll get it biked over to you,' 'Bike it over, I'll sign and bike it back,' 'Is it small enough for a bike, or shall we cab it round?' London in the mid-eighties buzzed and snarled to the sound of 550cc Hondas and Kawasaki 750s swooping and skidding around you, clipping your wing-mirrors, revving at the traffic lights and terrifying the citizenry with their desperado devilry.

I shall divert for a revealing story that a friend told me round about this time. Her aunt had been checked into Moorfields Eye Hospital, where she was due for a corneal graft, cataract operation or similarly routine, but nonetheless delicate, ophthalmic procedure. She was lying in bed wondering what was up, when the consultant came in.

'Ah, Miss Tredway, how do you do? You've had the operation explained? What we do is we cut out your nasty cloudy old lens and replace it with a shiny new donor one. Simple as can be. Trouble is, we don't have any donor eyes in at the moment.'

'Oh.'

'I shouldn't worry, though.' He went to the window and looked out over the City Road. 'It's raining, so it won't be very long.'

You know there is something amiss when a doctor can absolutely guarantee that if the roads are slippery a fatal accident will be sure to befall a despatch rider somewhere in the city and that a fresh, healthy pair of young eyes will soon be speeding their way to the operating theatre packed in a cool-box. A cool-box bungeed to the pillion of a motorcycle in all probability . . .

Well, that was London in the pre-fax, pre-internet eighties. Couriers and cars did the work, and it was matter in the form of massy atoms, rather than content in the form of massless electrons, that had to be conveyed from place to place.

But I was telling you about The Stinker. It was inevitable that sooner or later in my career as a literary critic I would open a courier's package (ooer, now but shush) and find a book about which there could be nothing good to say.

'Well, if you haven't anything nice to say, then don't say anything,' is the recommendation of most mothers, and as always their advice is worth considering. The difficulty comes when, as mentioned, iron has entered the soul and charity, compassion and fellow-feeling have fled it.

I shall refrain from naming names and titles, but The Stinker was the one that propelled me into meanness. I sharpened the nib, dipped it in the most caustic solution available and set forth to make my feelings known. Just as when a beautiful person is beautiful in all their lineaments – hair, nose, ankles, eyelashes and nape – so when a writer is bad they seem to strike one as bad in every particular, from style and syntax to moral outlook and spiritual worth. There will be those reading this book who have come to that same conclusion about me, although it is probable that they will have cast it down in disgust before getting this far. Unless they are reading it for review, of course, in which case I shall have cause to shudder. Or rather my mother will, since I do not read reviews.

I might have hoped that the nameless author of the nameless book that I so mercilessly tore into never read my review either, but I happen to know that they did. Oh, I was witty, devastating and – to anyone who read the piece – incontestably convincing and incontrovertibly correct. I adduced quotations with which to condemn the poor author out of his or her own mouth, I questioned their sanity, sense and intellect. I 'proved' that their book was not only bad but wicked, not only imperfect but opportunistic, creepy and deluded. All of which I sincerely believed it to be. It really was a most awful piece of work, this book. Had it been cack-handed and incompetent but well-intentioned and unobjectionable in disposition, I am sure I would have let it be. Since it was The Stinker, however, no feature redeemed it, and I let myself go. I mustn't overstate things. You should understand that plenty of worse reviews were written of that book and of other books that week, plenty of meaner and more disapproving pieces are written about books *every* week. Nonetheless, my article would certainly cause anyone who read it to wince and to feel for the author. Why am I lingering on this book and my review of it?

In a long life of offering up works for public scrutiny I have had my own share of negative critical notices. I no longer look, and my friends know better than to commiserate with (or occasionally to congratulate) me on a review that I will never read. But in all the years during which I could not resist checking my reviews and on reading them felt myself punched and lowered and dispirited by the savageries or cruel perspicacities levelled at me, I never felt a tenth as chronically dreadful as I did in the weeks following the publication of my assault on The

Stinker. I lay awake at night picturing his or her reaction. On the cowardly level I imagined that one day, when I least expected it, I would be waylaid by this now wholly deranged and indigent ex-author and have a quart of actual vitriol flung at my face as revenge for the quart of virtual vitriol I had flung in theirs. In less egoistic moods, I pictured their misery and humiliation and I felt like the worst kind of bully. What right had I to make them unhappy? What business of mine was it to hold up to the light their infelicities of phrasing or falsities of reasoning? Where the fuck, in other words, did I get off?

Any number of reviewers and critics will tell you that if someone chooses to present a work for money then the public should be warned before making an expenditure that they cannot recall. If you writers and performers don't like the heat, they say, you can get out of the kitchen. What right, they will add, turning the question around, do practitioners of theatre, literature, film, television or any other art have to be immune from informed opinion? Are they only to be lauded and applauded, pampered, praised and petted?

I cannot deny a single word of these and many other of the cogent *plaidoyers* routinely offered by criticism's apologists. There are all kinds of responses and attitudes that can justify the art and practice of reviewing, but none of them, not a one, addresses the question of how you live with yourself if your wicked wit, shrewd insight and scornful judgement will have hurt someone, will have them crying themselves to sleep. Or worse still, how you can live with yourself if you realize that you have become the kind of person who does not even *care* that they regularly cause pain, suffering, discouragement and loss of self-regard in those trying to earn a living in their field?

It is weak, it is wussy, it is probably a betrayal of everything the Cambridge literary ethos from Leavis to Kermode stands for, but I am much less interested in artistic standards, literary values, aesthetic authenticity and critical candour than I am in the feelings of others. Or in my own feelings, I suppose I should say, for I cannot bear to feel that I have offended or that I have enemies. It *is* weak, it *is* wussy, but there you are. And for that reason I was relieved when Alan Coren took over the *Listener* and suggested that I move away from literary reviewing and contribute instead a weekly column on general topics that might appeal to me. From that day on I have only agreed to review a book, film or television programme if one proviso is understood and accepted by the editor commissioning me: the review will be favourable or, if the product is so dreadful that even I cannot find a good word to say about it, there will be no article. I am less fastidious about kindness to the digital devices, smartphones and computer peripherals I sometimes review, but then their origins are usually so much more corporate and so much less personal. However, if it ever got back to me that the designers of a camera or the authors of a new piece of software were weeping because of something cruel I had said, then I would probably pack in my geek reviews too.

Most of all I refuse to say anything bad about the work of a friend. My literary integrity can go hang, but friendship is sacred. Of course, by telling you this, it allows you – were you so minded – to look back at the blurbs and jacket quotes I have given for writers I have known and speculate that when I wrote, 'Brilliant, harrowing, lung-achingly funny'

I might really have been thinking, 'Grisly, horrible, arse-seepingly incompetent'. You will never know.

One of Alan Coren's favourite academic stories was one of mine too. It concerns a don, often identified as Sir Arthur Quiller-Couch, that great moustachioed Edwardian doyen of letters, author of children's adventure stories and responsible as 'Q' for the great edition of the *Oxford Book of English Verse*. Apparently he was welcoming a new Fellow to the Senior Combination Room at Jesus, the Cambridge College where he roosted for the last thirty years of his life.

'We're delighted to have you here,' he said, putting an arm round the young man's shoulder, 'but a word of advice. Don't try to be clever. We're all clever here. Only try to be kind, a little kind.'

Like most university stories, this one is variously attributed and it probably never even happened but, as the Italians say, *se non è vero, è ben trovato* – even if it isn't true, it's well founded.

I wrote a weekly *Listener* column for another year. The *Tatler* smelling duties lasted only a few months before Boxer and I parted by mutual consent: the puns were threatening my sanity. I continued meanwhile to tap away at the keyboard for other publications as often as I was asked to. I seemed to be in almost limitless demand and, so long as I didn't have to breach my peculiar rules on reviewing, all was well.

Confirmed Celibate

How did it all begin? Why did editors fasten upon me in the first place? What motivated Mark Boxer to be in touch? Why did Russell Twisk make an approach? Well, it is possible that I owed my journalistic career, such as it was, to a man called Jonathan Meades. If you watch good television you will know who I mean. He wears charcoal suits and sunglasses and talks about architecture, food and culture high and low as brilliantly as any man alive. For many years he was *The Times*'s restaurant critic, and there are many who might think that, *pace* Giles Coren and his generation, he has never been surpassed in that field. In the mid-eighties he had some kind of position on the *Tatler*, 'features editor' is I think the proper description. He got hold of my telephone number somehow, perhaps from Don Boyd, who knew everybody.

'Forgive me for calling out of the blue,' he said. 'My name is Jonathan Meades and I work for the *Tatler* magazine. I got your number perhaps from Don Boyd, who knows everybody.'

'Hello. How can I help?'

'I am putting together an article in which people write about something they *don't* do. Gavin Stamp, for example, is telling us why he doesn't drive, and Brian Sewell is giving us a piece about never going on holiday. I wondered if you might be able to weigh in?'

'Gosh! Er . . .'

'So. Is there anything you don't do?'

'Hm,' I scrabbled frantically around in the recesses of my mind. 'I'm afraid I can't really think of anything. Well I don't strangle kittens or rape nuns, but I'm assuming this is about things we . . .'

'. . . about things we don't do which most of humanity does, exactly. Nothing?'

'Oh!' A thought suddenly struck me. 'I don't do *sex*. Would that count, do you think?'

A pause followed that made me wonder if the line had gone dead.

'Hello? . . . Jonathan?'

'Four hundred words by Friday afternoon. Can't offer more than two hundred pounds. Deal?'

I cannot entirely understand, to this day, why I withheld my body from sexual congress with another for as long as I did. Kim and I had been partners in a complete and proper sense at Cambridge and for a month or so afterwards. Since then I had become less and less interested in sex while Kim had pursued a more conventional and fulfilled erotic career and had by now found himself a new partner, a handsome Greek-American called Steve. Kim and I still adored each other and still shared the Chelsea flat. He had Steve and I had . . . I had my work.

If I have a theory to explain the celibacy that began in 1982 and was not to end until 1996 it is that during that period work took the place of everything else in my life. Whatever effect multiple school expulsions, social and academic failures and the final degradation of imprisonment may have had on me, I think it true that my last-gasp escape into Cambridge and the discovery that there was work I could do and be valued for doing galvanized me into an orgy of concentrated labour from which I could not and would not be diverted, not even by the prospect of sexual or romantic fulfilment. Perhaps career, concentration, commitment and creation had become my new drugs of choice.

Work can be an addiction like any other. Love of it can

be a home-wrecker, an obsession that bores, upsets, insults and worries those close to you. We all know that drugs, alcohol and tobacco are Bad, but work, we are brought up to believe, is Good. As a result the world is full of families who are angry at being abandoned and breadwinners who are even more angry because their hours of labour are not sufficiently appreciated. 'I do it for you!' they cry. While it may be true that work puts meat on the table, everyone around them knows that hard workers do it for themselves. Most children of workaholics would rather see less money and more of their parent.

Within a year of leaving Cambridge, friends and family were already referring to my apparent inability to use the word 'no'. I soon began to hear myself described as a workaholic. Kim preferred the word 'ergomaniac' partly because he was a classical scholar and partly I suspect because the 'maniac' part better expressed the absurd frenzy with which I was starting to throw myself into every offer that came my way. To this day I am often reminded by those about me that I don't have to say yes to everything and that there are such things as holidays. I don't believe them, of course, no matter how many times they assure me it is true.

The question that most troublingly refuses to go away is whether my productivity, ubiquity and well . . . career harlotry . . . have stopped me from realizing what, in the world of fathers, teachers and grown-ups in general, might be called My Full Potential. Hugh and Emma, to name the two most obvious of my contemporaries, have never been as recklessly carefree, prodigal and improvident with their talents as I have. I want to say that they have always had reason to believe in their talents more than I have in mine.

But then I also want to say that I have had more fun than they have and that:

> For when the One Great Scorer comes
> To write against your name,
> He marks – not that you won or lost,
> But how you played the Game.

Which is all very well, but while I may want to say all kinds of things, I am not sure that they would necessarily be true. I will not go so far as to claim that, when falling asleep every night, I mourn lost opportunities. 'Every night' would be an exaggeration. There is a vision that comes to me often though.

I picture myself at the surface of an ocean: the course of my life is played out as a descent to the sea bed. As I drop down I clutch at and try to reach blurred but alluring images representing the vocation of writer, actor, comedian, film director, politician or academic, but they all writhe and ripple flirtatiously out of reach, or rather it would be truer to say that I am afraid to leap forward and hug one of them to me. By being afraid to commit to one I commit to none and arrive at the bottom empty and unfulfilled. This is a self-aggrandizing, pitiful and absurd fantasy of regret, I know, but it is a frequent one. I close whatever book I have been reading in bed, and that same film plays out again and again in my mind before I sleep. I know that I have a reputation for cleverness and articulacy, but I also know that people must wonder why I haven't quite done better with my life and talents. A jack of so many trades and manifestly a master of none. In my perkier moods I am entirely pleased with this outcome, for I refuse to stand on a carpet in a headmaster's study and endure wise shakings of the head and heavy school-report pronouncements about my shortcomings. Such attitudes are grotesque, impudent and irrelevant. 'Could do better' is a meaningless conclusion. 'Could be happier' is the only one that counts. I have had five times the opportunities and experiences accorded to most, and if the result is a disappointment to posterity, well prosperity can eat it. In less perky moods, of course, I entirely concur with the judgements of the head-shakers and school-report pronouncers. What a waste. What a fatuous, selfish, air-headed, indolent and insulting waste my life has been.

While it is not exactly counterintuitive it may perhaps be less than immediately obvious to point out that it is a great deal more conceited of me to bemoan my life as a waste than for me to be more or less satisfied at the way it has turned out. Any regret at my lack of achievement suggests that I really believe that I had in me the ability, should I have concentrated on any one thing, to have written a *great* novel or to have been a *great* actor, director, playwright, poet or statesman or whatever else I might delude myself I had the potential for. Whether or not I have the ability to be any of those things, I do know that I lack the ambition, concentration, focus and above all *will* without which such talents are as useless as an engine without fuel. Which is not to say that I am lazy or unambitious in the short term. You might say I am good at tactics but hopeless at strategy, happy to slog away at whatever is in front of me but unable to take a long view, plan ahead or imagine the future. A good golfer, they say, has to picture his swing before he addresses the ball in order to drive. My whole life has been an adventure in hit and hope.

But sex. Yes, we have to return, I fear, to sex. We were discussing that commission for the *Tatler*. I wrote the article for Jonathan Meades, outlining my distaste for being cursed by nature with an urgent instinct to rummage about in the 'damp, dark, foul-smelling and revoltingly tufted areas of the human body that constitute the main dishes in the banquet of love' and my sense that the whole business was humiliating, disgusting and irksome. I suggested that a life without sex and without the presence of a partner offered numerous benefits. The celibate life allowed productivity, independence and ease free from the pressures of placating and accommodating the will and desires of another: released from the degrading imperatives of erotic congress, a new and better kind of life could be lived. Sex was an overrated bore. 'Besides,' I confessed as I ended the article, 'I'm scared that I may not be very good at it.'

The piece was quoted and reproduced in whole or in part in several newspapers, and for the next twelve years it was rare for this particular C-word not to be attached to me much as macrobiotic is attached to Gwyneth Paltrow and tantric to Sting. I joined Cliff Richard and Morrissey as one of celibacy's peculiar poster children. Profilers, chat show hosts and interviewers in the years to come would regularly ask if I was still keeping it up, ho-ho, whether I would recommend sexual abstinence as a way of life and how I coped with the loneliness of the single state. I had created a rod for my own back with this article but have never regretted writing it. It was, more or less, inasmuch as these things ever are, true. I *did* find the business of eros a nuisance and an embarrassment. I *did* enjoy the independence and freedom afforded me by being unattached and I *was* afraid that I might not be very good at sex. Am I going to deny my terror of rejection, or my low sense of my own physical worth?

With the passing of each year the odds against me ever forging a full relationship lengthened as I felt myself less and less practised in the arts of love and less and less confident about how I would ever go about finding a partner, even supposing that I wanted one. There was just so much to *do*. I was rehearsing in London prior to going down to Chichester to start *Forty Years On*, I was working on *Me and My Girl*, chugging out journalism and taking enthusiastic steps in another medium: radio.

Characters and the Corporation

Ever since I can remember I have loved radio, especially the kind of talk radio that only the BBC Home Service, later Radio 4, provides. Throughout my insomniac youth I listened through the day right up to the national anthem, when I would retune to the BBC World Service. 'England made me,' Anthony Farrant says to himself in the Graham Greene novel of that title. England made me too, but it was an England broadcast on 1500 metres Long Wave.

I wrote this as the opening of an article on the World Service for *Arena* magazine.

BBC World Service. The News, read by Roger Collinge . . . The warm brown tones trickle out of Bush House like honey from a jar: rich and resonant on the Long and Medium Waves for domestic listeners or bright and sibilant on the Short Wave for a hundred million Anglophone citizens of the world for whose benefit the precious signal is bounced off the atmosphere from relay station to relay station, through ionospheric storms and the rude jostling traffic of a hundred thousand intrusive foreign transmissions, to arrive fresh and crackling on the veranda table. Oh, to be in England, now that England's gone. This World Service, this little Bakelite gateway into the world of Sidney Box, Charters and Caldicott, Mazawattee tea, Kennedy's Latin Primer and dark, glistening streets. An England that never was, conjured into the air by nothing more than accents, March tunes and a meiotic, self-deprecating style that in its dishonesty is brassier and brasher than Disneyland. A Mary Poppins service, glamorous in its drab severity, merry in its stern routine and inexhaustible resource: a twinkling authoritarian that fulfils our deepest fantasy by simply staying, even though the wind changed long ago. Ooh, I love it . . .

I'm sure I knew what I meant at the time by the World Service's 'dishonesty', but the truth is I still adored and valued radio above television. Radio 4's mix of comedy, news, documentary, drama, magazine, panel game and quirky discussion is unique and was central to the fashioning of my outlook and manner. I grew up to the sound of warmly assured and calmly authoritative BBC voices vibrating the fabric speaker covers of valve wireless sets manufactured by Bush, Ferguson, Roberts and Pye. One of my first-ever memories is sitting under my mother's chair in our house in Chesham while she tapped away on her typewriter with characters from *The Archers* arguing about dairy cattle in the background. *My Music*, *My Word!*, *A Word in Edgeways*, *Stop the Week*, *Start the Week*, *Any Answers*, *Any Questions*, *Twenty Questions*, *Many a Slip, Does the Team Think?, Brain of Britain, From Our Own Correspondent, The Petticoat Line, File on Four, Down Your Way, The World at One, Today, PM, You and Yours, Woman's Hour, Letter from America, Jack de Manio Precisely, The Men from the Ministry, Gardener's Question Time, The Burkiss Way, The Jason Explanation, Round Britain Quiz, Just a Minute, I'm Sorry I Haven't a Clue, Desert Island Discs* and a hundred other dramas, comedies, quizzes and features have amused, amazed, enriched, enraged, informed and inflamed me from the earliest age. My voice, I think, owes more to the BBC microphone and the dusty, slow-to-warm-up Mullard valve than to the accents and tones of my family, friends and school fellows. Just as there are the lazily sucked bones of Wodehouse, Wilde and Waugh in my writing style, if style is the right word for it, so the intonations of John Ebden, Robert Robinson, Franklin 'Jingle' Engelmann, Richard 'Stinker' Murdoch, Derek Guyler, Margaret Howard, David Jacobs, Kenneth Robinson, Richard Baker, Anthony Quinton, John Julius Norwich, Alistair Cooke, David Jason, Brian Johnston, John Timpson, Jack de Manio, Steve Race, Frank Muir, Dennis Norden, Nicholas Parsons, Kenneth Williams, Derek Nimmo, Peter Jones, Nelson Gabriel, Derek Cooper, Clive Jacobs, Martin Muncaster and Brian Perkins have penetrated my brain and being to the extent that – much as heavy-metal pollutants get into the hair and skin and nails and tissue – they have become a physical as well as an emotional and intellectual part of me. We are all the sum of countless influences. I like to believe that Shakespeare, Keats, Dickens, Austen, Joyce, Eliot, Auden and the great and noble grandees of literature have had their effect on me, but the truth is they were distant uncles and aunts, good for a fiver at Christmas and a book token on birthdays, while Radio 4 and the BBC World Service were my mother and father, a daily presence and constant example.

I believed from the earliest age that I would be quite content to work in radio all my life. If I could just be a continuity announcer or regular broadcaster of some kind, how happy I would be. My dislike of my facial features and physical form contributed to this ambition. I had, as the tired old joke goes, a good face for radio. Announcers and broadcasters have no need of make-up or costume. For one who believed that any attempt at prettification on my part would only draw attention to my cursed deficiencies, a life in front of the microphone seemed like the perfect career. How much more realistic for me a national radio station than irrational venustation.

My first visits to Broadcasting House, the home of BBC Radio in Portland Place, had been as early as 1982, when I played a fictional news reporter for a Radio 1 programme called, I *think*, B15. The basement studios in Broadcasting House were all Bx, and I honestly cannot remember the value of the x which gave this programme its name. In its short run B14 or B12 or whatever it may have called itself was presented by David 'Kid' Jensen, an amiable Canadian disc jockey best known, according to a friend of mine who is very keen on this kind of thing, for being the least objectionable presenter of *Top of the Pops* in all its long history. My character on *Bwhatever*, Bevis Marchant, had his own little slot called *Beatnews*, a rather obvious parody of Radio 1's ludicrously urgent, trivial and self-important *Newsbeat*. Within two weeks of me contributing to this programme Margaret Thatcher had dispatched a task force to recapture the Falkland Islands, and a week later I was taken off the air. My parody of Brian Hanrahan and others was deemed insensitive. I shouted over an electric egg beater in a bucket to recreate the sound of reporting live from a helicopter. I was in fact mocking the grandiose, faux-butch reporting style, not making light of the danger that the military were in, but that has always been too complicated a distinction for stupid people to understand. There was a war on, I was trying to be funny, therefore I had contempt for the sacrifice and bravery of the troops. My levity was tantamount to treason and must be stopped. I think I am angrier about that now than I ever was at the time. Pomposity and indignation grow in old age, like nostril hairs and earlobes.

Not long after *Beatnews* a BBC producer called Ian Gardhouse was in touch with me about contributing to a Radio 4 programme of his called *Late Night Sherrin*. Ned Sherrin was a well-known broadcaster who had started life as a television producer, first at Val Parnell's ATV and then at the BBC. His most famous achievement in that phase of his life had been *That Was The Week That Was*, usually referred to as *TW3*, the live comedy show that had launched the satire boom and David Frost. Since then Nedwin, as I liked to call him, had given the world *Up Pompeii!*, *Side by Side by Sondheim* and a slew of collaborations with Caryl Brahms and others. Trained as a lawyer, he was known for his love of Tin Pan Alley, rich gossip and comely young men. He received his education at Exeter College, Oxford, where he read law, but before that he had been a boy at the most excellently named educational establishment in the history of the world – Sexey's School in Somerset.

I took to Ned straight away. He was like a stern aunt who twinkled and giggled after a little too much gin.

The idea behind *Late Night Sherrin* was to have a hero or heroine guest of the week who would be twitted and teased by Ned and an assortment of young witty types of which I was to be one. Ned called us his 'young turks'. *Late Night Sherrin* morphed, for reasons neither I nor Ian Gardhouse can remember, into *And So to Ned*. They were both live, late-night shows. The routine was for us all to meet for supper high up in the St George's Hotel just by Broadcasting House. The motive behind this, according to Ian, was so that he and Ned could keep an eye on the guests of the week and make sure they stayed relatively sober, a stratagem that failed riotously in the cases of Daniel Farson and Zsa Zsa Gabor.

After *And So to Ned*'s short life came *Extra Dry Sherrin*, whose format I cannot remember as being any different from the others: possibly it had live music or no live music or three guests instead of two. *Extra Dry Sherrin* lasted one series before Ian welcomed me into a new Sherrin-free, live 100-minute programme called *The Colour Supplement* – as the name suggests this was a Sunday 'magazine' show comprising a variety of features, one of which would be a section I could create and shape for myself in any way I chose. Each week I performed a kind of monologue as a different character: an estate agent, an architect, a journalist – I cannot remember the whole gallery. Their surnames usually came from Norfolk villages, so I do recall a Simon Mulbarton, a Sandy Crimplesham and a Gerald Clenchwarton.

It was unfortunate that the pay packets offered proved that the rest of the world held radio in no real esteem. I had grown up hearing Kenneth Williams and others bemoaning in quavering comic tones the insultingly nugatory fees they had been offered for their services and I soon found out that, compared to her brash younger brother, Television, Dame Wireless did indeed live the most frugal and threadbare existence. This never worried me: I would have done it for free, but it was sometimes hard to persuade Richard Armitage that hours composing broadcast monologues, taking parts in comedies and dramas and guesting on panel games were not a waste of time or beneath – as he seemed to think – my dignity. Radio is the poor relation of television insofar as monetary considerations go, but a rich one where it matters – in terms of depth and intimacy.

The writer Tony Sarchet and producer Paul Mayhew-Archer asked me to play an earnest investigative reporter called David Lander in *Delve Special*, a new comedy series they were creating. It was essentially a parody of *Checkpoint*, the very popular Radio 4 programme which featured doughty New Zealander Roger Cook inquiring into a different con, scam or swindle each week. The first part of the programme would catalogue the miseries of the unfortunates who had been exploited and ripped off: they might have had their house destroyed by expensive but incompetent pebble-dashing, been duped into buying a non-existent time-share villa, invested their savings in a – there were any number of ways that innocent lambs could be fleeced by rascally villains, the door-stepping confrontations with whom formed the second and most compulsively enjoyable part of the programme. Cook was famous for getting chi-iked, insulted, jostled, roughed up and even seriously assaulted by the angry subjects of his exposés. *Delve Special* barely had to exaggerate the stories that *Checkpoint* and its successor, John Waite's *Face the Facts*, already provided. Over the next three years we made four series and then, when Roger Cook jumped to television, we jumped with him, being screened for a run of six programmes on Channel 4 as *This Is David Lander*, for which I wore a quite monstrous blond wig. When my workload was simply too heavy to allow me to do a second series, Tony Slattery stepped in, and the show was retitled *This Is David Harper*.

One of the pleasures of making *Delve* for radio, aside from not having to wear a wig or care how I looked at all, was working with the guest performers who came along to play the victims and perpetrators. Brenda Blethyn, Harry Enfield, Dawn French, Andrew Sachs, Felicity Montagu, Jack Klaff, Janine Duvitski and many others came into the studio and gave of their brilliant best. Actually, 'into the studio' is not quite accurate. In order to achieve aural verisimilitude Paul Mayhew-Archer would often place us in the street, on the roof of Broadcasting House, in broom cupboards, catering areas, offices, corridors and hallways so that he and his engineer could capture the authentic tone and atmosphere of the scene. Location radio drama is not common, and the 'Sir, sir! It's a lovely day, can we have our lessons outside?' sort of mood that it engendered made the recordings about as larky as such sessions can ever be.

Meanwhile, still with radio, *The Colour Supplement* soon folded. Ian invited me to participate in yet another piece of Sherrinry, this time a live Saturday-morning show called *Loose Ends*, or 'Loose Neds' as the regular contributors preferred to call it. Over the years these included Victoria Mather, Carol Thatcher, Emma Freud, Graham Norton, Arthur Smith, Brian Sewell, Robert Elms and Victor Lewis-Smith. The format was always the same. Around the table, whose top was laid with green baize cloth, sat the regular contributors and a couple of guest authors, actors or musicians who had some new release to plug. Ned would open with a monologue in which the week's news was jokily reviewed. He was always very good at crediting the monologue's author; in the early years this was usually Neil Shand or Alistair Beaton, his collaborator on a pair of satirical Gilbert and Sullivan adaptations, *The Ratepayer's Iolanthe* and *The Metropolitan Mikado*, romping satires on the Ken Livingstone–Margaret Thatcher face-off which played to great applause in the mid-eighties. After the monologue, Ned introduced some feature which would have been pre-recorded by a regular contributor.

'Carol, I believe you went off to investigate this phenomenon?'

'Well, Ned . . .' Carol would say and give a little preamble to her recorded passage.

'Emma, you braved the dawn on Beachy Head to get a first-hand view, is that right?'

'Well, Ned . . .'

I christened Emma, Carol and Victoria the WellNeds, and they stayed with the programme for as long as anyone.

For my first few contributions to *Loose Ends* I presented a range of characters much as I had on *The Colour Supplement*. One week there was a news story about an academic who had been made to watch hours and hours of television in order to compile a report on whether or not the programming was injurious to the British public, especially its youth. There was much talk in those days about the evils of scenes of violence in cop shows and their deleterious influence on the impressionable minds of the young. For reasons which now seem difficult to reconstruct imaginatively, *Starsky and*

Hutch of all programmes was singled out as a major culprit, a symbol of all that was wrong. 'The Nice Mr Gardhouse', as Ned called Ian, suggested that I do a piece as an academic forced to watch television, so I tapped away that Friday afternoon and came in the next day with a piece written in the persona of a Professor Donald Trefusis, extraordinary Fellow of St Matthew's College, Cambridge, philologist and holder of the Regius Chair of Comparative Linguistics. Trefusis, it turned out, was indeed horrified at the violence of British television. The violence done to his sensibilities and the sensibilities of a young and vulnerable generation by Noel Edmonds and Terry Wogan and others made him shudder and shake. Thank goodness, he concluded, for the jolly car-chases and fight scenes where actors dressed as policemen pretend to shoot each other – without innocent merriment of that kind television would be insupportably damaging to the young.

Heavy steamroller irony, I suppose, but issuing from the querulous mouth of a gabbling tweedy don too old to care whom he might offend, it seemed to work well, well enough at any rate to encourage me to keep the character and try something similar the following week. Soon Trefusis became my sole weekly contributor. A paragraph of introduction would suggest the fiction that I, Stephen Fry, had gone round to his rooms at St Matthew's to interview him. The Professor started to get a trickle of fan mail. One piece, in which he savagely tore into the fad for Parent Power in education, turned the trickle into a flood of hundreds of letters, most of them asking for a transcript of the talk, or 'wireless essay' as he preferred to call them. Trefusis's age and perceived wisdom and authority allowed me to be ruder and more savagely satirical than I could ever have been in my own vocal persona. The British are like that, especially the middle-class Radio 4 audience: a young snappy, angry person annoys them, and they shout at the radio for him to show some respect and get the spiritual and intellectual equivalent of a haircut. But let the same sentiments exactly, word for word, be uttered in high academic tones, as if by a compound of G. E. Moore, Bertrand Russell and Anthony Quinton, and they will roll on to their tummies and purr.

For the next four or five years I fed *Loose Ends* on an almost exclusive diet of Trefusis. Just occasionally I might appear in the guise of another character. Ned's favourite alternative to the Professor was Rosina, Lady Madding, a kind of crazed old Diana Cooper figure. Her voice was a compound of Edith Evans and my prep-school elocution teacher:

I hope you don't mind sitting in here, at my age you get rather fond of draughts. I know you young people feel the cold terribly, but I'm afraid I rather like it. That's right. Yes, it *is* nice, isn't it? Though I wouldn't really call it a cushion, Pekinese is a more common name for them. No, well never mind, he was very old – just throw him on the fire would you?

Colonel and Mrs Chichester

In April 1984 I drove down to Sussex to start my summer of *Forty Years On*. I'll run through the cast list.

Paul Eddington had been promoted to the part that he had watched John Geilgud play nearly sixteen years earlier, that of the headmaster. Eddington was, of course, a big star of television situation comedy, well known and

loved as Penelope Keith's harassed husband in *The Good Life*
and more recently as Jim Hacker, the hopeless and hapless
Minister for Administrative Affairs in the immensely
popular *Yes, Minister*. He had been very friendly during
the rehearsals in London, but I couldn't help being slightly
in awe of him. I had never worked in daily proximity with
someone quite so famous before.

John Fortune took the role of Franklin that Paul had
played in the original production. John was one of the
greats of Cambridge comedy with John Bird, Eleanor
Bron and Timothy Birdsall back in the late fifties. He
had created with Eleanor Bron the legendary (and wiped)
series *Where Was Spring?* His partnership with John Bird
was to achieve great prominence again in the late nineties
and beyond with their wildly intelligent and prescient
satirical contributions to *Bremner, Bird and Fortune*.

Annette Crosby played the school matron. She is now
best known as Victor Meldrew's wife in *One Foot in the
Grave*, but I remembered her as a fiercely glamorous
Queen Victoria in *Edward VII* and an almost impossibly
perky and delicious Fairy Godmother in the *The Slipper
and the Rose*. Doris Hare appeared as the old grandmother.
She was seventy-nine and a magisterial trouper of the old
school, much loved for her years of playing Reg Varney's
mother in *On the Buses*. A fine young actor called Stephen
Rashbrook took the part of the head prefect, while the
rest of the school were played by local West Sussex boys.

The Chichester Festival, begun in the sixties by Leslie
Evershed-Martin and Laurence Olivier, presented each
year a long summer of plays and musicals in a large,
purpose-built, thrust-stage theatre. The 1984 season offered
The Merchant of Venice, *The Way of the World* and *Oh, Kay!*

as well as the *Forty Years On* that I had come down for. A tent, since replaced by a fully fledged second house called the Minerva, served as a space for smaller experimental productions. As a gig, as a booking, Chichester was much prized by old-school actors who liked the relaxed atmosphere of a prosperous south-coast town, a long season in repertory that didn't make too many demands and the security of guaranteed festival attendance. This regular local audience was known collectively as Colonel and Mrs Chichester on account of their severe and hidebound tastes – Rattigan seemed to be the only post-war playwright they were able to stomach. Colonel and Mrs Chichester were not afraid to impart the exciting news that they went to the theatre to be *entertained*.

Patrick Garland was a delightful director, courteous, intelligent, benign and delicately tactful. In rehearsal, he had an endearing habit of addressing the perplexed boys in the cast as if they were members of an Oxbridge common room. 'Forgive my mentioning it, gentlemen, but I do feel myself constrained to observe that the dilatory nature of the communal egress immediately consequent upon Paul's second act exordium is injurious to the pace and dynamism of the scene. I should be so grateful if this deficiency were remedied. With grateful thanks.'

The play's designer was Peter Rice, whose son Matthew soon became a lifelong friend. When not assisting his father he dug the garden of the little house he had hired for the season, shot rabbits and pigeons, skinned and plucked same and cooked them into exquisite suppers. He played the piano, sang songs, sketched and painted. His voice was not unlike Princess Margaret's: high, grand and piercing. Perhaps he had spent too much time in her presence, being a close friend of her son, David Linley, with whom he had been at Bedales.

Unlike Matthew, whose cottage was a charming rural retreat in the Earl of Bessborough's estate, I had taken a rather dull modern flat a short walk from the Festival Theatre. I devoted my spare time to the script of *Me and My Girl*. Once or twice Mike Ockrent came down to work on it with me. Robert Lindsay had been duly cast as Bill, and the part of Sally was to be taken by Leslie Ash, subject to her taking lessons in tap and singing. The major character role of Sir John had been given to Frank Thornton, better known as the Grace Brothers floorwalker Captain Peacock in *Are You Being Served?* The show's opening was all set for autumn in Leicester if I could just deliver a final rehearsal script within the next month.

My parents came down to Chichester from Norfolk for *Forty Years On*'s first night. I proudly introduced them to Alan Bennett and Paul Eddington. Alan in turn introduced us to his friends Alan Bates and Russell Harty.

'I love a play where there are laughs and sobs,' said Alan Bates, in a much camper voice than I would have imagined could ever issue from the lips of *The Go-Between*'s Ted Burgess and *Far From the Madding Crowd*'s Gabriel Oak, two of the manliest men in all of British film. 'I mean, you've got to have a giggle and a gulp, haven't you, or what's the theatre for?'

Russell Harty, with anagrammatic *diablerie*, referred to Alan Bates as Anal Beast, or, in mixed company, Lana Beast.

I think I was disappointing as Tempest. In my mind I believed that I could play the part and play it with brilliance, but something held me back from being any better than competent. I was OK. Perfectly good. *Fine*.

That last is the worst word in theatre. When friends come backstage and use the word 'fine' about a play, a production or your performance you know they hated it. Often they preface it, out of nowhere, with the word 'no', which is fantastically revealing.

'No, it was *fine*!'

'No, really, I thought it was . . . you know . . .'

Why would they open a sentence with 'No' when they have not even been asked a question? There can be only one explanation. As they walk along the backstage corridors towards your dressing-room they have said inside their own head, 'God, that stank. Stephen was embarrassingly awful. The whole thing was *ghastly*.' Then they enter and, as if answering and contradicting themselves, they instantly say, 'No, I thought it was great . . . no, really, I . . . mmm . . . I liked it.' I know this is right because I so often catch myself doing exactly the same thing without meaning to. 'No . . . really, it was fine.'

The production as a whole was considered a success, however. Colonel and Mrs Chichester enthused, and word soon got out that we were going to 'transfer'.

'Excellent news,' Paul Eddington said to me one evening as we stood waiting to go on. I nearly wrote 'as we stood in the wings', but Chichester had an apron stage that thrust out into the auditorium on three sides, so we must have been standing behind the set.

'Ooh!' I said. 'What good news?'

'It's official. We are going to transfer.'

'Wow!' I did a little dance. I had no idea what he was talking out.

It took me two days to work out the meaning of 'transfer'. The boys in the cast seemed to know, the women who served in the cafeteria knew, the tobacconist on the corner and the landlady of my flat knew, everyone knew except me.

'Wonderful news about the transfer,' said Doris Hare. 'The Queen's, I believe.'

'Er . . . ?' Did a transfer mean a royal visit? Now I was even more puzzled.

'I've played most of the houses on the Avenue, but this will be the first time I've played the Queen's.'

The Avenue? I pictured us in some tree-lined boulevard giving an outdoor performance to a bored and affronted monarch. The idea seemed grotesque.

Later, Patrick said to me, 'You will have heard the good news about the transfer?'

'Indeed. Yup. Great, isn't it?'

'This will be your West End debut, I think?'

So *that* is what it meant! The production would be *transferred* from Chichester to the West End. A transfer. Of course. D'uh.

I finished the Chichester season in a frenzy. Mike Ockrent came to collect my final draft of *Me and My Girl* a week before we closed.

Back in London I decided, since Kim and Steve were so happy together at Draycott Place, that it was time for me to move out of Chelsea and set up on my own. For a hundred pounds a week I found myself the tenant of a furnished one-bedroom flat in Regent Square, Bloomsbury. Just me and the new love of my life.

Computer 2

Early in the year I had called Hugh up excitedly. 'I've just bought a Macintosh. Cost me a thousand pounds.'

'*What?*'

Hugh enjoyed about a week of relaying the news of my fantastic expenditure on something as absurd and unworthy of outlay as a raincoat before he discovered that this Macintosh was a new type of computer.

I was more insanely in love with this strangely beautiful piece of technology than anything I had ever owned before. It had a cable leading out of it that ended in a device called a 'mouse'. The screen was *white* when you started it all up and loaded the system disk. The text that came up was black on white, like paper, instead of the fuzzily glowing green or orange on black offered by all other computers. An arrow on the screen could be activated by moving the mouse on the desk next to the computer. Images of a floppy disk and a dustbin appeared on screen and all along the top were words which, when clicked on with the mouse, pulled down a kind of graphical roller-blind on which menu options were written. You could double-click on pictures of documents and folders and windowpanes would open. I had never seen or imagined anything like it. Nor had anyone. Only Apple's short-lived Lisa computer had used this way of doing things before and it had never had a place in the consumer or home market.

While it was being developed this graphical user interface had been referred to as WIMP, standing for Windows, Icons, Menus, Pointing-device. I was instantly a slave to its elegance, ease, usefulness and wit. Most of you reading this will be too young to imagine a time when computers could have been presented in any other fashion, but this was new and revolutionary. Extraordinarily, it didn't catch on for ages. For years and years after the January 1984 release of the Apple Macintosh the rivals – IBM, Microsoft, Apricot, DEC, Amstrad and others – all dismissed the mouse, the icon and the graphical desktop as 'gimmicky', 'childish' and 'a passing fad'. Well, I shall refrain from going too deeply into the subject. I am fully aware of how minority a sport my love of all this dorky wizardry is. All you need know is that I, my 128 kilobyte Macintosh, Imagewriter bitmap printer and small collection of floppy disks were all very, *very* happy together. What possible need could I have for sex or human relationships when I had this?

Hugh, Katie and Nick Symons shared a house in Leighton Grove, Kentish Town; I had my Bloomsbury flat; Kim stayed on in Chelsea. We all saw each other as much as possible, but I was about to be busy performing eight times a week on the West End stage.

Richard Armitage had arranged with Patrick and the *Forty Years On* producers that in November I would be released from the run of the play for a few days, so that I could travel up to Leicester for the opening of *Me and My Girl*: this contractual clause was insisted upon not because Richard kindly believed I should have the treat of attending the first night of a musical to which I had contributed a script, but because he wanted to be sure that I would be on hand should the dress rehearsal and opening demonstrate a need for urgent, unforeseen rewrites.

We had participated in some strange conversations over the preceding months in which Richard had proved himself capable of changing hats mid-sentence, shuttling between his identity as the show's producer, the heir and manager of the composer's estate and, not least so far as I was concerned, my agent. 'I have had a word with myself,' he would say, 'and I have agreed to my outrageous demands as to your financial participation in this project. I wanted to cut you out of any backend, but I absolutely insisted, so much to my annoyance you have points in the show, which pleases me greatly.'

Early on in the rehearsal process Leslie Ash had not responded well to her dance and vocal lessons and by mutual agreement she had dropped out of the cast. I sat in Richard's office one afternoon as he rubbed his chin anxiously. Who on earth could we cast as Sally?

'What about Emma?' I said. 'She sings wonderfully and, while she may not have done any tap dancing, she's surely the kind of person who can do anything she turns her mind to.'

Richard's personality once more split before my eyes. 'Of course. Brilliant. I want her,' he said, before riposting, 'Well, if you do, you'll damned well have to pay through the nose for her. Oh now, come on, be reasonable. She has no experience, no real name. That's as maybe, she is one of the greatest talents of her generation and, as such, she'll cost you.'

I left Richard to wrestle the matter. I understood that he fell short of actually beating himself up and managed before too long to end his tense negotiations by shaking his hand on a deal satisfactory to both of him.

Emma duly joined the cast. She knew Robert Lindsay well, having worked at the Royal Exchange in Manchester, where Robert had presented his excellently received Hamlet. In fact I believe I am right in saying that Emma and Robert had known each other *very* well back then. Really jolly well indeed. Oh yes.

Forty Years On had to undergo one or two cast changes for its West End run. John Fortune and Annette Crosbie were unavailable for the transfer, and their roles went to David Horovitch and Emma's mother, Phyllida Law. The boys were recast too: the local Chichester lads who had thrown themselves into their roles with such aplomb and good spirits were now replaced by London stage-school professionals, who were just as sparky and cheerful and a great deal more streetwise and experienced.

The day before the opening, during the interval between the technical run and the evening dress rehearsal, I walked out of the Queen's Theatre stage door with David Horovitch and a group of these boys, heading for a pasta restaurant that they with their Soho savvy had recommended. Alan Bennett was out in the street, attaching bicycle clips to his trousers.

'Are you going to join us for spaghetti?' I asked him.

'Yes, do!' said the boys.

'Oh no,' said Alan, in slightly shocked tones, as if we were inviting him to a naked orgy in an opium den. 'I shall cycle home and have a poached egg.' Alan Bennett is always excellent at being as much like Alan Bennett as you could reasonably hope. A keen mind, a powerful artistic sensibility, a fierce political and social conscience – but a man of bicycle clips and poached eggs. Is it any wonder that he is so loved?

My name was now up in neon on Shaftesbury Avenue. I was too embarrassed to take a picture, which now, of course, I regret. I do have a photograph of the first-night party. I should imagine I was very happy. I had every reason to be.

Paul Eddington was happy too, enjoying a ripe and fruity time in his career. He had just been elected to the Garrick Club, which gave him enormous pleasure, and he and Nigel Hawthorne had been paid a large sum of money for a TV commercial, which pleased him almost as much.

'A *very* large sum,' he said happily. 'It's to advertise a new Cadbury's chocolate bar called Wispa. Nigel whispers in my ear in his Sir Humphrey character – half a day's work for the most extraordinary fee.'

'Gosh,' I said, 'and do Tony Jay and Jonathan Lynn get a good wedge too?'

'Ah!' Paul winced slightly at my mention of the names of the writers and creators of *Yes, Minister*, a mention I had not made mischievously but out of genuine curiosity as to how these things worked. 'Yes. Nigel and I had a twinge of guilt about that, so we're sending them each a case of claret. Jolly good claret.'

There is a chasm between writers and performers: for each, life often looks better across the divide, and while I am sure Tony and Jonathan were pleased to receive their case of jolly good claret, I cannot doubt that they may have preferred the kind of remuneration Paul and Nigel were enjoying. As I was to discover, however, writing has its rewards too.

One night, as the curtain came down, Paul whispered in my ear with delighted triumph, 'I can tell you now. It's official. I'm Prime Minister.'

That night the final episode of *Yes, Minister* had been broadcast. It ended with Jim Hacker succeeding to the leadership of his party and the country. Keeping the secret, Paul told me, had been the hardest job he had ever had.

I settled into the run of the play. There were six evening performances a week with matinees on Wednesdays and Saturdays. I would be saying the same lines to the same people, wearing the same clothes and handling the same props eight times a week for the next six months. Next door in the Globe Theatre (now called the Gielgud) a show set in a girls' school called *Daisy Pulls it Off* was running, and the cast of schoolgirls and schoolboys in each got on *very well together*, as you might imagine. Each Wednesday afternoon in the interval between matinee and evening performance there would be a backstage school feast, the boys hosting in the Queen's one week, the girls in the Globe the next. Further along the street stood the Lyric Theatre, where Leonard Rossiter was playing Truscott in a revival of Joe Orton's *Loot*. One evening we were stunned to hear that he had collapsed and died of a heart attack just before going on. Only a few months earlier both Tommy Cooper and Eric Morecambe had also died on stage. A small selfish and shameful part of me regretted the certainty that I would now never meet or work with those three geniuses at least as much as I mourned their passing or felt for the desolation such sudden deaths must have brought their families.

November came, and it was time for me to go up to Leicester for the opening of *Me and My Girl*. The plan was to arrive on Thursday for the dress rehearsal, stay on Friday for the first night and be back in London in time for the Saturday matinee and evening shows of *Forty Years On*. Who meanwhile would be taking my place as Tempest? I was horrified to discover that it would be Alan Bennett himself, reprising his original performance from 1968. Horrified, because I would, naturally, miss the chance to see him.

He came into the dressing-room I shared with David Horovitch on the Monday evening of that week.

'Oh, Stephen, I've got a funny request. I don't know if you'll want to accede, but I'll put it to you anyway.'

'Yes?'

'I know you aren't going till Thursday, but would you mind if I went on as Tempest on the Wednesday matinee and evening as well?'

'Oh goodness, not at all. Not *at all*.' The dear fellow was obviously a little nervous and wanted to dip his toes in the water and feel his way back into the role with a smaller matinee audience. The wonderful part of it all was that I could now be in that audience and watch him. For two performances. It is not often that an actor gets to see a production he is in, and while many prefer not to watch someone else playing their own part, especially if it is a master like Bennett, I was too much the fan to care if the comparison cast me in the shade. Which I knew it would. After all, he wrote Tempest for himself and he was Alan, for heaven's sake, Bennett.

I watched him both times and went round to the dressing-room.

'Oh, Alan, you were astounding. Astounding.'

'Ooh, do you think so, really?'

'I'm so pleased you were on today, but you know,' I said, 'you absolutely didn't need to ease yourself in with a matinee performance, you were perfect from the start.'

'Oh, that isn't why I asked if I could go on today.'

'It isn't?'

'To be honest, no.'

'Well, then why?'

'Well, you know I've got this film?'

Indeed I did know. Alan had written the screenplay for a film called *A Private Function*, which starred Maggie Smith, Michael Palin and Denholm Elliott. I was planning to catch it over the weekend.

'You see,' he said, 'it's the Royal Command premiere this evening, and I wanted a solid excuse not to have to go . . .'

It is a very Bennetty kind of shyness that sees performing on stage in front of hundreds of strangers as less stressful than attending a party.

Leicester passed in a blur. The dress rehearsal of *Me and My Girl* seemed fine, but without an audience it was impossible to tell whether any of the slapstick and big comic routines would really work. Robert and Emma were wonderful together. Robert's comedy business with his cloak, with his bowler hat, with cigarettes, cushions and any other props that came his way was masterly. I hadn't seen physical comedy this good outside silent pictures.

I went round the dressing-rooms with good-luck bottles of champagne, cards, bunches of roses and expressions of faith, hope and gratitude.

'Well, we are waiting for the final director now . . .' said Frank Thornton, adding in his most lugubrious manner the answer to my unspoken question, '. . . the audience!'

'Ah!' I nodded at this wise actorly thought.

In the end the final director jerked up their thumbs with a loud 'Lambeth Walk' 'Oi!'. They stood and cheered at the end for what seemed like half an hour. It was a most wonderful triumph, and everybody hugged each other and sobbed with joy just as they do in the best Hollywood backstage musicals. Mike Ockrent's magical and comically detailed direction, Gillian Gregory's choreography, Chris Walker's arrangements and a chorus and cast that threw themselves body and soul into every second of the two hours' running time ensured as happy an evening as I can remember in the theatre.

I would not want to be misunderstood. Musicals are still not quite my thing, and I am sure there are plenty of you who will wince at the thought of pearly kings and queens and larky high kicks accompanying a 1930s rum-ti-tum-ti score. Nonetheless I was pleased to be involved with something so alien to my usual tastes and which bubbled and bounced with such unaffected lightness of touch and warm silliness and unapologetic high spirits. We bucked the trend for self-regarding, high-toned, through-sung operatic melodramas. Not just bucked, buck-and-winged. I liked the fact that we were presenting an evening that paid homage to the origins of the word 'musical' as an adjective not a noun. From its beginnings the genre was Musical Comedy, and we had all hoped that there was still a demand for that kind of theatre. At the party I leant forward to a beaming Richard Armitage.

'Do you think,' I yelled in his ear, flaunting my theatrical jargon, 'that we will transfer?'

'Sure of it,' said Richard. 'Thank you, m'dear. My father is looking down and winking.'

I turned away, a tear in my eye. I knew how important it is for men to feel that they have finally earned the approval of their fathers.

Conspicuous Consumption

Country Cottages, Cheques, Credit Cards and Classic Cars

Back in London, the run of *Forty Years On* continued through Christmas and the New Year. I had started to cross off the days on a chart in the dressing-room like a prisoner scratching on the wall of his cell. There is something quite dreadful about what enforced repetition of action and speech does to the brain. Experienced stage actors all know how common it is to suffer a kind of out-of-body experience on stage where you look down and helplessly watch yourself from above. The moment comes to speak your lines and you will either freeze and dry up or say the same speech three or four times in a row without noticing. Only a pinch or a kick from a fellow actor can save you.

There was one scene in *Forty Years On* in which I had to tick a boy off for something or other. I would strike the corner of a desk hard with my index finger in time to the rhythms of my reprimand. One half-empty matinee I looked down and saw that the varnish on the desk had been worn away by the striking of my finger. For some reason this upset me greatly, and I resolved that evening to strike another part of the desk. When the moment came I raised my hand, aimed a good six inches to the left of the scuff mark and brought my finger down with a bang *on exactly the usual place*. For the next few days I tried again and again, but some form of extreme and insane muscle-memory insisted that my finger had always to hit the same spot. This disturbed me deeply, and I began to look upon the two or three weeks remaining as a hideous incarceration from which I would never escape. I didn't share this sense of suffocating torment with David, Phyllida or Paul, as they seemed, with their greater experience, serene and at ease.

Doris Hare, who was eighty by this time, had more energy than the rest of us put together. She was the only principal in the cast who didn't go straight home as soon as the show ended. She and I would go most nights to Joe Allen's. Doris had a way of entering the restaurant that made one convinced that it was not a woollen shawl about her neck, but a fox fur fastened with an emerald clasp, and that her companion was not a gawky and self-conscious young actor but a sleek compound of Noël Coward, Ivor Novello and Binkie Beaumont.

'The secret, dear,' she would tell me, 'is to enjoy yourself. Why would we be in the theatre if we didn't love every minute of it? Casting, rehearsals, matinees, touring . . . it's all *marvellous*.' And she meant it.

Joe Allen's, an American diner-style restaurant, is a popular hangout for actors, dancers, agents, producers and playwrights. The famously rude waiters and waitresses are often drawn from the ranks of showbusiness themselves. An American producer is notorious for once having got impatient at the slow service. He clicked his fingers for a waiter, calling out, 'Actor! Oh, Actor!'

I sat there in Joe Allen's one evening with Russell Harty, Alan Bennett and Alan Bates. All eyes were upon our table until suddenly heads swung towards the door. Laurence Olivier and Dustin Hoffman walked in. Our table no longer existed.

'Well, that's us told,' said Russell.

Olivier walked past, beaming at everyone in a general way.

'Why don't you go and say hello to him?' Alan Bennett said to Russell. 'You know him well.'

'I couldn't do that. Everyone would say, "Look there goes that odious Russell Harty sucking up to Larry Olivier."'

Harty and Bennett were very good friends. They each had a house in North Yorkshire. Alan would drive them up in his car at weekends. On one such journey, so the story goes, Alan said, 'Why don't we play a game of some kind to beguile the hours?'

'What about Botticelli?' said Russell.

'Ooh no! That's too competitive.'

They thought for a while, then Alan piped up, 'I know. We each have to think of the person whose underpants we would least like to have to wear on our head.'

'Colin Welland,' said Russell without a moment's hesitation.

'Ooh, that's not fair,' said Alan, 'you've won already.'

On another occasion, as they were driving through Leeds, Russell wound down the window and called out to a morose-looking woman waiting for a bus in the pelting rain, 'Hello, love! All right?'

As she looked up in bewilderment he wound the window back up, leant back and said with great satisfaction, 'The privilege of being able to cast a golden ray of sunshine into an otherwise dull and unremarkable existence.'

As soon as I was free from the fetters of *Forty Years On* my life seemed to triple in speed and intensity. I moved out of the Bloomsbury flat and into a large furnished house in Southgate Road on the fringes of the de Beauvoir Estate between Islington and the Balls Pond Road. Nick Symons,

Hugh, Katie and I shared this excellently eccentric house for the better part of a year. It looked, to Hugh's approving eye, like the kind of house the Rolling Stones might have rented in 1968. It was crammed to every corner with Benares brass trays, alabaster lamps, buhl cabinets, stuffed birds and waxed flowers in glass domes, lacquer screens, papier-mâché bowls, mahogany chiffoniers, oil paintings of varying quality in chipped gilt plaster frames, indecipherable objects of sinister Dutch treen, impossible silvered wallpaper and madly tarnished mirrors. Our landlord, who dropped by only occasionally, was a spongey-nosed individual by the name of Stanley. He seemed very relaxed and unconcerned about a group of what were little more than students living their disordered lives amongst his antique bibelots and whatnots.

The second series of *Alfresco* had been aired nationally by this time, making not the slightest dent upon the public consciousness. I was busy enough with the *Listener*, radio, tweaks for *Me and My Girl*'s West End transfer and my first proper film role. Directed by Mike Newell, the picture was called *The Good Father*, adapted from a Peter Prince novel by Christopher Hampton.

At the read-through I glanced nervously around and tried to look as if I belonged at the table. There was Simon Callow, whose controversial new book *Being An Actor* had served as the first blast of the trumpet against the monstrous regiment of tyrannical stage directors; next to him sat one of my favourite actresses, Harriet Walter; next to her, Joanne Whalley, who was just about to make a name and earn enduring teenage-fantasy status for herself bringing Michael Gambon off in *The Singing Detective*; and next to her sat one half of the National

Theatre of Brent, Jim Broadbent. And finally there was the film's star, Anthony Hopkins, a man from whom charisma, power and virility radiated with a force that was frankly frightening. I had been faintly obsessed with him ever since his blue eyes burnt out of the screen at me in Richard Attenborough's *Young Winston*.

Too late for the preliminary introductions, Miriam Margolyes had burst in like a beaming pinball just in time for the start of the read. When it was over she approached me.

'How do you do? I'm Mir . . .' She stopped and plucked at her tongue with her thumb and forefinger, '. . . Miriam Margolyes. Sorry about that, I was licking my girlfriend out last night and I've still got some cunt hairs in my mouth.' Miriam is perhaps the kindest, most loyal and incorruptibly decent person on the whole Equity roll, but she is certainly not someone to take out to tea with the archdeacon.

In the film I played a man called Creighton, divorced and beaten down by the crushing weight of life, children and alimony. I had only one scene, but since it was with Hopkins himself it was in my mind as good a role as Michael Corleone and Rhett Butler combined. The plot required me to have been at school with Simon Callow, which wounded me a little, as I knew he was a good eight years older than me. To someone in their twenties, eight years is a lifetime. I knew that I was not the type ever to be asked to play lissom youths or handsome lovers, but it did seem a little hard to be plunged into middle age for my first-ever film role.

People are strange about casting.

We hold a party at Southgate Road about this time. I go

David Lander, earnest investigative reporter in a badly behaved blond wig.

The Crystal Cube, with Emma and Hugh.

The Crystal Cube. The warty look was created using Rice Krispies. True story.

The man who put the turd in *Saturday Live*. I cannot recall a single thing about that sketch. Why the rolled-up trouser leg?

As Lord Melchett in *Blackadder*

More *Saturday Live*: with Hugh, Harry Enfield and Ben Elton. Why the electric carving knife, if that's what it is? I remember *nothing* of this moment.

DON'T DO IT
Stephen Fry

Studied indifference: Stephen Fry

Lord Hailsham, you may remember, sent letters to important people in the Cabinet earlier this year telling them he strongly disapproved of 'having sex'. Quintin and I have had our disagreements over the years – we could never agree about John Denver, for instance – but on the subject of sex we are as of one mind.

I haven't – and I can't speak for Hailsham here – had sex for four years. This didn't begin as a conscious embrace of the virtues of celibacy, nor was I forced to make myself unavailable because no one wanted me. Less an oil-painting and more an oil-slick I may be, but I think that if I wanted intimate carnal congress I could find it without paying. I gave coitus the red card for utilitarian reasons: the displeasure, discomfort and aggravation it caused outweighed any momentary explosions of pleasure, ease or solace. A simple calculus of felicity.

Sex does not enrich or deepen a relationship, it permanently cheapens and destabilises one. Everyone I know who is unfortunate enough to have a sex-mate, joy-partner, bed-friend, love-chum, call them what you will, finds that – after a week or two of long blissful afternoons of making the beast with two backs, or the beast with one back and a funny-shaped middle or the beast with legs splayed in the air and arms gripping the sides of the mattress – the day dawns when Partner A is keen for more swinking, grinding and sweating and Partner B would rather turn over and catch up with Jeeves and Bertie. Dismal weeks follow. A finds it difficult to meet B's eye after 9.00 in the evening, B announces in a nonchalant voice that he or she is 'completely bushed' just so that A will know that 'it isn't on tonight', and before they are a month older, nasty cracks appear.

I yield to no one in my admiration of the erotic capabilities of the human body. The contemplation of the erotic is a joyous frame in life's rich comic strip. But let it not be supposed that there is anything erotic about coition. A walk, a smile, a gait, a way of flicking the hair away from the eyes, the manner in which clothes encase the body, these can be erotic, but I would be greatly in debt to the man who could tell me what could ever be appealing about those damp, dark, foul-smelling and revoltingly tufted areas of the body that constitute the main dishes in the banquet of love. These zones, when interfered with, will of course produce all kinds of chemical reactions in the body: the blood will course, the breath will quicken and the heart will pound. Once under the influence of the drugs supplied by one's own body, there is no limit to the indignities, indecencies and bestialities to which the most usually rational and graceful of us will sink.

Let's face it, we have outgrown the functional necessity for these lusts. There was a time when Man did not connect the act of intercourse with the production of babies. There is no obvious reason to suppose that a penetration one summer leads to a baby next spring. And so in the past we *had* to keep rogering blindly away all the time and Dame Nature was kind enough at least to make it spasmodically pleasurable. We have inherited this instinct to rut as we have inherited other instincts once necessary for survival: the instincts to fight and quarrel and frighten and conquer. But these vestigial urges have no place in a rational, intelligent community that can determine its own destiny.

I concede that it is healthy to remember and respect our origins and the duality of our nature, but we still have eating and sleeping and defecating – these are far less under our control and serve to remind us quite painfully enough of the physicality and baseness of the flesh that houses and imprisons our great creating minds. We have no need of the moist, infected pleasures of the bedroom to humiliate us more.

Besides, I'm scared that I may not be very good at it.

Photo Tim Platt/*Tatler*
©Condé Naste Publications Ltd.
Words Stephen Fry/*Tatler*
©Condé Naste Publications Ltd.

The Tatler celibacy article.

From *Forty Years On*, Chichester, 1984. Self, Doris Hare, Paul Eddington and John Fortune.

First-night party f[...] the *Forty Years* [...] 'transfer', Quee[...] Theatre, London, 198[...] Katie Kelly (back to [...] shiny bun), boys fr[...] the cast, self, Hu[...] Laurie, sister J[...]

(*Left and bottom*)
Celebrating Christopher
Richardson's birthday
and Uppingham School
leaving party –
I remember that
Paul Smith shirt . . .

Emma.

Me and My Girl. Robert Lindsay and Emma Thompson.

The French's acting edition of
Me and My Girl.

Me and My Girl. Emma's dressing-room on the first night.

One hour before *Me and My Girl*'s Broadway opening. Between my cousin
Danny and his grandmother, Great-Aunt Dita.

Experimenting with a new pair of glasses in the kitchen of my parents' house in Norfolk.

around with a Nebuchadnezzar of champagne topping up the guests and trying not to breathe in the fumes myself being well aware of what my allergy to champagne might bring on. As I pass by, an actor friend asks what I am up to and I mention *The Good Father*.

'What sort of role?'

'Oh, I play this rather defeated father and husband who's going through a divorce.'

'You!' the actor is unable or unwilling to hide the contempt, outrage and disapproval in his voice. 'What the hell would *you* know about that?'

I grin tightly and move on. So I should be playing nothing but celibate gay men? Is that how acting works? I suppose the actor, who is married, with a second child on the way and not very much in demand, is peeved that he should be out of work while juicy parts are going to lucky buggers like me: his savage titter of disbelief must be his way of coping. People who didn't go to drama school, have enormous holes in their Chekhov technique and are given parts that they cannot possibly play out of any true experience must be excessively aggravating to proper actors. I can see that, but I am still a little hurt.

We are rather excited tonight to have Kate Bush at the party. Hugh has just been in a video of her newest song. Two Nebuchadnezzars of champagne last the evening perfectly, and for those, like me, who don't drink it, we are all still of an age where guests bring bottles and there is enough red wine to keep us merry too. Talking of red wine, parked in the street outside the house is my new pride and joy, a claret-coloured Daimler Sovereign. How perfect is my life. I want to weep when I look back. Enough money to keep me in cigarettes, shirts and a nice new car, but not so much as to isolate me from this charmed studenty existence of Bohemian house-sharing and irresponsible fun. Experiences are still new and exciting, my palate is not jaded, life is not stale.

We were happy and lucky, but this was Thatcher's Britain, and we did not let a moment pass without giving Thatcher's Britain a searing indictment. Forgive the phrase. We were still children really and Thatcher's Britain seemed to us to be something that needed searingly to be indicted, the searinglier the better. You might imagine that it had treated us so well that we should be on our knees thanking it for the film roles, job opportunities, affordable property prices, Daimler Sovereigns and burgeoning prosperity that had come our way with a minimum of effort. We certainly did not see it that way. Firstly, our educations and upbringings had been received under Labour and Edward Heath's more liberal and consensus-based dispensations. The new callousness and combative certainty of Thatcher and her cabinet of vulgar curiosities were alien to the values we grew up with, and it smelt all wrong. I know that if you are flourishing in a regime you are supposed not to bellyache about it. Seems ungrateful. Cake and eat it. Biting the hand that feeds. The moral high ground is easy to perch on if you're in a cashmere sweater. Chattering classes. Trendy liberals. Bah. I do see that. Bad enough from someone in an ordinary job, but to hear searing indictments of Thatcher's Britain from an *actor* . . .

The world finds it difficult to credit the breed with enough brains or the qualities of seriousness, understanding and worldly experience required for a political statement to which they can attach the slightest value. Daffy airheaded twazzocks, every one of them, is more or less the accepted view; one from which it is hard to dissent, and I speak as a fully paid-up member of Equity and the Screen Actors Guild myself. This is partly because, love them/us as I do – hard to find a kinder, funnier, more loyal bunch, etc., etc. – there are probably more embarrassing featherheads and ludicrous naifs in the acting profession than in any other. Perhaps because to penetrate a role properly you first have to empty the brain of all cynicism and self-awareness and such irrelevant impedimenta as logic, reason and empirical sense. Certainly some, but not all, of the very best actors I have known are innocent of any such encumbrances. I have noticed that, whenever I have made the mistake of getting myself embroiled in some public controversy or other, the side that holds the opposing view will always refer to me as an actor. It successfully devalues whatever it is I might have said. I have spent more time writing than acting, but 'After all, he's only a writer,' doesn't have quite the same sneering finality as 'Why should we pay any attention to the views of an *actor*?' I am not always such an imbecile as to be surprised by that, or even aggrieved. We all choose whatever weapons are at hand in a fight and when we get close in we jab and kick at the weakest and most vulnerable parts.

I mention all this because I am teeing up a section in which I have to take you through more sickening examples of my good fortune, dissipation, wanton wastefulness and sheer cheapness of spirit and lowness of social or moral tone.

Me and My Girl transferred to the Adelphi Theatre. Matthew Rice, David Linley and I made our way on foot from the stage door in Maiden Lane to the first-night party at Smith's in Covent Garden. As we walked, paparazzi closed in on David like wasps at a picnic. 'This way, Lord Linley.' Flash. 'Lord Linley, Lord Linley!' Flash, pop, flash. Every now and then he would bat them away with a growl. They would shrink back, mass and swarm again. This continued for the length of our walk.

'What can it be like?' I asked David.

'You'll know soon enough,' he said.

This was a charming remark, but not one I could set much store by. My name was beginning to mean a little more in the world, but there was still no danger of photographers shouting it out on the red carpet. As soon as I had understood that a few appearances on television, especially in a show like *Alfresco* which appealed to so few, would not generate instant fame, I had relaxed into life and work without troubling myself too much about the whole business. Letters had started to come in, a few from *Alfresco* . . . watchers, I won't say fans, and some from *Loose Ends* listeners or readers of the magazines for which I wrote. Once or twice I would be stopped in the street.

'You're that . . . that man . . .' Fingers would be clicked and feet stamped at the effort of memory.

'I know I look like him, but I'm not,' I tried saying once or twice. I soon learnt that whether or not they knew my name or where they had seen me they knew perfectly well that I was not anybody's doppelgänger. For good or ill my features are unmistakable, and since that time I have accepted that pretending not to be me is no good. Some can get away with it, but not I. Sunglasses, pulled-down beanies and muffled-up scarves make no difference. I might as well be carrying a sign with my name on.

As 1985 wore on, and *Me and My Girl* clearly established itself as a major hit, royalty statements from Noel Gay Music began to arrive. The 'backend' that Richard Armitage the agent had strong-armed Richard Armitage the producer into accepting was beginning to bear fruit.

Martin Bergman said to me with his usual assured omniscience, 'Oh yes, Stephen, you'll get at least a million out of it, no question.'

I didn't believe him for a second, but the weekly arrival of cheques was a delightful new feature of my life.

The first thing I did as soon as I fully understood that my 'net worth' was increasing was to sign up for every conceivable kind of plastic. When you applied for a Diner's Club card you could ask to be sent two, one for personal use and one for business. I needed no such distinction to be made in my life, but two cards, hurrah! I had a gold American Express Card, at that time the ultimate status symbol, as well as an ordinary green one. I had the usual bank card, two Mastercards (Access, your flexible friend, being one) and two Visa cards. Added to these were sundry store, subscription and membership cards. Do you remember Clifton James as Sheriff J.W. Pepper in *Live and Let Die* and *The Man With the Golden Gun*? Big, pot-bellied American in a Hawaiian shirt forever chewing and dabbing his brow with a bandana? There's a scene where he takes out his wallet, and its concertinaed compartments flip down almost to the ground exposing dozens of credit cards. That was my wallet.

Why? Well, I am distrustful of too much certainty in self-analysis, but I do not think this fatuous and infantile display of 'worth' can have been unconnected to the crime that got me arrested. Aged seventeen, I had run riot around England with someone else's credit cards – a Diner's Club and an Access card. That is what had got me sent to Pucklechurch prison.[†] I suppose eight years later I still found it hard to believe that I merited my own cards. I was now creditworthy. These cards were daily reminders that the long nightmare was over and that I was at last a proper, decent citizen solidly placed on the right side of the law. Not that this was to be anything like an endpoint for me. By no means. The same old self-destructive urges were only just below the surface. In all too short a time those same credit cards, symbols of legitimacy and respectability or not, would be chopping endless lines of far from legal and less than respectable cocaine.

For the meantime I clung to these tokens of worth, worthiness, credit and credibility. I spent £7,000 on a laser printer for my Macintosh computer. It was a staggering sum and in the eyes of most people unjustifiable and absurd. No one had ever seen before such extraordinary print clarity and quality from a computer. The standard machines were the dot-matrix kind, usually taking special paper that had punched holes down the sides; they produced type that was composed, as the name suggests, of dots, resulting in a fuzzy, low resolution. In the radio studio I was now able to brandish Trefusis scripts that looked as if they had been professionally typeset. With great solemnity I would tell the guests and contributors around the *Loose Ends* table that I wrote my script in longhand and then dropped it off at the printer's who produced three copies, one for Ian Gardhouse, one for the sound engineer and one for me. I would be stared at as if I were tragically and perhaps dangerously insane, but the fact that they could swallow such a ludicrous story shows how rare laser-printed pages were back then.

I became the first non-businessperson I knew to have a carphone. I would sit in traffic, wallowing back against the Connollized leather of the Sovereign, and call people for the sheer pleasure of being able to say, 'Hang on, the lights are turning green,' and hearing my interlocutor turn green too, with envy. Of course, they probably just thought, 'What a wanker,' but I was too happy to care.

I decided that I should have a house in the country. Look, I can't keep apologizing, but I will say one more time, I know how horrible this must be to read. A cat that keeps falling on its feet, even one that had a rather problematic kittenhood, does not make a very interesting or admirable hero. I have to lay out the facts as I recall them in the full knowledge that they reflect little or no credit on me. The cash was flying in, and I was a victim of nothing but my own saucer-eyed cupidity and trashy delight in the riches the world seemed so keen to offer me.

Having run away as a child from what I could now see was a blissful country home, I wanted to make one of my own. The country meant only one thing to me, Norfolk. There was one small problem, however. I knew that my parents, particularly my father, hated display and swagger and swank. I was too embarrassed to let them know quite how much I was earning. It seemed obscene and unjustified. My father I associated with a crippling work ethic and a contempt for money, or at least a complete lack of interest in it. For me to be running about the garden of life with my pinny spread open to catch all the gold coins raining down on me would have struck him, I believed, as grotesque and disgusting. This would be income almost as dishonestly come by in his eyes, or so I told myself, as the money I used to steal in my badolescence.

Stephen's way with embarrassing problems has ever been either to run away or, as in this case, to lie his way out of trouble. You do not need to have lived many years on the planet to know that this means to lie your way *into* trouble. I decided to tell my parents that I wanted to buy a place in Norfolk which I would open as a restaurant. It seemed less sybaritic and self-indulgent than to buy one purely as a second home. My parents appeared to believe me, or at least were as usual kind enough to pretend to and not call the lie at once.

I am the world's quickest and least patient shopper. I pluck from shelves like a *Supermarket Sweep* contestant on crystal meth. I never try clothes on for size. Queues and waiting drive me insane with impatience. It turned out that I was like this with houses too. I contacted a Norfolk estate agent and bought the third house I looked at. The first two were tempting but needed too much work. The one I settled on was a solid six-bedroom farmhouse, originally sixteenth-century but mostly overclad with Victorian brick in the rather yellowy grey characteristic of that part of Norfolk. I showed my parents round. Restaurant tables were imagined in the large dining-room and drawing room, and there was talk of the knocking-through of hatches, the construction of a bar and cold room and the hiring of a chef and waiting staff. Tactfully this was never really mentioned again. It was obvious that the house was for me to live in, and that if I ever did entertain the notion of being a restaurateur it was no more than a passing fantasy. Embarrassed by how inappropriate the house was for my age and single state, I told people

that I had a 'country cottage' in Norfolk. Just a little place
for weekends.

So there I was, a celibate man with a ludicrously big
house and a ludicrously big car. *A* ludicrously big car? It
was surely time to put that right. I embarked upon what
was to turn into a six- or seven-year classic-car spending
spree, starting with an early seventies Aston Martin V8.
It was a garish Yeoman Red when I bought it, so I had it
resprayed a sleek and understated Midnight Blue. I cannot
remember which I loved more, my little house in the
country, my Aston Martin, my Apple computer or my
gold AmEx card. What a styleless arsehole I was, what
a prodigal tit, what a flash fuckhead. I look back and see
only waste, vanity, emptiness and puerile conceit. That I
was happy offers me no compensation now.

In the replay of regret that flickers through my mind
I picture how I might have used the money that poured
in so prodigiously. Wasn't I happy enough in London?
Hugh, Katie, Nick and I loved Southgate Road and
now we were ready to pool our resources and buy our
own house together. Why did I need a large place in the
country too? I loved my Daimler Sovereign, why should
I need another car and another and another? A man can
only drive one vehicle at a time, for heaven's sake. I loved
my Macintosh, so why did I need to replace it every time
Apple came up with a new model? Why did I need *any* of
the baubles I spunked my money on? What the hell was
I playing at? I could have saved the money, invested it,
husbanded it. I might just as well tell myself that I could
have sung Don Giovanni at Covent Garden or opened
the batting at Lord's. As Dirty Harry tells Hal Holbrook
in *Magnum Force*, 'A man's gotta know his limitations.' I

will never be provident, prudent or prescient. Never. I do not have it in my genes to be so. I believe that change, improvement, heuristic development and the acquisition and advancement of learning and wisdom through experience are all possible and desirable. I also believe that leopards will always be spotty, skunks smelly and Stephens idiotically wasteful and extravagant. Some things are not susceptible to change.

'You'll never have to work again,' someone said to me at a party. To me this was like being congratulated on becoming tetraplegic – 'Hurrah! You'll never have to walk again! You can stay in bed all day.' Perhaps that is why I spent money so freely, so that I always had the incentive to work.

Another incentive to work was the example of Ben Elton. The second series was the last the world ever saw of *Alfresco*, but between putting the finishing touches to the final sketch of the hundred or so he wrote for it and completing his co-authorship of the second series of *The Young Ones* he had somehow contrived to write all six episodes of an entirely new comedy drama of his own invention which he called *Happy Families*. It starred Jennifer Saunders in the five roles of an old grandmother and her four lost granddaughters. Ade Edmondson, shortly to become Jennifer's real-life husband, played the hapless grandson who must search the world to reunite them all. I was cast as the same nonchalantly callous Dr de Quincy I had played in a few *Alfresco* sketches, with Hugh as Jim, my Kiplingesque friend and companion. The series was directed by *The Young Ones* producer-director, Paul Jackson. During the shoot, which took place in and around Denstone in Staffordshire, not five minutes from the charms of Uttoxeter and the horrors of Alton Towers, Paul mentioned that next year he would be putting together a new live comedy show for Channel 4. He wondered if Hugh and I would be interested in contributing to it. We conferred nervously with each other in the bar that evening. The new world of youthful stand-up comedy was going to be represented on this 'edgy' 'alternative' and 'ground-breaking' show. Stand-up was another string to Ben Elton's bow: he appeared regularly compèring at the Comedy Store and he was certainly going to do a session or two in the new series. Other comedy teams would be appearing, such as Mark Arden and Steve Frost, who performed as the Oblivion Boys, and Rik Mayall and Ade Edmondson, who had come together again, this time as the Dangerous Brothers. Hugh and I wondered if we would stick out like sore and inappropriately tweedy thumbs. Despite our characteristic fears and forebodings we decided that we should do the show. In the end, somewhere at the bottom of our churning wells of nonsense Hugh and I knew that we could and should do comedy together. It was a kind of destiny.

Back in London after filming, Hugh, Katie, Nick Symons and I each bought a share in a large house in St Mark's Rise, Dalston. Situated just off the Sandringham Road, which on account of its predominantly drug-dealing Yardie population was known as Da Front Line, the house was in need of some repair, and we set about improving it straight away. Which is to say we hired a team of perky young plasterers and decorators to do it for us. They were very good, and I should tell you about them.

Oh my God, Stephen is going to talk about the quality of work done by the team who came to decorate his house. WTF?

As they say on helplines, bear with me caller . . .

One of the plasterers, Martin, was really very, very expert indeed. Marvellous at ceiling roses and all kinds of moulded ornamental plasterwork. The other two, Paul and Charlie, were more than competent at the rendering, skimming, bonding, sanding, painting and other ancillary skills that might be expected from a general builder, but they had another quality. They were quite extraordinarily funny. I brought them coffee, as you do when you have the builders in, and I chatted with them in what I hoped was a friendly and unpatronizing manner but just couldn't get over how much they made me laugh. They had been at the University of East Anglia in Norwich, which seat of higher education they had quickly vacated, dropping out and moving to London, working in the building trade and wondering if comedy might ever be an attainable goal. Charlie was the lead singer in a punk outfit which apparently had a cult following. Paul entertained our household with impressions of London types, the especial favourite being a Greek cockney who had an eccentric way with very cockneyfied English. This character was based on a real-life Hackney kebab-shop owner called Adam. Hugh and I believed that, excellent as Paul and Charlie were with the bonding, skimming, rendering and so forth, they really should have a stab at making their way in comedy. Paul wasn't sure he would like performing but thought that perhaps, one day, he might see if he could make it as a writer.

The most successful comedy writer I knew lived just up the road in Islington. He was Douglas Adams. The success of the radio series, books and television adaptation of *The Hitchhiker's Guide to the Galaxy* had earned him international regard, reputation and riches. He was a gigantic man, at least three inches taller than me, although it seemed much more. When he ran up and down the stairs the whole house shook. He was curious about and amused by all kinds of inanimate articles and objects, by living plants and creatures, by himself, by other people, by the world and by the whole universe. The most fundamental laws, principles and accepted systems that underlie everything and are taken for granted by almost all of us were to him fascinating, funny and appealingly odd. More than anyone I have ever known he combined childlike simplicity with a great sophistication of understanding and intelligence.

Almost every day when I was not working I would go round to his house off Upper Street and, like a shy schoolboy, ask his wife, Jane, if he might be free to play. He was never free to play, of course, being eternally under the shadow of a writing deadline and so, naturally, we would play. Douglas's remark about deadlines has become the final word on the subject. 'I love deadlines, I love the whooshing sound they make as they fly by.'

In what manner did we play? What was the substance of our play? Scalextric? Trains? Jam sessions? Dressing up? No – I fear that you might already have guessed. Douglas was the only person I knew who, like me, owned a Macintosh computer. Like me, he upgraded to a new machine every time Apple brought one out. Like me, he more than just liked it, he loved it, believed in it, wanted to shout out its pioneering, world-changing importance from the rooftops. Like me, he could not believe how so many people could be chained to IBM-compatibles running CP/M or the new operating system, MS-DOS, both of which did nothing but put text up on the screen. We believed that the mouse, icons, drop-down menus and whole graphical-desktop idea *had* to be the way forward and were easily upset and enraged by those who failed to see it. Like all fanatics we must have been quite dreadfully boring, boorish and bothersome. Together we moved from the 512 'Big Mac' to the Mac Plus with its magical SCSI connectors and thence to the all-colour Mac II and beyond. Douglas could well afford it, and I was beginning, as *Me and My Girl* money continued to roll in, to be able to match his spending pound for pound. Bliss was it in that dawn to be alive, but to be monied was very heaven.

Any meaningful kind of internet was, of course, years off. Not only was there no World Wide Web, even servers, services and protocols like WAIS, Gopher, Veronica, Jughead, SuperJANET and Archie, most of them now long moribund, were then a futurist's dream. There had been Prestel, an early online service run by the Post Office which ran very happily on my old BBC Micro and allowed simple mail and messaging, and there was also Compuserve, a commercial online service that the ordinary enthusiast could log on to using a simple acoustic coupler modem. The exciting parts of the burgeoning internet, like electronic mail, Telnet and FTP, were tantalizingly out of reach, available only to those in academia and government. Most of Douglas's and my time was spent downloading small programs (especially kinds called 'inits') and trying them out on our machines until they crashed. There was no real purpose behind it all. If Jane asked us why we needed to do what we did and what the *point* was, which as a keen-brained, hard-nosed realist of a barrister she did from time to time, we would look at each other in wonderment.

'Point?' Douglas would roll the word round in his mouth as if it was new to him.

I would quote King Lear's 'Reason not the need'.

For some people, computers, digital devices and machines of that nature will be functional objects whose purpose is to serve by performing specifically needed tasks. If there is a little tweaking required to ensure that such functions can better be fulfilled, then so be it: let there be a little tweaking. For other people, people like Douglas and me, the tweaking *is* the function. Using a computer to write a book, fill in tax returns or print out an invoice is something you *could* do, but how much less fun than messing around. People like Douglas and me bond with digital devices as owners bond with dogs. Unless you are blind, or a shepherd, policeman or security guard, dogs do not have a function, they are there to be loved, tickled and patted – to bring joy. I suppose the more common affliction of this kind is the one people have with cars. Rowan Atkinson, Steve Coogan and Robbie Coltrane, for example. They use their cars to go to the shops, drive home and so forth, of course they do, but that is not what dominates their attitude and relationship to them. If you have not been blessed or cursed with deeply emotional feelings for machines you will set me down as a dork and a geek, much as you might set them down as petrol-heads and boy racers. Enthusiasts are used to being mocked, maligned and misunderstood. We don't really mind. In truth, there is every probability that Douglas and I relished being esoteric hobbyists who spoke a recondite language and devoted hours to fruitless projects. I am ashamed to confess that a little bit of regret entered the soul when Microsoft finally got the point and started to offer their own graphical interface. They called it Windows, and by 1992 version 3.1 had reached the stage where it was almost usable. Another three years were to pass before Windows 95 could finally be called an operating system, rather than an add-on to MS-DOS. That was eleven years after the introduction of the Mac, a lifetime in computer terms, and Douglas and I felt on the one hand vindicated and on the other a little deflated, as though the crowd had found their way into the secret garden. One of the most unattractive human traits, and so easy to fall into, is resentment at the sudden shared popularity of a previously private pleasure. Which of us hasn't been annoyed when a band, writer, artist or television series that had been a minority interest of ours has suddenly achieved mainstream popularity? When it was at a cult level we moaned at the philistinism of a world that didn't appreciate it, and now that they *do* appreciate it we're all resentful and dog-in-the-manger about it. I am old enough to remember the cool long-haired boys at school who were seriously annoyed by the success of *Dark Side of the Moon*. They went around muttering 'sell-out' when a month before they had bored anyone they could find on the subject of the misunderstood brilliance of Pink Floyd and how the world was too stupid to recognize their genius.

Douglas and I had years of lonely pleasure ahead of us, however, and the two- or three-year period of our intense visiting, disk swapping and techie chatter counts as among the happiest of my life.

Douglas's writing routine was painful in the extreme.

Sue Freestone, his publisher at Heinemann, would come round and beg, often almost with tears welling in her eyes, for pages from his printer. Douglas would hurl himself downstairs to the coffee machine, hurl himself back up again, thump to his desk and sit in front of the computer. After an hour or so twiddling with the screensaver, the wallpaper, the title of the file, the placement on the desktop of the folder the file was stored in, the formatting, the font, the size, the colour, the margins and the stylesheets, he might type a sentence. He would look at it, change it to italics, swap the word order around, get up, stare at it some more. Hum, curse, growl and groan and then delete it. He would try another sentence. He would look at this one and now perhaps give a little puff of pleasure. He would stand up, stride across the room and hurl himself down to the kitchen, where Sue and I would be gossiping and smoking around the table, and make himself another incredibly strong coffee.

'Dare I ask?' Sue would say.

'Going well. I have the first sentence!'

'Oh.' It would be perhaps July with the new novel already overdue the previous September. One sentence written so far. Sue would smile tightly. 'Well, that's a start at least . . .'

Douglas would nod enthusiastically and fling himself back up the stairs, coffee dripping in his wake. We would hear the feet thump across the floor above our heads and then an agonized cry of 'No! Hopeless!' would tell us that the proud first sentence was not, after all, up to snuff, and a banging on the keyboard would register its angry deletion. An author's day is tough enough, but the writing life of Douglas Adams was excruciating in a manner quite unlike anyone else's I have ever known.

Carlton Club Crustiness

Ben Elton, meanwhile, whose creative flow knew no constrictions of the smallest kind, could not be expected to be content with his thousand *Alfresco* sketches, two series of *The Young Ones,* the creation of a whole new comedy drama serial and the prospect of Paul Jackson's Channel 4 show. On his return from *Happy Families* filming in Staffordshire he immediately started work as a co-author on a new BBC situation comedy. Actually, to call it new would be wrong; it was in truth a second series, but one which wholly reworked the original.

The Black Adder, starring Rowan Atkinson and written by him and his long-time collaborator and fellow Oxonian Richard Curtis, had been broadcast two or even three years earlier and, although crammed from end to end with simply superb performances and brilliant comic scenes, had been generally regarded as something of a disappointment. The BBC decided that, whatever else the show's qualities might be, it was certainly too expensive to continue with: its producer John Lloyd was later to describe it as 'the show that looked a million dollars and cost a million pounds'.

Rowan had already at this stage decided that, even if it did get picked up for a second series, he would no longer be a writer on it, which left his co-creator Richard Curtis to decide whether he wanted to go it alone or find a collaborator. He opted for the latter course, and the writer he chose was Ben Elton. Richard Armitage, who was Rowan Atkinson's agent, believed that *Blackadder* certainly had potential enough to justify his pressuring the BBC to relent, but he entertained the gravest doubts about Ben Elton's suitability for the project. He called me into his office.

'Elton,' he said. 'Richard Curtis seems to want to work with him on the next *Blackadder*.'

'That's a brilliant idea!'

'Really? What about all those farting jokes?' Richard had still not forgiven Ben for Colonel Sodom and his exploding bottom in *There's Nothing to Worry About*.

'No, Ben is perfect for this, honestly.'

'Hm . . .' Richard sucked at his Villiger cigar and pondered deeply for a while.

Ben is sweet-natured, kind, honest and true. He is one of the most extraordinarily gifted people I have ever met. As much as he is gifted he seems cursed with a woeful talent for causing people to disapprove of him and to wrinkle their nose in distaste and scorn. They distrust what they see as his faux Cockney accent (it isn't faux, he has always talked that way, as do his brother and sister), the earnest self-righteousness of his political views and the (perceived) unctuous manner in which he expresses them. Ben is all kinds of things but has never been a fool and knows this very well, yet the one accomplishment he seems not to have been granted is the ability to do anything about it. Richard Armitage was certainly one of those who found him hard to take, but he was too shrewd not to see that, if the decade could be said to have a comedy pulse, then no one had their finger on it more surely than this same Benjamin Charles Elton with his growly and unlovable accent and his predilection, to Richard's mind, for bottom, penis and wind-expulsion humour.

'You really think so?' He looked at me with the blend of disbelief and disappointment you might expect to see on the face of the secretary of a Pall Mall gentlemen's club on hearing a member recommend Pete Doherty for election to the wine committee.

I was flattered to have my opinion so valued. My contribution to the success of *Me and My Girl*, which had made Richard the happiest man in London, and the fact that I could be taken to any weekend gathering or dinner party without letting the side down, had led him to rely on me as a kind of intermediary between his world and the brave new one that was springing up around him.

'Absolutely,' I said. 'There really is going to be another series is there?'

'The question,' said Richard, snatching blindly at the receiver hanging on the complicated switchboard behind his right shoulder, 'is whether we can persuade the BBC to give it a second chance. They want to decimate the budget.'

'That's not too bad. Only ten per cent.'

'Hey?'

'To decimate means to take away one in ten . . .'

This kind of footling pedantry makes most people want to give me a good kicking, but Richard always enjoyed it. 'Ha!' he said and then, as a voice came on the line, 'Get me John Howard Davies. By the way,' he added to me as I stood up to leave, 'we must talk about *Me and My Girl* on Broadway some time soon. Farewell.'

I was not, of course, privy to Richard Curtis, Rowan, Ben and John Lloyd's discussions as they created the second *Blackadder* series, but I do know that the decision to reduce the scale of the show was, from Ben's point of view, a *comic* necessity; the fact that from the BBC's it was a *financial* one might be regarded as a rare and happy collision of interests. When the executives saw the scripts that Ben and Richard came up with they breathed a sigh of relief. The budget was more than decimated, it was at the very least quartered.

It is not my job to speak for Ben, but this is how I interpret his conviction that it was comically necessary to pare the show back. *The Black Adder* had been shot on a grand scale, with many filmed exteriors and imposing locations. There were extras everywhere, there were populous battle scenes and much riding on horses and clanking of armour. The footage for each episode was edited and then shown to an audience, whose laughter was recorded on to the track. The resultant programme was without atmosphere, but more importantly without *focus*. I have a theory about situation comedy that I trot out to anyone who is prepared to listen or, in your case, to read. I see sitcoms as like a tennis match, where the most important thing for the spectator is to be able to *see the ball*. It does not matter how athletic, supple, graceful, fast and skilful the players are – if you can't see the ball all their athleticism is just so much meaningless gesture, inexplicable running and swiping and stroking; the moment you see the ball it all makes sense. The problem with *The Black Adder*, I thought, was that you never saw the ball. Wonderful and delightful were the mad shouting, conspiratorial whispering, machiavellian plotting, farcical hiding, dramatic galloping and wicked sword thrusting, but the ball of what was at stake from moment to moment, what the characters were thinking or saying or intending, was lost in the wealth of background: sentries at every gate, sweeping vistas, busy pages, squires and stewards busily paging, squiring and stewarding and, without meaning to, all taking the audience's eye off the ball. Ben wanted the whole thing stripped down to the essentials and he felt it imperative that the shows should be performed in front of an audience and taped in the true multi-camera studio-based sitcom style that had given us *Fawlty Towers*, *Dad's Army* (which he venerated) and all the great classics of television comedy.

I do not go so far as to claim that I was instrumental in the series going forward, but I do know that Richard Armitage's influence over the BBC was enormous – aside from anything else his boyhood friend Bill Cotton, the Managing Director of Television and Kingmaker in General, was one of the most powerful men in the corporation. They were both children of 1930s music stars. Billy Cotton the bandleader and Noel Gay the tunesmith were best friends who ran Tin Pan Alley, and their sons were best friends who ran much in the succeeding world of popular entertainment. Rowan and Ben were my friends, and I could not have been more pleased that the idea of a historical comedy series using their unique talents would be given another chance. I thought no more about it, other than nursing to myself the happy thought that I might have been responsible for persuading Richard Armitage that Ben was a good choice.

It came as a great surprise therefore to be asked if I would consider playing a regular character in the series. The first I heard about it was during the course of what Ben liked to call a 'crusty'.

For all his (utterly mistaken) reputation as a joyless, puritanical socialist Ben has always been, since I first knew him, inordinately fond of old-fashioned and very English style, manners and grandeur. He adores P. G. Wodehouse and Noël Coward and has a passion for English history. I share much of this. I love the world of clubland, old established five-star hotels, the streets of St James's and mad traditional institutions from Lord's cricket ground to the Beefsteak, from Wilton's to Wartski's, from Trumper's of Jermyn Street to the Sandpit of the Savile Club.

Perhaps, as we were both from European Jewish families who escaped Nazi persecution, the ability to penetrate even occasionally and tangentially the fastnesses of the Establishment makes us feel more strongly anchored to the codes and culture we could so easily never have known. Perhaps, as with my insane collection of credit cards, being recognized by the hall porters and headwaiters of London's smartest institutions helped convince me that I was not about to be arrested.

Since leaving university I had been a member of the Oxford and Cambridge Club in Pall Mall, a classic St James's palace of smoking rooms, dimpled and winged leather armchairs and grand marble staircases. Fiery torches on the outside wall throw their flames upwards in the evenings, and in the courts below can be heard the thump and clack of racquet and billiard balls. You had to be a member of either of the universities to join, of course, but more surprisingly, given the seventy-year co-educational status of both establishments, it was a male-only club, with women grudgingly being allowed to visit in a special wing and drawing-room reserved for them. Perhaps the greatest privilege of membership for me was the availability of other clubs in London and around the world. Reciprocal arrangements came into force during August when the Oxford and Cambridge closed for staff holidays. During that time the Reform Club (forever associated in my mind with Phileas Fogg in *Round the World in Eighty Days*), the Traveller's Club (home of the private oratory of the mysterious and sinister Monsignor Alfred Gilbey), the RAF Club, the Naval and Military (usually referred to as the 'In and Out'), the absurdly named East India, Devonshire, Sports and Public Schools Club in St James's Square and half a dozen others opened their doors to bereft Oxford and Cambridge members in need of clubly pampering. The Carlton Club, a High Tory edifice in St James's Street, more or less opposite the triple ancient glories of wine merchants Berry Bros and Rudd, Lock the hatter and Lobb the boot-maker, was also on the list of establishments offering us August and august hospitality.

I had taken Ben Elton to the Oxford and Cambridge, and he had revelled in the wonders and absurdities of it. The lecterns on the dining-room tables for those solitary lunchers or diners who wanted to read, the strange brass and mahogany weighing machines with an ancient book next to them in which members could record their weight, the library, the barber shop and the billiard-room had all appealed to his fondness for the dottily traditional. His word for it all was 'crusty', crusty as in old port and crusty as in the crabby and cantankerous old men that infest such places.

I called him up one day in the late July of '85.

'Ben, time for a crusty.'

'You're on, Bing, and that's perfect because I want

to talk to you anyway.' Ben always called me Bing or Bingable and does so to this day. I cannot quite remember why.

'If we make it next week,' I said, 'I can offer you all kinds of clubs, but the one I think we'd enjoy most is the Carlton.'

'I love the name already.'

We met for a preliminary gargle at the Ritz on the evening of the following Thursday. You may think it wrong, or hypocritical, or snobbish, or grotesque, or pathetic for two such figures in their twenties to swan about as if they were characters in a Wodehouse or Waugh novel, and perhaps it was. I would try and ask you to believe that there was an element – I won't say of irony – of *playfulness* perhaps, of self-conscious awareness of the ridiculous nature of what we were doing and the ludicrous figures that we cut. Two Jewish comics pretending to be *flâneurs* of the old school. Ben was more obviously a visitor to this world, I more inexcusably connected to it or more successfully, and therefore more creepily, giving off an air of belonging. I was a genuine member, after all, of a London club and over the next decades I was to join at least four more as well as half a dozen of the new kind of members-only media watering holes that were about to burst into the world of Soho bohemia.

We strolled down St James's Street, and I told Ben about Brooks's and White's, the Whig and Tory bastions that glowered across the street at each other. White's was and is the most aristocratic and exclusive of all the London clubs, but the Carlton, which we were now approaching, remains the most overtly political.

We crossed the threshold, and I waved what I hoped

was a nonchalant hand towards the uniformed porter in his mahogany guichet.

'Oxford and Cambridge,' I said. 'I have my membership card somewhere . . .'

'That's all right, sir,' said the porter, his eyes taking Ben in without flickering. Ben was, as he knew one had to be in such places, dressed in a suit and tie, but there are suits and ties and there are ways of wearing suits and ties. My charcoal tailor-made three-piece, New and Lingwood shirt with faintly distressed silk Cherubs tie looked as if they belonged, whereas Ben's Mr Byrite appearance suggested (and I mean this warmly and lovingly) a bus-driver reluctantly togged up for his sister's wedding.

We ascended to the first-floor dining-room. Ben nearly exploded as we passed the bust of a woman at the foot of the stairs.

'Bing,' he hissed, 'that's Thatch!'

'Of course it is,' I said with what I hoped was blithe ease. 'This is the Carlton Club after all.'

As we sat down I broke the news that I had brought him to the very citadel of modern Conservatism, the club where the present-day party had been born and constituted. Margaret Thatcher's image was certainly represented, as were those of all the Tory leaders since Peel. Ben was dazed and delighted to find himself right plumb spang in the centre of the enemy's camp. We both felt childishly mischievous, like children who have found the key to their parents' drinks cabinet.

'Not many people about,' said Ben.

'Well, being August, most of the members will be out of town. They'll be returning from the Riviera in time for the grouse.'

'We shall go up to the moors ourselves next week,' said Ben. 'I shall be your scamp.'

Scamp was the word Ben used as a generic term for a mixture of Oxford scout, Cambridge gyp, manservant, old retainer and loyal page. We maintained a peculiar fiction of myself as a crusty old country squire and Ben as my trusty scamp. Crusty and Trusty.

'Anyway,' I said. 'Here it is, the Carlton Club. The beating heart of the Establishment. But when I called you up, you said you wanted to talk to me?'

'That's right. Thing is, Bing. As you know, Dickie C and I have been working on this new *Blackadder*.'

'Indeed,' I said.

'Well, there's a part in it for you.'

'Really?'

'I won't lie to you,' he said. 'It's not like the greatest character in the world. He's called Lord Melchett and he stands behind the Queen and sucks up to her. He and Blackadder hate each other. He's a kind of chamberlain figure, you know?'

'Ben, of course I'll do it,' I said.

'Yeah? That's great!'

I could see out of the corner of my eye that an ancient gentleman a couple of tables away had been having difficulty accepting Ben's vowel sounds as they ricocheted off the portraits of Wellington and Churchill and into his disbelieving ears. For the past ten minutes he had been spluttering and growling into his soup with growing venom. He looked up at Ben's last exclamation, and I recognized the blotched, jowly and furious countenance of the Lord Chancellor, Quintin Hogg, now Lord Hailsham. He had his napkin tucked into his shirt collar like Oliver Hardy and his mixed expression of outrage, disbelief and reluctant desire to know more put me in mind of a maiden aunt who has just had a flasher open his raincoat at her in the church tea-rooms.

All in all, our Carlton Club adventure was one of the happier and more memorable evenings of my life.

Courtly Comedy

It is probable that if you have bothered to buy, steal or borrow this book you will have watched or at least know about *Blackadder* but you will forgive me if I describe its principal features for the benefit of Americans and others who may be less familiar. The second series of this 'historical sitcom' is set in Elizabethan England with Rowan Atkinson in the title role of Edmund, Lord Blackadder, a suave, scheming, manipulative and attractively amoral courtier. Tony Robinson and Tim McInnerny play his grubby servant Baldrick and idiot friend Lord Percy respectively, as they had in the first series. In the royal court Miranda Richardson plays the young Queen Elizabeth, Patsy Byrne her breast-fixated nurse and I the character Ben had described to me, Lord Melchett – a sort of William Cecil, Lord Burghley figure, all forked beard, forked tongue and fur-lined cloak.

We rehearsed at the BBC's North Acton rehearsal rooms, just as I had for *The Cellar Tapes*, *The Crystal Cube* and the 'Bambi' episode of *The Young Ones*. The director was the very charming and capable Mandy Fletcher. I ought to explain the difference between a director for multi-camera television and a film or theatre director. In the latter two worlds the director is absolute monarch, in charge of all the creative decisions and ultimately responsible for what is seen on screen or stage. In television it is the *producer* who takes that role. Our producer was John Lloyd. Mandy's job was to think about how the cameras would move and be coordinated in order best to capture what John and the cast constructed. Which is not to downplay her role and her skill, it is just that most people might think the director is the one running the show in terms of script, performance, comic ideas, directing the actors and so on. All that, especially since neither Richard Curtis nor Ben Elton liked to attend rehearsals, came from our producer.

When histories of British television comedy are written, the name of John Lloyd is certain to figure prominently. A graduate of Cambridge and the Footlights, he was a contemporary of his friend and occasional collaborator Douglas Adams. After Cambridge he moved to BBC radio, where he created *The News Quiz*, *Quote Unquote* and other quizzes and comedy shows before making the move to television with *Not the Nine O'Clock News*. Richard Curtis was the lead writer on that show, and Rowan Atkinson one of its stars. It was natural, then, that John should produce Rowan and Richard's *The Black Adder*. The year after that he produced the first series of *Spitting Image*, which he continued to work on until the end, as well as producing the subsequent three major series of *Blackadder*, including its occasional minor outbursts in charitable or other specials. In 2003 he and I started work on another child of his fertile mind, *QI*. As it happens, although he will not thank me for pointing it out, he had worked as a script consultant on a couple of episodes of *Alfresco* too, so it can be seen that my career has run in harness with his for the best part of thirty years. He is, I should point out at this stage, quite mad.

Success has a dozen parents and failure is an orphan, as I mentioned before when talking about the genesis of the 'Bambi' episode of *The Young Ones*. As it happened, although we had no idea while we were rehearsing it, *Blackadder II* turned out to be a great success with the public. I have no more authority in pronouncing why this was than anyone else might have, connected or unconnected to it. What Ben Elton brought to the party in terms of energy, fantastic wordplay, brilliant anachronisms and general *jeux d'esprit* cannot be overestimated, as cannot Richard Curtis's ear, wit and skill nor his uncanny understanding of Rowan's range and power. The transformation of Tony Robinson's Baldrick from a rather smart sidekick in the first series to a most terrifyingly dim-witted lowlife in the second was also crucial for the show's success. Tim McInnerny's Lord Percy was divine, as was Patsy Byrne's Nursie. Many would cite Miranda Richardson's performance as a young and terrifyingly unstable Queenie as one of the absolute highlights of that series and among the best comic characterizations ever seen on British television.

We had the most marvellous guests too. Tom Baker played a seadog called Captain Redbeard Rum. His performance was superb, and he himself was entirely charming. While a scene that didn't involve him was being rehearsed he would disappear and return with a tray fully laden with sweets, crisps, chocolates, sandwiches, nuts and snacks, which he would hand round to everyone in the room, often nipping off again to reload. During his *Doctor Who* days he had been quite the party animal in the pubs and clubs of London and often used to fetch up at the North Acton rehearsal rooms at three or four in the morning, where friendly security guards would admit him and let him sleep on a rehearsal mat until morning. Production assistants would arrive and wake him up for work. He had a way of gazing at you with grave bulging eyes that made it rather hard to determine whether he thought you an idiot or a god.

Miriam Margolyes made an appearance as the puritanical face-slapping Lady Whiteadder in a show called 'Beer'. Rik Mayall's Captain Flashheart exploded into the world like a firework display and, to my especial delight, Hugh appeared as a guest twice, firstly as one of Blackadder's flatulent drinking companions in 'Beer' and then, more magnificently, as a deranged Germanic super-villain and master of disguise in the final episode, at the conclusion of which we all somehow ended up dead.

Having bowed and paid due homage to all these great contributors I have to turn to what was for me the real miracle: Rowan Atkinson's performance as Edmund. I would watch him in rehearsal, and my mouth would drop open in stunned admiration. I had never before come close to such an extraordinary comic talent. I had seen him on stage at Edinburgh and laughed until I weed, I had admired him in *Not the Nine O'Clock News* and I had watched his rather disturbing character in the first series, but the Edmund of *Blackadder II* was a revelation. The urbanity, sarcasm, vocal control, minimalism and physical restraint were not sides of Rowan I had ever seen before. This Edmund was sexy, assured, playful, dynamic, debonair, soigné and charismatic.

Rowan, it is well known, is a private and unassuming

figure. He read Electrical Engineering at Newcastle before completing a Masters degree at the Queen's College, Oxford, and has always retained something of the manner of a quiet and industrious scientist about him. It is hard when meeting him to see quite where the comedy comes from. When making the best man's speech at his wedding some years later I tried to explain this. I said that it was as if the Almighty had suddenly noticed he had a full decade's allocation of comic talent, a supply that he had forgotten to dole out more or less evenly amongst the population as was His usual divine practice. For a joke he decided to give the whole load to the least likely person he could find. He looked down at the north-east of England and saw a diffident, studious young engineer wandering the streets of Jesmond, dreaming of transistors and tractors, and zapped him full of all that comedy talent. He gave him none of the usual showbiz pizzazz or yearning for fame, adulation and laughter, just the gigantic consignment of talent alone. I still wake up at night sometimes with a surge of shame fearing that I expressed this thought badly and that it sounded less affectionate and admiring than it might, that it somehow ignored the skill, concentration, commitment and conscious application of that talent that makes Rowan the authentic comic genius he is. Aside from all of this he is a delightful, kindly, sweet-natured and wise individual whose personal human qualities quite match his comic attainments.

When Rik Mayall came to rehearsals for his episode in *Blackadder II*, the contrast between his style and Rowan's was astonishing. It was like seeing a Vermeer next to a van Gogh, one all exquisite detail with the subtlest and most invisible working and the other a riot of wild and thickly applied brushstrokes. Two utterly different aesthetics, each outstandingly brilliant. With Rik you could see the character grow out of his own personality. Flashheart was an emphasized and extreme version of Rik. In Rowan's case it was as if Blackadder was somehow conjured up from nowhere. He emerged from Rowan like an extra limb. I am as capable of envy and resentment as the next man, but when you are in a room with two people who possess an order of talent that you know you can never even dream of attaining, it is actually a relief to be able to do no more than lean back and admire like a dewy-eyed groupie.

My make-up on *Blackadder II* was done by a divinely pretty girl called Sunetra Sastry. From a Brahmin-caste Indian family, she was bright, funny and as captivatingly alluring as any girl I had met for years. I was quite seriously considering asking her out on a date, when Rowan timidly approached me one morning during rehearsals for the second episode and asked if I would mind swapping make-up artists with him. Since he had grown his own beard for the part, unlike me, who had to have my large excrescence glued on with spirit gum every week, I thought this rather odd: his make-up sessions lasted as long as it took to powder the tip of his nose.

'Don't you like the one you've got?' I said.

'N-no, it's not that, she's splendid. It's just that well . . .' He gave me a look of uncharacteristic intensity.

'Oh!' I said, as the penny dropped. 'My dear fellow. Of course. Yes.'

All ideas of my asking Sunetra out left me, and over the course of the remaining five weeks I watched as she and Rowan grew closer and closer. They had been together for five years before they at last married in New York City. As the best man, I flew out to be there and record the ceremony on eight-millimetre film. They now have two children and twenty years of marriage behind them, but I still sometimes wonder what would have happened if I had been bold enough and quick enough on my feet to have asked Sunetra out straight away.

'Oh, you should have done!' Sunetra often says to me. 'I'd have gone out with you.' But I know how happy she is and how right it was that I stayed silent.

Hang on, Stephen, you're gay, aren't you? Indeed I am, but, as I was to tell a newspaper reporter some years later, I am only '90 per cent gay', which is of course pretty damned gay, but every now and again on my path through life I have met a woman in the 10 per cent bracket. Caroline Oulton at Cambridge was one, although I never told her so, and Sunetra another.

The *Blackadder* rehearse-record rhythms somehow made the time fly by. On Tuesday morning we would read through the script, with Richard and sometimes Ben in attendance. John would wince and clutch his brow and shake his head at the dire impossibility of it all – not the most tactful way to endear himself to the writers or indeed the performers. He never meant to transmit disapproval or disappointment, the tutting and moaning were just his way of gearing himself up for the work of the week ahead. Next, each scene, starting at the beginning, would slowly have 'legs' put on it. As the show was blocked out in this fashion, Mandy would make notes and build up her camera script, and John would grimace and sigh and smoke and pace and growl. His perfectionism and refusal to be satisfied was part of the reason *Blackadder* worked.

Every line, plot twist and action was taken, rubbed between his fingers, sniffed and passed, rejected or pulled in for servicing and improvement. We would all join in the process of joke polishing or 'fluffing', as John called it. I relished participating in these sessions which over the years became an absolute characteristic of *Blackadder* rehearsals. Visiting guest actors would often sit for hours working on a crossword or reading a book as we built up the epithets and absurd similes.

I picture Richard and Ben reading this and snorting with outrage. 'Hang on, we presented you with the scripts and devised the characters and the style. Don't go pretending that it was all your work.' Ben and Richard did indeed create the style, the storylines and most of the jokes. We added and subtracted in rehearsal, but they were the writers, there can be no doubt of that. My admiration for their work was and is extreme and unconditional. Nonetheless, as anyone who spent any time in *Blackadder* rehearsals then or later will confirm, the days were always a constant coffee and cigarettes grind of tweaking, refinement and emendation.

Sunday was the taping night, the night we performed the show in front of an audience. Ben would act as warm-up man, introducing the characters and setting the series in context. This was important, for there was always a detectable air of disappointment emanating from the audience. No part of the current series would yet have been broadcast, so they would be staring at an unfamiliar set and fretting at the absence of the characters they had known from the previous series. When they came to *Blackadder II* they were sorry not to have Brian Blessed there as the King; when they came to *Blackadder the Third* recordings they missed Queenie; and when they arrived for recordings of *Blackadder Goes Forth* they wanted to see Prince George and Mrs Miggins.

For all that, it was a happy experience. The Saturday after the taping of the last episode of *Blackadder II* Richard Curtis held a party at his house in Oxfordshire. It was a glorious summer's day, and, as we all wanted to watch television, Richard unwound an extension cord and put the set on a wooden chair in the shade of an apple tree. We sat on the grass and watched *Live Aid* all the way through to the end of the American broadcast from Philadelphia.

'We should do something similar,' Richard said.

'How's that?' I wasn't sure what he could mean.

'Comedians can raise money too. Look at what John Cleese did for Amnesty with those Secret Policeman's Balls.'

'So you mean a Comedians' Live Aid show?'

Richard nodded. He had already been germinating Comic Relief in his head for some time. Now, almost twenty-five years later, he has devoted six or seven months of his time every other year to an organization that, love or loathe the enforced custardy jollities of its biennial television pratfest, has raised hundreds of millions of pounds to comfort those who have sorely needed it.

Coral Christmas, Cassidy, C4, Clapless Clapham, Cheeky Chappies and Coltrane's Cock

With *Blackadder II* in the can, I was called up by Richard Armitage.

'Happy to say that they want to put on *Me and My*

Girl in Australia. Mike will need you there to help with changes that we can try out for Broadway.'

I didn't really believe that Broadway would happen. How could Americans possibly respond to Cockney capers and rhyming slang with anything other than blank stares and fidgety coughs? Australia seemed like a wonderful idea, however, and Mike and I flew out with the rest of the core production team to rehearse an Australian cast in the Melbourne Arts Centre. I wish I remembered more about the production. I think I fiddled about with the lyrics a little and changed one or two scenes, but that is all that springs to mind. It was towards the end of the year, and Mike and I decided that it would be fun to stay on and Christmas up in Queensland. He chose Hamilton, one of the Whitsunday Islands of the Coral Reef. I spent almost all of Christmas Day in my hotel room shivering, throbbing and shaking with sunstroke and sunburn, much to the amusement of Billy Connolly and Pamela Stephenson, who were staying in the same hotel.

Back in England Hugh and I turned our minds to the Channel 4 show that Paul Jackson had mentioned to us. Seamus Cassidy, the young commissioner at C4, was anxious for something akin to America's long-running *Saturday Night Live*. Our show, he decided, was to be called *Saturday Live*. I thought of him ever after, not unaffectionately, as Shameless Cassidy.

Stand-up was taking over the world. Our brand of sketch comedy, it seemed to Hugh and me, was in danger of looking more and more dated as each month passed, certainly as far as the prospect of live TV was concerned. The problem with being a duo rather than a solo performer is that you speak to each other, rather than out front to the audience. We had in the past written a certain number of sketches, the Shakespeare Masterclass for example, in which the audience could be directly addressed, but for much of our time we played characters locked in mini-dramas with a fourth wall between us and the watching world. Out of some act of rare reckless abandonment we decided that before putting ourselves in front of the cameras for this new show we should practise by performing in a comedy club. One of the premiere venues at that time was Jongleurs in Clapham, and thither we went for one night, sandwiched between a young Julian Clary and Lenny Henry. Julian performed as 'The Joan Collins Fan Club' in those days and shared the stage with his little terrier 'Fanny the Wonderdog'. He did very well, I recall. When Hugh and I left the stage after our fifteen minutes and puffed out our usual 'Christ they hated us' (Hugh) and 'It wasn't so bad' (me), we stayed back to watch Lenny. I remember thinking how wonderful it must be to be known and loved by an audience. All your work is done before you go on stage. Lenny entered to an enormous cheer and, or at least so it seemed to me, only had to open his mouth to have the audience writhing with joy and drumming their feet on the floor with approval. Hugh and I were unknown, *Blackadder II* hadn't aired yet, and *The Crystal Cube* and *Alfresco* had been watched by seven people, all of whom wanted to kill us. That night at Jongleurs we sweated blood as we treated the audience to our exquisitely wrought phrases, cunning jokes and deft characterizations only to be rewarded with vague titters and polite but sporadic applause. Lenny came on, did a bird call, boomed a hello and the building almost collapsed. This is to take nothing away from him at all. He had built up a rapport over the years and he had the gift that can guarantee a good time in a comedy club. He was relaxed and he made the audience relax. Hugh and I might have hidden our nerves and anxiety as best we could, but from the beginning we were *working* the audience rather than welcoming them with any confidence into our world. A tense audience might admire our writing and performing, but they are never going to give us the great rolling waves of love they sent out to Lenny. Later, when we were familiar figures and went on stage to gusts of welcome, I would remember that night at Clapless Clapham, as I always thought of it, and thank my lucky stars that I no longer had to prove myself in quite the same way. Yet, having said that, there came an evening some years later where I was able clearly to witness the reverse effect. I directed a number of 'Hysteria' benefit shows for the Terrence Higgins Trust in the late eighties and early nineties. For the third one I had the duty of welcoming on to the stage a very well-known comic. He entered to a thunderous ovation – they were *so* pleased to see him. He exited to only a . . . *respectable* level of applause. The next act was new. No one out there had any idea who he was or what they might expect. I did my best as compère to get the audience on his side.

'Dear ladies, darling gentlemen, I have no doubt in the world that you will give the next artist your warmest and wildest welcome. He is a brilliant young comic, I know you'll adore him – please greet the wonderful Eddie Izzard!' They were polite and they did their best, but they would so much rather have screamed a John Cleese or Billy Connolly on to the stage.

I stood in the wings and watched as Eddie left the stage

to a *gigantic* round of applause. How much better to go on to polite clapping and off to roars than, as the established comic had, to go on to roars and off to polite clapping.

Saturday Live was a bear garden: transmitted live from the biggest studio in London Weekend Television's South Bank studios, it featured a large central stage, side stages for the bands, random giant inflatables floating above and a vast arena for the audience of groundlings, mostly young fashion-conscious people who milled about getting in the way of the cameras and harassed floor managers in a style that was becoming the established fashion in hip youth TV, a style that veered between sulky disaffection and hysterical whooping adulation. Hugh was convinced that they were more interested in how their hair looked on screen than in anything we might be saying or doing to try and amuse them.

A month or so earlier we had gone to the Comedy Store to see a new comedian about whom we had heard great things. His name was Harry Enfield and he performed a stand-up routine as a most marvellously curmudgeonly and perverse old gentleman, a character he had consciously modelled on the persona Gerard Hoffnung adopted in his legendary interviews with Charles Richardson. Harry worked on *Spitting Image* as an impressionist and had, like us, been booked for *Saturday Live*. He had bumped into and become friends with Paul Whitehouse and Charlie Higson, our painter-decorators, and together Harry and Paul had developed a character based on Adam, Paul's Graeco-Cockney kebab-shop owner. Now named Stavros, he was working well as a puppet on *Spitting Image*, and Harry fancied the idea of trying him out in the flesh for *Saturday Live*.

Hugh and I rather envied Harry the stability of having one returning character. Each week for the twelve of the first run of *Saturday Live* we had to think of something new to do. Each week the blank sheet of paper and accusatory pen, or rather the blank screen, flashing cursor and accusatory keyboard. The sketches that seemed to work best in the insanely hot, loud and unstable atmosphere of the studio were the ones, as we had imagined, where Hugh and I talked out to the audience. We developed a line of talk-show parodies where Hugh played a character called Peter Mostyn, who interviewed me in increasingly strange formats.

'Hello and welcome to *Stealing a Car Stereo With*. I'm Peter Mostyn and tonight I'll be stealing a car stereo with Nigel Davenant, Shadow Home Secretary and Member of Parliament for South Reason. Nigel, hello and welcome to *Stealing a Car Stereo With* . . .' and so on.

I remember that Mostyn sketch with especial clarity (most of our *Saturday Live* experiences are a blur of jumbled memories: the brain can be kind that way) because it allowed us to film away from the feared studio audience and down in the LWT underground car park. With the show being live it was rather tense. We had some sort of iron punch with which to smash the nearside window of a car and pull out the radio. Rather than using the friable and safe sugar glass usually favoured as a prop we were going to do it on the real thing, a car belonging to someone in the production crew.

'Right – so, Shadow Home Secretary, have you ever stolen a car stereo before?'

'Ooh, not since I was a young parliamentary assistant.'

'Feeling confident?'

'Give it a damned good go, anyway . . .'

'That's the spirit! This is the kind of tool most car thieves use. One firm blow and then, quick as you can, out with the stereo. But while you're doing that, let me ask you, was politics always your first love?'

'Oh, no, Susanna was my first love, then a boy called Tony and *then* politics.'

'Right, has politics changed much since you first entered the house as a young man after that by-election in 1977?'

And, which was the purpose of these sketches, Hugh would continue an earnest and commonplace interview as if we were doing the most normal thing in the world. Later scenarios included 'Introducing My Grandfather To', 'Photocopying My Genitals With' and 'Flying a Light Aircraft Without Having Had Any Formal Instruction With'.

It took about six heavy bangs on the glass to smash the window that night, I recall. I could clearly hear the alarmed voice of Geoff Posner, the director, in the earpieces of the two cameramen and assistant floor manager each time the punch bounced harmlessly off the window. 'Jesus! Hell! Oh, for fuck's sake!'

Hugh improvised nobly. 'Would you say, Nigel, that new European lamination standards have succeeded in toughening glass since your early days stealing car stereos?'

'That's . . . *bang* . . . right, Peter. I would . . . *bang* . . . say . . . exactly . . . *bang* . . . that. Plus I've lost a lot of strength in my arms due to *bang* . . . *Crash!!* . . . ah, that's got it . . .' What I had lost a lot of strength in my arms due to I fortunately never had to declare.

The only other sketch I remember with any clarity is

seared into my memory like a brand because it necessitated a visit to a hypnotist.

I am not able, as I have discussed before, to sing. By which I mean I am *really* not able to sing, much as I am not able to fly through the air by flapping my arms. *Not. Able.* It is not a question of me doing it *badly* but a question of me not being able to do it *at all*. I have told you what my singing voice does to those cocky and wrong-headed fools who have skipped about the place proclaiming, 'Why, that's nonsense! *Everyone* can sing . . .' Hugh, as we know, sings marvellously, as he does most things marvellously, but Stephen just plain doesn't. I *think* I can sing when I'm on my own, in the shower for instance, but there is no way of testing it. If I imagine for a second that there is anybody in the house, or in the garden, or within a hundred yards of me, I freeze up. And that would include a microphone, so my singing is like a physicist's quantum event: any observation fatally alters its outcome.

Well, came the day in the middle of the second series of *Saturday Live* that I found that Hugh had painted me, or I had painted myself, into a dreadful corner. Somehow a routine had been written in which it was essential for me to sing. Hugh was performing some other crucial function in the sketch, and I could not but accept that I was going to have to sing. Live. On television.

For three days I was in a complete panic, trembling, sweating, moaning, yawning, needing a pee every ten minutes – all the symptoms of extreme nervous tension. At last Hugh could take it no more.

'All right then. We'll just have to write another sketch.'

'No, no! I'll be fine.' Annoyingly it was a good sketch.

Much as I dreaded the prospect of its approach, I knew that we *should* do it. 'Really. I'll be fine.'

Hugh took in my quaking knees, ashen complexion and terrified countenance. 'You won't be fine,' he said. 'I can see that. Look, it's obviously psychological. You can hammer out a tune on a piano, you can tell one song from another. You're obviously not tone deaf.'

'No,' I said, 'the problem is I am tone *dumb*.'

'Psychological. What you should do is see a hypnotist.'

At three o'clock next afternoon I rang the doorbell of the Maddox Street consulting rooms of one Michael Joseph, Clinical Hypnotist.

He turned out to be Hungarian by birth. Hungarian, I suppose because of my grandfather, is my favourite accent in all the world. I shan't attempt to write 'Vot' for 'What' and 'deh' for 'the', you will just have to imagine a voice like George Solti's weaving its way into my brain.

'Tell me the issue that brings you here,' he asked, expecting, I imagine, smoking or weight control or something along those lines.

'I have to sing tomorrow night.'

'Excuse me?'

'Tomorrow night I have to sing. Live on television.'

I outlined the nature of the problem. 'You say you can never sing, you have never sung?'

'Well, I think it must be a mental block. I have a good enough ear to be able usually to recognize some keys. E flat major, C minor and D major, for instance. But the moment I have to sing in front of anybody else I just get a hammering in my ears, my throat constricts, my mouth goes dry and the most tuneless, arrhythmic horror comes out.'

'I see, I see. Perhaps you should put the palms of your

hands on your knees, that would be pleasantly comfortable, I think. You know, if you feel your hands on your legs, it is amazing how they seem almost to melt into the flesh, is it not? Soon it is hard to tell which is your hands and which is your legs, don't they? They are as one. And as this is happening it now feels as if you are being lowered down a well, haven't you? Down into the dark. But my voice is like the rope that keeps you confident that you will not be lost. My voice will be able to pull you back up, but for the moment it is dropping you down and down and until you are in the warm and in the dark. Yes? No?'

'Mm . . .' I felt myself slipping into a state – not of unconsciousness, for I was fully awake and aware – of willing relaxation and contented stupor. Light closed around me until I was snug and securely held in the well of darkness and warmth that he had described.

'Tell me when it was that you decided that you could not sing?'

And now, quite unexpectedly, there popped fully formed into my head a perfectly clear memory of cong. prac.

Congregational practice is held every Saturday morning in the prep school gym/chapel/assembly hall. The music master, Mr Hemuss, takes us through the hymns that will be sung in tomorrow's service. It is my first term. I am seven years old and just getting used to boarding 200 miles from home. I stand at the end of a row with a hymnbook in my hand joining in as the school sings its way through the first verse of 'Jerusalem the Golden'. Kirk, the duty prefect, saunters up and down the aisles, making sure everyone is behaving. Suddenly he stops right next to me and holds up his hand.

'Sir, sir . . . Fry is singing flat!'

There is tittering. Mr Hemuss calls for hush. 'On your own then, Fry.'

I don't know what singing flat means, but I know it must be terrible.

'Come on,' Hemuss strikes his hand down on the keyboard to sound a chord and belts out the opening line in a strong tenor, 'Jerusalem the golden . . .'

I try to pick it up from there. 'With milk and honey blest . . .' The school erupts with hoots of derisive laughter as a husky tuneless squeak emerges from me.

'Yes, well. In future I think it would be better if you mimed,' says Mr Hemuss. Kirk grins triumphantly and moves on, and I am left alone, hot, pink and quaking with humiliation, shame and terror.

The memory shrinks and moves away as Michael Joseph's reassuring Magyar tones continue to solace me. 'It has been a painful memory, but now it is one that makes you smile. For you can see that this is what has been locking up the music inside you all these years. Tomorrow evening you have to sing, yes?'

'Yes.' My voice seeming to come from a long way away.

'When you have to sing, is there a . . . how you say . . . a *cue*? Is there some cue for you to sing?'

'Yes. My friend Hugh turns to me and says, "Hit it, bitch."'

'"Hit it, bitch?"'

'"Hit it, bitch."'

'Very good. "Hit it, bitch." So. Tomorrow, when you stand before the audience you will feel confident, happy and filled with belief in your ability to triumph in this moment. And when you hear the words "Hit it, bitch" all tensions and fears will melt away. This is the signal for you to be able easily to sing the song you need to sing. No fear, no tightness in the throat. Ease, confidence, assurance. Repeat that to me.'

'When I hear the words "Hit it, bitch" all tensions and fears will melt away. It is the signal for me to be able to sing the song I need to sing. No fear. No tightness in the throat. Ease. Confidence. Assurance.'

'Excellent. And now I shall pull on the rope and bring you up to the surface. As I pull I count down from twenty. When I reach "ten" you will begin to awaken, refreshed and happy, quite able to remember our conversation and all its details. At "five" your eyes will begin to open. So. Twenty, nineteen . . .'

I stumbled away, rather amazed that this memory of cong. prac. had been revealed and fully confident that I would indeed be able to sing when the moment came. I believe I even hummed to myself as I walked from Maddox Street to the Oxford Street tube station.

The following evening I told Hugh that, if he muffed his cue and said 'Hit it, baby,' or 'Cue it, bitch,' or anything like that, then our whole enterprise would fail. All was well, the moment came, Hugh delivered the line correctly, and sounds came out of my mouth in more or less the right order and employing more or less the correct musical pitches.

Did the experience unlock singing for me? Absolutely not. I am as hopeless as ever I was. At weddings and funerals I still prefer to mime. At John Schlesinger's funeral at a synagogue in St John's Wood some years ago the person I stood next to said to me encouragingly, 'Come on, Stephen – you're not singing. Have a go!'

'Believe me, Paul, you don't want me to,' I said. Besides, I was having a much better time listening to *him*.

'No. Go on!'

So I joined in the chorus.

'You're right,' Paul McCartney conceded. 'You can't sing.'

I suppose, in career terms, *Saturday Live* was a good move. It was watched by a large audience and generally went down well. It was especially successful for Ben, who moved from being a regular contributor to permanent host. His sign-off, 'My name's Ben Elton, good night!', became the catchphrase of the show until Harry and Paul, tiring of the very successful Stavros, devised a new character for Harry to play. They came up with a loud-mouthed Sarf London plasterer who fanned his wad of dosh at the audience and shouted 'Loadsamoney!' with gleeful, exultant braggadocio. He seemed to symbolize the second act of the Thatcher play, an era of materialism, greed and contempt for those left behind. As with Johnny Speight and Warren Mitchell's Alf Garnett, much of the audience seemed either to be deaf to or chose to disregard Paul and Harry's satirical intent, raising Loadsamoney to almost folk-heroic status.

Ben, Harry, Hugh and I fell into the habit of winding down, after the recordings, in a Covent Garden club called the Zanzibar, usually bringing with us the guest comedians or musicians of the week.

Wedged in a semicircle of banquette one night, I had the opportunity of observing Robbie Coltrane's romantic and poetic seduction technique. He picked up the hand of the girl sitting next to him.

'What fine, delicate hands you have,' he said.

'Why thank you,' said the girl.

'I love women with small hands.'

'You do?'

'I do. They make my cock look so much bigger.'

The Zanzibar swarmed with media people. Jimmy Mulville was often there. This sharp, witty, fast-brained Liverpudlian had been something of a legend in Cambridge, having left the year I arrived. He had gone up to read Latin and Ancient Greek, and a less likely Cambridge classicist you could never hope to meet. The rumour was that his father, a docker from Walton, had come home one night when Jimmy was seventeen and said, 'You'd better do well in your A levels and that, son, because I've just been to the bookies and put down a bet on you getting all A grades and a scholarship to Cambridge. Got a good price too.'

'Christ, Dad!' Jimmy is reported to have said in shock. 'How much did you bet?'

'Everything,' came the reply. 'So get studying.'

They say that today's schoolchildren now suffer more exam pressure than my generation ever did, and generally I have no doubt that this is true, but I don't suppose many have had to endure pressure of the kind Jimmy did that year. He duly obliged with the straight As and the scholarship.

It is too good a story for me to check up and risk the disappointment of it being proved a distortion or exaggeration. What is certainly true is that, when Jimmy arrived at Jesus in 1975, he brought a wife with him. It is not uncommon for people of a working-class background to wed before they are twenty, but it is very uncommon for students to be married, and how the young Mrs Mulville coped at Cambridge I do not know. Jimmy became President of the Footlights in 1977 and by the time I am writing about he was starring in and writing the Channel 4 comedy *Who Dares Wins* with his Cambridge contemporary Rory McGrath. He would go on to found Hat Trick, one of the first independent television production companies, famous for bringing shows like *Have I Got News for You* to television and slightly less famous for giving shows like my own *This Is David Lander* an airing.

Who Dares Wins had established itself as something of a cult, singled out as being responsible for the post-closing-time scheduling slot that Channel 4 made its own. Its beery style was not very close to the kind of thing Hugh and I did, but for me the flashes of brilliance in the writing more than made up for its laddish manner. It gave the world one of my favourite jokes. There is something very pleasing about one-word punchlines.

The show nearly always ended with a long, complex party scene, shot in a one-camera single take. In one of these episodes Jimmy approaches Rory and picks up a can of beer. Just as he's bringing it up to his lips, Rory warns him, 'Um, I've been using that as an ashtray actually.' Jimmy gives him a hard look, says, 'Tough,' and swigs.

Another occasional habitué of the Zanzibar was the remarkable Peter Bennett-Jones, also a Cambridge graduate, and now one of the most powerful managers, agents and producers in British television and film. I remember helping to give him the bumps outside the club at half past two on the morning of his thirtieth birthday and watching in alarm as he dropped to the pavement and announced that he would now do thirty press-ups.

'You're an old man!' I said. 'You'll give yourself a heart attack.'

P B-J, as he is universally known, did the thirty and then another twenty, just because.

A friend of mine claims that he was at a loose end in

Hong Kong years ago. A hotel concierge recommended a restaurant.

'Go Kowloonside and ask for Chou Lai's.'

On the quay at Kowloon he was pointed to a junk that was just leaving. He leapt aboard.

'Chou Lai's?' he asked. Everyone on board nodded.

After half an hour's chugging through choppy waters he was dropped off on an island. Nothing. He thought he had been (almost literally) shanghaied. After what seemed an eternity another junk phutted its way to the jetty.

'Chou Lai?' called the skipper, and once more my friend hopped aboard.

An hour followed in which he ploughed deeper through the South China Sea, beginning to fear for his life. At last he was deposited on yet another island, but this time there was at least a restaurant, strung with lights and vibrating with music. Chou Lai himself came forward, a bonhomous fellow with an eyepatch that completed the superbly Condradian feel of my friend's adventure.

'Hello, very welcome. Tell me, you American?'

'No, I'm English as a matter of fact.'

'English! Ah! You know P B-J?'

One wonders how many perplexed English customers had been asked that question without having the slightest idea who or what a 'P B-J' might be. My friend did know but doubted Chou Lai could possibly mean the same one. It turned out he certainly did.

'Yeah! Pe'er Be'ett-Joes!'

My friend had a free dinner and a ride back to Kowloon in Chou Lai's private launch.

There you have Peter Bennett-Jones: with his long lean frame, a line in crumpled linen suits and a ripely old-fashioned 'dear old boy' manner, he looks and sounds the part of a superannuated colonial district commissioner from the pages of Somerset Maugham, yet is younger than Mick Jagger and as sharp, clever and powerful a force in London's media world as you could find.

I was fortunate or unfortunate enough to miss the evening at the Zanzibar when Keith Allen, one of the pioneers of alternative comedy and a man I was to come to know well, stood up on the bar and began to throw bottles back and forth, destroying much of the stock as well as most of the mirrors and fittings. Keith did get arrested and on his return from a short stretch found himself permanently banned, or Zanzibarred as I preferred to put it. The owner, Tony Macintosh, was good-natured enough not to exclude him from his new establishment, the Groucho, which he and Mary-Lou Sturridge were on the point of opening in Soho.

My years of hurling myself headlong into the world of Soho Bohemia were still ahead of me, but I was beginning to look at figures like Keith Allen with a kind of admiration tinged with fear. They seemed to own the London in which I still felt like a shy visitor, a London which was beginning to vibrate with enormous energy. I was afraid to enter the fashionable nightclubs like the Titanic and the Limelight; after all, they seemed to be about nothing but dancing and getting drunk, neither of which I was very interested in, and even the Zanzibar was not a place I would ever dream of visiting except in a group, but a demon in me whispered that it was wrong for me to be nothing but a machine for churning out words. 'You owe it to yourself to live a little, Harry. . .' as Clint breathes to himself in *Dirty Harry*.

*

Who was I at this time? I still found that people were bothered by my front, my ease, my apparent – oh, I don't know – effortlessness, invulnerability, lack of need? Something in me riled . . . no not riled, sometimes riled perhaps, but mostly intrigued or baffled . . . something in me intrigued or baffled, triggered a mixture of exasperation and curiosity.

How could somebody be so muffled up against the cruel winds of the world, so armed against the missiles of fate, so complete? Be *great* to see them drunk. See their guard down. Find out what makes them tick.

I really do believe that there are those who would like and trust me better if they saw me weeping into a whisky, making a fool of myself, getting aggressive, maudlin and drunkenly out of control. I have never found those states in others anything other than tiring, awkward, embarrassing and fantastically dull, but I am quite sure that people would cherish a view of me in that condition at least once in a while. As it happens I am almost never out of control no matter how much I drink. My limbs may well lose coordination, but they have so little to begin with that it is hard to tell the difference. But I certainly never become aggressive or violent or weepy. This is clearly a fault.

Back then I could see that outsiders looking in on the Stephen Fry they encountered saw a man who had drawn life's winning lottery ticket. I did not seem to have it in me to project the vulnerability, fear, insecurity, doubt, inadequacy, puzzlement and inability to cope that I so very often felt.

The signs were writ large for those with the wit to read. The cars alone screamed so much, surely? An Aston Martin, a Jaguar XJ12, a Wolseley 15/50, an Austin Healey

100/6 in concourse condition, an Austin Westminster, an MG Magnette, an MGB roadster . . .

People saw me riding around in these woody, leathery chariots and thought them the automobile equivalent of the tweed jacket and cavalry twills in which I still dressed myself. 'Good old Stephen. He's from another world, really. Quintessentially English. Old-fashioned values. Cricket, crosswords, classic cars, clubland. Bless.' Or they thought, 'Pompous, smug Oxbridge twat in his young fogey brogues and snobby cars. What a git.' And I thought, 'What a fraud. Half-Jewish poof who doesn't really know what he's doing or who he is but is still the same sly, skulking, sweet-scoffing teenager he ever was, never quite fitting in. Destroyed by love, incapable of being loved, unworthy of being loved.'

Till the day I die people will always prefer to see me as strong, comfortable and English, like a good leather club chair. I have learned long ago not to fight it. Besides, and this is more than a question of good manners (although actually good manners are reason enough), why should anyone bleat on about what they feel inside all the time? It isn't dignified, it isn't interesting and it isn't attractive.

Any armchair psychologist can see that someone with my history of teenage *Sturm* and adolescent *Drang* (the needy sugar addiction, alienation, wild moods, unhappy sensualism, blighted romance, thieving, expulsions, fraud and imprisonment[†]) who is suddenly given a new lease of life and the chance to work and make a preposterous amount of money, might well respond as I did and make a series of silly and self-conscious attempts at display, to prove to himself and to the family whose life he made such a misery that he was now *someone*. Someone who *belonged*.

Look, I have cars and credits cards and club memberships and a country house. I know the name of the head waiter at Le Caprice. I am stitched into England like Connollized leather into the seat of an Aston.

If asked, I would have told you that I was happy. I was happy. I was content, certainly, which is to happy what Pavillon Rouge is to Château Margaux, I suppose, but which will have to do for most of us.

Saturday Live was adjudged a hit, and perhaps as a result of our appearances on it Hugh and I were summoned once more to Jim Moir's office to see if we couldn't waggle our cocks in the air and get someone to kneel and suck, or 'put a show together', as other, lesser comedy executives might have put it.

After the BBC's lack of interest in *The Crystal Cube*, we were leery about high-concept programmes and determined that we should have a shot at committing to screen what we knew best, sketch comedy.

'Excellent,' said Richard Armitage. 'You can do that next year. But first Stephen . . .' He rubbed his hands together, and his eyes gleamed. 'Broadway.'

Clipper Class, Côte Basque and Choreography

Mike Ockrent and I flew to New York together in clipper class, PanAm's equivalent of business, where you could eat and drink and smoke until your eyes, liver and lungs bubbled. We had a few days, and our job was to dazzle Richard's potential financiers and co-producers. Robert Lindsay was already there. This was my first-ever trip to the United States, and I had to keep hugging myself. I had often fantasized about America as a child and felt that, when I got there, I should find that I already knew it and love it all the more for that.

I shan't distress you too much with my thoughts about the Manhattan skyline. If you haven't visited New York City yourself, you have seen it in film and television and you know that there are a lot of very, very tall buildings crowded together on a relatively small island. You will know there are long tunnels and rattly bridges. There is a central oblong park, wide avenues that run arrow-straight down from one end to the other, rhythmically intersected by numbered streets. You will know that the avenues also have numbers, except when they are called Madison, Park, Lexington, Amsterdam or West End. You will know there is just one exception, one daring diagonal thoroughfare that carves its way down from the top-left corner of the island, ignoring the symmetry of the grid, creating squares, circuses and slivered scalenes of open space as it slices its way south-west – Verdi Square, Dante Park, Columbus Circle, Madison Square, Herald Square, Union Square. You will know that this outlaw diagonal is called Broadway. You will know too that where Broadway meets 42nd Street at Times Square, the heart of New York theatre beats and has done so for a hundred years.

I walked around the theatre district, rubbernecking the neon, bowing to the statue of George M. Cohan ('Give my regards to Broadway' it says on the plinth, and to this day I get a lump in my throat every time I see that – more out of veneration for James Cagney's impersonation of him than out of love or knowledge of Cohan himself), seating myself in the Carnegie Deli to write postcards, subjecting myself to the overwhelming rudeness of the waiters and trying to make sense of a Reuben Special. Everything in New York is *exactly* what you expect and yet it still astonishes you. Had I come to Manhattan and found that the avenues were winding and bendy, the buildings low and squat and the people slow, drawling and kindly and that there was no trace of that fabled charge of energy that you drew from the very pavements as you walked on them, then I would have had cause to blink and shake my head in wonder. As it is, the town was precisely what I knew it would be, what legend, fable, literature and Tin Pan Alley had long reported it to be, down to the clouds of steam blooming from the manholes, the boatlike wallow of the huge chequer cabs as they bounced and flipped their tyres on the great iron sheets that seemed to have been casually slung by a giant on to the surface of the street and the strange smoky whiff at every street corner that turned out, on inquiry, to be the smell of new-baked pretzel. Just what I had always known. Yet every five steps I took I could not but stop and grin and gasp and stretch my eyes at the theatre of it all, the noise and rudeness and vitality. Affirmation of what we absolutely expect comes as more of a shock than disaffirmation.

Richard's possible colleagues for the Broadway production were two Americans, James Nederlander, who seemed to own half the theatres in America, and Terry Allen Kramer, who seemed to own half the real estate in Manhattan. They were serious and hard-boiled business people. They had it in their heads that the British couldn't choreograph, and when an American producer has an idea in their head, nothing can shift it, not Mr Muscle, not TNT, not electric-shock treatment.

Jimmy Nederlander was convinced he knew the secret of a good musical.

'It's gotta have heart,' he told me over lunch at the Côte Basque on 55th Street, with Terry, Mike and Robert. 'I saw your show in London and I said to my wife, "Honey, this show has got fucking heart. It's got fucking heart, we should do it." She agreed.'

'It's gotta have proper choreography too,' growled Terry.

Terry Allen Kramer liked to say that, while she wasn't the richest woman in America, she certainly paid more tax than any woman in America. She had at one time owned majority shares in Columbia Pictures as well as having large quantities of oil money and property, including the block on which the Côte Basque, made famous by Truman Capote, stood.

When I had arrived there for the lunch appointment I had found myself almost paralysed by the snootiness of the waiters. New York is an infinitely ritzier and more class-bound city than London. White-gloved, liveried and top-lofty elevator attendants, doormen, chauffeurs and *maîtres d'* can make life hell for those without social confidence. Adrift on an alien shore, all the ease I had amassed over the years that allowed me to meet a headwaiter's eye squarely at the Ritz or Le Caprice now deserted me. Abroad is bloody, as George VI liked to say. Abroad, no matter how high you have climbed the ladders at home, forces you to slide down the snakes and start again.

'Yessssss?' hissed the waiter who floated up to me as I had glanced with overdone nonchalance around the dining-room, the very effort of projecting a casual proprietorial air betraying all the illness at ease and inferiority I was feeling.

'Oh, um, well. I'm meeting some people for lunch, I'm afraid I'm a little early . . . should I . . . er . . . sorry.'

'Name?'

'Stephen Fry. Sorry.'

'Let me see . . . I find no reservation under that name.'

'Oh. Sorry! No, that's *my* name, sorry.'

'Uh! And in what name is the reservation?'

'I think probably in the name of Kramer. Sorry. Do you have a table in the name of Terry Allen Kramer?'

It was as if the current had suddenly been switched on. A smile lit up the waiter's whole countenance, his body language transformed itself from drooping contempt to drooling abasement, quivering attention and hysterical respect.

'Sir, I'm *sure* Mrs Kramer would *love* for you to be seated and maybe have a glass of champagne or a cocktail? Would you like something to read while you wait? Mrs Kramer is usually ten minutes late, so perhaps some olives? An ashtray? *Anything*? Anything at all? Thank you, sir.'

Lordy. And indeed she had been ten minutes late, sweeping in and gathering up Jimmy Nederlander, Mike Ockrent and Robert Lindsay, who by this time had joined me on the uncomfortable anteroom sofa.

A telephone had been brought to the table and plugged into a socket by the wall for her as we sat down. Through this she had hollered instructions to minions at her office during the course of lunch.

When it came time for pudding she looked around the table. 'Who wants dessert? You guys want dessert?'

I nodded with enthusiasm, and she loudly clapped her hands. 'André, get the pastry cart.'

Le chariot à pâtisseries was duly wheeled before us loaded with exquisite *délices*. Terry Allen Kramer pointed at one more than ordinarily luxurious tower of cream, glazed pastry and crystallized fruits. 'What's that?' she barked.

André went into his spiel. 'Madame, it is a *mousseline* of *almandine* and *nougatine* whipped into a *sabayon* of *praline* and *souffline* . . .' and so forth. Cutting him short, Terry positioned her hand over the pristine surface of this gorgeous creation and with one long pull dug up a great scoop of it, sucked it from her fingers with a loud smack, cocked her head to one side, thought for a moment and then said, turning her head away from the waiter as she did so, 'Take it away, it's shit.'

Robert and I stared with open mouths. Mike later suggested that she did this to impress us with her ruthlessness, to make us aware that we were expendable and that she took no prisoners. I simply thought it was the single most ghastly thing I had ever seen a human do, and I had once seen a man take out his cock and piss all over the desk of a four-star hotel lobby, splashing a receptionist and two bystanders.

Terry noticed that we were looking at her and smiled grimly. 'The dessert was shit. Shit is shit. Did I say about how important the choreography is?'

If that lunch had been a test we somehow passed it, and Terry and Jimmy duly agreed to pony up.

I went back to England, and Hugh and I set about starting to write for next year's pilot of a Fry and Laurie TV sketch show.

'We should do a tour,' Hugh said.

'A tour?'

'If we agree to a live show around the country then that will force us to write material for it. We're not allowed to do Shakespeare Masterclass, or Dracula . . . only new material.'

Although we were not really well known and certainly nothing like as famous as Harry and Ben were becoming, there was a sizeable enough demand for us in college and university towns, it seemed, and a tour was arranged. We wrote and stared out of the window and paced up and down and bought Big Macs and looked out of the window and went for walks and tore at our hair and swore and watched television and bought more Big Macs and swore again and wrote and screamed with horror as the clock showed that another day was over and we looked at what we had written and groaned and agreed to meet again first thing next day whosever turn it was agreeing to arrive with some coffee and Big Macs.

After we had assembled some material I had to go back to New York for *Me and My Girl* rehearsals. The plan was for me to return after the opening. We would tour and record a one-off Fry and Laurie pilot show to be screened at Christmas and followed the next year by a series.

Me and My Girl rehearsed in Manhattan somewhere down near the Flatiron Building. I had never seen such facilities or met with such order in the course of a theatrical venture. There was a dance room, a song room and even a book room, a huge space dedicated to rehearsing my bits and my bits alone. I even had my own writer's room off it, handsomely supplied with desk, electric typewriter, stationery and coffee percolator. Mike Ockrent led the same production team, but only Robert remained from the British cast. Enn Reitel had taken over from him in London, and would be followed by Gary Wilmot, Karl Howman, Brian Conley, Les Dennis and many others in the course of its long run. Here in New York Robert had

Maryann Plunkett, whom I had seen in *Sunday in the Park with George*, playing opposite him as Sally and George S. Irving as Sir John.

I stayed at the Wyndham, an old-fashioned actor's hotel on 58th Street whose rooms were spacious chintzy suites with bathrooms and fittings that believed it was still 1948. By each bed was a white telephone with no dial or buttons. When you picked up the receiver it connected you to the front desk. 'I'd like to make a call,' you would tell the operator. You gave the number you wanted and hung up. Five minutes or half an hour later, according to whim or luck, the phone would ring, and you would be through. Most nights at about two or three I would be jerked awake by the phone's crashing buzz.

'Yes?'

'Your call to Rome, Italy . . .'

'I didn't ask for a call to Rome.'

'My mistake. Wrong number. Thank you.'

At breakfast I fell into the habit of chatting with some of the long-term guests, almost all of them actors or theatre people. A favourite was Raymond Burr, enormously bulky but very kindly and cheerful, despite the habitually tired bloodhound droop of his eyes. He went so far as to ask my advice about doing more *Perry Mason* on television.

'Do young people remember it?'

'Well, I have to confess it was before my time,' I said to him. 'But I loved *Ironside*.'

'Why thank you. They don't want to do more *Ironside*, but there is talk of more *Perry Mason*. You never saw it?'

'I'm sure television could do with a really good legal series. He was a lawyer, that is right?'

'Oh my. I shall have to tell the producers. I met a smart young Englishman and he had barely heard of Perry Mason. Oh my.'

If Raymond Burr wasn't available for conversation I had in another corner of the breakfast room Broadway's ancient royal couple, Hume Cronyn and Jessica Tandy. They spoke to me through each other.

'Oh look, honey, here's the English fellow. I wonder how his rehearsals are going.'

'Not too bad,' I would reply. 'The cast seem amazing to me.'

'He says the cast is amazing! Is he confident of a hit I wonder?'

'Oh well, you know. It's pretty much in the lap of the gods. By which I mean the lap of the critics I suppose.'

'He's calling the critics gods, honey, did you hear that? Gods!'

And so on.

Once rehearsals kicked in, I saw something of the American work ethic. Competition for parts in the chorus was so tough that they never relaxed. During time off the boys and girls were teaching each other new steps, practising vocal scales and warming up or down according to the time of day. And drinking water all the time. We are now so used to it all over the western world that one has to remind oneself that there was a time when young Americans didn't feel naked without a bottle of water in their hands.

I also saw something of the meaning of the star system. It is a kind of paradox of America, the republic that freed itself of the inequitable shackles of monarchy, class and social rank, that it chooses to privilege stars with a status far beyond that of any European duke or prince. As with any true aristocracy, the principles of *noblesse oblige* apply to stars. Robert told me of the time they all went upstate to film a TV commercial. It was a long and tiring day in humid summer, chorus members were clanking around in medieval armour, pearly suits and fur-lined cloaks, and take after take was called for. As the shoot wore on Robert noticed a diminution in friendliness towards him that he could not understand. He asked Maryann Plunkett whether he had done something wrong.

'Everyone is very tired and very hot, and I think they'd like it to be over.'

'Well, yes, me too,' said Robert, 'but how is that my fault?'

'Robert, you're the star! You're the company leader. *You* decide if it's time for everyone to wrap and go home.'

'B-but . . .' Robert, of course, had been brought up in the self-consciously 'we're all mates here' cooperative atmosphere of British theatre, where no one would ever *dare* pull starry rank. Because we have a class system in Britain we go out of our way to make sure that it is made plain that everyone is absolutely equal. Because America doesn't, they seem to revel in the power, status and prestige that achievement can bring.

'Robert, it's your duty to make decisions for us . . .'

Swallowing nervously, and grateful that none of his British contemporaries were witnessing the moment, he spoke up to the director in front of everyone. 'Right, Tommy. One more take only and then everyone needs to get out of costume and be on their way.'

'Sure, Bob,' said the director. 'Absolutely. Whatever you say.'

Everybody smiled, and Robert learned the duties and responsibilities of stardom.

Me and My Girl tried out in downtown Los Angeles, in the Dorothy Chandler Pavilion, then best known as the location of the annual Academy Awards ceremony. I stayed at the Biltmore Hotel off Pershing Square, almost near enough the theatre to walk. This was Los Angeles, of course, and, as everyone knows, walking is never done there. Besides, when you have rented a bright-red convertible Mustang you want to use it at every opportunity. There was really very little for me to do other than attend the early performances and occasionally offer new snatches of dialogue as required. After a week at the Biltmore, charming as it was, I thought I might as well blow all my per diems on a weekend at the Bel-Air Hotel. For the low, low price of $1,500 a night I had a little bungalow and a beautiful garden in which my own private hummingbird flitted about just for me. On the second night I invited the chorus, who somehow jammed themselves in, drank $600 worth of wine and liquor and vamoosed in a cloud of kisses and extravagant gratitude.

LA was our only try-out town, and the show had gone well enough in front of a mostly elderly subscription audience. Broadway was next, and from here there was no escape and no second chances. It is a known oddity of the New York theatre world that a production is made or broken almost solely by its review in the *New York Times*. It is the paper, incidentally, not the reviewer, that wields this terrible power. As Bernard Levin once observed, a Barbary Ape could hold the post of *Times* reviewer and still have the power to close a show. Frank Rich was the current Barbary Ape that we had to please, and there was no knowing until the night whether his thumb would go up or down. If it went down the whole production would fold, Jimmy, Terry and Richard would lose their money, and the cast would all be fired. Humiliation all round.

We had already earned a certain measure of ill will in the town by being the first show to open in the Marriott Marquis Theatre, built as part of a major Times Square reconstruction project. To make way for an enormous new hotel, the much loved Helen Hayes Theatre had been pulled down to such a howl of impassioned protest that the Marriott group promised to integrate a new theatre into the development, and the Marquis was it.

At the dress rehearsal nerves were frayed, and Jimmy Nederlander and Terry Allen Kramer, being denied, as producers, any other outlet for their tension than the pleasure of firing people, had scented blood. Their old insecurity on the issue of the dance numbers resurfaced, and, sitting behind them, I heard mutters and growls about Gillian Gregory, the choreographer. How they thought firing her the day before previews began could possibly help I do not know, but I suppose plenty of shows had been rescued in shorter time than that. I assume they liked the idea of bringing in Tommy Tune or Bob Fosse or some other legend of dance, having them work everyone eighteen hours a day for three days and then telling the world how they had fired asses and saved the show. American entertainment tycoons do like to see themselves cast in the mythological tough uncompromising sonofabitch mould. Theatre people hate dramatics – they get enough of that at work; non-theatre people dramatize everything around them.

I caught hold of Richard Armitage and mentioned that I had heard grumblings.

'Hm,' he said. 'I shall have to do something about that.'

We sat and watched an energetic but somehow spiritless dress rehearsal. The new theatre smelled of carpet glue and wood varnish. It had fluorescent strips for house lights, which meant that they couldn't be faded up or down, but only flickered on and off, killing the atmosphere. Even when they went out the exit signs were so brightly lit you could easily read your programme from their lurid spill. The doors at the back of the auditorium were horribly over-sprung such that, no matter how gently you tried to close them, they made a terrible bang, and if people didn't know about them and let them go without care it was as if a gunshot had gone off. The dancing had been, to my untutored non-specialist eye, spectacular, but Terry Allen Kramer scribbled savagely in her notebook every time a leg kicked or a body twirled.

When finally the curtain came down for the ending she stood and opened her mouth.

'The choreo . . .'

Richard's voice drowned her out. 'Damn. Well, those house lights are a disaster. And the doors and the exit signs. But there's nothing we can do about that in time for the first preview. Just nothing. It would take a miracle.'

Terry uttered a harsh bark. 'Nothing? Ha! That's what *you* think! There's *plenty* we can do. Bill Marriott is a personal friend. I don't care if I have to wake him up, he'll goddamn sort this out. Someone get me to a phone *right now*!'

Off she went, steaming and puffing like the iron-clad destroyer she was. Orders were issued and issues ordered, Bill Marriott was jerked from his European slumbers and in under an hour electricians were being elevated to the ceiling on scissor-lifts and men in white overalls were removing door springs at the back of the house. In her commanding glory, Terry had forgotten all about the choreography.

I shook Richard by the hand. 'Masterly,' I said. 'If I had a hat, I'd take it off to you.'

By the first preview the atmosphere of the show began to be restored. The doors were now, of course, whisper quiet, the exit signs glowed gently and the house lights were warm and sweetly controllable. I had moved out of the Wyndham and was staying in a most glorious apartment on 59th Street, Central Park South, with a matchless view of the park and Fifth Avenue. It belonged to Douglas Adams, who, with typical generosity, had told me to make free of it. I held a nervous party there the evening of the first night. My parents had flown over, as had Hugh. My Great-Aunt Dita, who had escaped the Nazis in Salzburg and come over to America in the 1940s, was a formidable and terrifying presence. She offered Hugh one of her untipped Pall Mall cigarettes.

'That's very kind,' said Hugh, taking out a full-strength, but filtered, Marlboro Red, 'I prefer these.'

'You some kind of health nut?' said my Aunt, thrusting her pack towards him. 'Take.' Hugh, being the polite fellow he is, took one.

Neither Mike Ockrent nor I could face being in the auditorium with the first-night audience. The knowledge that Frank Rich had already been and written his review and that it would be out in just a few hours was almost more than we could bear. We paced up and down in the foyer, consuming gin and tonic after gin and tonic, becoming more and more hysterical with panic, terror and a sense of the absurdity of this whole venture. Our pacing routes would converge, and we kept bumping into each other, which caused us to burst into fresh fits of manic laughter.

'We are at the first night of our own Broadway show,' Mike kept saying, shaking his head in disbelief. 'It can't be true. Someone is going to wake me up.'

I repeated those lines from *The Producers* that everybody quotes at first nights.

Wow, this play wouldn't run a night.

A night? Are you kidding? This play's guaranteed to close on page four.

How could this happen? I was so careful. I picked the wrong play, the wrong director, the wrong cast. Where did I go right?

And so on.

Years later, Mike would collaborate with Mel Brooks on *The Producers'* reinvention as a stage musical, only to be struck down with incurable leukaemia before he had the chance to see it open as the biggest Broadway hit of its day.

During the second half, just after the audience had gone back in from the interval, Ralph Rosen, the company's general manager, waddled in his amiable flat-footed way across the lobby to whisper to us the news that a friend of a friend had a friend whose friend was dating a friend at the *New York Times* and that their friend had seen an advance copy of the Frank Rich review and that it was good. It was more than good. It was a rave. Ralph solemnly shook our hands. He was the most quiet-spoken, honourable and matter-of-fact person I had met in America. If he said a thing was so, then it was so and not otherwise.

By the time we all assembled upstairs for the party

Richard had a copy in his hands and a wetness in his eyes once more.

At the Antoinette Perry Awards later that year *Me and My Girl* was nominated for thirteen Tonys. We failed to pick up ten of them, my category included, but Robert and Maryann each won for best performance in a musical and, perhaps most pleasingly of all, Gillian Gregory won for best choreography. I don't know if to this day she is aware how adeptly Richard saved her from being pointlessly and unjustifiably fired.

I got back to England still shaken by my good fortune. *Me and My Girl* was running in the West End and on Broadway, there were productions in Tokyo, Budapest, Australia, Mexico – I have forgotten the other territories. The show would run on Broadway for the next three and a half years and in the West End for another six. In the meantime there was *Fry and Laurie* to look forward to, another *Blackadder* and . . . and . . . who knew what else? It seemed that I was an insider, a showbusiness somebody.

In August 1987 I was at home in Norfolk congratulating myself on having given up smoking for ten days. Hugh, Kim and other friends came up to help me celebrate my thirtieth birthday, and within ten minutes of their arrival I was back on the cigarettes.

My roaring twenties were over, and next month Hugh and I would start work on our BBC pilot, which we planned to call *A Bit of Fry and Laurie*. My bank balance was good and getting ever better. I had cars, certainty and a slowly growing name. I was the luckiest person I knew.

Never one to take stock or make inventories I do recall standing in the garden of the Norfolk house watching the sun set and feeling that I had finally arrived. I do not believe that I actually crowed over the remains of my miserable past self, but I came perhaps as close to exultation as a person can.

When someone exults, Fate's cruel lips curl into a smile.

C

Back in London some weeks later an actor friend asked me if I fancied a line. I did not even know what he meant but I said that I certainly would like one, because he had asked in a way that made 'a line' sound intriguing and wicked and fun. I thought perhaps he was going to tell me a quite appalling joke or pick-up line. Instead, he took a packet of folded paper from his pocket, dug out some white powder and chopped it up into two lines on the surface of a smoked-glass coffee table. He asked me if I had a ten-pound note. I produced one, and he rolled it up tight and put it to one nostril. He sniffed up half of his line, applied the rolled-up ten-pound note to the other nostril and sniffed up the other half. I came forward, took the tube, knelt down and did the same, reproducing his actions as carefully as I could. The powder stung my nostrils enough to produce a few tears in my eyes. I went back to my chair, and we sat and talked for a while. After twenty or thirty minutes we did the same thing again. And then a third time. By now I was buzzing and garrulous and wide awake and happy.

I did not know it but this was to mark the beginning of a new act of my life. The tragedy and farce of that drama are the material for another book.

In the meantime, thank you for your company.

Acknowledgements

Some of the characters who feature in this book have been kind enough to read it and correct lapses in my memory. I am especially grateful to Kim and Ben and the Nice Mr Gardhouse, but my gratitude reaches out to many others. It is very hard to know whether people will be more offended by inclusion or exclusion from these pages. Full as the book is, it would have been twice the length if I could have given space to everyone who was important in my younger life.

I thank Don Boyd for leading me to the kind and helpful Philip Wickham of the University of Exeter's Bill Douglas Centre for the History of Cinema and Popular Culture, which houses a Don Boyd archive where invaluable *Gossip* material was made available to me.

To Anthony Goff, my agent, to Jo Crocker, my tireless and loving assister, to Christian Hodell and to Louise Moore at Penguin go the warmest and most affectionate and grateful thanks too, but I reserve my deepest acknowledgements for the dedicatee of this book, the colleague without whom I would never have been in a position to write it and without whose friendship my life would have been unimaginably poorer.

Index

By Jussi Adler-Olsen . . .

'She scratched her fingertips on the smooth walls until they bled, and pounded her fists on the thick panes until she could no longer feel her hands. At least ten times she had fumbled her way to the steel door and stuck her fingernails in the crack to pry it open . . .'

Merete Lynggard vanished five years ago. Everyone says she's dead. Everyone says the case is a waste of time. Everyone except Copenhagen detective Carl Mørck. Turning over this old case he thinks he's found a clue missed by his predecessors. It takes him on a journey, one that upsets his superiors, that troubles his colleagues, that causes him to break rules. But at the end of it a woman waits who has been missing for five years . . .

'Gripping story-telling'
Guardian

'Though he never said anything, I knew Garv blamed me. And that was OK, because I blamed me too.'

One day Maggie Walsh walks out on her husband of nine years and runs away to Hollywood. There she joins her best friend Emily, who is busily pitching scripts to studios, mixing with movie stars and generally living the heck out of the dream. Maggie should be enjoying herself but she can't stop thinking about her husband Garv and the life she's run away from. Is her sojourn in the City of Angels a once-in-a-lifetime journey of self-discovery, or is she simply hiding from the one thing she cannot face?

'Filled with wonderful warm characters and dialogue that leaps off the pages. Keyes is a superior storyteller'
Irish Independent

Everyone knows the real Silvia, don't they?

Silvia Shute lies in hospital in a coma. Family and friends
gather at her bedside, each thinking they know the real Silvia.
But do they? For Silvia hides a secret. One she can never tell.
And as her visitors congregate so the truth about Silvia is slowly
revealed. Again, and again, and again . . .

**'Hilarious. Chortle-out-loud turns of phrase,
razor-sharp observations'**
Stylist